BEN JONSON

Selected Works

BEN JONSON

Selected Works

Edited by

DAVID McPHERSON

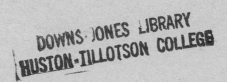
HOLT, RINEHART AND WINSTON, INC.

New York Chicago San Francisco Atlanta
Dallas Montreal Toronto London Sydney

Library of Congress Catalog Card Number: 70-187113
ISBN: 0-03-083113-X

PRINTED IN THE UNITED STATES OF AMERICA

2 3 4 5   065   9 8 7 6 5 4 3 2 1

PREFACE

If we read Ben Jonson's plays apart from his poetry or his masques apart from his literary criticism, we may find ourselves not giving sufficient attention to his impressive versatility as a writer and to the interconnections between his works in the various genres. The purpose of this anthology is to make available between the same covers two of his best plays (*Volpone* and *Bartholomew Fair*), one of his better masques (*The Masque of Queens*), a fairly extensive sampling of his poetry, a big chunk of his literary criticism, and, for biographical interest, selections from his conversations with Drummond—all in modernized text accompanied by rather full biographical and critical introductions, notes, and bibliographies.

Deciding which plays to include was difficult. Any anthology of Jonson must, I think, include *Volpone,* his best-known play. With room for only one other play, however, does one choose *The Alchemist* or *Bartholomew Fair*? Most anthologists would have chosen *The Alchemist,* but it is similar to *Volpone* in that both are constructed around the grand schemes of two or three characters. The structure of *Bartholomew Fair* is not as neat; its apparent chaos, which imitates the chaos of a real fair, conceals principles of organization that are as interesting in their own way as the precision of the other two plays.[1] More important, both *Volpone* and *The Alchemist* are in verse, whereas *Bartholomew Fair* is in the

---

[1] See Richard Levin, "The Structure of *Bartholomew Fair,*" PMLA 80 (1965): 172–79.

magnificent baroque prose that Jonas Barish has so brilliantly taught us to appreciate.[2]

My introduction to *The Masque of Queens* attempts to describe briefly what masques must have been like in performance, but even an extended description is bound to be a pitiful substitute for the experience itself. It seemed best, therefore, to choose a masque that reads well as poetry. Both recent editions of Jonson's complete masques mention the merits of *The Masque of Queens* in this regard.[3] I have abridged Jonson's account of his sources because the general reader does not need it and may be distracted by the bristling array of Latin quotations.

As for the poems, my care was not only to include most of the perennial favorites but also to see that the principal kinds of poems he wrote are represented: epigram, epistle, elegy, song, ode. From Jonson's scattered literary criticism I have chosen the Induction to *Every Man Out of His Humor* (1599) to illustrate his early comic theory and other prologues to demonstrate its development. But the bulk of this section is from *Timber, or Discoveries,* from which I have selected virtually all of the passages that relate directly to literary criticism. In *Conversations with Drummond* most of my deletions fall into two categories: repetitious passages and jokes that have little point for the modern reader.

In summary, my effort has been to choose representative and interesting works and passages and to edit them for a reader who has had little or no previous acquaintance with Jonson. My hope is that each reader will become, as I am, a devoted member of "the Tribe of Ben."

DAVID MC PHERSON

University of California
Santa Barbara

[2] *Ben Jonson and the Language of Prose Comedy* (Cambridge, Mass.: Harvard University Press, 1960).

[3] Herford and Simpson (abbreviated hereafter as H&S) II.279–80 (see Selected Bibliography) and Stephen Orgel, ed., *Ben Jonson: The Complete Masques* (New Haven, Conn.: Yale University Press, 1969), p. 37.

CONTENTS

GENERAL INTRODUCTION

Ben Jonson began his literary career as an intolerant idealist and crusader. He saw rampant moral corruption and hypocrisy in society, and like his character Asper in *Every Man Out of His Humor*, he was determined to "strip the ragged follies of the time,/ Naked, as at their birth" and "print wounding lashes in their iron ribs."[1] He saw rampant corruption and hypocrisy also in literature; he was furious "that such lean, ignorant, and blasted wits,/ Such brainless gulls, should utter their stolen wares/ With such applauses in our vulgar ears."[2] And he saw an inseparable connection between these two forms of corruption: "Wheresoever manners and fashions are corrupted, language is. It imitates the public riot. The excess of feasts and apparel are the notes of a sick state; and the wantonness of language, of a sick mind."[3]

Jonson's goal, noble and ambitious, was "to raise the despised head of poetry again, and stripping her out of those rotten and base rags wherewith the times have adulterated her form, restore her to her primitive habit, feature, and majesty, and render her worthy to be embraced and kissed of all the great and master-spirits of our world" (Epistle Dedicatory, *Volpone*). He sought to achieve this goal by keeping always in mind the purpose of literature as expounded by the great Roman poet and critic Horace: "Poets would either profit or delight,/ Or mixing sweet and fit, teach life the right," as Jonson himself translated ("Horace, Of the Art of Poetry,"

---

[1] Induction, lines 17–18 (see Literary Criticism section).

[2] *Every Man In His Humor*, H&S V.iii.335–37–1601 quarto only. I consistently modernize the text.

[3] *Discoveries*, H&S 954–58 (see Literary Criticism section).

477–78–H&S VIII.327). Jonson repeats this familiar credo in four different prologues and prefaces. But whereas Horace gives poets the choice of providing profit *or* delight, Jonson emphasizes moral profit. In the preface to *The Masque of Queens,* for example, he speaks of "that rule of the best artist, to suffer no object of delight to pass without his mixture of profit and example." Nearly all writers in the Renaissance paid lip service to the idea of literature as a moral teacher and most believed it, but few believed it with the pugnacious intensity of Ben Jonson.

Like many crusaders, Jonson was egotistical and quarrelsome, but his idealism gave a kind of savage energy to his works. There were periods in his life when he was more inclined to be tolerant of human weakness than he was when he was dispensing "wounding lashes" early in his career; he learned to laugh not only at others but at himself. His best works, however, never cease to possess that fierce energy. As Coleridge remarked, "In Ben Jonson you have an intense and burning art."[4] At the same time one is always conscious when reading Jonson that the artist is in command of his material. As Jonas Barish puts it, Jonson is "a volcano . . ., but a volcano kept under strictest control."[5]

I. LIFE

The intensity, the fierceness, the obsessive quality in Jonson's works must be, to some extent, a disciplined, artistic version of the sensational and even violent events that filled his own life. He told Drummond[6] that his grandfather had gained an estate under Henry VIII, but that his father, a minister, had lost it. He also said that his father had died a month before he was born (in 1572 or 1573), and that his mother had married a bricklayer. If this is true, Jonson could justifiably claim to have been up and then down on the wheel of fortune before he was even born, since being the stepson of a bricklayer was considerably different from being the son of a minister with an estate.

[4] *The Table Talk and Omniana of Samuel Taylor Coleridge,* ed. T. Ashe (London: George Bell and Sons, 1896), p. 194.

[5] *Ben Jonson: A Collection of Critical Essays* (Englewood Cliffs, N.J.: Prentice-Hall, Inc., 1963), p. 12.

[6] Drummond's reports are not to be trusted implicitly, for reasons set forth in my introduction to Jonson's *Conversations with Drummond.*

The bricklayer and his newly acquired family lived near Westminster Abbey and its Westminster School, one of the best in the nation. Luckily, Jonson was sent to this school, although probably by a benefactor rather than by his stepfather. Through an even greater stroke of luck his master at the school was William Camden, who at that very time must have been writing his *Britannia* (1586), a work that established him as the leading historical and antiquarian scholar in England. Under Camden the boy received the grounding in Latin and Greek that enabled him to become one of the most learned writers of the period, and the warm tone of Jonson's later dedications to Camden indicates that the boy learned not only grammar but also personal loyalty and devotion to the life of the mind. Dedicating *Cynthia's Revels* to Camden, Jonson calls himself *Alumnus olim, aeternum Amicus* ("Once a pupil, a friend forever") [see H&S IV.4].

After years of hard work and high hopes of entering Oxford or Cambridge on a scholarship, Jonson one day found himself out of school altogether. Worse still, he found himself laying bricks with his stepfather. Thomas Fuller says Jonson kept up his studies, "a trowell in his hand,...a book in his pocket" (H&S XI.509). How long Jonson laid bricks is uncertain. At some point he must have either abandoned or interrupted his apprenticeship to go as a soldier to Flanders. He told Drummond that he had killed an enemy soldier there in hand-to-hand combat.

Jonson turned up at age twenty-four or twenty-five as an actor and playwright in the account books of Philip Henslowe, theatrical entrepreneur. Henslowe was not long in wishing that he had never seen the burly young man. In 1597, his first year of association with the manager, Jonson was jailed for completing a play (begun by Thomas Nashe) that the Queen's Privy Council suspected was "a lewd play" full of "seditious and slanderous matter" (H&S I.217). Henslowe's company was also in trouble for playing it. But Jonson was out of jail in a few weeks and Henslowe hired him again. The manager operated a play "factory" in which two or more writers collaborated on a script in order to turn it out rapidly. Jonson had married in 1594 and he fed himself and his family by means of this work, which he must have detested. Somehow he found time to write the first play he thought worth saving, *Every Man In His Humour* (1598). It was performed not by Henslowe's company but by the Lord Chamberlain's Men, with an actor named William Shakespeare taking one of the roles.

Success seemed assured for Jonson, but a few days after the play opened he quarreled with a fellow actor named Gabriel Spencer. They fought a duel and Spencer was killed. Jonson was in jail again, and this time he escaped hanging only by pleading benefit of clergy. He received the felon's brand on his thumb, and all his goods were confiscated. As a result he was arrested for debt in early 1599 and thrown in jail again—his third incarceration in eighteen months.

Henslowe was very irritated at the loss of Gabriel Spencer, who was apparently a good actor. Writing to his son-in-law, the great actor Edward Alleyn, the manager complained, "It is for me hard and heavy since you were with me; I have lost one of my company which hurteth me greatly—that is, Gabrell, for he is slayen in Hogsden Fields by the hands of Benjamin Jonson, bricklayer."[7] But, unbelievably, the manager took Jonson in once again, and he borrowed money from Henslowe three times in late 1598 and in 1599 against plays not yet written (*Diary*, pp. 96, 123, 124).

He did not care to preserve any of these plays; in fact, everything he wrote for Henslowe has been lost. The next three plays he saved were written for other companies: *Every Man Out of His Humour* (1599), for Shakespeare's company, and *Cynthia's Revels* (1600) and *Poetaster* (1601), for the resurgent companies of boy actors who played in indoor theaters where admission prices were higher and audiences were therefore wealthier and more sophisticated. Jonson labeled these three plays "comicall satyres," indicating their debt to the verse satire of ancient Rome and to the Elizabethan imitations thereof, which were then quite popular with many educated readers. Traditionally this satire was marked by the author's anger—real or pretended—at the abuses he saw around him. The leading Roman satirist of this kind, Juvenal, wrote that in view of the extreme corruption of men "it is difficult *not* to write satire." Jonson found this attitude congenial to his temperament. The trouble was that the spokesman he created in each of these plays—Asper in *Every Man Out*, Crites in *Cynthia's Revels*, and Horace in *Poetaster*—managed to sound more arrogant than angry. Jonson's enemies identified him with these spokesmen and saw in the plays not a justified condemnation of vice but an arrogant claim of superiority by a man they understandably viewed as nothing but a quondam bricklayer, now a hack writer for Henslowe.

[7] Modernized from *Henslowe's Diary*, ed. R. A. Foakes and A. T. Rickert (Cambridge, Eng.: Cambridge University Press, 1961), p. 286.

Two of his fellow playwrights, John Marston and Thomas Dekker, decided to satirize Jonson on the stage and so began writing *Satiromastix* ("The Satirist Whipped"). But Jonson, writing hastily, completed *Poetaster* first. One result of these plays was that Jonson fought physically with Marston; he told Drummond that he "beat him and took his pistol from him, wrote his *Poetaster* on him."

Jonson loftily and unilaterally called off this "War of the Theaters" in an Apologetical Dialogue appended to the printed version of *Poetaster* (1602). He announced that he was switching from comical satire to stately tragedy "that must and shall be sung high and aloof,/ Safe from the wolf's black jaw, and the dull ass's hoof" (lines 238–39). Unfortunately, however, *Sejanus* (1603), a tragedy scrupulously based on Roman history, was not a popular success, and worse, it got him in trouble not with other playwrights but with the powerful Earl of Northampton. Jonson said that he "was called before the Council for his *Sejanus* & accused both of popery and treason by him." Jonson was vulnerable to this accusation because he was in fact (he told Drummond) a Catholic from 1598 to 1610. Jonson's insistence on maintaining an illegal religion in the climate created by the Gunpowder Plot of 1605 was dangerous. He was called before the ecclesiastical authorities in 1606 to explain his absence from Anglican services, but he was apparently not jailed this time.

As far as we know, the last incarceration of Jonson had occurred a year earlier, in 1605. He had patched his quarrels with Marston and the two of them, along with George Chapman, wrote a comedy called *Eastward Ho,* which contained some jibes at the Scotchmen who had descended on London with King James in 1603. There was a report, Jonson told Drummond, that the three authors were to have their ears and noses slit, but through the intercession of some powerful noblemen they were released unmutilated.

Out of this chaos, astonishingly enough, came Jonson's comic masterpiece, *Volpone* (1606). It was apparently quite successful, since it was performed repeatedly in London and also for university audiences at Oxford and Cambridge. Jonson's best comedies followed in the next decade. There was *Epicoene* (1609), which Dryden commented on so thoroughly in the *Essay of Dramatic Poesy,* then *The Alchemist* (1610), which Coleridge singled out as having a "perfect plot" (*Table Talk,* p. 194). The second (and last) tragedy that he cared to preserve, *Catiline,* was played in 1611. Like

Sejanus it was based on extensive reading in Roman history, and like *Sejanus* it was not popular. But Jonson came back in 1614 with *Bartholomew Fair* and in 1616 with *The Devil Is an Ass*, both successful enough.

As far as drama was concerned, Jonson rested on his laurels from 1616 until 1626. Although he received support from many noblemen and knights, his fortunes were tied to the patronage of James I. At the very end of Queen Elizabeth's reign Jonson paid her some elaborate compliments in *Every Man Out* and *Cynthia's Revels*, but there is no indication that she was impressed. When she died in 1603, however, and the Scottish king James ascended the English throne, Jonson's fortunes began to rise almost immediately. For example, he was called on to write part of the King's coronation entertainment. Jonson's first masque for Queen Anne was performed in January 1605; he wrote twenty-four other such court entertainments during the twenty-three years of James' reign. A masque written by Jonson and designed by Inigo Jones became an annual feature of the winter festivities at court. Jonson was not paid enough for this annual masque to support himself all year—he received forty pounds (two or three thousand dollars, roughly, in modern buying power) for *Love Freed from Ignorance and Folly* (H&S, X.529)—but he gained esteem from being the chief poet at court, and noblemen supplemented the income he received from the royal family. The Earl of Pembroke, for example, gave Jonson twenty pounds annually to buy books.

The year 1616 was a milestone in Jonson's career not only because it saw the production of the last play he was to write for ten years but also because it saw the publication of his collected *Works*, which he himself probably selected and saw through the press. He told Drummond in 1619 that half of his comedies were not in print; for example, *The Case Is Altered* (1597) was published in 1609 under his name, but it does not appear in the 1616 folio. The folio did contain nine plays, the latest being *Catiline* (1611), all of the masques through 1616, and a considerable amount of nondramatic poetry.[8]

Prestige did not remove all the storm and stress from Jonson's life, however. He was a notorious tippler: Drummond says that

---

[8] *Bartholomew Fair* (1614) does not appear in this folio, but we must not infer that he was ashamed of it, since he told Drummond that he had written a defense of it.

Jonson told of being hauled dead drunk through the streets of Paris by the scapegrace son of Sir Walter Raleigh, whom Jonson accompanied to the Continent in 1613 as tutor. In his poems Jonson often extols temperance and order, but these virtues seem to have been cherished ideals rather than descriptions of his own daily life. He told Drummond that necessity had several times forced him to sell off his sizable library.

During the last ten years of James' reign, however, Jonson was at least free enough from financial need to devote much of his time to pursuits not directly related to literature. He took several months to walk all the way to Scotland and back in 1618–19. That feat shows that he was in good health, since he was forty-six at the time—a relatively old man by Elizabethan standards. He resided at Gresham College in London in 1620 and may have delivered rhetoric lectures there. He read widely in such subjects as geometry, architecture, and magnetism as well as in the humanities. *Timber, or Discoveries* consists largely of notes he took from his readings in the humanities during his later years.

A fire in 1623 destroyed the notes he had taken to that point, along with many works in progress which are described in the amusing poem "Execration upon Vulcan." There was a translation of Horace's *Ars Poetica*, which he later rewrote, his *English Grammar*, also redone, a verse account of his Scottish journey, a translation of a Latin prose romance commissioned by King James, and a history of the reign of Henry V.

Jonson fell upon evil days when King James died in 1625. James and Jonson were nearly the same age, and they shared an enthusiasm for erudite scholarship on the one hand and rank vulgarity on the other. Charles I was of another generation, and his effete taste was influenced by his French queen Henrietta Maria. Jonson suffered the ignominy of seeing his rival, the architect Inigo Jones, continue to design the annual masque while other poets were commissioned to do the writing. He was forced to begin writing comedies again, but they are feeble compared to his earlier ones. *The Staple of News* (1626), *The New Inn* (1629), *The Magnetic Lady* (1632), and *A Tale of a Tub* (1633) were labeled by Dryden as Jonson's "dotages," and the label has stuck. Nor were the plays popular when first produced; Jonson's ode "Come Leave the Loathed Stage" was occasioned by the failure of *The New Inn*. On the very day of the play's disastrous first performance the Chapter of Westminster sent "to Mr. Benjamin Jonson in his sickness and want" a gift of five pounds (H&S I.244).

This is one of many indications that Jonson was in ill health and perhaps in poverty during the last decade of his life.

All was not bleak, however. Jonson continued to write noble nondramatic poems, and there gathered around him many young poets and dramatists who revered him and wrote under his obvious influence. Jonson died in 1637 and was buried in Westminster Abbey, near his old schoolroom. Instead of an elaborate Latin epitaph there was inscribed only the brief, appropriate, and memorable phrase, "O rare Ben Jonson!"

II. JONSON'S REPUTATION

Throughout the seventeenth century Jonson was more popular than Shakespeare, or at any rate there were more allusions to Jonson. The habit of comparing the two writers soon formed, much to the detriment of Jonson's reputation. In his Preface to Shakespeare, Pope felt it necessary to criticize the feud between the partisans of the two authors: "Because *Ben Johnson* had much the most learning, it was said on the one hand that *Shakespear* had none at all; and because *Shakespear* had much the most wit and fancy, it was retorted on the other, that *Johnson* wanted both."[9] Pope's attack did no good. As Shakespeare was viewed more and more as that ideal of the nineteenth century, the poet of nature, Ben Jonson was viewed more and more as a cold intellectual.

This view has long been outmoded. As T. S. Eliot observed, there is a power animating Jonson's fictional characters "which comes from below the intellect."[10] He was a passionate man, he lived a passionate life, and he poured his emotions into his works. He may justly be charged with arrogance and vanity but not with lack of emotion. He had no use for soft and gooey emotion, for anything that smacked of sentimentality, but of pride and aspiration, greed and lust, zeal and energy, Jonson can tell us much. Furthermore, intellectuality and passion are by no means incompatible personality traits. I try to demonstrate, in the introductions before each section of this anthology, that the passion in Jonson's best works is disciplined; it is subordinated to the moral and artistic design of the whole.

[9] *Poetry and Prose of Alexander Pope,* ed. Aubrey Williams (Boston: Houghton Mifflin, 1969), p. 465.
[10] *Ben Jonson: A Collection of Critical Essays*, ed. Jonas A. Barish (Englewood Cliffs, N.J.: Prentice-Hall, Inc., 1963), p. 21.

III. FACTS AND REFERENCES

A NOTE ON THE TEXT

My modernized texts are invariably based on the first folio edition of the work in question. Details are given at the end of the introduction to each section.

SELECTED BIBLIOGRAPHY

Early Editions

The 1616 folio: in all probability printed under Jonson's own supervision. It includes all the plays he cared to preserve that had been written by about 1613, all the masques through 1616, and poems (*Epigrams, The Forest*) written at various stages of his career.

The 1640 folio: since Jonson died in 1637, this folio lacks the authority of the 1616 edition. Nevertheless, it is our only text for some of the works written in the last half of his career.

Modern Editions

The standard edition of Jonson's complete works—and the only one published in this century—is the invaluable *Ben Jonson*, edited by C. H. Herford, Percy Simpson, and Evelyn Simpson. 11 vols. Oxford: The Clarendon Press, 1925–52. Cited as H&S.

The reader is also referred to *Selected Works,* ed. Harry Levin. New York: Random House, Inc., 1938.

Other Scholarship and Criticism[11]

Armstrong, William A. "Ben Jonson and Jacobean Stagecraft." In *Jacobean Theatre*, edited by John Russell Brown, pp. 43–61. New York: St. Martin's Press, Inc., and London: Edward Arnold, 1960.

Bacon, Wallace A. "The Magnetic Field: The Structure of Jonson's Comedies." *HLQ* 19 (1956): 121–53.

Bamborough, J. B. *Ben Jonson.* London: Hutchinson University Library, 1970.

Barish, Jonas A. *Ben Jonson and the Language of Prose Comedy.* Cambridge, Mass.: Harvard University Press, 1960.

---

[11] The key to such abbreviations as *HLQ* and *SP* appears on page xix.

Barish, Jonas A., ed. *Ben Jonson: A Collection of Critical Essays.* Englewood Cliffs, N.J.: Prentice-Hall, Inc., 1963.

Baskervill, Charles. *English Elements in Jonson's Early Comedy.* Austin: University of Texas Press, 1911.

Beaurline, L. A. "Ben Jonson and the Illusion of Completeness." *PMLA* 84 (1969): 51–59.

Bentley, Gerald Eades. *Shakespeare and Jonson: Their Reputations in the Seventeenth Century Compared.* Chicago: The University of Chicago Press, 1945.

Boughner, Daniel C. *The Devil's Disciple: Ben Jonson's Debt to Machiavelli.* New York: Philosophical Library, 1968.

Bowers, Fredson Thayer. "Ben Jonson the Actor." *SP* 34 (1937): 392–406.

Chute, Marchette. *Ben Jonson of Westminster.* New York: E. P. Dutton & Co., Inc., 1953.

Eliot, T. S. "Ben Jonson." In *Selected Essays 1917–1932.* New York: Harcourt Brace Jovanovich, Inc., 1932; also in Barish, *Essays.*

Hays, H. R. "Satire and Identification: An Introduction to Ben Jonson." *Kenyon Review* 19 (1957): 267–83.

Jackson, Gabriele Bernhard. *Vision and Judgment in Ben Jonson's Drama.* New Haven, Conn., and London: Yale University Press, 1968.

Kay, W. David. "The Shaping of Ben Jonson's Career: A Re-examination of Facts and Problems." *MP* 67 (1970): 224–37.

Knights, L. C. *Drama and Society in the Age of Jonson.* London: Chatto & Windus Ltd., 1937.

Knoll, Robert E. *Ben Jonson's Plays: An Introduction.* Lincoln: University of Nebraska Press, 1964.

Noyes, Robert Gale. *Ben Jonson on the English Stage, 1660–1776.* Cambridge, Mass.: Harvard University Press, 1935.

Partridge, Edward B. *The Broken Compass: A Study of the Major Comedies of Ben Jonson.* London: Chatto & Windus Ltd., 1958.

Sackton, Alexander H. *Rhetoric as a Dramatic Language in Ben Jonson.* New York: Columbia University Press, 1948.

Thayer, C. G. *Ben Jonson: Studies in the Plays.* Norman: University of Oklahoma Press, 1963.

Townsend, Freda L. *Apologie for Bartholomew Fayre: The Art of Jonson's Comedies.* New York: Modern Language Association, 1947.

Wilson, Edmund. "Morose Ben Jonson." In *The Triple Thinkers,* rev. ed. New York: Oxford University Press, 1948; also in Barish, *Essays.*

KEY TO ABBREVIATIONS USED IN THIS BOOK

CL	*Comparative Literature*
EIC	*Essays in Criticism*
ELH	*English Literary History*
ELN	*English Language Notes*
H&S	Herford and Simpson, i.e., *Ben Jonson,* ed. C. H. Herford, Percy Simpson, and Evelyn Simpson. 11 vols. Oxford: The Clarendon Press, 1925–52.
HLQ	*Huntington Library Quarterly*
JEGP	*Journal of English and Germanic Philology*
MLN	*Modern Language Notes*
MLQ	*Modern Language Quarterly*
MLR	*Modern Language Review*
MP	*Modern Philology*
PMLA	Publications of the Modern Language Association
PQ	*Philological Quarterly*
RES	*Review of English Studies*
SEL	*Studies in English Literature*
ShS	*Shakespeare Survey*
SP	*Studies in Philology*

BEN JONSON

Selected Works

VOLPONE

INTRODUCTION

Volpone is a comedy, but a very strange one by ordinary standards. Although it is funny, it does not have a happy ending; there is no wedding, no feast, nor is either in prospect. Instead, there is severe punishment for the principal characters. The only morally upright characters, a young man and a young woman, are cleared of false accusations against them, but they are not allowed to fall in love as they might have in a more conventional comedy; there is no romance in *Volpone*. Jonson feared that the "boy gets girl" comedy provided pleasure without moral profit, and he was committed to providing both (Prologue, 6–8). His comic vision of human failings is not a tolerant one; on the contrary, at least in *Volpone* it is downright savage. Yet both the humor and the savagery are controlled and kept subservient to the moral purpose.

The moral theme that informs and unifies *Volpone* is that vice and folly are ultimately self-defeating. In the Epistle Dedicatory Jonson lists the duties of the comic poet, and the first is "to imitate justice." The central purpose in *Volpone* is to imitate justice, not the justice represented by the venal judges of Venice but poetic justice. In *Volpone* everybody gets exactly what he deserves. The punishments at the end are almost grotesquely appropriate to the vices and follies of the offenders. To take the most important examples, Mosca, who has lived by being a perfidious servant, is sentenced to the ultimate in servitude: slavery in the galleys. Since most of Volpone's wealth was gotten by feigning disease, he is sentenced to lie in prison until he is sick and lame indeed.

The operations of poetic justice are in a sense responsible for the humor in the play. The laughter is always at someone's expense, but we feel free to laugh because the victim usually deserves what he is getting. The basic deception that Volpone and Mosca practice is clearly a crime—namely, fraud—and yet we laugh, not only because the two schemers are so clever and so exuberant but also because the suckers, in their ghoulish greed, deserve to be swindled. We laugh at Corbaccio's near-deafness and at his near-blindness at the reading of the will (V.iii.63). The infirmities of age are not usually the subjects of mirth, but Corbaccio richly deserves our cruel laughter because he is so gleeful about Volpone's infirmities. Each horrendous symptom Mosca recites makes the old raven more joyful (I.iv.6–56). Volpone is a confidence man but such a delightful and flamboyant one that he almost has our sympathy. Yet he also deserves to be swindled, and thus we laugh when this supposed master schemer suffers petty humiliations such as the beating he receives from Corvino (II.iii) and the comic agonies he undergoes while being forced to hear Lady Wouldbe's chatter (III.iv). Lady Wouldbe is another case in point: because of her own loose morals she deserves to be told that her husband is cheating on her and to be embarrassed when she sallies forth to attack the unsuspecting Peregrine, thinking that he is a "lewd harlot, a base fricatrice,/ A female devil in a male outside" (IV.ii.55–56). Her husband, Sir Politic, a kind of Wouldbe Volpone, deserves to be plotted against and farcically exposed in his turtle shell (V.iv). In all these funny scenes the tendency toward pure farce, which is essentially amoral, is controlled by the strict application of poetic justice.

Contrasted to these funny but satiric scenes are the scenes involving Celia and Bonario. These two characters do not deserve the suffering they undergo; the scenes in which they suffer are therefore no laughing matter. Celia's only possible sin is dropping the handkerchief from her window down to Scoto-Volpone (II.ii), but for this minor act of flirtation Corvino "bewhores" her (II.v) in language that rivals the violence of Othello's attack on Desdemona. Bonario would apparently rather be convicted of serious crimes than question the authority of his father, and Celia asks that her persecutors be forgiven.

Celia and Bonario are innocent, but they are also ineffectual. It is not their own efforts that clear them of charges and bring punishment on the guilty; it is the fact that the rascals have fallen out among themselves. The ineffectuality of the only decent characters in the play makes us suspect that Jonson's view of the human predicament is quite savage and pessimistic, yet *Volpone* does not strike one as unbridled pessimism because poetic justice eventually operates just as powerfully for Celia and Bonario as it does for the rest of the characters. They are not warm and human enough to end up in each other's arms, but at the end they are at least freed from the control of vicious husbands and fathers. In melodrama the virtuous characters defeat evil; in the ironic comedy that is *Volpone* evil destroys itself.

The savage view of human vice implied by the characterization and the theme is also implied by the savage quality of many metaphors in the play; the imagery is often gross and nasty. The action literally revolves about Volpone's body, this piece of supposedly diseased flesh, as it lies on the couch at center stage. The Fox soliloquizes:

> Now, now my clients
> Begin their visitation! Vulture, kite,
> Raven, and gorcrow, all my birds of prey,
> That think me turning carcass, now they come
>
> (I.ii.87–90)

We first meet the three carrion-eating human birds as each in turn circles expectantly around the prospective meal of flesh (I.iii,iv,v). Many of the tropes, especially in the early scenes, have to do with feeding on human flesh. Mosca, who is once called, with grim aptness, a flesh-fly, praises Volpone because the old fox does not "devour/ Soft prodigals" (I.i.40); Androgyno defines a Puritan as "a precise, pure illuminate brother,/ Of those devour flesh, and sometimes one another" (I.ii.43–44). Volpone says that his confidence game is "better than rob churches, yet,/ Or fat, by eating once a month a man" (I.v.91–92).

The language is comic, it is nasty, and yet it is morally appropriate. For example, when Mosca covers Volpone with insults that are supposedly designed only to impress Corvino, we know (and Mosca knows) that the description is symbolically accurate: "The pox approach and add to your diseases,...Would you would once close/ Those filthy eyes of yours that flow with slime/ Like two frog-pits, and those same hanging cheeks,/ Covered with hide instead of skin..." (I.v.52–59). The grossness, the layer of what Alvin Kernan has called "primal stuff" in Jonson,[1] has weight and bulk,

---

[1] *The Cankered Muse: Satire in the English Renaissance* (New Haven, Conn.: Yale University Press, 1959), p. 168.

but it is not dead weight. It helps to make the play huge, grotesque,
and powerful. The very fact that we can talk about the imagery of
feeding on flesh or of disease indicates that the images fall into
patterns, and these patterns help to impose artistic order on the
primal stuff.

The language of the play is ordered and controlled by other
linguistic and rhetorical devices. The entire play, except for the
mountebank scene, is written in a fairly stringent blank verse. The
iambic pentameter beat gives even a slightly irregular line like
"Forbear, foul ravisher! libidinous swine" a feeling of hard and
definite form. Also important is Jonson's characteristic use of
allusion to create an atmosphere of corrupt splendor. When Volpone
woos Celia, for instance, he tries to lure her into bed by offering her
"a diamond [which] would have bought Lollia Paulina/ When she
came in like star-light, hid with jewels/ That were the spoils of
provinces" (III.vii.195–97). This is a magnificent distillation of a
long prose passage, much of which I omit, in Pliny's *Natural History*
(IX.xxxv):

> I myself have seen Lollia Paulina (late wife, and
> after widow, to Caius Caligula the emperor) when she
> was dressed and set out, not in stately wise, nor of
> purpose for some great solemnity, but only when she
> was to go unto a wedding supper. ...I have seen her, I
> say, so beset and bedecked all over with emeralds and
> pearls, disposed in rows, ranks, and courses one by
> another; round about the attire of her head,...at her
> ears pendant, about her neck in a carcanet, upon her
> wrist in bracelets, and on her fingers in rings; that she
> glittered and shone again like the sun as she went.
> The value of these ornaments, she estimated and
> rated at 400 hundred thousand Sestertii. ... Yet were
> not these jewels the gifts and presents of the prodigal
> prince her husband, but the goods and ornaments
> from her own house, fallen unto her by way of
> inheritance from her grandfather, which he had
> gotten together even by the robbing and spoiling of
> whole provinces.[2]

[2] Modernized from the translation of Philemon Holland, 1601, quoted in
Volpone, ed. Arthur Sale (London: University Tutorial Press, 1951), p. 157.

Jonson controls the tone not by an author-surrogate as in his "comicall satyres" but by irony. An instance of this kind of irony is the disparity between the magnificence of Volpone's language and the evident baseness of the values that underlie that language. His opening speech is both a morning prayer and an aubade, a dawn love lyric, but addressed to a heap of gold it is rank blasphemy. Even the uneducated part of the audience must have felt this. There is also irony in the fact that Volpone and Mosca sometimes sound like typical satiric spokesmen, as when Volpone gravely observes, "What a rare punishment/ Is avarice to itself" (I.iv.142–43) and Mosca says, "Hood an ass with reverend purple,/ So you can hide his two ambitious ears,/ And he shall pass for a cathedral doctor (I.ii.111–13)." But considering the character of the speakers of these *sentences*, as the Renaissance called moral maxims, we are obliged to see the pronouncements as something more complex than mere moral platitudes. Volpone's own avarice will in fact punish itself, and Mosca's own disguises do not, finally, prevent him from seeming an ass. The Venetian judge appropriately concludes the last scene with a stern moral expressed in a savage metaphor:

> Let all that see these vices thus rewarded
> Take heart and love to study 'em. Mischiefs feed
> Like beasts, till they be fat, and then they bleed.

FACTS AND REFERENCES

FIRST PERFORMANCE

Jonson in the 1616 folio gives 1605, but this would permit any date up to March 25, 1606 (the Elizabethans figured the year from one March 25 to the next). Certain topical references (e.g., the whale at Woolwich, II.i) point to early 1606 (modern reckoning). The play was first acted at the Globe by the King's Men.

SELECTED BIBLIOGRAPHY

Early Editions

Quarto, 1607 (facsimile available).

Folio, 1616 (basis for this edition).

Folio, 1640.

Modern Editions (other than H&S)

Barish, Jonas A., ed. Crofts Classics. New York: Appleton-Century-Crofts, 1958.

Brockbank, Philip, ed. The New Mermaids. London: Ernest Benn, Ltd., 1968.

Halio, Jay L., ed. The Fountainwell Drama Texts. Berkeley and Los Angeles: University of California Press, 1968.

Kernan, Alvin B., ed. The Yale Ben Jonson.[1] New Haven, Conn.: Yale University Press, 1962.

Rea, John D., ed. Yale Studies in English, no. 59. New Haven, Conn.: Yale University Press, 1919.

Sale, Arthur, ed. London: University Tutorial Press, 1951.

Other Scholarship and Criticism[2]

Barish, Jonas A. "The Double Plot in *Volpone*." MP 51 (1953): 83–92.

Davison, P. H. "*Volpone* and the Old Comedy." MLQ 24 (1963): 151–57.

Dessen, Alan C. "*Volpone* and the Late Morality Tradition." MLQ 25 (1964): 383–99.

Donaldson, Ian. "*Volpone*—Quick and Dead." EIC 21 (1971): 121–34.

Enright, D. J. "Poetic Satire and Satire in Verse: A Consideration of Jonson and Massinger." *Scrutiny* 18 (1952): 211–23.

Goldberg, S. L. "Folly into Crime: the Catastrophe of *Volpone*." MLQ 20 (1959): 233–42.

Hallett, Charles A. "The Satanic Nature of Volpone." PQ 49 (1970): 41–55.

Hawkins, Harriett. "Folly, Incurable Disease, and *Volpone*." SEL 8 (1968): 335–48.

Levin, Harry. "Jonson's Metempsychosis." PQ 22 (1943): 231–39.

---

[1] My text and notes are often indebted to this excellent edition.
[2] Many books listed in the Selected Bibliography following the General Introduction include discussions of *Volpone*.

Perkinson, Richard H. "*Volpone* and the Reputation of Venetian Justice." *MLR* 35 (1940): 11–18.

Putney, Rufus. "Jonson's Poetic Comedy." *PQ* 41 (1962): 188–204.

VOLPONE

Never, most equal Sisters, had any man a wit so presently
excellent as that it could raise itself; but there must come both
matter, occasion, commenders, and favorers to it. If this be
true, and that the fortune of all writers doth daily prove it, it
behooves the careful to provide well toward these accidents;   5
and, having acquired them, to preserve that part of reputation
most tenderly wherein the benefit of a friend is also defended.
Hence is it that I now render myself grateful and am studious
to justify the bounty of your act, to which, though your mere
authority were satisfying, yet, it being an age wherein poetry   10
and the professors of it hear so ill on all sides, there will a
reason be looked for in the subject. It is certain, nor can it
with any forehead be opposed, that the too much license of
poetasters in this time hath much deformed their mistress;
that, every day, their manifold and manifest ignorance doth   15

EQUAL—in merit, but also in justice (Latin *aequus*).   TWO . . . UNIVER-
SITIES—Oxford and Cambridge.   6. them—the favorers.   9. your
act—the favoring; the "love and acceptance shown to his poem."   11. professors—practitioners.   hear so ill—are spoken of so slightingly.   12. the
subject—poetry, which in this corrupt age must give reasons for its existence.
13. any forehead—the boldest audacity.   14. poetasters—petty poets.

stick unnatural reproaches upon her; but for their petulancy it
were an act of the greatest injustice either to let the learned
suffer, or so divine a skill (which indeed should not be
attempted with unclean hands) to fall under the least
contempt. For, if men will impartially, and not asquint, look   20
toward the offices and function of a poet, they will easily
conclude to themselves the impossibility of any man's being
the good poet without first being a good man. He that is said
to be able to inform young men to all good disciplines, inflame
grown men to all great virtues, keep old men in their best and   25
supreme state, or, as they decline to childhood, recover them
to their first strength; that comes forth the interpreter and
arbiter of nature, a teacher of things divine no less than
human, a master in manners; and can alone, or with a few,
effect the business of mankind: this, I take him, is no subject   30
for pride and ignorance to exercise their railing rhetoric upon.
But it will here be hastily answered that the writers of these
days are other things: that not only their manners, but their
natures, are inverted, and nothing remaining with them of the
dignity of poet but the abused name, which every scribe   35
usurps; that now, especially in dramatic, or, as they term it,
stage poetry, nothing but ribaldry, profanation, blasphemy, all
license of offense to God and man is practiced. I dare not deny
a great part of this, and am sorry I dare not, because in some
men's abortive features (and would they had never boasted   40
the light) it is overtrue; but that all are embarked in this bold
adventure for hell is a most uncharitable thought, and, uttered,
a more malicious slander. For my particular, I can (and from a
most clear conscience) affirm that I have ever trembled to
think toward the least profaneness, have loathed the use of   45
such foul and unwashed bawdry as is now made the food of
the scene. And, howsoever I cannot escape, from some, the
imputation of sharpness, but that they will say I have taken a
pride, or lust, to be bitter, and not my youngest infant but
hath come into the world with all his teeth; I would ask of   50
these supercilious politics, what nation, society, or general

16. for—because of. petulancy—insolence.   21. offices—duties.
40. abortive features—premature and deformed plays.   49. youngest infant—most recent play before *Volpone, Sejanus* (1603).   50. with all his
teeth—biting, satiric. *Sejanus* had gotten Jonson into trouble with the authorities.   51. politics—schemers.

order, or state I have provoked? what public person? whether I
have not in all these preserved their dignity, as mine own
person, safe? My works are read, allowed (I speak of those that
are entirely mine); look into them. What broad reproofs have I   55
used? where have I been particular? where personal? except to
a mimic, cheater, bawd, or buffoon, creatures for their
insolencies worthy to be taxed? Yet to which of these so
pointingly as he might not either ingenuously have confessed
or wisely dissembled his disease? But it is not rumor can make   60
men guilty, much less entitle me to other men's crimes. I know
that nothing can be so innocently writ or carried, but may be
made obnoxious to construction; marry, whilst I bear mine
innocence about me, I fear it not. Application is now grown a
trade with many, and there are that profess to have a key for   65
the deciphering of everything; but let wise and noble persons
take heed how they be too credulous, or give leave to these
invading interpreters to be overfamiliar with their fames, who
cunningly, and often, utter their own virulent malice under
other men's simplest meanings. As for those that will (by   70
faults which charity hath raked up, or common honesty
concealed) make themselves a name with the multitude, or (to
draw their rude and beastly claps) care not whose living faces
they entrench with their petulant styles, may they do it
without a rival, for me. I choose rather to live graved in   75
obscurity than share with them in so preposterous a fame. Nor
can I blame the wishes of those severe and wiser patriots, who,
providing the hurts these licentious spirits may do in a state,
desire rather to see fools, and devils, and those antique relics
of barbarism retrieved, with all other ridiculous and exploded   80
follies, than behold the wounds of private men, of princes, and
nations. For, as Horace makes Trebatius speak, among these,

54. allowed—accepted by the Master of Revels, the censor of the time.
55. entirely mine—*Eastward Ho* (1605), written by Jonson, Chapman, and
Marston, had not been "allowed"; the three writers had been jailed because
of passages considered insulting to King James. broad—indecent.
62. carried—conducted.   63. to construction—by interpretation.
64. Application—finding hidden allusions to particular persons.   65. there
are—there are those.   71. raked up—covered up.   74. styles—in the
usual sense and also Latin *stilus,* a sharp-pointed writing instrument capable of
intrenching a face.   78. providing—foreseeing.   79. fools, and devils—
the old-fashioned morality plays, which featured such characters. 80. exploded—the Latin sense, hooted and clapped off the stage.

—Sibi quisque timet, quamquam est intactus, et odit.

And men may justly impute such rages, if continued, to the
writer, as his sports. The increase of which lust in liberty,   85
together with the present trade of the stage, in all their
misc'line interludes, what learned or liberal soul doth not
already abhor? where nothing but the filth of the time is
uttered, and that with such impropriety of phrase, such plenty
of solecisms, such dearth of sense, so bold prolepses, so racked   90
metaphors, with brothelry able to violate the ear of a pagan,
and blasphemy to turn the blood of a Christian to water. I
cannot but be serious in a cause of this nature, wherein my
fame and the reputations of divers honest and learned are the
question; when a name so full of authority, antiquity, and all   95
great mark, is, through their insolence, become the lowest
scorn of the age; and those men subject to the petulancy of
every vernaculous orator that were wont to be the care of
kings and happiest monarchs. This it is that hath not only rapt
me to present indignation but made me studious heretofore   100
and by all my actions to stand off from them; which may most
appear in this my latest work (which you, most learned
Arbitresses, have seen, judged, and, to my crown, approved)
wherein I have labored, for their instruction and amendment,
to reduce not only the ancient forms but manners of the   105
scene: the easiness, the propriety, the innocence, and last, the
doctrine, which is the principal end of poesie, to inform men
in the best reason of living. And though my catastrophe may
in the strict rigor of comic law meet with censure, as turning
back to my promise; I desire the learned and charitable critic   110
to have so much faith in me to think it was done of industry:

83. *Sibi . . .odit*—from Horace (*Satires* II.i.23); translated by Jonson himself
(*Poetaster* III.v.41–42): "In satires, each man, though untouched, complains/
As he were hurt; and hates such biting strains."   84-85. men . . . sports—a
difficult passage. Perhaps: if such wounding writers continue their practices
(rages) they become fair game (sports) for the satirist.   87. misc'line interludes—mixed, jumbled plays (Latin *ludi miscelli*).   90. prolepses—anach-
ronisms (*OED*).   95. name—i.e., poet.   98. vernaculous—low-bred,
scurrilous (*OED*).   99. rapt—carried me by force.   105. reduce—
lead back, restore.   108. catastrophe—climax of the play.   109. comic
law—the dominant critical theories of the time.   109-110. as turning back
to my promise—as if I were turning my back on my promise ("to bring back
the ancient forms").   111. of industry—on purpose.

for with what ease I could have varied it nearer his scale (but
that I fear to boast my own faculty) I could here insert. But
my special aim being to put the snaffle in their mouths that
cry out, "We never punish vice in our interludes, &c," I took   115
the more liberty, though not without some lines of example
drawn even in the ancients themselves, the goings out of whose
comedies are not always joyful, but oft times the bawds, the
servants, the rivals, yea, and the masters are mulcted; and fitly,
it being the office of a comic poet to imitate justice, and   120
instruct to life, as well as purity of language, or stir up gentle
affections. To which I shall take the occasion elsewhere to
speak. For the present, most reverenced Sisters, as I have cared
to be thankful for your affections past, and here made the
understanding acquainted with some ground of your favors, let   125
me not despair their continuance, to the maturing of some
worthier fruits; wherein, if my Muses be true to me, I shall
raise the despised head of poetry again, and stripping her out
of those rotten and base rags wherewith the times have
adulterated her form, restore her to her primitive habit,   130
feature, and majesty, and render her worthy to be embraced
and kissed of all the great and master-spirits of our world. As
for the vile and slothful, who never affected an act worthy of
celebration, or are so inward with their own vicious natures as
they worthily fear her and think it a high point of policy to   135
keep her in contempt with their declamatory and windy
invectives, she shall out of just rage incite her servants (who
are *genus irritabile*) to spout ink in their faces that shall eat,
farther than their marrow, into their fames; and not Cinnamus
the barber with his art shall be able to take out the brands, but 140
they shall live, and be read, till the wretches die, as things
worst deserving of themselves in chief, and then of all
mankind.

> From my house in the Blackfriars,
> this 11. of February, 1607.

114. snaffle—bit for a bridle.   121. gentle—noble.   138. *genus
irritabile*—an irritable sort.   139. Cinnamus—barber-surgeon in Martial
(VI.1xiv.26), skilled in removing stigmata.   144-45. From . . . 1607—in
quarto only.

THE PERSONS OF THE PLAY

VOLPONE, *a Magnifico*
MOSCA, *his parasite*
VOLTORE, *an advocate*
CORBACCIO, *an old gentleman*
CORVINO, *a merchant*
AVOCATORI, *four magistrates*
NOTARIO, *the register*
NANO, *a dwarf*
CASTRONE, *an eunuch*
[SIR] POLITIC WOULDBE, *a knight*
PEREGRINE, *a gent[leman]-traveler*
BONARIO, *a young gentleman [son of Corbaccio]*
FINE MADAME WOULDBE, *the knight's wife*
CELIA, *the merchant's wife*
COMMENDATORI, *officers*
MERCATORI, *three merchants*
ANDROGYNO, *a hermaphrodite*
SERVITORE, *a servant*
GREGE
WOMEN

THE SCENE

Venice

Volpone—the fox. The suffix *-one* in Italian is augmentative; *volpe* is "fox," but *Volpone* is "big, bad fox." An Italian dictionary by Jonson's friend John Florio (*A World of Words*, 1598) defines *volpone* as "an old fox, an old Reynard, an old crafty, sly, subtle companion, sneaking lurking wily deceiver." Magnifico—nobleman. Mosca—fly, or "flesh-fly," as Voltore calls him (V.ix.1). Voltore—vulture. Corbaccio—raven. The suffix *-accio* has the connotation of messy. Corvino—carrion crow. Avocatori—properly, state prosecutors, but here, judges. Nano—Latin *nanus*, "dwarf." Politic Wouldbe—often called Sir Pol, Pol being a common name for parrots. Peregrine—a hawk used in falconry; also, literally, a traveler. Bonario—"honest, uncorrupt" (Florio). Celia—related to Latin *caelum*, "sky, heaven." Androgyno—from Greek *andros* ("man") and *gyne* ("woman"). Grege—crowd.

THE ARGUMENT

V olpone, childless, rich, feigns sick, despairs,
O ffers his state to hopes of several heirs,
L ies languishing; his Parasite receives
P resents of all, assures, deludes; then weaves
O ther cross plots, which ope themselves, are told.   5
N ew tricks for safety are sought; they thrive; when, bold,
E ach tempts th' other again, and all are sold.

2. state—estate.   5. ope—open. told—exposed.   7. sold—enslaved.

PROLOGUE

Now, luck God send us, and a little wit
  Will serve to make our play hit;
According to the palates of the season,
  Here is rhyme not empty of reason.
This we were bid to credit from our poet,   5
  Whose true scope, if you would know it,
In all his poems still hath been this measure:
  To mix profit with your pleasure;
And not as some, whose throats their envy failing,
  Cry hoarsely, "All he writes is railing,"   10
And when his plays come forth, think they can flout them,
  With saying, "He was a year about them."
To these there needs no lie but this his creature,
  Which was two months since no feature;
And though he dares give them five lives to mend it,   15
  'Tis known, five weeks fully penned it,
From his own hand, without a coadjutor,
  Novice, journeyman, or tutor.
Yet thus much I can give you as a token
  Of his play's worth: no eggs are broken,   20

1. God—the Quarto reading; changed to "yet." in the folio, presumably in
deference to censorship policy.   6. scope—aim.   8. profit ... pleasure—from Horace (*Ars Poetica* 343–44). See General Introduction.
12. a year—Jonson was notoriously slow in composing.   13. his creature—i.e., *Volpone.*   14. was ... no feature—did not exist.
17–18. coadjutor ... tutor—various forms of collaboration in authorship,
all common at the time.

Nor quaking custards with fierce teeth affrighted,
  Wherewith your rout are so delighted;
Nor hales he in a gull, old ends reciting,
  To stop gaps in his loose writing,
With such a deal of monstrous and forced action,   25
  As might make Bedlam a faction;
Nor made he 'his play for jests stol'n from each table,
  But makes jests to fit his fable.
And so presents quick comedy, refined,
  As best critics have designed;   30
The laws of time, place, persons he observeth,
  From no needful rule he swerveth.
All gall and copperas from his ink he draineth,
  Only a little salt remaineth,
Wherewith he'll rub your cheeks, till red with laughter,   35
  They shall look fresh a week after.

21. custards—fools (Kernan).   23. gull—simpleton, sucker. old ends—
lines from old plays, now clichés.   26. make Bedlam a faction—win the
support of the London insane asylum.   28. fable—plot.   29. quick—
alive, lively.   31. The laws of time, place, persons—fixtures of
Renaissance criticism. The law of time said the fictional action of a play
should take no more than one day. The place should be one city. Persons
should act and speak in a fashion appropriate to the comic type to which
each should belong, e.g., the jealous husband, the meal-cadging parasite.
32. From . . . swerveth—Sale wittily observes, "Whenever Jonson follows
classical (or neo-classical) rules, he and/or his dramatic spokesmen praise him
for doing so; whenever he does not [see above], they praise him for not doing
so."   33. gall and copperas—oak gall and iron sulphate, both used in
making ink.

ACT I
SCENE I

                    [*Volpone's house.*]
  Volpone. Good morning to the day; and next, my gold!
Open the shrine, that I may see my saint.
              [*Mosca opens a curtain disclosing piles of gold.*]
Hail the world's soul, and mine! More glad than is

3. world's soul—in astrology the world's soul is the sun, which Volpone is
here greeting, but in *The Masque of Beauty* (1.374) Jonson specifically equates
the world's soul with the Platonic harmony of the universe.

The teeming earth to see the longed-for sun
Peep through the horns of the celestial Ram,   5
Am I, to view thy splendor darkening his;
That lying here, amongst my other hoards,
Show'st like a flame by night, or like the day
Struck out of chaos, when all darkness fled
Unto the center. O thou son of Sol,   10
But brighter than thy father, let me kiss,
With adoration, thee, and every relic
Of sacred treasure in this blessed room.
                    [*Seizes and kisses pieces of treasure.*]
Well did wise poets by thy glorious name
Title that age which they would have the best,   15
Thou being the best of things, and far transcending
All style of joy in children, parents, friends,
Or any other waking dream on earth.
Thy looks when they to Venus did ascribe,
They should have giv'n her twenty thousand cupids,   20
Such are thy beauties and our loves! Dear saint,
Riches, the dumb god that giv'st all men tongues,
That canst do nought, and yet mak'st men do all things;
The price of souls; even hell, with thee to boot,
Is made worth heaven! Thou are virtue, fame,   25
Honor, and all things else. Who can get thee,
He shall be noble, valiant, honest, wise—
    Mosca. And what he will, sir. Riches are in fortune
A greater good than wisdom is in nature.
    Volpone. True, my beloved Mosca. Yet, I glory   30
More in the cunning purchase of my wealth
Than in the glad possession, since I gain
No common way: I use no trade, no venture;
I wound no earth with ploughshares; fat no beasts
To feed the shambles; have no mills for iron,   35

5. Peep . . . Ram—astrological language for the beginning of spring.
6. thy—the gold's.   his—the sun's.   8–9. day . . . chaos—the day the
earth was created.   10. son of Sol—the alchemists considered gold a
child of the sun.   15. that age—the Golden Age, during which (ironi-
cally) men did not covet gold but lived in simplicity and harmony.
17. style—form.   19. Venus . . . ascribe—following Homeric tradition the
Latin poets often called Venus golden (*aurea*).   31. purchase—thieves'
booty was called *purchase* in underworld jargon.   35. shambles—
slaughterhouse.

Oil, corn, or men, to grind 'em into powder;
I blow no subtle glass; expose no ships
To threat'nings of the furrow-facèd sea;
I turn no monies in the public bank,
Nor usure private—
    Mosca.   No, sir, nor devour   40
Soft prodigals. You shall ha' some will swallow
A melting heir as glibly as your Dutch
Will pills of butter, and ne'er purge for't;
Tear forth the fathers of poor families
Out of their beds, and coffin them, alive,   45
In some kind, clasping prison, where their bones
May be forthcoming, when the flesh is rotten.
But, your sweet nature doth abhor these courses;
You loathe the widow's or the orphan's tears
Should wash your pavements, or their piteous cries   50
Ring in your roofs, and beat the air for vengeance—
    Volpone. Right, Mosca, I do loathe it.
    Mosca.   And, besides, sir,
You are not like the thresher that doth stand
With a huge flail, watching a heap of corn,
And, hungry, dares not taste the smallest grain,   55
But feeds on mallows and such bitter herbs;
Nor like the merchant, who hath filled his vaults
With Romagnìa and rich Candian wines,
Yet drinks the lees of Lombard's vinegar.
You will not lie in straw, whilst moths and worms   60
Feed on your sumptuous hangings and soft beds.
You know the use of riches, and dare give, now,
From that bright heap, to me, your poor observer,
Or to your dwarf, or your hermaphrodite,
Your eunuch, or what other household trifle   65
Your pleasure allows maintenance—
    Volpone.   Hold thee, Mosca,
                          [*Gives him money.*]
Take of my hand; thou strik'st on truth in all,
And they are envious term thee parasite.

---

42. Dutch—proverbially fond of butter.   43. purge—take a laxative.
58. Romagnia—Rumney, a sweet Greek wine. Candian—Cretan.
63. observer—servant.   68. term—who term.

Call forth my dwarf, my eunuch, and my fool,
And let 'em make me sport. What should I do   [*Exit Mosca.*]   70
But cocker up my genius, and live free
To all delights my fortune calls me to?
I have no wife, no parent, child, ally,
To give my substance to; but whom I make
Must be my heir, and this makes men observe me.   75
This draws new clients, daily, to my house,
Women and men of every sex and age,
That bring me presents, send me plate, coin, jewels,
With hope that when I die (which they expect
Each greedy minute) it shall then return   80
Tenfold upon them; whilst some, covetous
Above the rest, seek to engross me, whole,
And counterwork the one unto the other,
Contend in gifts, as they would seem in love.
All which I suffer, playing with their hopes,   85
And am content to coin 'em into profit,
And look upon their kindness, and take more,
And look on that; still bearing them in hand,
Letting the cherry knock against their lips,
And draw it by their mouths, and back again.   90
How now!

71. cocker up—to pamper, spoil (a child). *OED* also gives, without convincing evidence, "to coddle up (an invalid) so as to restore him to
strength." genius—a classical belief: the tutelary god or attendant spirit
alloted to every person at birth.   75. observe—pay court to.
82. engross—monopolize.   88. bearing them in hand—leading them on.

ACT I
SCENE II

[*Re-enter Mosca with Nano, Androgyno, and Castrone.*]
  Nano. Now, room for fresh gamesters, who do will you to
                                                                    [know,
They do bring you neither play nor university show;
And therefore do entreat you that whatsoever they rehearse,

May not fare a whit the worse, for the false pace of the verse.
If you wonder at this, you will wonder more ere we pass,   5
For know, here is enclosed the soul of Pythagoras,   [*Pointing*
That juggler divine, as hereafter shall follow;   *to Androgyno.*]
Which soul, fast and loose, sir, came first from Apollo,
And was breathed into Aethalides, Mercurius his son,
Where it had the gift to remember all that ever was done.   10
From thence it fled forth, and made quick transmigration
To goldy-locked Euphorbus, who was killed in good fashion,
At the siege of old Troy, by the cuckold of Sparta.
Hermotimus was next (I find it in my charta)
To whom it did pass, where no sooner it was missing,   15
But with one Pyrrhus of Delos it learned to go afishing;
And thence did it enter the sophist of Greece.
From Pythagore, she went into a beautiful piece,
Hight Aspasia, the meretrix; and the next toss of her
Was again of a whore, she became a philosopher,   20
Crates the Cynic, as itself doth relate it.
Since, kings, knights, and beggars, knaves, lords, and fools gat
                                                          [it,
Besides ox and ass, camel, mule, goat, and brock,
In all which it hath spoke, as in the Cobbler's cock.
But I come not here to discourse of that matter,   25
Or his one, two, or three, or his great oath, "By Quater!"

4. false . . . verse—the meter of this interlude parodies that of some old morality plays.   6. Pythagoras—Greek philosopher of sixth century B.C.
He supported his belief in the transmigration of souls by recalling the bodies
his own soul had previously occupied.   Jonson drew the names and the
tone here from Lucian's dialogue "The Dream, or the Cock," which is itself
a satirical treatment of Pythagoras' claims.   8. fast and loose—referring
to a trick in which a belt was folded in a special way and a dagger inserted.
Bets were placed on whether the belt was fast or loose (around the dagger
or free of it).   9. Aethalides—herald for Jason's argonauts; he had from
his father, Mercury, the gift of remembering everything.   12. Euphorbus—
a Trojan hero (*Illiad* 17).   13. cuckold of Sparta—Menelaus, husband of
Helen.   14. Hermotimus—ancient Greek philosopher.   charta—papers
(perhaps Lucian's Dialogue).   21. Crates—cynic philosopher.
24. Cobbler's cock—in Lucian's dialogue the soul of Pythagoras is occu-
pying the body of a cock, who is describing his previous bodies to his
master, a cobbler.   26. "By Quater"—Pythagoras attached mystical
significance to numbers, especially the trigon or triangle of four, viz.,   *
                                                              * *
                                                           * * *
                                                        * * * *

His musics, his trigon, his golden thigh,
Or his telling how elements shift; but I
Would ask, how of late thou hast suffered translation,
And shifted thy coat in these days of reformation?   30
    Androgyno. Like one of the reformèd, a fool, as you see,
Counting all old doctrine heresy.
    Nano. But not on thine own forbid meats hast thou
                                      [ventured?
    Androgyno. On fish, when first a Carthusian I entered.
    Nano. Why, then thy dogmatical silence hath left thee?   35
    Androgyno. Of that an obstreperous lawyer bereft me.
    Nano. O wonderful change! When Sir Lawyer forsook
                                      [thee,
For Pythagore's sake, what body then took thee?
    Androgyno. A good, dull moyle.
    Nano.   And how! by that means
Thou wert brought to allow of the eating of beans?   40
    Androgyno. Yes.
    Nano.   But from the moyle into whom didst
                                     [thou pass?
    Androgyno. Into a very strange beast, by some writers
                                 [called an ass;
By others, a precise, pure, illuminate brother,
Of those devour flesh, and sometimes one another;
And will drop you forth a libel, or a sanctified lie,   45
Betwixt every spoonful of a nativity-pie.
    Nano. Now quit thee, for heaven, of that profane nation,
And gently report thy next transmigration.
    Androgyno. To the same that I am.
    Nano.   A creature of delight,
And (what is more than a fool) an hermaphrodite?   50
Now, 'pray thee, sweet soul, in all thy variation,

---

27. golden thigh—the followers of Pythogoras believed he had a golden
thigh.   30. reformation—the Reformation; here Jonson, a Catholic at this
time, begins to mingle satire on Protestants with Lucian's satire on
Pythagorean mysticism.   33. forbid meats—the Pythagoreans were for-
bidden to eat meat, fish, or beans and enjoined to a five-year silence.
34. Carthusian—a religious order famed for the severity of its diet.
39. moyle—mule.   43. precise . . . brother—i.e., a Puritan.   46. nativity-pie—the Puritans disliked the term Christmas pie because Christmas
contains the popish syllable *mas*.

Which body wouldst thou choose to take up thy station?
>   *Androgyno.* Troth, this I am in, even here would I tarry.
>   *Nano.* 'Cause here the delight of each sex thou canst vary?
>   *Androgyno.* Alas, those pleasures be stale and forsaken;   55
No, 'tis your fool wherewith I am so taken,
The only one creature that I can call blessed;
For all other forms I have proved most distressèd.
>   *Nano.* Spoke true, as thou wert in Pythagoras still.
This learnèd opinion we celebrate will,   60
Fellow eunuch, as behooves us, with all our wit and art,
To dignify that whereof ourselves are so great and special a
>   [part.

>   *Volpone.* Now, very, very pretty! Mosca, this
Was thy invention?
>   *Mosca.*   If it please my patron,
Not else.
>   *Volpone.* It doth, good Mosca.
>   *Mosca.*   Then it was, sir.   65

SONG

>   Fools, they are the only nation
>   Worth men's envy or admiration;
>   Free from care or sorrow-taking,
>   Selves and others merry making,
>   All they speak or do is sterling.   70
>   Your fool, he is your great man's dearling,
>   And your ladies' sport and pleasure;
>   Tongue and bable are his treasure.
>   E'en his face begetteth laughter,
>   And he speaks truth free from slaughter.   75
>   He's the grace of every feast,
>   And, sometimes, the chiefest guest:
>   Hath his trencher and his stool,
>   When wit waits upon the fool.
>   O, who would not be   80
>   Hee, hee, hee?
>   *One knocks without.*
>   *Volpone.* Who's that? Away! Look, Mosca.
>   [*Exeunt Nano and Castrone.*]

---

73. bable—the fool's scepter; also, slang for phallus.

    Mosca.   Fool, begone!
                              [*Exit Androgyno.*]
'Tis Signior Voltore, the advocate;
I know him by his knock.
    Volpone.   Fetch me my gown,
My furs, and night-caps; say my couch is changing,   85
And let him entertain himself awhile
Without i' th' gallery. [*Exit Mosca.*] Now, now, my clients
Begin their visitation! Vulture, kite,
Raven, and gorcrow, all my birds of prey,
That think me turning carcass, now they come.   90
I am not for 'em yet.   [*Enter Mosca.*]
              How now? the news?
    Mosca. A piece of plate, sir.
    Volpone.   Of what bigness?
    Mosca.   Huge,
Massy, and antique, with your name inscribed,
And arms engraven.
    Volpone.   Good! and not a fox
Stretched on the earth, with fine delusive sleights   95
Mocking a gaping crow? ha, Mosca!
    Mosca.   Sharp, sir.
    Volpone. Give me my furs. Why dost thou laugh so, man?
    Mosca. I cannot chose, sir, when I apprehend
What thoughts he has, without, now, as he walks:
That this might be the last gift he should give;   100
That this would fetch you; if you died today,
And gave him all, what he should be tomorrow;
What large return would come of all his ventures;
How he should worshipped be, and reverenced;
Ride with his furs, and foot-cloths; waited on   105
By herds of fools and clients; have clear way
Made for his moyle, as lettered as himself;
Be called the great and learnèd advocate:
And then concludes, there's nought impossible.

---

85. is changing—being changed.   89. gorcrow—carrion crow.
94–96. and not a fox . . . crow—Volpone is suggesting another coat of arms
for the plate: a picture illustrating Aesop's fable of the fox and the crow.
The crow, with a morsel of food in his beak, is praised by the fox for his
singing voice; when the crow opens his mouth to demonstrate, he drops the
food (see V.viii.13).

    Volpone. Yes, to be learnèd, Mosca.

    Mosca.   O, no; rich   110

Implies it. Hood an ass with reverend purple,

So you can hide his two ambitious ears,

And he shall pass for a cathedral doctor.

    Volpone. My caps, my caps, good Mosca. Fetch him in.

    Mosca. Stay, sir; your ointment for your eyes.

    Volpone.   That's true; 115

Dispatch, dispatch. I long to have possession

Of my new present.

    Mosca.   That, and thousands more,

I hope to see you lord of.

    Volpone.   Thanks, kind Mosca.

    Mosca. And that, when I am lost in blended dust,

And hundreds such as I am, in succession—   120

    Volpone. Nay, that were too much, Mosca.

    Mosca.   You shall live

Still to delude these harpies.

    Volpone.   Loving Mosca!

        [*After looking into a mirror, Volpone gets into bed.*]

'Tis well. My pillow now, and let him enter.   [*Exit Mosca.*]

Now, my feigned cough, my phthisic, and my gout,

My apoplexy, palsy, and catarrhs,   125

Help, with your forcèd functions, this my posture,

Wherein, this three year, I have milked their hopes.

He comes, I hear him—uh! uh! uh! uh! O—

111. Hood . . .purple—the academic gown worn by doctors of philosophy had a purple hood.   129. uh! uh! uh! uh! O—"uh! is a cough and O a groan" (Sale).

ACT I

SCENE III

                         [*Enter Mosca with Voltore.*]

    Mosca. You still are what you were, sir. Only you,

Of all the rest, are he commands his love,

And you do wisely to preserve it thus,

With early visitation, and kind notes

Of your good meaning to him, which, I know,   5

Cannot but come most grateful. Patron, sir.
Here's Signior Voltore is come—
    Volpone. *[Faintly.]*   What say you?
    Mosca. Sir, Signior Voltore is come this morning
To visit you.
    Volpone. I thank him.
    Mosca.   And hath brought
A piece of antique plate, bought of St. Mark,   10
With which he here presents you.
    Volpone.   He is welcome.
Pray him to come more often.
    Mosca.   Yes.
    Voltore.   What says he?
    Mosca. He thanks you and desires you see him often.
    Volpone. Mosca.
    Mosca.   My patron?
    Volpone.   Bring him near, where is he?
I long to feel his hand.
    Mosca.   *[Trying to guide Volpone's groping hands.]*
           The plate is here, sir.   15
    Voltore. How fare you, sir?
    Volpone.   I thank you, Signior Voltore.
Where is the plate? mine eyes are bad.
    Voltore. *[Putting it into his hands.]* I'm sorry
To see you still thus weak.
    Mosca. *[Aside.]*   That he is not weaker.
    Volpone. You are too munificent.
    Voltore.   No, sir; would to heaven
I could as well give health to you as that plate!   20
    Volpone. You give, sir, what you can. I thank you. Your
                   [love
Hath taste in this, and shall not be unanswered.
I pray you see me often.
    Voltore.   Yes, I shall, sir.
    Volpone. Be not far from me.
    Mosca. *[To Voltore.]*   Do you observe that, sir?
    Volpone. Hearken unto me still; it will concern you.   25
    Mosca. You are a happy man, sir; know your good.
    Volpone. I cannot now last long—

10. St. Mark—the piazza of St. Mark was famous for goldsmiths.

  Mosca.   You are his heir, sir.
  Voltore. Am I?
  Volpone.   I feel me going, uh! uh! uh! uh!
I am sailing to my port, uh! uh! uh! uh!
And I am glad I am so near my haven.   30
  Mosca. Alas, kind gentleman. Well, we must all go—
  Voltore. But, Mosca—
  Mosca.   Age will conquer.
  Voltore.   .   Pray thee, hear me.
Am I inscribed his heir for certain?
  Mosca.   Are you?
I do beseech you, sir, you will vouchsafe
To write me i' your family. All my hopes   35
Depend upon your worship. I am lost,
Except the rising sun do shine on me.
  Voltore. It shall both shine and warm thee, Mosca.
  Mosca.   Sir,
I am a man that have not done your love
All the worst offices. Here I wear your keys,   40
See all your coffers and caskets locked,
Keep the poor inventory of your jewels,
Your plate, and monies; am your steward, sir,
Husband your goods here.
  Voltore.   But am I sole heir?
  Mosca. Without a partner, sir, confirmed this morning; 45
The wax is warm yet, and the ink scarce dry
Upon the parchment.
  Voltore.   Happy, happy me!
By what good chance, sweet Mosca?
  Mosca.   Your desert, sir;
I know no second cause.
  Voltore.   Thy modesty
Is loth to know it; well, we shall requite it.   50
  Mosca. He ever liked your course, sir; that first took him.
I oft have heard him say how he admired
Men of your large profession, that could speak
To every cause, and things mere contraries,
Till they were hoarse again, yet all be law;   55
That, with most quick agility, could turn,

54. mere—absolute.

And re-turn; make knots, and undo them;
Give forkèd counsel; take provoking gold
On either hand, and put it up. These men,
He knew, would thrive with their humility.   60
And, for his part, he thought he should be bless'd
To have his heir of such a suffering spirit,
So wise, so grave, of so perplexed a tongue,
And loud withal, that would not wag, nor scarce
Lie still, without a fee; when every word   65
Your worship but lets fall, is a chequin!   *Another knocks.*
Who's that? One knocks. I would not have you seen, sir.
And yet—pretend you came and went in haste;
I'll fashion an excuse. And, gentle sir,
When you do come to swim in golden lard,   70
Up to the arms in honey, that your chin
Is borne up stiff with fatness of the flood,
Think on your vassal; but remember me:
I ha' not been your worst of clients.
     Voltore.   Mosca—
     Mosca. When will you have your inventory brought, sir?   75
Or see a copy of the will? [*Calling out to the one knocking.*]
                                          [Anon.
I'll bring 'em to you, sir. Away, be gone,
Put business i' your face.   [*Exit Voltore.*]
     Volpone.   Excellent, Mosca!
Come hither, let me kiss thee.
     Mosca.   Keep you still, sir.
Here is Corbaccio.
     Volpone.   Set the plate away.   80
The vulture's gone, and the old raven's come.

---

58. provoking—"provoke: to call to a judge or court to take up one's
cause" (*OED*).   63. perplexed—intricate, puzzling.   66. chequin—
gold coin.   67. I would not have you seen—a lie; he wants Corbaccio
to see Voltore.

ACT I

SCENE IV

Mosca. Betake you to your silence, and your sleep.
[*To the plate.*] Stand there and multiply. Now shall we see
A wretch who is indeed more impotent
Than this can feign to be, yet hopes to hop
Over his grave. [*Enter Corbaccio.*] Signior Corbaccio!   5
You're very welcome, sir.
    Corbaccio.   How does your patron?
    Mosca. Troth, as he did, sir; no amends.
    Corbaccio. [*Cupping his ear.*]   What? mends he?
    Mosca. [*Shouting.*] No, sir. He is rather worse.
    Corbaccio.   That's well. Where is he?
    Mosca. Upon his couch, sir, newly fall'n asleep.
    Corbaccio. Does he sleep well?
    Mosca.   No wink, sir, all this night,   10
Nor yesterday, but slumbers.
    Corbaccio.   Good! he should take
Some counsel of physicians. I have brought him
An opiate here, from mine own doctor—
    Mosca. He will not hear of drugs.
    Corbaccio.   Why? I myself
Stood by while 't was made, saw all th' ingredients,   15
And know it cannot but most gently work.
My life for his, 'tis but to make him sleep.
    Volpone. [*Aside.*] Ay, his last sleep, if he would take it.
    Mosca.   Sir,
He has no faith in physic.
    Corbaccio.   Say you, say you?
    Mosca. He has no faith in physic: he does think   20
Most of your doctors are the greater danger,
And worse disease t' escape. I often have
Heard him protest that your physician
Should never be his heir.
    Corbaccio.   Not I his heir?
    Mosca. Not your physician, sir.   25

---

2. multiply—probably a blasphemous echo of Gen. 1:28.   4. this—Volpone.   11. but slumbers—only dozes.

    Corbaccio.   O, no, no, no.
I do not mean it.
    Mosca.   No, sir, nor their fees
He cannot brook; he says they flay a man
Before they kill him.
    Corbaccio.   Right, I do conceive you.
    Mosca. And then, they do it by experiment,
For which the law not only doth absolve 'em,   30
But gives them great reward; and he is loth
To hire his death so.
    Corbaccio.   It is true, they kill
With as much license as a judge.
    Mosca.   Nay, more;
For he but kills, sir, where the law condemns,
And these can kill him too.
    Corbaccio.   Ay, or me,   35
Or any man. How does his apoplex?
Is that strong on him still?
    Mosca.   Most violent.
His speech is broken, and his eyes are set,
His face drawn longer than 't was wont—
    Corbaccio.   How? how?
Stronger than he was wont?
    Mosca.   No, sir; his face   40
Drawn longer than 't was wont.
    Corbaccio.   O, good.
    Mosca.   His mouth
Is ever gaping, and his eyelids hang.
    Corbaccio.   Good.
    Mosca. A freezing numbness stiffens all his joints,
And makes the color of his flesh like lead.
    Corbaccio.   'Tis good.
    Mosca. His pulse beats slow and dull.
    Corbaccio.   Good symptoms still. 45
    Mosca. And from his brain—
    Corbaccio.   Ha? How? not from his brain?
    Mosca. Yes, sir, and from his brain—

27. flay—skin alive.   46. not from his brain—perhaps Corbaccio thinks
from means away from, i.e., out of his head, and he is suddenly afraid
that Volpone will be unable to make a will (see 1.57). Mosca reassures the
old rascal that he simply meant proceeding from.

  Corbaccio.   I conceive you; good.

  Mosca. Flows a cold sweat, with a continual rheum,

Forth the resolvèd corners of his eyes.

  Corbaccio. Is't possible? Yet I am better, ha!   50

How does he with the swimming of his head?

  Mosca. O, sir, 'tis past the scotomy; he now

Hath lost his feeling, and hath left to snort;

You hardly can perceive him that he breathes.

  Corbaccio. Excellent, excellent; sure I shall outlast him! 55

This makes me young again, a score of years.

  Mosca. I was a-coming for you, sir.

  Corbaccio.   Has he made his will?

What has he given me?

  Mosca.   No, sir.

  Corbaccio.   Nothing? ha!

  Mosca. He has not made his will, sir.

  Corbaccio.   Oh, oh, oh.

What then did Voltore, the lawyer, here?   60

  Mosca. He smelled a carcass, sir, when he but heard

My master was about his testament;

As I did urge him to it for your good—

  Corbaccio. He came unto him, did he? I thought so.

  Mosca. Yes, and presented him this piece of plate. 65

  Corbaccio. To be his heir?

  Mosca.   I do not know, sir.

  Corbaccio.   True,

I know it too.

  Mosca. [*Aside.*] By your own scale, sir.

  Corbaccio.   Well,

I shall prevent him yet. See, Mosca, look,

Here I have brought a bag of bright chequins,

Will quite weigh down his plate.

  Mosca. [*Taking the bag.*] Yea, marry, sir.   70

This is true physic, this your sacred medicine;

No talk of opiates to this great elixir.

---

47. conceive—understand. 49. resolvèd—slackened. 50. Yet I am
better—fluid discharge from the brain was held to be the last stage of incurable apoplexy, and Corbaccio is delighted. 52. scotomy—dizziness
accompanied by dimness of sight (*OED*). 68. prevent—come before.
Used in this sense several times in the play. 70. marry—indeed.

Corbaccio. 'Tis *aurum palpabile*, if not *potabile*.

Mosca. It shall be ministered to him, in his bowl?

Corbaccio. Ay, do, do, do,

Mosca.   Most blessed cordial!   75
This will recover him.

    Corbaccio.   Yes, do, do, do.

    Mosca. I think it were not best, sir.

    Corbaccio.   What?

    Mosca.   To recover him.

    Corbaccio. O, no, no, no; by no means.

    Mosca.   Why, sir, this
Will work some strange effect if he but feel it.

    Corbaccio. 'Tis true, therefore forbear; I'll take my
                                 [venture;   80
Give me 't again.

    Mosca.   At no hand, pardon me;
You shall not do yourself that wrong, sir. I
Will so advise you, you shall have it all.

    Corbaccio. How?

    Mosca.   All, sir; 'tis your right, your own; no
                                      [man
Can claim a part; 'tis yours without a rival,   85
Decreed by destiny.

    Corbaccio.   How, how, good Mosca?

    Mosca. I'll tell you, sir. This fit he shall recover—

    Corbaccio. I do conceive you.

    Mosca.   And on the first advantage
Of his gained sense, will I re-importune him
Unto the making of his testament,   90
And show him this.   [*Points to the bag of gold.*]

    Corbaccio.   Good, good.

    Mosca.   'Tis better yet,
If you will hear, sir.

    Corbaccio.   Yes, with all my heart.

    Mosca. Now would I counsel you, make home with speed;
There, frame a will whereto you shall inscribe
My master your sole heir.   95

73. *aurum . . . potabile*—"gold which can be felt if not drunk." Gold dissolved in liquid was believed to be a universal remedy.   75. cordial—
medicine for the heart.

    Corbaccio.   And disinherit
My son?
    Mosca. O, sir, the better; for that color
Shall make it much more taking.
    Corbaccio.   O, but color?
    Mosca. This will, sir, you shall send it unto me.
Now, when I come to enforce, as I will do,
Your cares, your watchings, and your many prayers,   100
Your more than many gifts, your this day's present,
And, last, produce your will; where, without thought
Or least regard unto your proper issue,
A son so brave and highly meriting,
The stream of your diverted love hath thrown you   105
Upon my master, and made him your heir:
He cannot be so stupid, or stone dead,
But out of conscience and mere gratitude—
    Corbaccio. He must pronounce me his?
    Mosca.   'Tis true.
    Corbaccio.   This plot
Did I think on before.
    Mosca.   I do believe it.   110
    Corbaccio. Do you not believe it?
    Mosca.   Yes, sir.
    Corbaccio.   Mine own project.
    Mosca. Which, when he hath done, sir—
    Corbaccio.   Published me his heir?
    Mosca. And you so certain to survive him—
    Corbaccio.   Ay.
    Mosca. Being so lusty a man—
    Corbaccio.   'Tis true.
    Mosca.   Yes, sir—
    Corbaccio. I thought on that too. See, how he should be   115
The very organ to express my thoughts!
    Mosca. You have not only done yourself a good—
    Corbaccio. But multiplied it on my son?
    Mosca.   'Tis right, sir.
    Corbaccio. Still my invention.
    Mosca.   'Las, sir, heaven knows

---

96. color—appearance.   97. taking—attractive. but—only.
99. enforce—urge.

It hath been all my study, all my care,   120
(I e'en grow grey withal) how to work things—
    Corbaccio. I do conceive, sweet Mosca.
    Mosca.   You are he
For whom I labor here.
    Corbaccio.   Ay, do, do, do.
I'll straight about it.   [*Going.*]
[*Mosca now begins to speak too softly for Corbaccio to hear.*]
    Mosca.   Rook go with you, raven!
    Corbaccio. I know thee honest.   125
    Mosca.   You do lie, sir.
    Corbaccio.   And—
    Mosca. Your knowledge is no better than your ears, sir.
    Corbaccio. I do not doubt to be a father to thee.
    Mosca. Nor I to gull my brother of his blessing.
    Corbaccio. I may ha' my youth restored to me, why not?
    Mosca. Your worship is a precious ass—
    Corbaccio.   What sayst thou?   130
    Mosca. I do desire your worship to make haste, sir.
    Corbaccio. 'Tis done, 'tis done, I go.   [*Exit.*]
    Volpone. [*Leaping up.*]   O, I shall burst!
Let out my sides, let out my sides—
    Mosca.   Contain
Your flux of laughter, sir. You know this hope
Is such a bait it covers any hook.   135
    Volpone. O, but thy working, and thy placing it!
I cannot hold; good rascal, let me kiss thee.
I never knew thee in so rare a humor.
    Mosca. Alas, sir, I but do as I am taught;
Follow your grave instructions; give 'em words;   140
Pour oil into their ears, and send them hence.
    Volpone. 'Tis true, 'tis true. What a rare punishment
Is avarice to itself!
    Mosca.   Ay, with our help, sir.
    Volpone. So many cares, so many maladies,
So many fears attending on old age.   145

---

124. rook . . . you—may you be cheated.   128. my brother—Corbaccio's
son. blessing—cf. Jacob's gulling of Esau, Genesis 27.   134. flux—flow
(cf. *bloody flux*, a common medical term in Jonson's time).   141. Pour
. . . ears—deceive them with flattery.

Yea, death so often called on as no wish
Can be more frequent with 'em; their limbs faint,
Their senses dull, their seeing, hearing, going,
All dead before them; yea, their very teeth,
Their instruments of eating, failing them.   150
Yet this is reckoned life! Nay, here was one,
Is now gone home, that wishes to live longer!
Feels not his gout, nor palsy; feigns himself
Younger by scores of years, flatters his age
With confident belying it, hopes he may   155
With charms, like Aeson, have his youth restored;
And with these thoughts so battens, as if fate
Would be as easily cheated on as he,   *Another knocks.*
And all turns air! Who's that, there, now? a third?
    Mosca. Close to your couch again; I hear his voice.   160
It is Corvino, our spruce merchant.
    Volpone. [*Lies down.*]   Dead.
    Mosca. Another bout, sir, with your eyes. [*Applies*
                      [*ointment.*] Who's there?

156. Aeson—father of Jason, whose youth was restored by the magic of his
son's wife, Medea.   157. battens—grows fat.

ACT I

SCENE V

                                 [*Enter Corvino.*]
    Mosca. Signior Corvino! come most wished for! O,
How happy were you, if you knew it, now!
    Corvino. Why? what? wherein?
    Mosca.   The tardy hour is come, sir.
    Corvino. He is not dead?
    Mosca.   Not dead, sir, but as good;
He knows no man.   5
    Corvino.   How shall I do, then?
    Mosca.   Why, sir?
    Corvino. I have brought him here a pearl.
    Mosca.   Perhaps he has
So much remembrance left as to know you, sir.

He still calls on you, nothing but your name
Is in his mouth. Is your pearl orient, sir?

  Corvino. Venice was never owner of the like.   10
  Volpone. [*Faintly.*] Signior Corvino.
  Mosca.   Hark.
  Volpone.   Signior Corvino.
  Mosca. He calls you; step and give it him. He is here, sir.
And he has brought you a rich pearl. [*Volpone seizes the*
              [*pearl.*]

  Corvino.   How do you, sir?
Tell him it doubles the twelfth caract.

  Mosca.   Sir,
He cannot understand, his hearing's gone;   15
And yet it comforts him to see you—

  Corvino.   Say
I have a diamond for him, too.

  Mosca.   Best show 't, sir,
Put it into his hand; 'tis only there
He apprehends, he has his feeling yet.
See how he grasps it!

  Corvino. 'Las, good gentleman!   20
How pitiful the sight is!

  Mosca.   Tut, forget, sir.
The weeping of an heir should still be laughter
Under a visor.

  Corvino. Why, am I his heir?

  Mosca. Sir, I am sworn, I may not show the will
Till he be dead. But here has been Corbaccio,   25
Here has been Voltore, here were others too,
I cannot number 'em, they were so many,
All gaping here for legacies; but I,
Taking the vantage of his naming you,
"*Signior Corvino, Signior Corvino,*" took   30
Paper, and pen, and ink, and there I asked him
Whom he would have his heir? "*Corvino.*" Who
Should be executor? "*Corvino.*" And
To any question he was silent to,
I still interpreted the nods he made,   35
Through weakness, for consent; and sent home th' others,

23. visor—mask.

Nothing bequeathed them but to cry and curse. *They embrace.*
    Corvino. O, my dear Mosca. Does he not perceive us?
    Mosca. No more than a blind harper. He knows no man,
No face of friend, nor name of any servant,   40
Who 't was that fed him last, or gave him drink;
Not those he hath begotten, or brought up,
Can he remember.
    Corvino.   Has he children?
    Mosca.   Bastards,
Some dozen, or more, that he begot on beggars,
Gypsies, and Jews, and black-moors, when he was drunk.   45
Knew you not that, sir? 'Tis the common fable,
The dwarf, the fool, the eunuch are all his;
He's the true father of his family,
In all save me, but he has given 'em nothing.
    Corvino. That's well, that's well. Art sure he does not
                           [hear us?   50
    Mosca. Sure, sir? why, look you, credit your own sense.
                  [*Shouts in Volpone's ear.*]
The pox approach and add to your diseases,
If it would send you hence the sooner, sir;
For, your incontinence, it hath deserved it
Throughly and throughly, and the plague to boot—   55
You may come near, sir—Would you would once close
Those filthy eyes of yours that flow with slime
Like two frog-pits, and those same hanging cheeks,
Covered with hide instead of skin—Nay, help, sir—
That look like frozen dish-clouts set on end.   60
    Corvino. Or, like an old smoked wall, on which the rain
Ran down in streaks.
    Mosca.   Excellent, sir, speak out.
You may be louder yet; a culverin
Dischargèd in his ear would hardly bore it.
    Corvino. His nose is like a common sewer, still running.   65
    Mosca. 'Tis good! And what his mouth?
    Corvino.   A very draught.
    Mosca. O, stop it up—   [*Starting to smother him.*]
    Corvino.   By no means.

46. fable—story (perhaps true).   52. pox—syphilis.   63. culverin— kind
of gun.   66. draught—cesspool.

  Mosca.   Pray you, let me.
Faith, I could stifle him rarely with a pillow,
As well as any woman that should keep him.
  Corvino. Do as you will, but I'll be gone.
  Mosca.   Be so.   70
It is your presence makes him last so long.
  Corvino. I pray you, use no violence.
  Mosca.   No, sir? why?
Why should you be thus scrupulous, pray you, sir?
  Corvino. Nay, at your discretion.
  Mosca.   Well, good sir, be gone.
  Corvino. I will not trouble him now to take my pearl? 75
  Mosca. Puh! nor your diamond. What a needless care
           [*Taking the jewels.*]
Is this afflicts you! Is not all here yours?
Am not I here, whom you have made? Your creature?
That owe my being to you?
  Corvino.   Grateful Mosca!
Thou art my friend, my fellow, my companion, 80
My partner, and shalt share in all my fortunes.
  Mosca. Excepting one.
  Corvino.   What's that?
  Mosca.   Your gallant wife, sir.
       [*Exit Corvino hurriedly.*]
Now is he gone; we had no other means
To shoot him hence but this.
  Volpone.   My divine Mosca!
Thou hast today outgone thyself. (*Another knocks.*) Who's
            [there? 85
I will be troubled with no more. Prepare
Me music, dances, banquets, all delights;
The Turk is not more sensual in his pleasures
Than will Volpone. [*Exit Mosca.*] Let me see: a pearl!
A diamond! plate! chequins! good morning's purchase. 90
Why, this is better than rob churches, yet,
Or fat, by eating once a month a man.   [*Enter Mosca.*]
Who is't?
  Mosca. The beauteous Lady Wouldbe, sir,

---

75. take my pearl—Volpone has a death grip on the pearl and diamond.
92. fat—grow fat.

Wife to the English knight, Sir Politic Wouldbe—
This is the style, sir, is directed me—   95
Hath sent to know how you have slept tonight,
And if you would be visited?
    Volpone.   Not now.
Some three hours hence.—
    Mosca.   I told the squire so much.
    Volpone. When I am high with mirth and wine, then, then.
'Fore heaven, I wonder at the desperate valor   100
Of the bold English, that they dare let loose
Their wives to all encounters!
    Mosca.   Sir, this knight
Had not his name for nothing; he is *politic,*
And knows, howe'er his wife affect strange airs,
She hath not yet the face to be dishonest.   105
But had she Signior Corvino's wife's face—
    Volpone. Has she so rare a face?
    Mosca.   O, sir, the wonder,
The blazing star of Italy! a wench
O' the first year! a beauty ripe as harvest!
Whose skin is whiter than a swan, all over!   110
Than silver, snow, or lilies! a soft lip,
Would tempt you to eternity of kissing!
And flesh that melteth in the touch to blood!
Bright as your gold! and lovely as your gold!
    Volpone. Why had not I known this before?
    Mosca.   Alas, sir,   115
Myself but yesterday discovered it.
    Volpone. How might I see her?
    Mosca.   O, not possible;
She's kept as warily as is your gold;
Never does come abroad, never takes air
But at a window. All her looks are sweet   120
As the first grapes or cherries, and are watched
As near as they are.
    Volpone.   I must see her—
    Mosca.   Sir,
There is a guard, of ten spies thick, upon her;
All his whole household; each of which is set

122. near—closely.

Upon his fellow, and have all their charge,   125
When he goes out, when he comes in, examined.
  Volpone. I will go see her, though but at her window.
  Mosca. In some disguise then.
  Volpone.   That is true. I must
Maintain mine own shape still the same: we'll think.
               [*Exeunt.*]

129. mine own shape—my disguise as a sick man.

ACT II
SCENE I

     [*The Piazza, before Corvino's House.*]
     [*Enter Politic Wouldbe, Peregrine.*]
  Sir Politic. Sir, to a wise man, all the world's his soil.
It is not Italy, nor France, nor Europe,
That must bound me, if my fates call me forth.
Yet, I protest, it is no salt desire
Of seeing countries, shifting a religion,   5
Nor any disaffection to the state
Where I was bred, and unto which I owe
My dearest plots, hath brought me out; much less
That idle, antique, stale, grey-headed project
Of knowing men's minds, and manners, with Ulysses;   10
But a peculiar humor of my wife's,
Laid for this height of Venice, to observe,
To quote, to learn the language, and so forth—
I hope you travel, sir, with license?
  Peregrine.   Yes.
  Sir Politic. I dare the safelier converse—How long, sir,   15
Since you left England?
  Peregrine.   Seven weeks.
  Sir Politic.   So lately!
You ha' not been with my lord ambassador?

4. salt—wanton (cf. salacious). 8. dearest plots—most expensive pieces
of land. 10. Ulysses—famed as a traveler. 12. Laid . . . height—
sailed for this latitude. 13. quote—make notes. 14. license—pass-
port.

>   *Peregrine.* Not yet, sir.
>   *Sir Politic.*   'Pray you, what news, sir, vents
>   [our climate?

I heard, last night, a most strange thing reported
By some of my lord's followers, and I long   20
To hear how 'twill be seconded!
>   *Peregrine.*   What was't, sir?
>   *Sir Politic.* Marry, sir, of a raven, that should build

In a ship royal of the King's.
>   *Peregrine.* [*Aside.*] —This fellow,

Does he gull me, trow? or is gulled?—Your name, sir?
>   *Sir Politic.* My name is Politic Wouldbe.   25
>   *Peregrine.* [*Aside.*]   —O, that speaks him—

A knight, sir?
>   *Sir Politic.* A poor knight, sir.
>   *Peregrine.*   Your lady

Lies here, in Venice, for intelligence
Of tires, and fashions, and behavior
Among the courtesans? The fine Lady Wouldbe?
>   *Sir Politic.* Yes, sir, the spider and the bee ofttimes   30

Suck from one flower.
>   *Peregrine.*   Good Sir Politic!

I cry you mercy; I have heard much of you.
'Tis true, sir, of your raven.
>   *Sir Politic.*   On your knowledge?
>   *Peregrine.* Yes, and your lion's whelping in the Tower.
>   *Sir Politic.* Another whelp!
>   *Peregrine.*   Another, sir.
>   *Sir Politic.*   Now, heaven!   35

What prodigies be these? The fires at Berwick!
And the new star! These things concurring, strange!
And full of omen! Saw you those meteors?
>   *Peregrine.* I did, sir.
>   *Sir Politic.*   Fearful! Pray you, sir, confirm me,

Were there three porpoises seen above the bridge,   40
As they give out?
>   *Peregrine.*   Six, and a sturgeon, sir.

18.· vents—comes out of.   22. build—nest.   28. tires—dress.
34. Tower—of London; this and the other "prodigies" to follow are all recent
news to Jonson's audience.   36. fires at Berwick—ghost armies firing
near the Scottish border.

  Sir Politic. I am astonished!

  Peregrine.   Nay, sir, be not so;

I'll tell you a greater prodigy than these—

  Sir Politic. What should these things portend?

  Peregrine.   The very day

(Let me be sure) that I put forth from London,   45

There was a whale discovered in the river,

As high as Woolwich, that had waited there,

Few know how many months, for the subversion

Of the Stode fleet.

  Sir Politic. Is't possible? Believe it,

'Twas either sent from Spain, or the Archduke's!   50

Spinola's whale, upon my life, my credit!

Will they not leave these projects? Worthy sir,

Some other news.

  Peregrine. Faith, Stone the fool is dead,

And they do lack a tavern fool extremely.

  Sir Politic. Is Mas' Stone dead?

  Peregrine.   He's dead, sir; why, I hope 55

You thought him not immortal? [*Aside.*] —O, this knight,

Were he well known, would be a precious thing

To fit our English stage. He that should write

But such a fellow, should be thought to feign

Extremely, if not maliciously.—

  Sir Politic.   Stone dead!   60

  Peregrine. Dead. Lord, how deeply, sir, you apprehend

                      [it!

He was no kinsman to you?

  Sir Politic.   That I know of.

Well, that same fellow was an unknown fool.

  Peregrine. And yet you know him, it seems?

  Sir Politic.   I did so, Sir,

I knew him one of the most dangerous heads   65

Living within the state, and so I held him.

  Peregrine. Indeed, sir?

  Sir Politic.   While he lived, in action.

49. Stode—German port on the Elbe. 50. Archduke—ruler of the
Spanish Netherlands and enemy of England. 51. Spinola—Spanish general
credited with schemes for secret weapons. 55. Mas'—Master. 61. apprehend—both "feel" and "understand" (Kernan). 63. unknown—not
known for what he actually was.

He has received weekly intelligence,
Upon my knowledge, out of the Low Countries,
For all parts of the world, in cabbages;   70
And those dispensed, again, t' ambassadors,
In oranges, musk-melons, apricots,
Lemons, pome-citrons, and suchlike; sometimes
In Colchester oysters, and your Selsey cockles.
   Peregrine. You make me wonder!
   Sir Politic.   Sir, upon my knowledge.   75
Nay, I have observed him, at your public ordinary,
Take his advertisement from a traveler,
A concealed statesman, in a trencher of meat;
And, instantly, before the meal was done,
Convey an answer in a toothpick.
   Peregrine.   Strange!   80
How could this be, sir?
   Sir Politic.   Why, the meat was cut
So like his character, and so laid as he
Must easily read the cipher.
   Peregrine.   I have heard
He could not read, sir.
   Sir Politic.   So 'twas given out,
In policy, by those that did employ him;   85
But he could read, and had your languages,
And to 't, as sound a noddle—
   Peregrine.   I have heard, sir,
That your baboons were spies, and that they were
A kind of subtle nation near to China.
   Sir Politic. Ay, ay, your Mamuluchi. Faith, they had   90
Their hand in a French plot, or two; but they
Were so extremely given to women as
They made discovery of all; yet I
Had my advices here, on Wednesday last,
From one of their own coat, they were returned,   95
Made their relations, as the fashion is,
And now stand fair for fresh employment.

73. pome-citrons—a citrus fruit.   76. ordinary—tavern.   77. advertisement—information.   78. concealed statesman—spy.   82. character—
code.   85. policy—craftiness.   87. noddle—pate.   90. Mamuluchi—
slaves in Moslem countries.   93. made discovery of— revealed.
94. advices—dispatches.   96. relations—reports.

    Peregrine. [*Aside.*]   —'Heart!
This Sir Pol will be ignorant of nothing—
It seems, sir, you know all.
    Sir Politic.   Not all, sir. But
I have some general notions; I do love   100
To note and to observe: though I live out,
Free from the active torrent, yet I'd mark
The currents and the passages of things
For mine own private use; and know the ebbs
And flows of state.
    Peregrine.   Believe it, sir, I hold   105
Myself in no small tie unto my fortunes
For casting me thus luckily upon you,
Whose knowledge, if your bounty equal it,
May do me great assistance in instruction
For my behavior, and my bearing, which   110
Is yet so rude and raw—
    Sir Politic.   Why? came you forth
Empty of rules for travel?
    Peregrine.   Faith, I had
Some common ones, from out that vulgar grammar,
Which he that cried Italian to me, taught me.
    Sir Politic. Why, this it is that spoils all our brave bloods,   115
Trusting our hopeful gentry unto pedants,
Fellows of outside, and mere bark. You seem
To be a gentleman, of ingenuous race—
I not profess it, but my fate hath been
To be where I have been consulted with   120
In this high kind, touching some great men's sons,
Persons of blood and honor—
    Peregrine.   Who be these, sir?

---

97. 'Heart—by God's heart.   113. vulgar grammar—ordinary textbook.
118. ingenuous—noble.   119. I not profess it—I'm not a professional
educator.   121. this high kind—i.e., the education of gentlemen's sons.

ACT II
SCENE II

[*Enter Mosca and Nano, disguised as assistants (zanies).*]
Mosca. Under that window, there 't must be. The same.
                              [*They begin erecting a platform stage.*]
    Sir Politic. Fellows to mount a bank! Did your instructor
In the dear tongues never discourse to you
Of the Italian mountebanks?
    Peregrine.   Yes, sir.
    Sir Politic.   Why,
Here shall you see one.
    Peregrine.   They are quacksalvers,   5
Fellows that live by venting oils and drugs.
    Sir Politic. Was that the character he gave you of them?
    Peregrine. As I remember.
    Sir Politic.   Pity his ignorance.
They are the only knowing men of Europe!
Great general scholars, excellent physicians,   10
Most admired statesmen, professed favorites
And cabinet counselors to the greatest princes!
The only languaged men of all the world!
    Peregrine. And I have heard they are most lewd impostors,
Made all of terms and shreds; no less beliers   15
Of great men's favors than their own vile medicines;
Which they will utter upon monstrous oaths,
Selling that drug for twopence, ere they part,
Which they have valued at twelve crowns before.
    Sir Politic. Sir, calumnies are answered best with silence.   20
Yourself shall judge. Who is it mounts, my friends?
    Mosca. Scoto of Mantua, sir.
    Sir Politic.   Is't he? Nay, then
I'll proudly promise, sir, you shall behold
Another man than has been phantasied to you.

2–4. mount a bank—Sir Pol's etymology for mountebank is correct (*banco*,
"bench, portable stage").   3. dear—esteemed.   6. venting—vending.
14. lewd—ignorant.   15. terms and shreds—technical jargon and quotations shredded from context.   22. Scoto of Mantua—Italian enter-
tainer who had visited England in 1576.

I wonder, yet, that he should mount his bank   25
Here, in this nook, that has been wont t' appear
In face of the Piazza! Here he comes!
                    [*Enter Volpone, disguised as a Mountebank.*]
    Volpone. [*To Nano.*]   Mount, zany.
    Grege.   Follow, follow, follow, follow, follow.
                              [*Volpone mounts the stage.*]
    Sir Politic. See how the people follow him! He's a man
May write ten thousand crowns in bank here. Note,   30
Mark but his gesture. I do use to observe
The state he keeps in getting up!
    Peregrine.   'Tis worth it, sir.
    Volpone. Most noble gentlemen, and my worthy
patrons, it may seem strange that I, your Scoto
Mantuano, who was ever wont to fix my bank in face of   35
the public Piazza, near the shelter of the Portico to the
Procuratia, should now, after eight months' absence
from this illustrious city of Venice, humbly retire myself
into an obscure nook of the Piazza.
    Sir Politic. Did not I now object the same?   40
    Peregrine.   Peace, sir.
    Volpone. Let me tell you: I am not, as your
Lombard proverb saith, cold on my feet, or content to
part with my commodities at a cheaper rate than I
accustomed; look not for it. Nor that the calumnious   45
reports of that impudent detractor, and shame to our
profession, Alessandro Buttone I mean, who gave out, in
public, I was condemned *a sforzato* to the galleys, for
poisoning the Cardinal Bembo's—cook, hath at all
attached, much less dejected me. No, no, worthy   50
gentlemen; to tell you true, I cannot endure to see the
rabble of these ground *ciarlitani* that spread their cloaks
on the pavement as if they meant to do feats of activity,
and then come in lamely with their moldy tales out of
Boccaccio, like stale Tabarin, the fabulist: some of them   55

28. zany—assistant, clown.   42-43. I . . . feet—I'm not frightened.
48. *sforzato*—"Sfortzati, gally slaves, prisoners perforce" (Florio, 1598).
49. Bembo's—cook—the dash indicates that *cook* is a euphemism for
mistress.   50. attached . . . me—entangled me with the law.   52. ground
ciarlitani—charlatans who perform on the ground rather than on a "bank."
53. feats of activity—acrobatics.   55. fabulist—storyteller.

discoursing their travels, and of their tedious captivity in
the Turk's galleys, when, indeed, were the truth known,
they were the Christian's galleys, where very temperately
they eat bread, and drunk water, as a wholesome
penance, enjoined them by their confessors, for base   60
pilferies.

    Sir Politic. Note but his bearing and contempt of
these.

    Volpone. These turdy-facy-nasty-paty-lousy-fartical
rogues, with one poor groatsworth of unprepared anti-   65
mony, finely wrapped up in several *scartoccios,* are able,
very well, to kill their twenty a week, and play; yet these
meager, starved spirits, who have half stopped the organs
of their minds with earthy oppilations, want not their
favorers among your shriveled salad-eating artisans, who   70
are overjoyed that they may have their half-pe'rth of
physic; though it purge 'em into another world, 't makes
no matter.

    Sir Politic. Excellent! ha' you heard better language,
sir?   75

    Volpone. Well, let 'em go. And, gentlemen, honor-
able gentlemen, know that for this time our bank, being
thus removed from the clamors of the *canaglia,* shall be
the scene of pleasure and delight; for I have nothing to
sell, little or nothing to sell.   80

    Sir Politic. I told you, sir, his end.

    Peregrine. You did so, sir.

    Volpone. I protest, I and my six servants are not
able to make of this precious liquor so fast as it is
fetched away from my lodging by gentlemen of your   85
city, strangers of the Terra Firma, worshipful merchants,
ay, and senators too, who, ever since my arrival, have
detained me to their uses by their splendidous liberal-
ities. And worthily. For what avails your rich man to
have his magazines stuft with *moscadelli,* or of the purest   90
grape, when his physicians prescribe him, on pain of

59. eat—ate, prounced *et.*   66. *scartoccios*—"a coffin of paper for spice"
(Florio, 1598).   69. earthy oppilations—gross obstructions.   71. half-
pe'rth—half-pennyworth.   78. *canaglia*—"rascally people only fit for dog's
company" (Florio, 1598).   86. Terra Firma—Venice's possessions on the
mainland.   90. magazines—storehouses. *moscadelli*—muscatel wines.

death, to drink nothing but water cocted with aniseeds?
O health! health! the blessing of the rich! the riches of
the poor! who can buy thee at too dear a rate, since
there is no enjoying this world without thee? Be not   95
then so sparing of your purses, honorable gentlemen, as
to abridge the natural course of life—

    Peregrine. You see his end?

    Sir Politic.   Ay, is't not good?

    Volpone. For, when a humid flux, or catarrh, by the   100
mutability of air falls from your head into an arm or
shoulder, or any other part, take you a ducat, or your
chequin of gold, and apply to the place affected: see,
what good effect it can work. No, no, 'tis this blessed
unguento, this rare extraction, that hath only power to   105
disperse all malignant humors that proceed either of hot,
cold, moist, or windy causes—

    Peregrine. I would he had put in dry too.

    Sir Politic.   'Pray you, observe.

    Volpone. To fortify the most indigest and crude
stomach, ay, were it of one that through extreme   110
weakness vomited blood, applying only a warm napkin
to the place, after the unction and fricace; for the
vertigine in the head, putting but a drop into your
nostrils, likewise behind the ears; a most sovereign and
approved remedy: the *mal caduco,* cramps, convulsions,   115
paralyses, epilepsies, *tremor cordia,* retired nerves, ill
vapours of the spleen, stoppings of the liver, the stone,
the strangury, *hernia ventosa, iliaca passio*; stops a
dysenteria immediately; easeth the torsion of the small
guts; and cures *melancholia hypocondriaca,* being taken   120
and applied according to my printed receipt. [*Pointing
to his bill and his glass.*] For, this is the physician, this
the medicine; this counsels, this cures; this gives the

92. cocted—boiled.   105. *unguento*—salve.   106. humors—body
fluids.   109. crude—sour.   112. fricace—massage. 113. vertigine—
vertigo.   115. *mal caduco*—falling sickness.   116. *tremor cordia*—
heart palpitations. retired nerves—shrunken sinews.   118. strangury—
painful urination.   *hernia ventosa*—gaseous tumor.   *iliaca passio*—in-
testinal cramps.   120. *melancholia hypocondriaca*—"melancholy was
supposed to be seated in the hypochondria—the soft parts of the body below
the rib cartilages" (Brockbank).   121. receipt—recipe.

direction, this works the effect; and, in sum, both
together may be termed an abstract of the theoric and   125
practic in the Aesculapian art. 'Twill cost you eight
crowns. And, Zan Fritada, pray thee sing a verse,
extempore, in honor of it.

                           [*Nano prepares to sing.*]

Sir Politic. How do you like him, sir?
Peregrine.   Most strangely, I!
Sir Politic. Is not his language rare?
Peregrine.   But alchemy
I never heard the like, or Broughton's books.   130

SONG

    Had old Hippocrates or Galen,
    That to their books put med'cines all in,
    But known this secret, they had never,   135
    Of which they will be guilty ever,
    Been murderers of so much paper,
    Or wasted many a hurtless taper.
    No Indian drug had e'er been famèd,
    Tobacco, sassafras not namèd;   140
    Ne yet of guacum one small stick, sir,
    Nor Raymond Lully's great elixir.
    Ne had been known the Danish Gonswart,
    Or Paracelsus, with his long sword.

Peregrine. All this, yet, will not do; eight crowns is   145
high.
    Volpone. No more. Gentlemen, if I had but time to
discourse to you the miraculous effects of this my oil,
surnamed *Oglio del Scoto,* with the countless catalogue
of those I have cured of th'aforesaid, and many more   150
diseases; the patents and privileges of all the princes and

126. Aesculapian—Aesculapius was god of medicine.   127. Zan Fritada—
another famous zany.   129. But—except for.   130. Broughton—an
eccentric Puritan scholar of Hebrew.   133. Hippocrates or Galen—physicians of ancient Greece whose teachings were still followed in the Renaissance.   138. hurtless—harmless.   140. Tobacco, sassafras—both used
medicinally.   141. guacum—medicinal bark.   142. Lully—medieval
sage believed to have discovered the elixir of life.   143. Gonswart—unidenti-
fied.   144. Paracelsus—the Galen of the Renaissance; he was said to have
kept his quintessences in the pommel of his sword.

commonwealths of Christendom; or but the depositions
of those that appeared on my part, before the signiory of
the *Sanita* and most learned college of physicians; where
I was authorized, upon notice taken of the admirable   155
virtues of my medicaments, and mine own excellency in
matter of rare and unknown secrets, not only to disperse
them publicly in this famous city, but in all the
territories that happily joy under the government of the
most pious and magnificent states of Italy. But may   160
some other gallant fellow say, "O, there be divers that
make profession to have as good and as experimented
receipts as yours." Indeed, very many have assayed, like
apes, in imitation of that, which is really and essentially
in me, to make of this oil; bestowed great cost in   165
furnaces, stills, alembics, continual fires, and preparation
of the ingredients (as indeed there goes to it six hundred
several simples, besides some quantity of human fat, for
the conglutination, which we buy of the anatomists),
but, when these practitioners come to the last decoction,   170
blow, blow, puff, puff, and all flies in fumo. Ha, ha, ha!
Poor wretches! I rather pity their folly and indiscretion
than their loss of time and money; for those may be
recovered by industry; but to be a fool born is a disease
incurable. For myself, I always from my youth have   175
endeavoured to get the rarest secrets, and book them,
either in exchange or for money; I spared nor cost nor
labor where anything was worthy to be learned. And
gentlemen, honorable gentlemen, I will undertake, by
virtue of chemical art, out of the honorable hat that   180
covers your head to extract the four elements, that is to
say, the fire, air, water, and earth, and return you your
felt without burn or stain. For, whilst others have been
at the balloo, I have been at my book, and am now past
the craggy paths of study, and come to the flowery   185
plains of honor and reputation.

    Sir Politic. I do assure you, sir, that is his aim.

    Volpone. But to our price—

153-154. signiory of the *Sanita*—Venice's public health bureau.
168. simples—medicinal herbs.   170. decoction—boiling to extract the
essences.   171. in fumo—up in smoke.   184. balloo—Venetian game.

Peregrine.   And that withal, Sir Pol.

Volpone. You all know, honorable gentlemen, I
never valued this *ampulla,* or vial, at less than eight   190
crowns, but for this time I am content to be deprived of
it for six; six crowns is the price, and less in courtesy I
know you cannot offer me; take it or leave it, howsoever, both it and I am your service. I ask you not as the
value of the thing, for then I should demand of you a   195
thousand crowns; so the Cardinals Montalto, Farnese,
the great Duke of Tuscany, my gossip, with divers other
princes have given me; but I despise money. Only to
show my affection to you, honorable gentlemen, and
your illustrious state here, I have neglected the messages   200
of these princes, mine own offices, framed my journey
hither, only to present you with the fruits of my travels.
[*To Nano and Mosca.*] Tune your voices once more to
the touch of your instruments, and give the honorable
assembly some delightful recreation.   205

Peregrine. What monstrous and most painful circumstance
Is here, to get some three or four *gazets*!
Some three pence i' th' whole, for that 'twill come to.

SONG

You that would last long, list to my song,   210
Make no more coil, but buy of this oil.
Would you be ever fair? and young?
Stout of teeth? and strong of tongue?
Tart of palate? quick of ear?
Sharp of sight? of nostril clear?   215
Moist of hand? and light of foot?
Or I will come nearer to't,
Would you live free from all diseases?
Do the act your mistress pleases,
Yet fright all aches from your bones?   220
Here's a med'cine for the nones.

Volpone. Well, I am in a humor, at this time, to
make a present of the small quantity my coffer contains:

197. gossip—godfather or close friend.   207. *gazets*—Venetian coin worth a
penny.   211. coil—fuss.   214. Tart—keen.   220. aches . . . bones—
bone-ache was a synonym for venereal disease. *Aches* was pronounced *Hs.*
221. nones—nonce, i.e., for the occasion.

to the rich, in courtesy, and to the poor, for God's sake.
Wherefore, now mark: I asked you six crowns, and six   225
crowns at other times you have paid me; you shall not
give me six crowns, nor five, nor four, nor three, nor
two, nor one; nor half a ducat; no, nor a *moccenigo*.
Sixpence it will cost you, or six hundred pound—expect
no lower price, for by the banner of my front, I will not 230
bate a *bagatine*; that I will have, only, a pledge of your
loves, to carry something from amongst you to show I
am not contemned by you. Therefore, now, toss your
handkerchiefs, cheerfully, cheerfully; and be advertised
that the first heroic spirit that deigns to grace me with a 235
handkerchief, I will give it a little remembrance of
something beside, shall please it better than if I had
presented it with a double pistolet.

    Peregrine. Will you be that heroic spark, Sir Pol?
    [*Celia at the window throws down her handkerchief.*]
O see! the window has prevented you.   240

    Volpone. Lady, I kiss your bounty, and for this
timely grace you have done your poor Scoto of Mantua,
I will return you, over and above my oil, a secret of that
high and inestimable nature shall make you forever
enamored on that minute wherein your eye first de-   245
scended on so mean, yet not altogether to be despised,
an object. Here is a poulder concealed in this paper of
which, if I should speak to the worth, nine thousand
volumes were but as one page, that page as a line, that
line as a word: so short is this pilgrimage of man, which 250
some call life, to the expressing of it. Would I reflect on
the price? Why, the whole world were but as an empire,
that empire as a province, that province as a bank, that
bank as a private purse to the purchase of it. I will, only,
tell you: it is the poulder that made Venus a goddess   255
(given her by Apollo), that kept her perpetually young,
cleared her wrinkles, firmed her gums, filled her skin,
colored her hair; from her derived to Helen, and at the
sack of Troy unfortunately lost; till now, in this our age,
it was as happily recovered by a studious antiquary out   260

228. *moccenigo*—a coin worth perhaps nine gazets.   230. banner of my
front—sign hanging in front of the "banco."   231. *bagatine*—a tiny coin.
238. pistolet—Spanish gold coin.   247. poulder—powder.

of some ruins of Asia, who sent a moiety of it to the
court of France (but much sophisticated), wherewith the
ladies there now color their hair. The rest, at this
present, remains with me; extracted to a quintessence, so
that wherever it but touches in youth it perpetually   265
preserves, in age restores the complexion; seats your
teeth, did they dance like virginal jacks, firm as a wall;
makes them white as ivory, that were black as—

261. moiety—a portion.   262. sophisticated—adulterated.   267. virginal jacks—parts of a virginal (pianolike instrument).

ACT II

SCENE III

                                [Enter Corvino.]

Corvino.   *[Shouting up to Celia.]*
Blood o' the devil, and my shame! *[To Volpone on the*
                          [platform.] Come down here;
Come down! No house but mine to make your scene?
                            He beats
Signior Flaminio, will you down, sir? down? *away the*
What, is my wife your Franciscina, sir? *mountebank, &c.*
No windows on the whole Piazza, here,   5
To make your properties, but mine? but mine?
Heart! ere tomorrow I shall be new christened,
And called the Pantolone di Besogniosi
About the town.   *[Exit.]*
    Peregrine. What should this mean, Sir Pol?
    Sir Politic. Some trick of state, believe it. I will home.   10
    Peregrine. It may be some design on you.
    Sir Politic.   I know not.
I'll stand upon my guard.
    Peregrine.   It is your best, sir.
    Sir Politic. This three weeks all my advices, all my letters,
They have been intercepted.

1. Blood—the quarto reading changed to "Spite" in folio, presumably in deference to censorship policy.   3. Flaminio—famous Italian actor.
4. Franciscina—the amorous maid of the *commedia dell'arte.*   8. Pantalone—
the cuckolded husband, also a stock character.

Peregrine.   Indeed, sir?
Best have a care.
   Sir Politic. Nay, so I will.   [*Exit.*]
   Peregrine.   This knight,   15
I may not lose him for my mirth, till night.   [*Exit.*]

ACT II
SCENE IV

   [*Volpone's house. Enter Volpone and Mosca.*]
   Volpone. O, I am wounded!
   Mosca.   Where, sir?
   Volpone.   Not without;
Those blows were nothing; I could bear them ever.
But angry Cupid, bolting from her eyes,
Hath shot himself into me like a flame;
Where, now, he flings about his burning heat,   5
As in a furnace an ambitious fire
Whose vent is stopped. The fight is all within me.
I cannot live except thou help me, Mosca;
My liver melts, and I, without the hope
Of some soft air from her refreshing breath,   10
Am but a heap of cinders.
   Mosca.   'Las, good sir!
Would you had never seen her!
   Volpone.   Nay, would thou
Hadst never told me of her.
   Mosca.   Sir, 'tis true;
I do confess I was unfortunate,
And you unhappy; but I'm bound in conscience,   15
No less than duty, to effect my best
To your release of torment, and I will, sir.
   Volpone. Dear Mosca. shall I hope?
   Mosca.   Sir, more than dear,
I will not bid you to despair of aught
Within a human compass.   20
   Volpone.   O, there spoke

3. bolting—shooting arrows.   9. liver—supposed seat of violent passions.

My better angel. Mosca, take my keys,
Gold, plate, and jewels, all's at thy devotion;
Employ them how thou wilt; nay, coin me too,
So thou in this but crown my longings—Mosca?
    Mosca. Use but your patience.
    Volpone.   So I have.
    Mosca.   I doubt not   25
To bring success to your desires.
    Volpone.   Nay, then,
I not repent me of my late disguise.
    Mosca. If you can horn him, sir, you need not.
    Volpone.   True.
Besides, I never meant him for my heir.
Is not the color o' my beard and eyebrows   30
To make me known?
    Mosca.   No jot.
    Volpone.   I did it well.
    Mosca. So well, would I could follow you in mine,
With half the happiness; and, yet, I would
Escape your epilogue.
    Volpone.   But were they gulled
With a belief that I was Scoto?
    Mosca.   Sir,   35
Scoto himself could hardly have distinguished!
I have not time to flatter you now; we'll part,
And as I prosper, so applaud my art.   *[Exeunt.]*

22. devotion—disposal.   28. horn him—cuckold him.   34. your epilogue—
i.e., the beating.

ACT II
SCENE V

                [Corvino's House.]
                [Enter Corvino, Celia.]
    Corvino. Death of mine honor, with the city's fool?
A juggling, tooth-drawing, prating mountebank?
And at a public window? where, whilst he,

2. tooth-drawing—mountebanks were sometimes dentists.

With his strained action, and his dole of faces,
To his drug-lecture draws your itching ears,   5
A crew of old, unmarried, noted lechers
Stood leering up like satyrs: and you smile
Most graciously, and fan your favors forth,
To give your hot spectators satisfaction!
What, was your mountebank their call? their whistle?   10
Or were y' enamored on his copper rings?
His saffron jewel, with the toad stone in 't?
Or his embroidered suit, with the cope-stitch,
Made of a hearse cloth? or his old tilt-feather?
Or his starched beard? Well! you shall have him, yes.   15
He shall come home and minister unto you
The fricace for the mother. Or, let me see,
I think you'd rather mount? would you not mount?
Why, if you'll mount, you may; yes truly, you may,
And so you may be seen, down to th' foot.   20
Get you a cittern, Lady Vanity,
And be a dealer with the virtuous man;
Make one. I'll but protest myself a cuckold,
And save your dowry. I am a Dutchman, I!
For if you thought me an Italian,   25
You would be damned ere you did this, you whore!
Thou'dst tremble to imagine that the murder
Of father, mother, brother, all thy race,
Should follow as the subject of my justice!
    Celia. Good sir, have patience!
    Corvino.   What couldst thou propose   30
Less to thyself than in this heat of wrath,
And stung with my dishonor, I should strike [*Waves his*
                                            [*sword.*]

4. dole of faces—repertory of expressions.   12. toad stone—magic stone
supposedly taken from between the eyes of a toad.   13. cope-stitch—
fancy stitch on ceremonial garments.   14. tilt-feather—plume worn at
tilting, i.e., jousting.   15. starched beard—fashionable at this time.
17. fricace . . . mother—literally, massage for a diseased swelling of the womb;
but the massage Corvino has in mind would make a mother of Celia in another
sense (see IV.ii.55).   21. cittern—zither. Lady Vanity—wicked character
in the morality plays.   22. dealer—prostitute.   23. Make one—make a
deal. protest—declare.   24. save . . . dowry—an adulteress lost all of her
inheritance.   24–25. Dutchman . . . Italian—by reputation the Dutch were
phlegmatic, Italians vengeful.

This steel into thee, with as many stabs
As thou wert gazed upon with goatish eyes?
  Celia. Alas, sir, be appeased! I could not think 35
My being at the window should more now
Move your impatience than at other times.
  Corvino. No? not to seek and entertain a parley
With a known knave? before a multitude?
You were an actor with your handkerchief, 40
Which he, most sweetly, kissed in the receipt,
And might, no doubt, return it with a letter,
And point the place where you might meet: your sister's,
Your mother's, or your aunt's might serve the turn.
  Celia. Why, dear sir, when do I make these excuses? 45
Or ever stir abroad but to the church?
And that so seldom—
  Corvino.   Well, it shall be less;
And thy restraint before was liberty
To what I now decree, and therefore mark me.
First, I will have this bawdy light dammed up; 50
And till't be done, some two, or three yards off
I'll chalk a line, o'er which if thou but chance
To set thy desp'rate foot, more hell, more horror,
More wild, remorseless rage shall seize on thee
Than on a conjurer that had heedless left 55
His circle's safety ere his devil was laid.
Then, here's a lock which I will hang upon thee
And, now I think on't, I will keep thee backwards;
Thy lodging shall be backwards, thy walks backwards,
Thy prospect—all be backwards, and no pleasure 60
That thou shalt know but backwards. Nay, since you force
My honest nature, know it is your own
Being too open makes me use you thus.
Since you will not contain your subtle nostrils
In a sweet room, but they must snuff the air 65
Of rank and sweaty passengers—(*Knock within.*) One knocks.
Away, and be not seen, pain of thy life;
Not look toward the window; if thou dost—[*Celia starts to*
                [*leave.*]

Nay, stay, hear this, let me not prosper, whore,

50. light—window. 57. lock—chastity belt. 66. passengers—passers-by.

But I will make thee an anatomy,   70
Dissect thee mine own self, and read a lecture
Upon thee to the city, and in public.
Away! [*Exit Celia.*] Who's there? [*Enter servant.*]
    Servant.   'Tis Signior Mosca, sir.

70. anatomy—(1) a literal dissection, (2) a moral harangue.

ACT II

SCENE VI

    Corvino. Let him come in, his master's dead. There's yet
Some good to help the bad.   [*Enter Mosca.*]
                        My Mosca, welcome!
I guess your news.
    Mosca.   I fear you cannot, sir.
    Corvino. Is't not his death?
    Mosca.   Rather the contrary.
    Corvino. Not his recovery?
    Mosca.   Yes, sir.
    Corvino.   I am cursed,   5
I am bewitched, my crosses meet to vex me.
How? how? how? how?
    Mosca.   Why, sir, with Scoto's oil!
Corbaccio and Voltore brought of it,
Whilst I was busy in an inner room—
    Corvino. Death! that damned mountebank! but for the
                                   [law,   10
Now, I could kill the rascal; 't cannot be
His oil should have that virtue. Ha' not I
Known him a common rogue, come fiddling in
To th' *ostería,* with a tumbling whore,
And, when he has done all his forced tricks, been glád   15
Of a poor spoonful of dead wine, with flies in 't?
It cannot be. All his ingredients
Are a sheep's gall, a roasted bitch's marrow,
Some few sod earwigs, pounded caterpillars,

6. crosses—troubles.   14. *ostería*—inn.   19. sod—boiled.

A little capon's grease, and fasting spittle; 20
I know 'em to a dram.
    Mosca.   I know not, sir;
But some on 't, there, they poured into his ears,
Some in his nostrils, and recovered him,
Applying but the fricace.
    Corvino.   Pox o' that fricace.
    Mosca. And since, to seem the more officious 25
And flatt'ring of his health, there they have had,
At extreme fees, the college of physicians
Consulting on him how they might restore him;
Where one would have a cataplasm of spices,
Another a flayed ape clapped to his breast, 30
A third would ha' it a dog, a fourth an oil
With wild cats' skins. At last, they all resolved
That to preserve him was no other means
But some young woman must be straight sought out,
Lusty, and full of juice, to sleep by him; 35
And to this service, most unhappily
And most unwillingly, am I now employed,
Which here I thought to pre-acquaint you with,
For your advice, since it concerns you most,
Because I would not do that thing might cross 40
Your ends, on whom I have my whole dependence, sir.
Yet, if I do it not they may delate
My slackness to my patron, work me out
Of his opinion; and there all your hopes,
Ventures, or whatsoever, are all frustrate. 45
I do but tell you, sir. Besides, they are all
Now striving who shall first present him. Therefore,
I could entreat you, briefly, conclude somewhat.
Prevent 'em if you can.
    Corvino.   Death to my hopes!
This is my villainous fortune! Best to hire 50
Some common courtesan?
    Mosca.   Ay, I thought on that, sir.
But they are all so subtle, full of art,

20. fasting spittle—saliva of a fasting man. 22. on 't—of it. 29. cataplasm—poultice. 34. young woman—the remedy prescribed for King David (I Kings I:1–4). 42. delate—"to report, inform of (an offence, crime, fault)" (*OED*).

And age again doting and flexible,
So as—I cannot tell—we may perchance
Light on a quean may cheat us all.   55
    Corvino.   'Tis true.
    Mosca. No, no; it must be one that has no tricks, sir,
Some simple thing, a creature made unto it;
Some wench you may command. Ha' you no kinswoman?
God's so—Think, think, think, think, think, think, think, sir.
One o' the doctors offered there his daughter.   60
    Corvino. How!
    Mosca.   Yes, Signior Lupo, the physician.
    Corvino. His daughter!
    Mosca.   And a virgin, sir. Why, alas,
He knows the state of 's body, what it is;
That nought can warm his blood, sir, but a fever;
Nor any incantation raise his spirit;   65
A long forgetfulness hath seized that part.
Besides, sir, who shall know it? Some one or two—
    Corvino. I pray thee give me leave.   [*Walks aside.*]
                               If any man
But I had had this luck—The thing in 't self,
I know, is nothing—Wherefore should not I   70
As well command my blood and my affections
As this dull doctor? In the point of honor
The cases are all one of wife and daughter.
    Mosca. [*Aside.*] I hear him coming.
    Corvino.   She shall do 't. 'Tis
                                [done.
'Slight, if this doctor, who is not engaged,   75
Unless 't be for his counsel, which is nothing,
Offer his daughter, what should I that am
So deeply in? I will prevent him; Wretch!
Covetous wretch! Mosca, I have determined.
    Mosca. How, sir?
    Corvino.   We'll make all sure. The party you wot of   80
Shall be mine own wife, Mosca.
    Mosca.   Sir, the thing,
But that I would not seem to counsel you,

---

55. quean—whore.   61. Lupo—wolf.   75. 'Slight—by God's light.
78. prevent—Corvino adopts Mosca's word (line 49).   80. wot—know.

I should have motioned to you at the first;
And make your count, you have cut all their throats.
Why, 'tis directly taking a possession!   85
And in his next fit, we may let him go.
'Tis but to pull the pillow from his head,
And he is throttled; 't had been done before
But for your scrupulous doubts.
     Corvino.   Ay, a plague on 't,
My conscience fools my wit! Well, I'll be brief,   90
And so be thou, lest they should be before us.
Go home, prepare him, tell him with what zeal
And willingness I do it; swear it was
On the first hearing, as thou mayst do, truly,
Mine own free motion.
     Mosca.   Sir, I warrant you,   95
I'll so possess him with it that the rest
Of his starved clients shall be banished all;
And only you received. But come not, sir,
Until I send, for I have something else
To ripen for your good, you must not know 't.   100
     Corvino. But do not you forget to send now.
     Mosca.   Fear not.
                              [Exit Mosca.]

83. motioned—proposed.   90. wit—intelligence.

ACT II
SCENE VII

     Corvino. Where are you, wife? My Celia? wife?
               [Enter Celia crying.]   What, blubbering?
Come, dry those tears. I think thou thought'st me in earnest?
Ha? by this light I talked so but to try thee.
Methinks the lightness of the occasion
Should ha' confirmed thee. Come, I am not jealous.   5
     Celia. No?
     Corvino. Faith I am not, I, nor never was;
It is a poor unprofitable humor.
Do not I know if women have a will

They'll do 'gainst all the watches o' the world?
And that the fiercest spies are tamed with gold?   10
Tut, I am confident in thee, thou shalt see 't;
And see I'll give thee cause too, to believe it.
Come, kiss me. Go, and make thee ready straight
In all thy best attire, thy choicest jewels,
Put 'em all on, and, with 'em, thy best looks.   15
We are invited to a solemn feast
At old Volpone's, where it shall appear
How far I am free from jealousy or fear.   [*Exeunt.*]

ACT III

SCENE I

[*A street. Mosca alone.*]
   Mosca. I fear I shall begin to grow in love
With my dear self and my most prosp'rous parts,
They do so spring and burgeon; I can feel
A whimsy i' my blood. I know not how,
Success hath made me wanton. I could skip   5
Out of my skin, now, like a subtle snake,
I am so limber. O! your parasite
Is a most precious thing, dropped from above,
Not bred 'mongst clods and clodpolls, here on earth.
I muse the mystery was not made a science,   10
It is so liberally professed! Almost
All the wise world is little else in nature
But parasites or sub-parasites. And yet,
I mean not those that have your bare town-art,
To know who's fit to feed 'em; have no house,   15
No family, no care, and therefore mold
Tales for men's ears, to bait that sense; or get
Kitchen-invention, and some stale receipts

2. parts—(1) abilities, (2) genitalia.   4. whimsy—(1)dizziness, (2) a wench
(*Bartholomew Fair* II.iv), (3) whim.   9. clodpolls—numbskulls.
10. mystery—craft. science—branch of learning.   11. liberally—pertaining
to the seven liberal arts, the standard university curriculum.   14. town-
art—town as opposed to gown, i.e., university (?).   18. Kitchen-invention—
elaborate dishes. receipts—recipes.

To please the belly, and the groin; nor those,
With their court-dog-tricks, that can fawn and fleer,   20
Make their revènue out of legs and faces,
Echo my lord, and lick away a moth.
But your fine, elegant rascal, that can rise
And stoop, almost together, like an arrow;
Shoot through the air as nimbly as a star;   25
Turn short as doth a swallow; and be here,
And there, and here, and yonder, all at once;
Present to any humor, all occasion;
And change a visor swifter than a thought!
This is the creature had the art born with him;   30
Toils not to learn it, but doth practice it
Out of most excellent nature: and such sparks
Are the true parasites, others but their zanies.

21. legs—bows.   22. lick—flick (?).   moth—vermin.

ACT III

SCENE II

[*Enter Bonario.*]

Mosca. Who's this? Bonario? Old Corbaccio's son?
The person I was bound to seek. Fair sir,
You are happ'ly met.
        Bonario.   That cannot be by thee.
    Mosca. Why, sir?
        Bonario.   Nay, 'pray thee know thy way and leave me:
I would be loth to interchange discourse   5
With such a mate as thou art.
        Mosca.   Courteous sir,
Scorn not my poverty.
        Bonario.   Not I, by heaven;
But thou shalt give me leave to hate thy baseness.
    Mosca. Baseness?
        Bonario.   Ay, answer me, is not thy sloth
Sufficient argument? thy flattery?   10
Thy means of feeding?

6. mate—base fellow.

    Mosca.   Heaven be good to me!
These imputations are too common, sir,
And eas'ly stuck on virtue when she's poor.
You are unequal to me, and howe'er
Your sentence may be righteous, yet you are not ,   15
That ere you know me, thus proceed in censure.
St. Mark bear witness 'gainst you, 'tis inhuman.   [*He cries.*]
    Bonario. [*Aside.*] What? does he weep? the sign is soft
                                     [and good.
I do repent me that I was so harsh.
    Mosca. 'Tis true that swayed by strong necessity,   20
I am enforced to eat my carefull bread
With too much obesquy; 'tis true, beside,
That I am fain to spin mine own poor raiment
Out of my mere observance, being not born
To a free fortune; but that I have done   25
Base offices, in rending friends asunder,
Dividing families, betraying counsels,
Whispering false lies, or mining men with praises,
Trained their credulity with perjuries,
Corrupted chastity, or am in love   30
With mine own tender ease, but would not rather
Prove the most rugged and laborious course,
That might redeem my present estimation,
Let me here perish, in all hope of goodness.
    Bonario. [*Aside.*]—This cannot be a personated passion—   35
I was to blame, so to mistake thy nature;
Pray thee forgive me and speak out thy business.
    Mosca. Sir, it concerns you, and though I may seem
At first to make a main offence in manners,
And in my gratitude unto my master,   40
Yet, for the pure love which I bear all right,
And hatred of the wrong, I must reveal it.
This very hour your father is in purpose
To disinherit you—
    Bonario.   How!

---

14. unequal—above, socially; also, unjust.   21. carefull—hard-won.
22. obesquy—obsequiousness.   23. fain—obliged.   24. mere observance—absolute parasitism.   28. mining—undermining.   32. Prove—
take.   33. estimation—reputation.   39. main—major.

Mosca.   And thrust you forth
As a mere stranger to his blood; 'tis true, sir.   45
The work no way engageth me, but as
I claim an interest in the general state
Of goodness and true virtue, which I hear
T' abound in you, and for which mere respect,
Without a second aim, sir, I have done it.   50
    Bonario. This tale hath lost thee much of the late trust
Thou hadst with me; it is impossible.
I know not how to lend it any thought
My father should be so unnatural.
    Mosca. It is a confidence that well becomes   55
Your piety; and formed, no doubt, it is
From your own simple innocence, which makes
Your wrong more monstrous and abhorred. But, sir,
I now will tell you more. This very minute
It is, or will be doing; and if you   60
Shall be but pleased to go with me, I'll bring you,
I dare not say where you shall see, but where
Your ear shall be a witness of the deed;
Hear yourself written bastard and professed
The common issue of the earth.
    Bonario.   I'm mazed!   65
    Mosca. Sir, if I do it not, draw your just sword
And score your vengeance on my front and face;
Mark me your villain. You have too much wrong,
And I do suffer for you, sir. My heart
Weeps blood in anguish—
    Bonario.   Lead, I follow thee.   [*Exeunt.*]   70

---

49. for . . . respect—for this reason only.   56. piety—filial love and reverence.   65. common . . . earth—of unknown or obscure parentage.
67. score—mark.   front—forehead.

ACT III
SCENE III

[*Volpone's house.*]

Volpone.   Mosca stays long, methinks.   Bring forth your
                                                    [sports
And help to make the wretched time more sweet.
                    [*Enter Nano, Castrone, Androgyno.*]
    Nano.   Dwarf, fool, and eunuch, well met here we be.
A question it were now, whether of us three,
Being, all, the known delicates of a rich man,   5
In pleasing him, claim the precedency can?
    Castrone.   I claim for myself.
    Androgyno.   And so doth the fool.
    Nano.   'Tis foolish indeed, let me set you both to school.
First for your dwarf, he's little and witty,
And everything, as it is little, is pretty;   10
Else, why do men say to a creature of my shape,
So soon as they see him, "It's a pretty little ape"?
And, why a pretty ape? but for pleasing imitation
Of greater men's action, in a ridiculous fashion.
Beside, this feat body of mine doth not crave   15
Half the meat, drink, and cloth one of your bulks will have.
Admit your fool's face be the mother of laughter,
Yet, for his brain, it must always come after;
And though that do feed him, it's a pitiful case
His body is beholding to such a bad face.   *One knocks.*   20
    Volpone.   Who's there? My couch, away, look, Nano, see;
Give me my caps first—go, inquire.
                        [*Exeunt Castrone, Androgyno.*]
                        [*Volpone leaps into his bed.*]
                            Now Cupid
Send it be Mosca, and with fair return.
    Nano.   It is the beauteous madam—
    Volpone.   Wouldbe—is it?
    Nano.   The same.
    Volpone.   Now, torment on me; squire her in,   25

---

4. whether—which.   5. known delicates—acknowledged morsels.
15. feat—neat, pretty.   23. fair return—good profit (from a commercial
venture).

For she will enter, or dwell here forever.
Nay, quickly, that my fit were past. I fear   [*Exit Nano.*]
A second hell too: that my loathing this
Will quite expel my appetite to the other.
Would she were taking, now, her tedious leave.   30
Lord, how it threats me, what I am to suffer!

28. this—Lady Wouldbe.   29. the other—Celia.

ACT III

SCENE IV

                              [*Enter Nano with Lady Wouldbe.*]
      Lady Wouldbe. [*To Nano.*] I thank you, good sir. Pray
                                        [you signify
Unto your patron I am here—This band
Shows not my neck enough.—I trouble you, sir;
Let me request you bid one of my women
Come hither to me. In good faith, I am dressed   5
Most favourably today! It is no matter;
'Tis well enough. [*Enter 1st Woman.*] Look, see these
                                        [petulant things!
How they have done this!
      Volpone. [*Aside.*]   —I do feel the fever
Ent'ring in at mine ears. O for a charm
To fright it hence—
      Lady Wouldbe. Come nearer. Is this curl   10
In his right place? or this? Why is this higher
Than all the rest? You ha' not washed your eyes yet?
Or do they not stand even i' your head?
Where's your fellow? Call her.   [*Exit 1st Woman.*]
      Nano. [*Aside.*]   Now, St. Mark
Deliver us! Anon she'll beat her women   15
Because her nose is red. [*Re-enter 1st Woman with 2nd*
                                        [*Woman.*]
      Lady Wouldbe.   I pray you, view
This tire, forsooth; are all things apt, or no?
      1st Woman. One hair a little, here, sticks out, forsooth.

2. band—ruff.

  Lady Wouldbe. Dost so, forsooth? And where was your
                 [dear sight
When it did so, forsooth? What now! Bird-eyed?   20
And you too? Pray you both approach and mend it.
Now, by that light, I muse you're not ashamed!
I, that have preached these things, so oft, unto you,
Read you the principles, argued all the grounds,
Disputed every fitness, every grace,   25
Called you to counsel of so frequent dressings—
  Nano. [*Aside.*] More carefully than of your fame or
                  [honor.
  Lady Wouldbe. Made you acquainted what an ample
                  [dowry
The knowledge of these things would be unto you,
Able, alone, to get you noble husbands   30
At your return; and you, thus, to neglect it!
Besides, you seeing what a curious nation
Th' Italians are, what will they say of me?
"The English lady cannot dress herself."
Here's a fine imputation to our country!   35
Well, go your ways, and stay i' the next room.
This fucus was too coarse, too; it's no matter.
Good sir, you'll give 'em entertainment?
        [*Exit Nano with Women.*]
  Volpone. The storm comes toward me.
  Lady Wouldbe.   How does my Volp?
  Volpone. Troubled with noise, I cannot sleep; I dreamt 40
That a strange fury entered, now, my house,
And, with the dreadful tempest of her breath,
Did cleave my roof asunder.
  Lady Wouldbe.   Believe me, and I
Had the most *fearful* dream, could I remember 't—
  Volpone. [*Aside.*] Out on my fate! I ha' giv'n her the
                [occasion 45
How to torment me. She will tell me hers.
  Lady Wouldbe. Methought the golden mediocrity,
Polite, and delicate—
  Volpone.   Oh, if you do love me,

---

20. Bird-eyed—startled (?). 32. curious—fastidious. 37. fucus—makeup. 47. golden mediocrity—Aristotle's Golden Mean: "nothing to excess."

No more; I sweat, and suffer, at the mention
Of *any* dream; feel how I tremble yet.   50
                    [*Placing her hand on his heart.*]
    Lady Wouldbe. Alas, good soul! the passion of the heart,
Seed-pearl were good now, boiled with syrup of apples,
Tincture of gold, and coral, citron-pills,
Your elecampane root, myrobalanes—
    Volpone. [*Aside.*] Ay me, I have ta'en a grasshopper by
                                          [the wing! 55
    Lady Wouldbe. Burnt silk and amber. You have muscadel
Good in the house—
    Volpone.   You will not drink and part?
    Lady Wouldbe. No, fear not that. I doubt we shall not
                                          [get
Some English saffron, half a dram would serve,
Your sixteen cloves, a little musk, dried mints,   60
Bugloss, and barley-meal—
    Volpone. [*Aside.*]   She's in again.
Before I feigned diseases, now I have one.
    Lady Wouldbe. And these applied with a right scarlet
                                          [cloth.
    Volpone. [*Aside.*] Another flood of words! a very
                                          [torrent!
    Lady Wouldbe. Shall I, sir, make you a poultice?
    Volpone.   No, no, no.   65
I'm very well, you need prescribe no more.
    Lady Wouldbe. I have, a little, studied physic; but now
I'm all for music, save, i' the forenoons
An hour or two for painting. I would have
A lady, indeed, to have all letters and arts,   70
Be able to discourse, to write, to paint,
But principal, as Plato holds, your music,
And so does wise Pythagoras, I take it,
Is your true rapture, when there is concent
In face, in voice, and clothes, and is, indeed,   75
Our sex's chiefest ornament.
    Volpone.   The poet
As old in time as Plato, and as knowing,

---

51. passion of the heart—heartburn.   52–61. Seed-pearl . . . barley-meal—
a catalog of popular remedies.   74. concent—harmony.   76. The
poet—Sophocles (*Ajax* 293).

Says that your highest female grace is silence.
    Lady Wouldbe. Which o' your poets? Petrarch? or
                           [Tasso? or Dante?
Guarini? Ariosto? Aretine?   80
Cieco di Hadria? I have read them all.
    Volpone. [*Aside.*]   Is everything a cause to my
                            [destruction?
    Lady Wouldbe. I think I ha' two or three of 'em about
                              [me.
    Volpone. [*Aside.*]   The sun, the sea, will sooner both
                            [stand still
Than her eternal tongue! Nothing can scape it.   85
    Lady Wouldbe. Here's *Pastor Fido*— [*Producing a book.*]
    Volpone. [*Aside.*]   Profess obstinate silence.
That's now my safest.
    Lady Wouldbe.   All our English writers,
I mean such as are happy in th' Italian,
Will deign to steal out of this author, mainly;
Almost as much as from Montagniè.   90
He has so modern and facile a vein,
Fitting the time, and catching the court-ear.
Your Petrarch is more passionate, yet he,
In days of sonneting, trusted 'em with much.
Dante is hard, and few can understand him.   95
But for a desperate wit, there's Aretine!
Only, his pictures are a little obscene—
You mark me not?
    Volpone.   Alas, my mind's perturbed.
    Lady Wouldbe. Why, in such cases, we must cure
                            [ourselves,
Make use of our philosophy—
    Volpone.   O'y me!   100
    Lady Wouldbe. And as we find our passions do rebel,
Encounter 'em with reason, or divert 'em

---

79. your poets—she names Italian writers of the Middle Ages and Renaissance, hardly contemporary with Plato.   86. *Pastor Fido—The Faithful
Shepherd*, Guarini's pastoral tragicomedy (1590).   90. Montagniè—the
French essayist Montaigne.   94. trusted . . . much—provided them (English
writers) with matter to translate or imitate.   96. desperate—outrageous.
Aretine . . . obscene—Pietro Aretino wrote sonnets to accompany a series of
pictures on the positions in love-making.

By giving scope unto some other humor
Of lesser danger: as, in politic bodies
There's nothing more doth overwhelm the judgment,   105
And clouds the understanding, than too much
Settling and fixing, and, as 'twere, subsiding
Upon one object. For the incorporating
Of these same outward things into that part
Which we call mental, leaves some certain feces   110
That stop the organs, and, as Plato says,
Assassinates our knowledge.
    Volpone. [*Aside.*]   Now, the spirit
Of patience help me!
    Lady Wouldbe. Come, in faith, I must
Visit you more adays and make you well;
Laugh and be lusty.
    Volpone. [*Aside.*] My good angel save me!   115
    Lady Wouldbe. There was but one sole man in all the
                                       [world
With whom I e'er could sympathize; and he
Would lie you often, three, four hours together
To hear me speak, and be sometimes so rapt,
As he would answer me quite from the purpose,   120
Like you, and you are like him, just. I'll discourse,
An 't be but only, sir, to bring you asleep,
How we did spend our time and loves together,
For some six years.
    Volpone.   Oh, oh, oh, oh, oh, oh.
    Lady Wouldbe. For we were *coaetanei,* and brought up—   125
    Volpone. Some power, some fate, some fortune rescue
                                            [me!

125. coaetanei—of the same age.

ACT III
SCENE V

[*Enter Mosca.*]

Mosca. God save you, madam!

Lady Wouldbe.   Good sir.

Volpone.   Mosca, welcome!
Welcome to my redemption.

Mosca.   Why, sir?

Volpone.   Oh,
Rid me of this my torture quickly, there,
My madam with the everlasting voice;
The bells in time of pestilence ne'er made   5
Like noise, or were in that perpetual motion!
The cock-pit comes not near it. All my house,
But now, steamed like a bath with her thick breath.
A lawyer could not have been heard; nor scarce
Another woman, such a hail of words   10
She has let fall. For hell's sake, rid her hence.

Mosca. Has she presented?

Volpone.   Oh, I do not care;
I'll take her absence upon any price,
With any loss.

Mosca.   Madam—

Lady Wouldbe.   I ha' brought your patron
A toy, a cap here, of mine own work—

Mosca.   'Tis well.   15
I had forgot to tell you I saw your knight
Where you'd little think it—

Lady Wouldbe.   Where?

Mosca.   Marry,
Where yet, if you make haste, you may apprehend him,
Rowing upon the water in a gondole,
With the most cunning courtesan of Venice.   20

Lady Wouldbe. Is't true?

Mosca.   Pursue 'em, and believe your eyes.
Leave me to make your gift. [*Exit Lady Wouldbe.*]   I knew
                                        ['twould take.

---

5. bells . . . pestilence—outbreaks of the plague were frequent, during which time death knells sounded almost continuously.   7. cock-pit—where cock fights were held.   12. presented—i.e., a gift.

For lightly, they that use themselves most license,
Are still most jealous.
    Volpone.   Mosca, hearty thanks
For thy quick fiction and delivery of me.   25
Now to my hopes, what sayst thou? [*Re-enter Lady Wouldbe.*]
    Lady Wouldbe.   But do you hear, sir?
    Volpone. Again! I fear a paroxysm.
    Lady Wouldbe.   Which way
Rowed they together?
    Mosca.   Toward the Rialto.
    Lady Wouldbe. I pray you lend me your dwarf.
    Mosca.   I pray you, take him.
                      [*Exit Lady Wouldbe.*]
Your hopes, sir, are like happy blossoms: fair,   30
And promise timely fruit, if you will stay
But the maturing; keep you at your couch.
Corbaccio will arrive straight with the will;
When he is gone, I'll tell you more.   [*Exit Mosca.*]
    Volpone.   My blood,
My spirits are returned; I am alive;   35
And, like your wanton gamester at primero,
Whose thought had whispered to him, not go less,
Methinks I lie, and draw—for an encounter.
            [*He draws the curtains across his bed.*]

23. lightly—commonly.   28. Rialto—bridge over the Grand Canal.
36. primero—a fashionable card game somewhat like poker; Volpone uses its
technical terms (*Go less, lie, draw,* and *encounter*) to speak of the seduction of
Celia.

ACT III

SCENE VI

        [*Mosca leads Bonario in and hides him.*]
    Mosca. Sir, here concealed you may hear all. But pray
                       [you
                    One knocks.
Have patience, sir; the same's your father knocks.
I am compelled to leave you.
    Bonario.   Do so. Yet
Cannot my thought imagine this a truth.

1. here concealed—behind the door opening onto the stage.

ACT III

SCENE VII

[*Mosca lets Corvino and Celia in.*]

Mosca. Death on me! you are come too soon, what
                                                    [meant you?
Did not I say I would send?
    Corvino.   Yes, but I feared
You might forget it, and then they prevent us.
    Mosca. Prevent! [*Aside.*] —Did e'er man haste so for his
                                                    [horns?
A courtier would not ply it so for a place.—   5
Well, now there's no helping it, stay here;
I'll presently return.   [*He moves toward Bonario.*]
    Corvino.   Where are you, Celia?
You know not wherefore I have brought you hither?
    Celia. Not well, except you told me.
    Corvino.   Now I will:
Hark hither.   [*He leads her aside and whispers to her.*]
    Mosca. [*To Bonario.*] Sir, your father hath sent word,   10
It will be half an hour ere he come;
And therefore, if you please to walk the while
Into that gallery—at the upper end
There are some books to entertain the time.
And I'll take care no man shall come unto you, sir.   15
    Bonario. Yes, I will stay there. [*Aside.*] I do doubt this
                                                    [fellow. [*Exit.*]
    Mosca. [*To Volpone.*] There, he is far enough; he can
                                                    [hear nothing.
And for his father, I can keep him off.
    Corvino. Nay, now, there is no starting back, and
                                                    [therefore
Resolve upon it: I have so decreed.   20
It must be done. Nor would I move 't afore,
Because I would avoid all shifts and tricks,
That might deny me.

3. prevent—see I.iv.68; II.vi.49, 78.   5. place—office.   7. presently—
immediately.   9. except . . . me—unless you were to tell me.   21. move—
propose.

  Celia.   Sir, let me beseech you,
Affect not these strange trials; if you doubt
My chastity, why, lock me up forever;   25
Make me the heir of darkness. Let me live
Where I may please your fears, if not your trust.
  Corvino. Believe it, I have no such humor, I.
All that I speak I mean; yet I am not mad;
Not horn-mad, see you? Go to, show yourself   30
Obedient, and a wife.
  Celia.   O heaven!
  Corvino.   I say it,
Do so.
  Celia. Was this the train?
  Corvino.   I've told you reasons:
What the physicians have set down; how much
It may concern me; what my engagements are;
My means, and the necessity of those means   35
For my recovery; wherefore, if you be
Loyal and mine, be won, respect my venture.
  Celia. Before your honor?
  Corvino.   Honor! tut, a breath.
There's no such thing in nature; a mere term
Invented to awe fools. What, is my gold   40
The worse for touching? clothes for being looked on?
Why, this 's no more. An old, decrepit wretch,
That has no sense, no sinew; takes his meat
With others' fingers; only knows to gape
When you do scald his gums; a voice, a shadow; 45
And what can this man hurt you?
  Celia.   Lord, what spirit
Is this hath entered him?
  Corvino.   And for your fame,
That's such a jig; as if I would go tell it,
Cry it, on the Piazza! Who shall know it
But he that cannot speak it, and this fellow,   50
Whose lips are i' my pocket? Save yourself
—If you'll proclaim 't, you may—I know no other
Should come to know it.

---

32. train—trap. 48. jig—comic dance; hence, a trifle.

    Celia.   Are heaven and saints then nothing?
Will they be blind, or stupid?
    Corvino.   How?
    Celia.   Good sir,
Be jealous still, emulate them, and think   55
What hate they burn with toward every sin.
    Corvino. I grant you. If I thought it were a sin
I would not urge you. Should I offer this
To some young Frenchman, or hot Tuscan blood
That had read Aretine, conned all his prints,   60
Knew every quirk within lust's labyrinth,
And were professed critic in lechery;
And I would look upon him, and applaud him,
This were a sin; but here, 'tis contrary,
A pious work, mere charity, for physic   65
And honest policy to assure mine own.
    Celia. O heaven! canst thou suffer such a change?
    Volpone. Thou art mine honor, Mosca, and my pride,
My joy, my tickling, my delight! Go, bring 'em.
    Mosca. Please you draw near, sir.
    Corvino.   Come on, what—   70
You will not be rebellious? By that light—
                      [*He drags her to the bed.*]
    Mosca. [*To Volpone.*] Sir, Signior Corvino, here, is come
                               [to see you.
    Volpone. Oh!
    Mosca.   And hearing of the consultation had,
So lately, for your health, is come to offer,
Or rather, sir, to prostitute—
    Corvino.   Thanks, sweet Mosca.   75
    Mosca. Freely, unasked, or unentreated—
    Corvino.   Well.
    Mosca. As the true, fervent instance of his love,
His own most fair and proper wife, the beauty
Only of price in Venice—
    Corvino.   'Tis well urged.
    Mosca. To be your comfortress, and to preserve you.   80

---

60. prints—the pornographic pictures mentioned by Lady Wouldbe.
61. quirk—twist.   62. critic—expert.   79. Only of price—of unique
worth (?).

    Volpone. Alas, I'm past already! Pray you, thank him
For his good care and promptness; but for that,
'Tis a vain labor e'en to fight 'gainst heaven;
Applying fire to a stone, uh, uh, uh, uh!
Making a dead leaf grow again. I take   85
His wishes gently, though; and you may tell him
What I've done for him. Marry, my state is hopeless!
Will him to pray for me, and t' use his fortune
With reverence when he comes to't.
    Mosca.   Do you hear, sir?
Go to him with your wife.
    Corvino. [*To Celia.*] Heart of my father!   90
Wilt thou persist thus? Come, I pray thee, come.
Thou seest 'tis nothing, Celia. By this hand [*Raising his hand.*]
I shall grow violent. Come, do 't, I say.
    Celia. Sir, kill me rather. I will take down poison,
Eat burning coals, do anything—
    Corvino.   Be damned!   95
Heart! I will drag thee hence home by the hair,
Cry thee a strumpet through the streets, rip up
Thy mouth unto thine ears, and slit thy nose,
Like a raw rotchet!—Do not tempt me, come.
Yield, I am loth—Death! I will buy some slave   100
Whom I will kill, and bind thee to him, alive;
And at my window hang you forth, devising
Some monstrous crime, which I, in capital letters,
Will eat into thy flesh with aquafortis,
And burning cor'sives, on this stubborn breast.   105
Now, by the blood thou hast incensed, I'll do 't!
    Celia. Sir, what you please, you may; I am your martyr.
    Corvino. Be not thus obstinate, I ha' not deserved it.
Think who it is entreats you. Pray thee, sweet;
Good faith, thou shalt have jewels, gowns, attires,   110
What thou wilt, think and ask. Do, but go kiss him.
Or touch him, but. For my sake. At my suit.
This once. [*She refuses.*] No? Not? I shall remember this.
Will you disgrace me thus? D' you thirst my undoing?
    Mosca. Nay, gentle lady, be advised.

---

99. rotchet—a fish.   104. aquafortis—nitric acid.   105. cor'sives—
corrosives.

Corvino.   No, no.   115
She has watched her time. God's precious, this is scurvy,
'Tis very scurvy; and you are—
    Mosca.   Nay, good sir.
    Corvino. An errant locust, by heaven, a locust! Whore,
Crocodile, that hast thy tears prepared,
Expecting how thou'lt bid 'em flow.
    Mosca.   Nay, pray you, sir!   120
She will consider.
    Celia.   Would my life would serve
To satisfy.
    Corvino. 'Sdeath! if she would but speak to him,
And save my reputation, 'twere somewhat;
But spitefully to effect my utter ruin!
    Mosca. Ay, now you've put your fortune in her hands.   125
Why i' faith, it is her modesty, I must quit her.
If you were absent, she would be more coming;
I know it, and dare undertake for her.
What woman can before her husband? Pray you,
Let us depart and leave her here.
    Corvino.   Sweet Celia,   130
Thou may'st redeem all yet; I'll say no more.
If not, esteem yourself as lost. [*She begins to leave with him.*]
                Nay, stay there.
                    [*Exit Mosca and Corvino.*]
    Celia. O God, and his good angels! whither, whither,
Is shame fled human breasts? that with such ease
Men dare put off your honors, and their own?   135
Is that, which ever was a cause of life,
Now placed beneath the basest circumstance,
And modesty an exile made, for money?
    Volpone. Ay, in Corvino, and such earth-fed minds,
That never tasted the true heaven of love.   *He leaps*   140
Assure thee, Celia, he that would sell thee,   *off from*
Only for hope of gain, and that uncertain,   *his couch.*
He would have sold his part of Paradise
For ready money, had he met a cope-man.
Why art thou mazed to see me thus revived?   145

---

118. errant—either wandering or arrant, i.e., outright.   119. Crocodile—
supposed to attract victims by weeping piteously.   126. quit—acquit, excuse.   144. cope-man—dealer.

Rather applaud thy beauty's miracle;
'Tis thy great work, that hath, not now alone,
But sundry times raised me in several shapes,
And, but this morning, like a mountebank,
To see thee at thy window. Ay, before   150
I would have left my practice for thy love,
In varying figures I would have contended
With the blue Proteus, or the hornèd flood.
Now, art thou welcome.

> *Celia.*   Sir!

> *Volpone.*   Nay, fly me not.

Nor let thy false imagination   155
That I was bed-rid, make thee think I am so:
Thou shalt not find it. I am, now, as fresh,
As hot, as high, and in as jovial plight
As when in that so celebrated scene
At recitation of our comedy,   160
For entertainment of the great Valois,
I acted young Antinous, and attracted
The eyes and ears of all the ladies present,
T' admire each graceful gesture, note, and footing.

SONG   165

> Come, my Celia, let us prove,
> While we can, the sports of love;
> Time will not be ours forever,
> He, at length, our good will sever;
> Spend not then his gifts in vain.   170
> Suns that set may rise again;
> But if once we lose this light,
> 'Tis with us perpetual night.
> Why should we defer our joys?
> Fame and rumor are but toys.   175
> Cannot we delude the eyes

148. raised me—like a conjurer raising a spirit.   152. figures—shapes.
153. Proteus—god who could change himself into any shape.   hornèd flood—
the river god Achelous, who as bull, serpent, and man-bull fought Hercules.
158. jovial plight—"happy condition, but Jove and his love for earthly maidens
is referred to" (Kernan).   161. Valois—Venice in 1574 entertained Henry
of Valois, who had just become Henry III, King of France.   162. Antinous—
a beautiful youth, favorite of the emperor Hadrian.   166. prove—try.

　　Of a few poor household spies?
　　Or his easier ears beguile,
　　Thus removèd by our wile?
　　'Tis no sin love's fruits to steal, 　　　　　　　　　180
　　But the sweet thefts to reveal:
　　To be taken, to be seen,
　　These have crimes accounted been.
　Celia.　Some serene blast me, or dire lightning strike
This my offending face.
　　Volpone.　　　　　　Why droops my Celia?　　　185
Thou hast in place of a base husband found
A worthy lover; use thy fortune well,
With secrecy and pleasure.　See, behold,

　　　　　　　　　　　　　[Pointing to his hoard.]

What thou art queen of; not in expectation,
As I feed others, but possessed and crowned.　　　190
See, here, a rope of pearl, and each more orient
Than that the brave Egyptian queen caroused;
Dissolve and drink 'em.　See, a carbuncle
May put out both the eyes of our St. Mark;
A diamond would have bought Lollia Paulina　　　195
When she came in like star-light, hid with jewels
That were the spoils of provinces; take these,
And wear, and lose 'em; yet remains an earring
To purchase them again, and this whole state.
A gem but worth a private patrimony　　　　　　200
Is nothing; we will eat such at a meal.
The heads of parrots, tongues of nightingales,
The brains of peacocks, and of estriches
Shall be our food, and, could we get the phoenix,
Though nature lost her kind, she were our dish.　　205

177. household spies—Corvino has an intelligence network (see I.v.123–6).
178. his—Corvino's. 　　　　184. serene—evening mist, thought poisonous.
191–92. pearl . . . caroused—Cleopatra drank a huge pearl dissolved in vinegar
in order to meet Antony's challenge that she spend ten million sesterces on
one meal. 　　　　193. carbuncle—a red gem. 　　　　194. put out . . . St. Mark—
perhaps alluding to a statue in St. Mark's Cathedral that had gems for eyes.
195. Lollia Paulina—wife of the Emperor Caligula who wore huge ropes of
splendid jewels. 　　　　204. phoenix—mythical Arabian bird; every 500 years it
burned and arose anew from its own ashes. 　　　205. kind—species; since only
one was believed to exist at a time, to dine upon it would be to make the kind
extinct.

    Celia. Good sir, these things might move a mind affected
With such delights; but I, whose innocence
Is all I can think wealthy, or worth th' enjoying,
And which, once lost, I have nought to lose beyond it,
Cannot be taken with these sensual baits.   210
If you have conscience—
    Volpone.   'Tis the beggar's virtue;
If thou hast wisdom, hear me, Celia.
Thy baths shall be the juice of July-flowers,
Spirit of roses, and of violets,
The milk of unicorns, and panthers' breath   215
Gathered in bags and mixed with Cretan wines.
Our drink shall be preparèd gold and amber,
Which we will take until my roof whirl round
With the vertigo; and my dwarf shall dance,
My eunuch sing, my fool make up the antic.   220
Whilst we, in changèd shapes, act Ovid's tales,
Thou like Europa now, and I like Jove,
Then I like Mars, and thou like Erycine;
So of the rest, till we have quite run through,
And wearied all the fables of the gods.   225
Then will I have thee in more modern forms,
Attirèd like some sprightly dame of France,
Brave Tuscan lady, or proud Spanish beauty;
Sometimes unto the Persian Sophy's wife,
Or the Grand Signior's mistress; and, for change,   230
To one of our most artful courtesans,
Or some quick Negro, or cold Russian;
And I will meet thee in as many shapes;
Where we may, so, transfuse our wand'ring souls [*Kissing her.*]
Out at our lips and score up sums of pleasures,   235
          That the curious shall not know
          How to tell them as they flow;
          And the envious, when they find
          What their number is, be pined.

213. July flowers—gillyflowers.   215. panthers' breath—panthers were believed to draw victims by their sweet-scented breath.   220. antic—jig.
221–23. Ovid's tales . . . Erycine—*The Metamorphoses*; stories such as Jove's
amours (in the form of a bull) with the maiden Europa and Mars' amours
with Venus (Erycine).   229. Sophy—Shah.   230. Grand Signior—Turk-
ish Sultan.   232. quick—lively.   237. tell—count.   239. pined—
consumed with envy.

  Celia. If you have ears that will be pierced, or eyes   240
That can be opened, a heart may be touched,
Or any part that yet sounds man about you;
If you have touch of holy saints, or heaven,
Do me the grace to let me 'scape. If not,
Be bountiful and kill me. You do know   245
I am a creature hither ill betrayed
By one whose shame I would forget it were.
If you will deign me neither of these graces,
Yet feed your wrath, sir, rather than your lust—
It is a vice comes nearer manliness—   250
And punish that unhappy crime of nature,
Which you miscall my beauty: flay my face,
Or poison it with ointments for seducing
Your blood to this rebellion. Rub these hands
With what may cause an eating leprosy,   255
E'en to my bones and marrow; anything
That may disfavour me, save in my honor;
And I will kneel to you, pray for you, pay down
A thousand hourly vows, sir, for your health;
Report, and think you virtuous—
  Volpone.   Think me cold,   260
Frozen, and impotent, and so report me?
That I had Nestor's hernia thou wouldst think.
I do degenerate and abuse my nation
To play with opportunity thus long;
I should have done the act, and then have parleyed. 265
Yield, or I'll force thee.   *[He seizes her.]*
  Celia.   O! just God!
  Volpone.   In vain—
  Bonario. Forbear, foul ravisher! libidinous swine! *He*
Free the forced lady, or thou diest, impostor. *leaps out from*
But that I am loth to snatch thy punishment *where Mosca*
Out of the hand of justice, thou shouldst yet *had placed* 270
Be made the timely sacrifice of vengeance,   *him.*
Before this altar, and this dross, thy idol. *[Points to the gold.]*
Lady, let's quit the place, it is the den
Of villainy; fear nought, you have a guard;
And he ere long shall meet his just reward.   275

---

257. disfavour—disfigure.   262. Nestor's hernia—impotence of old age.

[*Exeunt Bonario & Celia.*]

Volpone.   Fall on me, roof, and bury me in ruin!
Become my grave, that wert my shelter! O!
I am unmasked, unspirited, undone,
Betrayed to beggary, to infamy—

ACT III

SCENE VIII

[*Enter Mosca, bleeding.*]

Mosca. Where shall I run, most wretched shame of men,
To beat out my unlucky brains?
   Volpone.   Here, here.
What! dost thou bleed?
   Mosca.   O, that his well-driven sword
Had been so courteous to have cleft me down
Unto the navel, ere I lived to see   5
My life, my hopes, my spirits, my patron, all
Thus desperately engagèd by my error.
   Volpone. Woe on thy fortune!
   Mosca.   And my follies, sir.
   Volpone. Th' hast made me miserable.
   Mosca.   And myself, sir.
Who would have thought he would have hearkened so?   10
   Volpone. What shall we do?
   Mosca.   I know not; if my heart
Could expiate the mischance, I'd pluck it out.
Will you be pleased to hang me, or cut my throat?
And I'll requite you, sir. Let's die like Romans,
Since we have lived like Grecians.   *They knock without.*   15
   Volpone.   Hark! who's there?
I hear some footing; officers, the *Saffi*,
Come to apprehend us! I do feel the brand
Hissing already at my forehead; now,
Mine ears are boring.

15. Grecians—sensualists.   16. *Saffi*—"Saffo, a catchpole, or sergeant"
(Florio, 1598).   19. are boring—are being bored.

Mosca.   To your couch, sir; you
Make that place good, however. Guilty men [*Volpone lies*
                                       [*down.*]   20
Suspect what they deserve still. [*Mosca opens door.*] Signior
                                        [Corbaccio!

20. however—whatever you do.

ACT III
SCENE IX

[*Enter Corbaccio and behind him, eavesdropping, Voltore.*]
    Corbaccio. Why, how now, Mosca?
    Mosca.   O, undone, amazed, sir.
Your son, I know not by what accident,
Acquainted with your purpose to my patron,
Touching your will, and making him your heir,
Entered our house with violence, his sword drawn,   5
Sought for you, called you wretch, unnatural,
Vowed he would kill you.
    Corbaccio.   Me?
    Mosca.   Yes, and my patron.
    Corbaccio. This act shall disinherit him indeed.
Here is the will.
    Mosca.   'Tis well, sir.
    Corbaccio.   Right and well.
Be you as careful now for me.
    Mosca.   My life, sir,   10
Is not more tendered; I am only yours.
    Corbaccio. How does he? Will he die shortly, think'st
                                     [thou?
    Mosca.   I fear
He'll outlast May.
    Corbaccio. Today?
    Mosca. [*Shouting.*] No, last out May, sir.
    Corbaccio. Couldst thou not gi' him a dram?
    Mosca.   O, by no means, sir.
    Corbaccio. Nay, I'll not bid you.

1. amazed—in a maze.

    Voltore. [*Stepping forward.*]   This is a knave, I see.   15
    Mosca. [*Aside.*] How! Signior Voltore! Did he hear me?
    Voltore.   Parasite!
    Mosca. Who's that? O, sir, most timely welcome—
    Voltore.   Scarce
To the discovery of your tricks, I fear.
You are his, only? And mine, also, are you not?
                                [*Corbaccio walks aside.*]
    Mosca. Who? I, sir?
    Voltore.   You, sir. What device is this   20
About a will?
    Mosca.   A plot for you, sir.
    Voltore.   Come,
Put not your foists upon me; I shall scent 'em.
    Mosca. Did you not hear it?
    Voltore.   Yes, I hear Corbaccio
Hath made your patron, there, his heir.
    Mosca.   'Tis true,
By my device, drawn to it by my plot,   25
With hope—
    Voltore. Your patron should reciprocate?
And you have promised?
    Mosca.   For your good I did, sir.
Nay, more, I told his son, brought, hid him here,
Where he might hear his father pass the deed;
Being persuaded to it by this thought, sir: 30
That the unnaturalness, first, of the act,
And then his father's oft disclaiming in him,
Which I did mean t' help on, would sure enrage him
To do some violence upon his parent.
On which the law should take sufficient hold,   35
And you be stated in a double hope.
Truth be my comfort, and my conscience,
My only aim was to dig you a fortune
Out of these two old, rotten sepulchres—
    Voltore. I cry thee mercy, Mosca.
    Mosca.   Worth your patience,   40
And your great merit, sir. And see the change!

22. foists—tricks; but literally stenches, farts (which explains why Voltore
"scents 'em").   32. in—of.   36. stated—enstated.

  Voltore. Why, what success?

  Mosca.   Most hapless! you must help, sir.

Whilst we expected th' old raven, in comes

Corvino's wife, sent hither by her husband—

   Voltore. What, with a present?

  Mosca.   No, sir, on visitation;   45

I'll tell you how anon—and staying long,

The youth he grows impatient, rushes forth,

Seizeth the lady, wounds me, makes her swear—

Or he would murder her, that was his vow—

T' affirm my patron to have done her rape,   50

Which how unlike it is, you see! and hence,

With that pretext he's gone t' accuse his father,

Defame my patron, defeat you—

   Voltore.   Where's her husband?

Let him be sent for straight.

   Mosca.   Sir, I'll go fetch him.

   Voltore. Bring him to the *Scrutineo.*

   Mosca.   Sir, I will.   55

   Voltore. This must be stopped.

   Mosca.   O, you do nobly, sir.

Alas, 'twas labored all, sir, for your good;

Nor was there want of counsel in the plot.

But Fortune can, at any time, o'erthrow

The projects of a hundred learned clerks, sir.   60

   Corbaccio. [*Rejoining the others.*] What's that?

   Voltore. [*To Corbaccio.*] Will 't please you, sir, to go

                [along?

       [*Exeunt Corbaccio and Voltore.*]

   Mosca. [*To Volpone.*] Patron, go in and pray for our

                [success.

   Volpone. Need makes devotion; heaven your labor bless!

---

41. success—result. 55. *Scrutineo*—the Venetian Senate House.
60. clerks—scholars.

ACT IV
SCENE I

[*A street in Venice.*]
[*Enter Sir Politic and Peregrine.*]

    Sir Politic. I told you, sir, it was a plot; you see
What observation is! You mentioned me
For some instructions: I will tell you, sir,
Since we are met here in this height of Venice,
Some few particulars I have set down   5
Only for this meridian, fit to be known
Of your crude traveler; and they are these.
I will not touch, sir, at your phrase, or clothes,
For they are old.
    Peregrine.   Sir, I have better.
    Sir Politic.   Pardon,
I meant as they are themes.
    Peregrine.   O, sir, proceed.   10
I'll slander you no more of wit, good sir.
    Sir Politic. First, for your garb, it must be grave and
                                      [serious,
Very reserved and locked; not tell a secret
On any terms, not to your father; scarce
A fable but with caution; make sure choice   15
Both of your company and discourse; beware
You never speak a truth—
    Peregrine.   How!
    Sir Politic.   Not to strangers,
For those be they you must converse with most;
Others I would not know, sir, but at distance,
So as I still might be a saver in 'em.   20
You shall have tricks, else, passed upon you hourly.
And then, for your religion, profess none,
But wonder at the diversity of all;

1. it—the mountebank scene (?).   2. mentioned—asked.   4. height—
latitude.   6. meridian—locality.   8. your—the impersonal use common
in Jonson, but Peregrine peversely takes it personally.   10. themes—topics.
11. slander . . . wit—accuse you of being witty.   12. garb—bearing.   20. be
a saver in 'em—save myself from loss caused by them (a gambling term).

And, for your part, protest were there no other
But simply the laws o' th' land, you could content you.   25
Nick Machiavel and Monsieur Bodin both
Were of this mind. Then must you learn the use
And handling of your silver fork at meals,
The metal of your glass (these are main matters
With your Italian), and to know the hour   30
When you must eat your melons and your figs.
      Peregrine. Is that a point of state too?
      Sir Politic.   Here it is.
For your Venetian, if he see a man
Preposterous in the least, he has him straight;
He has, he strips him. I'll acquaint you, sir.   35
I now have lived here 'tis some fourteen months;
Within the first week of my landing here,
All took me for a citizen of Venice,
I knew the forms so well—
      Peregrine. [*Aside.*] And nothing else.
      Sir Politic. I had read Contarini, took me a house,   40
Dealt with my Jews to furnish it with movables—
Well, if I could but find one man, one man
To mine own heart, whom I durst trust, I would—
      Peregrine. What, what, sir?
      Sir Politic.   Make him rich, make him a fortune:
He should not think again. I would command it.   45
      Peregrine. As how?
      Sir Politic.   With certain projects that I have,
Which I may not discover.
      Peregrine. [*Aside.*] If I had
But one to wager with, I would lay odds, now,
He tells me instantly.
      Sir Politic.   One is, and that
I care not greatly who knows, to serve the state   50
Of Venice with red herrings for three years,
And at a certain rate, from Rotterdam,

---

26. Machiavel—Machiavelli had an undeserved reputation for atheism. Bodin—
French political thinker who advocated religious toleration.   28. fork—not
common in England at this time.   29. metal—material.   40. Contarini—
his treatise on the Venetian Republic, translated into English in 1599.
41. movables—movable (as distinguished from built-in) furnishings.   47. discover—reveal.

Where I have correspondence. There's a letter
[*Showing a greasy paper.*]
Sent me from one o' th' States, and to that purpose;
He cannot write his name, but that's his mark.   55
    Peregrine. He is a chandler?
    Sir Politic.   No, a cheesemonger.
There are some other too with whom I treat
About the same negotiation;
And I will undertake it: for 'tis thus
I'll do 't with ease, I've cast it all. Your hoy   60
Carries but three men in her, and a boy;
And she shall make me three returns a year.
So, if there come but one of three, I save;
If two, I can defalk. But this is now
If my main project fail.
    Peregrine.   Then you have others?   65
    Sir Politic. I should be loath to draw the subtle air
Of such a place without my thousand aims.
I'll not dissemble, sir; where'er I come
I love to be considerative, and 'tis true
I have at my free hours thought upon   70
Some certain goods unto the state of Venice,
Which I do call my cautions; and, sir, which
I mean, in hope of pension, to propound
To the Great Council, then unto the Forty,
So to the Ten. My means are made already—   75
    Peregrine. By whom?
    Sir Politic.   Sir, one that though his place be obscure,
Yet he can sway, and they will hear him. He's
A *commendatore.*
    Peregrine.   What, a common sergeant?
    Sir Politic. Sir, such as they are put it in their mouths
What they should say, sometimes, as well as greater.   80

---

54. one o' th' States—a member of the Dutch Estates-General, their governing
body.   56. chandler—a candle merchant; Sir Pol's paper is presumably
greasy.   60. cast—calculated. hoy—Dutch coastal boat.   63. save—avoid
loss (see line 20).   64. defalk—cut expenses (and thus survive).   69. considerative—thoughtful.   72. cautions—precautions.   74–75. Great . . .
Ten—"the ruling bodies of Venice in order of importance" (Kernan).
79–80. such . . . say—common men, such as sergeants, sometimes put words
in the mouths of the great (i.e., influence them).

I think I have my notes to show you— [*Searching his pockets.*]
    Peregrine.   Good sir.
    Sir Politic. But you shall swear unto me, on your gentry,
Not to anticipate—
    Peregrine.   I, sir?
    Sir Politic.   Nor reveal
A circumstance—My paper is not with me,
    Peregrine. O, but you can remember, sir.
    Sir Politic.   My first is   85
Concerning tinderboxes. You must know
No family is here without its box.
Now, sir, it being so portable a thing,
Put case that you or I were ill affected
Unto the state; sir, with it in our pockets   90
Might not I go into the Arsenal?
Or you? Come out again? And none the wiser?
    Peregrine. Except yourself, sir.
    Sir Politic.   Go to, then. I therefore
Advertise to the state how fit it were
That none but such as were known patriots,   95
Sound lovers of their country, should be suffered
T' enjoy them in their houses; and even those
Sealed at some office, and at such a bigness
As might not lurk in pockets.
    Peregrine.   Admirable!
    Sir Politic. My next is, how t' inquire, and be resolved   100
By present demonstration, whether a ship
Newly arrived from Syria, or from
Any suspected part of all the Levant,
Be guilty of the plague. And where they use
To lie out forty, fifty days, sometimes,   105
About the *Lazaretto* for their trial,
I'll save that charge and loss unto the merchant,
And in an hour clear the doubt.
    Peregrine.   Indeed, sir!
    Sir Politic. Or—I will lose my labor.
    Peregrine.   My faith, that's much.
    Sir Politic. Nay, sir, conceive me. 'Twill cost me, in
                                      [onions, 110

89. Put case—Say, for example.   98. Sealed—registered under seal.
101. present—immediate.   106. *Lazaretto*—quarantine islands.

Some thirty livres—
    Peregrine.   Which is one pound sterling.
    Sir Politic. Beside my waterworks.   For this I do, sir:
First, I bring in your ship 'twixt two brick walls—
But those the state shall venture. On the one
I strain me a fair tarpaulin, and in that   115
I stick my onions, cut in halves; the other
Is full of loopholes, out at which I thrust
The noses of my bellows; and those bellows
I keep, with waterworks, in perpetual motion,
Which is the easiest matter of a hundred.   120
Now, sir, your onion, which doth naturally
Attract th' infection, and your bellows blowing
The air upon him, will show instantly
By his changed color if there be contagion,
Or else remain as fair as at the first.   125
Now 'tis known, 'tis nothing.
    Peregrine.   You are right, sir.
    Sir Politic. I would I had my note. [*Searching his*
                          [*pockets.*]
    Peregrine.   Faith, so would I.
But you ha' done well for once, sir.
    Sir Politic.   Were I false,
Or would be made so, I could show you reasons
How I could sell this state, now, to the Turk—   130
Spite of their galleys, or their—
           [*Still frantically searching his pockets.*]
    Peregrine.   Pray, you, Sir Pol.
    Sir Politic. I have 'em not about me.
    Peregrine.   That I feared.
They're there, sir?   [*Pulling a book from Sir Pol's pocket.*]
    Sir Politic.   No, this is my diary,
Wherein I note my actions of the day.
    Peregrine. Pray you let's see, sir. What is here?—
                    ["*Notandum,* 135
A rat had gnawn my spur leathers; notwithstanding,
I put on new and did go forth; but first
I threw three beans over the threshold. Item,
I went and bought two toothpicks, whereof one

111. livres—French coin.   128. false—traitorous.

I burst, immediately, in a discourse   140
With a Dutch merchant 'bout *ragion del stato*.
From him I went and paid a *moccenigo*
For piecing my silk stockings; by the way
I cheapened sprats, and at St. Mark's I urined."
Faith, these are politic notes!
    Sir Politic.   Sir, I do slip   145
No action of my life, thus, but I quote it.
    Peregrine. Believe me it is wise!
    Sir Politic.   Nay, sir, read forth.

141. *ragion del stato*—political affairs.   143. piecing—mending.
144. cheapened—bargained for.   146. thus . . . it—without noting it in this manner.

ACT IV
SCENE II

    [*Enter Lady Wouldbe, Nano, and two Women.*]
    Lady Wouldbe. Where should this loose knight be, trow?
                       [Sure, he's housed.
    Nano. Why, then he's fast.
    Lady Wouldbe.   Ay, he plays both with me.
I pray you stay. This heat will do more harm
To my complexion than his heart is worth.
I do not care to hinder, but to take him.   5
How it comes off!   [*Rubbing her makeup.*]
    1st Woman. My master's yonder.   [*Pointing.*]
    Lady Wouldbe.   Where?
    2nd Woman. With a young gentleman.
    Lady Wouldbe.   That same's the
                       [party!
In man's apparel! Pray you, sir, jog my knight.
I will be tender to his reputation,
However he demerit.
    Sir Politic.   My lady!
    Peregrine.   Where?   10
    Sir Politic. 'Tis she indeed; sir, you shall know her. She is,

2. plays both—i.e., fast and loose (see I.ii.8n).   10. demerit—errs.

Were she not mine, a lady of that merit
For fashion, and behavior, and for beauty
I durst compare—
    Peregrine.   It seems you are not jealous,
That dare commend her.
    Sir Politic.   Nay, and for discourse—   15
    Peregrine. Being your wife, she cannot miss that.
    Sir Politic. [*The parties join.*]   Madam,
Here is a gentleman; pray you, use him fairly;
He seems a youth, but he is—
    Lady Wouldbe.   None?
    Sir Politic.   Yes, one
Has put his face as soon into the world—
    Lady Wouldbe. You mean, as early? But today?
    Sir Politic.   How's this?   20
    Lady Wouldbe. Why, in this habit, sir; you apprehend me!
Well, Master Wouldbe, this doth not become you.
I had thought the odor, sir, of your good name
Had been more precious to you; that you would not
Have done this dire massàcre on your honor,   25
One of your gravity, and rank besides!
But knights, I see, care little for the oath
They make to ladies, chiefly their own ladies.
    Sir Politic. Now, by my spurs, the symbol of my
                        [knighthood—
    Peregrine. [*Aside.*] Lord, how his brain is humbled for
                        [an oath!   30
    Sir Politic. I reach you not.
    Lady Wouldbe.   Right, sir, your policy
May bear it through thus. [*To Peregrine.*] Sir, a word with
                        [you.
I would be loath to contest publicly
With any gentlewoman, or to seem
Froward, or violent, as *The Courtier* says.   35
It comes too near rusticity in a lady,
Which I would shun by all means. And, however
I may deserve from Master Wouldbe, yet
T' have one fair gentlewoman, thus, be made

---

31. reach—understand. policy—craft.   35. Froward—perverse. *The
Courtier*—a book by Castiglione on noble conduct.

Th' unkind instrument to wrong another,   40
And one she knows not, ay, and to persèver,
In my poor judgment, is not warranted
From being a solecism in our sex,
If not in manners.
     Peregrine.   How is this!
     Sir Politic.   Sweet madam,
Come nearer to your aim.
     Lady Wouldbe.   Marry, and will, sir.   45
Since you provoke me with your impudence
And laughter of your light land-siren here,
Your Sporus, your hermaphrodite—
     Peregrine.   What's here?
Poetic fury and historic storms!
     Sir Politic. The gentleman, believe it, is of worth,   50
And of our nation.
     Lady Wouldbe. Ay, your Whitefriars nation!
Come, I blush for you, Master Wouldbe, ay;
And am ashamed you should ha' no more forehead
Than thus to be the patron, or St. George,
To a lewd harlot, a base fricatrice,   55
A female devil in a male outside.
     Sir Politic.   Nay,
And you be such a one, I must bid adieu
To your delights. The case appears too liquid.   [*Exit.*]
     Lady Wouldbe. Ay, you may carry't clear, with your
                                [state-face!
But for your carnival concupiscence,   60
Who here is fled for liberty of conscience,
From furious persecution of the marshal,
Her will I disc'ple.

47. light—immoral. land-siren—the sirens who lured Ulysses toward the rocks
were sea-sirens.   48. Sporus—a young favorite of Nero's, emasculated at the
emperor's command. With Sporus dressed as a woman, the two were "married" in a public ceremony.   51. Whitefriars—the "red light" district of
London.   53. forehead—modesty.   55. fricatrice—massage artist;
slang for whore.   57. And you be such a one—presumably addressed to
Peregrine, since Sir Pol believes his wife's story (see V.iv.35).   58. liquid—
clear, as the next line implies.   59. state-face—serious countenance.
60. carnival—fleshy.   61–62. liberty . . . marshall—Lady Wouldbe com-
pares this prostitute (as she thinks) to a Puritan fled England and its Earl
Marshall, a court official.   63. disc'ple—discipline.

Peregrine.　　This is fine, i' faith!
And do you use this often? Is this part
Of your wit's exercise, 'gainst you have occasion?　　65
Madam—
　　Lady Wouldbe. Go to, sir.
　　Peregrine.　　　　　Do you hear me, lady?
Why, if your knight have set you to beg shirts,
Or to invite me home, you might have done it
A nearer way by far.
　　Lady Wouldbe. This cannot work you
Out of my snare.
　　Peregrine.　　Why, am I in it, then?　　70
Indeed, your husband told me you were fair,
And so you are; only your nose inclines—
That side that's next the sun—to the queen-apple.
　　Lady Wouldbe. This cannot be endured by any patience.

64. use this—act like this.　　65. 'gainst . . . occasion—in case you need it.
69. nearer—more direct.　　73. queen apple—her nose is red on one side.

ACT IV
SCENE III

[*Enter Mosca.*]

　　Mosca. What's the matter, madam?
　　Lady Wouldbe.　　　　　If the Senate
Right not my quest in this, I will protest 'em
To all the world no aristocracy.
　　Mosca. What is the injury, lady?
　　Lady Wouldbe.　　　　Why, the callet
You told me of, here I have ta'en disguised.　　5
　　Mosca. Who? This! What means your ladyship? The
　　　　　　　　　　　　　　[creature
I mentioned to you is apprehended, now
Before the Senate. You shall see her—
　　Lady Wouldbe.　　　　Where?

4. callet—whore.

  Mosca. I'll bring you to her. This young gentleman,
I saw him land this morning at the port.   10
  Lady Wouldbe. Is't possible? How has my judgment
               [wandered!
Sir, I must, blushing, say to you, I have erred;
And plead your pardon.
  Peregrine.   What, more changes yet?
  Lady Wouldbe. I hope y' ha' not the malice to remember
A gentlewoman's passion. If you stay   15
In Venice, here, please you to use me, sir—
  Mosca. Will you go, madam?
  Lady Wouldbe.   Pray you, sir, use me. In faith,
The more you see me, the more I shall conceive
You have forgot our quarrel.
    [*Exeunt Lady Wouldbe, Mosca, Nano, and Women.*]
  Peregrine.   This is rare!
Sir Politic Wouldbe? No, Sir Politic Bawd,   20
To bring me, thus, acquainted with his wife!
Well, wise Sir Pol, since you have practiced thus
Upon my freshmanship, I'll try your salt-head,
What proof it is against a counterplot.   [*Exit.*]

16. use me—a sexual innuendo here. In the quarto the word is used a
third time instead of "see" (line 18).   23. salt-head—(1) seasoned experience, (2) salaciousness.

ACT IV
SCENE IV

    [*The Scrutineo, the Venetian court of law.*]
    [*Enter Voltore, Corbaccio, Corvino, and Mosca.*]
  Voltore. Well, now you know the carriage of the business,
Your constancy is all that is required,
Unto the safety of it.
  Mosca.   Is the lie
Safely conveyed amongst us? Is that sure?
Knows every man his burden?
  Corvino.   Yes.
  Mosca.   Then shrink not.   5

1. carriage—management. 5. burden—refrain.

 Corvino. [*Aside to Mosca.*] But knows the advocate the
              [truth?
 Mosca.   O sir,
By no means. I devised a formal tale
That salved your reputation. But be valiant, sir.
 Corvino. I fear no one but him, that this his pleading
Should make him stand for a co-heir—
 Mosca.   Co-halter!   10
Hang him, we will but use his tongue, his noise,
As we do Croaker's here.   [*Pointing to Corbaccio.*]
 Corvino.   Ay, what shall he do?
 Mosca. When we ha' done, you mean?
 Corvino.   Yes.
 Mosca.   Why, we'll think:
Sell him for mummia, he's half dust already.
    [*Turns away from Corvino and speaks to Voltore.*]
Do not you smile to see this buffalo,   15
How he doth sport it with his head?—I should,
If all were well and past. [*To Corbaccio.*] Sir, only you
Are he that shall enjoy the crop of all,
And these not know for whom they toil.
 Corbaccio.   Ay, peace.
 Mosca. [*To Corvino.*] But you shall eat it.—Much!—[*To*
       [*Voltore.*] Worshipful sir, 20
Mercury sit upon your thund'ring tongue,
Or the French Hercules, and make your language
As conquering as his club, to beat along,
As with a tempest, flat, our adversaries;
But much more yours, sir.
 Voltore.   Here they come, ha' done. 25
 Mosca. I have another witness if you need, sir,
I can produce.
 Voltore. Who is it?
 Mosca.   Sir, I have her.

---

7. formal—convincing because of its outward form. 14. mummia—
mummy dust was highly prized as a medicine. 15. buffalo—alluding to
Corvino's horns. 20. Much!—fat chance! 21. Mercury—god of
eloquence and thievery. 22. French Hercules—also a symbol of eloquence.

ACT IV
SCENE V

[*Enter four Avocatori, Bonario, Celia, Notario, Commendatori,
and Others.*]

1st Avocatore. The like of this the Senate never heard of.

2nd Avocatore. 'Twill come most strange to them when
[we report it.

4th Avocatore. The gentlewoman has been ever held
Of unreprovèd name.

3rd Avocatore.   So the young man.

4th Avocatore. The more unnatural part, that of his
[father.   5

2nd Avocatore. More of the husband.

1st Avocatore.   I not know to give
His act a name, it is so monstrous!

4th Avocatore. But the impostor, he is a thing created
T' exceed example.

1st Avocatore. And all after-times!

2nd Avocatore. I never heard a true voluptuary   10
Described but him.

3rd Avocatore. Appear yet those were cited?

Notario. All but the old magnifico, Volpone.

1st Avocatore. Why is not he here?

Mosca.   Please your
[fatherhoods,
Here is his advocate. Himself's so weak,
So feeble—

4th Avocatore. What are you?

Bonario.   His parasite,   15
His knave, his pander! I beseech the court
He may be forced to come, that your grave eyes
May bear strong witness of his strange impostures.

Voltore. Upon my faith and credit with your virtues,
He is not able to endure the air.   20

2nd Avocatore. Bring him, however.

3rd Avocatore.   We will see him.

4th Avocatore.   Fetch him.

12. magnifico—nobleman.

 Voltore. Your fatherhoods' fit pleasures be obeyed,
But sure the sight will rather move your pities
Than indignation. May it please the court,
In the meantime he may be heard in me!   25
I know this place most void of prejudice,
And therefore crave it, since we have no reason
To fear our truth should hurt our cause.
  3rd Avocatore.   Speak free.
  Voltore. Then know, most honored fathers, I must now
Discover to your strangely abusèd ears   30
The most prodigious and most frontless piece
Of solid impudence, and treachery,
That ever vicious nature yet brought forth
To shame the state of Venice. This lewd woman,
        [Pointing to Celia.]
That wants no artificial looks or tears   35
To help the visor she has now put on,
Hath long been known a close adulteress
To that lascivious youth, there; *[Pointing to Bonario.]* not
        [suspected,
I say, but known, and taken, in the act,
With him; and by this man, the easy husband,   40
       [Pointing to Corvino.]
Pardoned; whose timeless bounty makes him now
Stand here, the most unhappy, innocent person
That ever man's own goodness made accused.
For these, not knowing how to owe a gift
Of that dear grace but with their shame, being placed 45
So above all powers of their gratitude,
Began to hate the benefit, and in place
Of thanks, devise t' extirp the memory
Of such an act. Wherein, I pray your fatherhoods
To observe the malice, yea, the rage of creatures   50
Discovered in their evils; and what heart
Such take, even from their crimes. But that anon
Will more appear. This gentleman, the father,
       [Pointing to Corbaccio.]

---

31. frontless—shameless. 35. wants—lacks. 37. close—secret.
41. timeless—ill-timed. 44. owe—own. 45. dear grace—Corvino's
pardon of them. 48. extirp—root out.

Hearing of this foul fact, with many others,
Which daily struck at his too tender ears,   55
And grieved in nothing more than that he could not
Preserve himself a parent (his son's ills
Growing to that strange flood) at last decreed
To disinherit him.
   1st Avocatore. These be strange turns!
   2nd Avocatore. The young man's fame was ever fair and
                [honest. 60

   Voltore. So much more full of danger is his vice,
That can beguile so under shade of virtue.
But as I said, my honored sires, his father
Having this settled purpose—by what means
To him betrayed, we know not—and this day   65
Appointed for the deed, that parricide,
I cannot style him better, by confederacy
Preparing this his paramour to be there,
Entered Volpone's house—who was the man,
Your fatherhoods must understand, designed   70
For the inheritance—there sought his father.
But with what purpose sought he him, my lords?
I tremble to pronounce it, that a son
Unto a father, and to such a father,
Should have so foul, felonious intent: 75
It was, to murder him! When, being prevented
By his more happy absence, what then did he?
Not check his wicked thoughts; no, now new deeds—
Mischief doth ever end where it begins—
An act of horror, fathers! He dragged forth   80
The agèd gentleman, that had there lain bed-rid
Three years, and more, out off his innocent couch,
Naked, upon the floor, there left him; wounded
His servant in the face; and, with this strumpet,
The stale to his forged practice, who was glad   85
To be so active—I shall here desire
Your fatherhoods to note but my collections
As most remarkable—thought at once to stop
His father's ends, discredit his free choice

85. stale—prostitute used as a decoy by thieves. forged practice—con-
trived plot.   87. collections—conclusions.

In the old gentleman, redeem themselves 90
By laying infamy upon this man,
To whom, with blushing, they should owe their lives.
    1st Avocatore. What proofs have you of this?
    Bonario.   Most honored fathers,
I humbly crave there be no credit given
To this man's mercenary tongue.
    2nd Avocatore.   Forbear. 95
    Bonario. His soul moves in his fee.
    3rd Avocatore.   O, sir!
    Bonario.   This fellow,
For six sols more would plead against his Maker.
    1st Avocatore. You do forget yourself.
    Voltore.   Nay, nay, grave fathers,
Let him have scope. Can any man imagine
That he will spare's accuser, that would not 100
Have spared his parent?
    1st Avocatore.   Well, produce your proofs.
    Celia. I would I could forget I were a creature!
    Voltore. Signior Corbaccio!
    4th Avocatore.   What is he?
    Voltore.   The father.
    2nd Avocatore. Has he had an oath?
    Notario.   Yes.
    Corbaccio.   What must I do now?
    Notario. Your testimony's craved.
    Corbaccio. [*Cupping his ear.*]   Speak to the knave? 105
I'll ha' my mouth first stopped with earth. My heart
Abhors his knowledge. I disclaim in him.
    1st Avocatore. But for what cause?
    Corbaccio.   The mere portent of nature.
He is an utter stranger to my loins.
    Bonario. Have they made you to this?
    Corbaccio.   I will not hear thee, 110
Monster of men, swine, goat, wolf, parricide!
Speak not, thou viper.
    Bonario.   Sir, I will sit down,

---

90. gentleman—i.e., Volpone.   97. sols—French coins of small worth.
107. his knowledge—knowing him.   disclaim—deny kinship.
108. mere portent—absolute freak.   110. made—shaped.

And rather wish my innocence should suffer,
Than I resist the authority of a father.

    Voltore. Signior Corvino!
    2nd Avocatore.   This is strange.
    1st Avocatore.   Who's this?   115
    Notario. The husband.
    4th Avocatore.   Is he sworn?
    Notario.   He is.
    3rd Avocatore.   Speak, then.
    Corvino. This woman, please your fatherhoods, is a whore
Of most hot exercise, more than a partridge,
Upon recòrd—
    1st Avocatore. No more.
    Corvino.   Neighs like a jennet.
    Notario. Preserve the honor of the court.
    Corvino.   I shall,   120
And modesty of your most reverend ears.
And, yet, I hope that I may say these eyes
Have seen her glued unto that piece of cedar,
That fine, well-timbered gallant; and that here
                      [*Tapping his forehead.*]
The letters may be read, thorough the horn,   125
That make the story perfect.
    Mosca.   Excellent, sir.
                 [*Mosca and Corvino whisper.*]
    Corvino. There is no shame in this now, is there?
    Mosca.   None.
    Corvino. [*To the court.*] Or if I said I hoped that she
                   [were onward
To her damnation, if there be a hell
Greater than whore and woman; a good Catholic   130
May make the doubt.
    3rd Avocatore. His grief hath made him frantic.
    1st Avocatore. Remove him hence.   *She swoons.*

---

118. partridge—proverbially lecherous bird.   119. jennet—used in a
similar context in *Othello* I.i.113.   124. well-timbered—well-built. here—
his forehead, making the V with his fingers to signify horns.   125. letters . . .
horn—punning on cuckold's horn and hornbook, an ABC book, the leaves of
which were protected with transparent sheets of horn.   126. perfect—
complete.   130. Catholic—the quarto reading is "Christian."

2nd Avocatore. Look to the woman.

Corvino. Rare!
Prettily feigned! Again!

4th Avocatore. Stand from about her.

1st Avocatore. Give her the air.

3rd Avocatore. [*To Mosca.*] What can you say?

Mosca. My wound,
May 't please your wisdoms, speaks for me, received   135
In aid of my good patron, when he missed
His sought-for father, when that well-taught dame
Had her cue given her to cry out a rape.

Bonario. O most laid impudence! Fathers—

3rd Avocatore. Sir, be silent,
You had your hearing free, so must they theirs.   140

2nd Avocatore. I do begin to doubt th' imposture here.

4th Avocatore. This woman has too many moods.

Voltore. Grave fathers,
She is a creature of a most professed
And prostituted lewdness.

Corvino. Most impetuous,
Unsatisfied, grave fathers!

Voltore. May her feignings   145
Not take your wisdoms; but this day she baited
A stranger, a grave knight, with her loose eyes
And more lascivious kisses. This man saw 'em
Together on the water in a gondola.

Mosca. Here is the lady herself that saw 'em too,   150
Without; who, then, had in the open streets
Pursued them, but for saving her knight's honor.

1st Avocatore. Produce that lady.

2nd Avocatore. Let her come.

4th Avocatore. These things.
They strike with wonder!

3rd Avocatore. I am turned a stone!

---

139. laid—planned.   140. free—without interruption.   146. but—
only.   baited—enticed.   151. Without—outside the courtroom.

Damned deeds are done with greatest confidence.

    1st Avocatore. Take 'em to custody, and sever them.

                [Celia and Bonario are taken out.]

    2nd Avocatore. 'Tis pity two such prodigies should live.   55

    1st Avocatore. Let the old gentleman be returned with

                                      [care.

I'm sorry our credulity wronged him.

                  [Exeunt Officers with Volpone.]

    4th Avocatore. These are two creatures!

    3rd Avocatore.   I have an earthquake in me!

    2nd Avocatore. Their shame, even in their cradles, fled

                                [their faces.

    4th Avocatore. *[To Voltore.]* You've done a worthy

                      [service to the state, sir,   60

In their discovery.

    1st Avocatore. You shall hear ere night

What punishment the court decrees upon 'em.

    Voltore. We thank your fatherhoods.—

                  [Exeunt Court Officials.]

                      How you like it?

    Mosca.   Rare.

I'd ha' your tongue, sir, tipped with gold for this;

I'd ha' you be the heir to the whole city;   65

The earth I'd have want men, ere you want living.

They're bound to erect your statue in St. Mark's.

                  [Voltore moves to one side.]

Signior Corvino, I would have you go

And show yourself, that you have conquered.

    Corvino.   Yes.

    Mosca. It was much better that you should profess   70

Yourself a cuckold, thus, than that the other

Should have been proved.

    Corvino.   Nay, I considered that.

Now, it is her fault.

    Mosca.   Then, it had been yours.

    Corvino. True. I do doubt this advocate still.

    Mosca.   I' faith,

You need not; I dare ease you of that care.   75

    Corvino. I trust thee, Mosca.

---

55. prodigies—evil portents, monsters.   66. want living—lack a livelihood.

Mosca.   As your own soul, sir.
                                              [*Exit Corvino.*]
Corbaccio.   Mosca!
Mosca. Now for your business, sir.
Corbaccio.   How! Ha' you business?
Mosca. Yes, yours, sir.
Corbaccio   O, none else?
Mosca.   None else, not I.
Corbaccio. Be careful then.
Mosca.   Rest you with both your eyes, sir.
Corbaccio. Dispatch it.
Mosca.   Instantly.
Corbaccio.   And look that all   80
Whatever be put in: jewels, plate, moneys,
Household stuff, bedding, curtains.
Mosca.   Curtain-rings, sir;
Only the advocate's fee must be deducted.
Corbaccio. I'll pay him now; you'll be too prodigal.
Mosca. Sir, I must tender it.
Corbaccio.   Two chequins is well?   85
Mosca. No, six, sir.
Corbaccio.   'Tis too much.
Mosca.   He talked a great while,
You must consider that, sir.
Corbaccio.   Well, there's three—
Mosca. I'll give it him.
Corbaccio.   Do so, and there's for thee.
                              [*Gives Mosca money and exits.*]
Mosca. Bountiful bones! What horrid, strange offense
Did he commit 'gainst nature in his youth,   90
Worthy this age? [*To Voltore.*] You see, sir, how I work
Unto your ends; take you no notice.
Voltore.   No,
I'll leave you.
Mosca. All is yours, [*Exit Voltore.*]—the devil and all,
Good advocate!—[*To Lady Wouldbe.*] Madam, I'll bring you
                                              [home.
Lady Wouldbe. No, I'll go see your patron.

79. Rest . . . eyes—don't worry about a thing.   85. tender—pay.
91. age—old age.

   Mosca.   That you shall not.   95
I'll tell you why: my purpose is to urge
My patron to reform his will, and for
The zeal you've shown today, whereas before
You were but third or fourth, you shall be now
Put in the first; which would appear as begged   100
If you were present. Therefore—
    Lady Wouldbe.   You shall sway me.
                                        [Exeunt.]

ACT V

SCENE I

                     [Volpone's house. Enter Volpone.]
    Volpone. Well, I am here, and all this brunt is past.
I ne'er was in dislike with my disguise
Till this fled moment. Here, 'twas good, in private,
But in your public—*Cavè,* whilst I breathe.
'Fore God, my left leg 'gan to have the cramp,   5
And I apprehended, straight, some power had struck me
With a dead palsy. Well, I must be merry
And shake it off. A many of these fears
Would put me into some villainous disease
Should they come thick upon me. I'll prevent 'em.   10
Give me a bowl of lusty wine to fright
This humor from my heart. Hum, hum, hum!   *He drinks.*
'Tis almost gone already; I shall conquer.
Any device, now, of rare, ingenious knavery
That would possess me with a violent laughter,   15
Would make me up again. So, so, so, so.   *Drinks again.*
This heat is life; 'tis blood by this time! Mosca!

---

3. fled moment—last episode.   4. *Cavè*—beware.

ACT V

SCENE II

[*Enter Mosca.*]

Mosca. How now, sir? Does the day look clear again?
Are we recovered? and wrought out of error
Into our way, to see our path before us?
Is our trade free once more?
    Volpone.   Exquisite Mosca!
    Mosca. Was it not carried learnedly?
    Volpone.   And stoutly.   5
Good wits are greatest in extremities.
    Mosca. It were a folly beyond thought to trust
Any grand act unto a cowardly spirit.
You are not taken with it enough, methinks?
    Volpone. O, more than if I had enjoyed the wench.   10
The pleasure of all womankind's not like it.
    Mosca. Why, now you speak, sir! We must here be fixed;
Here we must rest. This is our masterpiece;
We cannot think to go beyond this.
    Volpone.   True,
Th'ast played thy prize, my precious Mosca.
    Mosca.   Nay, sir,   15
To gull the court—
    Volpone. And quite divert the torrent
Upon the innocent.
    Mosca.   Yes, and to make
So rare a music out of discords—
    Volpone.   Right.
That yet to me 's the strangest; how th'ast borne it!
That these, being so divided 'mongst themselves,   20
Should not scent somewhat, or in me or thee,
Or doubt their own side.
    Mosca.   True, they will not see't.
Too much light blinds 'em, I think. Each of 'em
Is so possessed and stuffed with his own hopes
That anything unto the contrary,   25
Never so true, or never so apparent,

21. or . . . or—either . . . or.

Never so palpable, they will resist it—
   Volpone. Like a temptation of the devil.
   Mosca.   Right, sir.
Merchants may talk of trade, and your great signiors
Of land that yields well; but if Italy   30
Have any glebe more fruitful than these fellows,
I am deceived. Did not your advocate rare?
   Volpone. O—"My most honored fathers, my grave fathers,
Under correction of your fatherhoods,
What face of truth is here? If these strange deeds   35
May pass, most honored fathers"—I had much ado
To forbear laughing.
   Mosca.   'T seemed to me you sweat, sir.
   Volpone. In troth, I did a little.
   Mosca.   But confess, sir;
Were you not daunted?
   Volpone.   In good faith, I was
A little in a mist, but not dejected;   40
Never but still myself.
   Mosca.   I think it, sir.
Now, so truth help me, I must needs say this, sir,
And out of conscience for your advocate:
He's taken pains, in faith, sir, and deserved,
In my poor judgment, I speak it under favor,   45
Not to contrary you, sir, very richly—
Well—to be cozened.
   Volpone.   Troth, and I think so too,
By that I heard him in the latter end.
   Mosca. O, but before, sir, had you heard him first
Draw it to certain heads, then aggravate,   50
Then use his vehement figures—I looked still
When he would shift a shirt; and doing this
Out of pure love, no hope of gain—
   Volpone.   'Tis right.
I cannot answer him, Mosca, as I would,
Not yet; but for thy sake, at thy entreaty,   55

---

31. glebe—soil.   45. under favor—with permission.   50–51. Draw . . .
figures—rhetorical terms: *heads*, topics; *aggravate*, emphasize; *figures*, figures
of speech.   51–52. looked . . . shirt—his gestures made him look as if he
were changing his shirt.   54. answer—repay.

I will begin e'en now to vex 'em all,
This very instant.

    Mosca.   Good, sir.

    Volpone.   Call the dwarf
And eunuch forth.

    Mosca.   Castrone! Nano!

                    [*Enter Castrone and Nano.*]

    Nano.   Here.

    Volpone. Shall we have a jig now?

    Mosca.   What you please, sir.

    Volpone.   Go,
Straight give out about the streets, you two,   60
That I am dead; do it with constancy,
Sadly, do you hear? Impute it to the grief
Of this late slander.   [*Exeunt Castrone and Nano.*]

    Mosca.   What do you mean, sir?

    Volpone.   O,
I shall have instantly my vulture, crow,
Raven, come flying hither on the news   65
To peck for carrion, my she-wolf and all,
Greedy and full of expectation—

    Mosca. And then to have it ravished from their mouths?

    Volpone. 'Tis true. I will ha' thee put on a gown,
And take upon thee as thou wert mine heir;   70
Show 'em a will. Open that chest and reach
Forth one of those that has the blanks. I'll straight
Put in thy name.

    Mosca.   It will be rare, sir.

    Volpone.   Ay,
When they e'en gape, and find themselves deluded—

    Mosca. Yes.

    Volpone. And thou use them scurvily! Dispatch,   75
Get on thy gown.

    Mosca.   But what, sir, if they ask
After the body?

    Volpone. Say it was corrupted.

    Mosca. I'll say it stunk, sir; and was fain t' have it
Coffined up instantly and sent away.

62. Sadly—seriously.   70. take upon thee—pretend. as—as if.
78. fain—obliged.

Volpone. Anything, what thou wilt. Hold, here's my will.   80
Get thee a cap, a count-book, pen and ink,
Papers afore thee; sit as thou wert taking
An inventory of parcels. I'll get up
Behind the curtain, on a stool, and hearken;
Sometime peep over, see how they do look,   85
With what degrees their blood doth leave their faces.
O, 'twill afford me a rare meal of laughter!
    Mosca. Your advocate will turn stark dull upon it.
    Volpone. It will take off his oratory's edge.
    Mosca. But your *clarissimo,* old round-back, he   90
Will crump you like a hog-louse with the touch.
    Volpone. And what Corvino?
    Mosca.   O sir, look for him
Tomorrow morning with a rope and dagger
To visit all the streets; he must run mad.
My lady too, that came into the court   95
To bear false witness for your worship—
    Volpone.   Yes,
And kissed me 'fore the fathers, when my face
Flowed all with oils—
    Mosca.   And sweat, sir. Why, your gold
Is such another med'cine, it dries up
All those offensive savors! It transforms   100
The most deformèd, and restores 'em lovely
As 'twere the strange poetical girdle. Jove   *Cestus.*
Could not invent t' himself a shroud more subtle
To pass Acrisius' guards. It is the thing
Makes all the world her grace, her youth, her beauty.   105
    Volpone. I think she loves me.
    Mosca.   Who? The lady, sir?
She's jealous of you.
    Volpone.   Dost thou say so?   [*Knocking without.*]
    Mosca.   Hark,
There's some already.

81. count-book—account-book.   83. parcels—parts (of his possessions).
90. *clarissimo*—nobleman.   91. crump you—curl up.   102. poetical
girdle—worn by Venus; it restored beauty and passion even to the old.
102–4. Jove . . . guards—Acrisius kept this daughter Danaë locked in a tower
of brass, but Jove penetrated it (and her) in the form of a shower of gold.
106. She—Lady Wouldbe (?).   107. jealous of you—wants you all for herself.

Volpone.   Look!

Mosca. [*Peering out.*] It is the vulture;
He has the quickest scent.

Volpone.   I'll to my place,
Thou to thy posture.

Mosca.   I am set.

Volpone.   But Mosca,   110
Play the artificer now, torture 'em rarely.

110. posture—role.

ACT V
SCENE III

[*Enter Voltore.*]

Voltore. How now, my Mosca?

Mosca. [*Writing.*]   Turkey carpets, nine—

Voltore. Taking an inventory? That is well.

Mosca. Two suits of bedding, tissue—

Voltore.   Where's the will?
Let me read that the while.

[*Enter bearers carrying Corbaccio in a chair.*]

Corbaccio.   So, set me down,
And get you home.   [*Exeunt bearers.*]

Voltore.   Is he come now, to trouble us?   5

Mosca. Of cloth of gold, two more—

Corbaccio.   Is it done, Mosca?

Mosca. Of several vellets, eight—

Voltore.   I like his care.

Corbaccio. Dost thou not hear?

[*Enter Corvino.*]

Corvino.   Ha! Is the hour come, Mosca?

Volpone. [*Aside.*] Ay, now they muster.

Peeps from behind a traverse.

Corvino.   What does the advocate here,
Or this Corbaccio?

3. tissue—cloth woven with gold.   9. *traverse*—screen or curtain.

  Corbaccio.   What do these here?
            [*Enter Lady Wouldbe.*]
  Lady Wouldbe.   Mosca!   10
Is his thread spun?
  Mosca.   Eight chests of linen—
  Volpone. [*Aside.*]   O,
My fine Dame Wouldbe, too!
  Corvino.   Mosca, the will,
That I may show it these and rid 'em hence.
  Mosca. Six chests of diaper, four of damask—There.
     [*Gives them the will and continues to write.*]
  Corbaccio. Is that the will?
  Mosca.   Down-beds, and bolsters—
  Volpone. [*Aside.*]   Rare! 15
Be busy still. Now they begin to flutter;
They never think of me. Look, see, see, see!
How their swift eyes run over the long deed
Unto the name, and to the legacies,
What is bequeathed them there.
  Mosca.   Ten suits of hangings— 20
  Volpone. [*Aside.*] Ay, i' their garters, Mosca. Now their
               [hopes
Are at the gasp.
  Voltore. Mosca the heir!
  Corbaccio.   What's that?
  Volpone. [*Aside.*] My advocate is dumb; look to my
             [merchant.
He has heard of some strange storm, a ship is lost,
He faints; my lady will swoon. Old glazen-eyes 25
He hath not reached his despair, yet.
  Corbaccio.   All these
Are out of hope; I'm sure the man.
  Corvino.   But, Mosca—
  Mosca. Two cabinets—
  Corvino.   Is this in earnest?
  Mosca.   One
Of ebony—
  Corvino. Or do you but delude me?
  Mosca. The other, mother of pearl—I am very busy. 30

14. diaper—cloth with patterned weave.

Good faith, it is a fortune thrown upon me—
Item, one salt of agate—not my seeking.

    Lady Wouldbe. Do you hear, sir?

    Mosca.   A perfumed box—Pray you forbear,
You see I'm troubled—made of an onyx—

    Lady Wouldbe.   How!

    Mosca. Tomorrow, or next day, I shall be at leisure   35
To talk with you all.

    Corvino.   Is this my large hope's issue?

    Lady Wouldbe. Sir, I must have a fairer answer.

    Mosca.   Madam!
Marry, and shall: pray you, fairly quit my house.
Nay, raise no tempest with your looks; but hark you,
Remember what your ladyship offered me   40
To put you in an heir; go to, think on 't.
And what you said e'en your best madams did
For maintenance, and why not you? Enough.
Go home and use the poor Sir Pol, your knight, well,
For fear I tell some riddles. Go, be melancholic.   45

                        [Exit Lady Wouldbe.]

    Volpone. *[Aside.]* O my fine devil!

    Corvino.   Mosca, pray you a word.

    Mosca. Lord! Will not you take your dispatch hence yet?
Methinks of all you should have been th' example.
Why should you stay here? With what thought? What
                         [promise?
Hear you: do not you know I know you an ass,   50
And that you would most fain have been a wittol
If fortune would have let you? That you are
A declared cuckold, on good terms? This pearl,
You'll say, was yours? Right. This diamond?
I'll not deny't, but thank you. Much here else?   55
It may be so. Why, think that these good works
May help to hide your bad. I'll not betray you,
Although you be but extraordinary,
And have it only in title, it sufficeth.

---

32. salt—saltshaker.   38. fairly—completely.   40. remember . . . you—
Lady Wouldbe has evidently offered her favors to Mosca (see I.vi.101).
51. wittol—willing cuckold.   58–59. Although . . . title—although you're
a cuckold in name but not in fact.

Go home, be melancholic too, or mad.   [*Exit Corvino.*]   60
    Volpone. [*Aside.*] Rare Mosca! How his villainy
                                    [becomes him!
    Voltore. Certain he doth delude all these for me.
    Corbaccio. Mosca the heir? [*Still straining to read the*
                                    [*will.*]
    Volpone. [*Aside.*]   O, his four eyes have found it!
    Corbaccio. I'm cozened, cheated, by a parasite slave!
Harlot, th'ast gulled me.
    Mosca.   Yes, sir. Stop your mouth,   65
Or I shall draw the only tooth is left.
Are not you he, that filthy, covetous wretch
With the three legs, that here, in hope of prey,
Have, any time this three year, snuffed about
With your most grov'ling nose, and would have hired   70
Me to the pois'ning of my patron, sir?
Are not you he that have, today, in court,
Professed the disinheriting of your son?
Perjured youself? Go home, and die, and stink.
If you but croak a syllable, all comes out.   75
Away, and call your porters! Go, go, stink. [*Exit Corbaccio.*]
    Volpone. [*Aside.*] Excellent varlet!
    Voltore.   Now, my faithful Mosca,
I find thy constancy.
    Mosca.   Sir?
    Voltore.   Sincere.
    Mosca.   A table
Of porphyry—I mar'l you'll be thus troublesome.
    Voltore. Nay, leave off now, they are gone.
    Mosca.   Why, who are you?   80
What! Who did send for you? O, cry you mercy,
Reverend sir! Good faith, I am grieved for you,
That any chance of mine should thus defeat
Your—I must needs say—most deserving travails.
But I protest, sir, it was cast upon me,   85
And I could, almost, wish to be without it,
But that the will o' th' dead must be observed.
Marry, my joy is that you need it not;

---

65. Harlot—originally applied to men.   68. three legs—his own plus a cane.
79. mar'l—marvel.

You have a gift, sir—thank your education—
Will never let you want while there are men 90
And malice to breed causes. Would I had
But half the like, for all my fortune, sir.
If I have any suits—as I do hope,
Things being so easy and direct, I shall not—
I will make bold with your obstreperous aid; 95
Conceive me, for your fee, sir. In meantime,
You that have so much law, I know ha' the conscience
Not to be covetous of what is mine.
Good sir, I thank you for my plate; 'twill help
To set up a young man. Good faith, you look 100
As you were costive; best go home and purge, sir. [*Exit*
[*Voltore.*]
   Volpone. Bid him eat lettuce well! My witty mischief,
       [*Coming from behind curtain.*]
Let me embrace thee. O that I could now
Transform thee to a Venus—Mosca, go,
Straight take my habit of *clarissimo,* 105
And walk the streets; be seen, torment 'em more.
We must pursue as well as plot. Who would
Have lost this feast?
   Mosca.   I doubt it will lose them.
   Volpone. O, my recovery shall recover all.
That I could now but think on some disguise 110
To meet 'em in, and ask 'em questions.
How I would vex 'em still at every turn!
   Mosca. Sir, I can fit you.
   Volpone.   Canst thou?
   Mosca.   Yes, I know
One o' th' *commendatori,* sir, so like you;
Him will I straight make drunk, and bring you his habit. 115
   Volpone. A rare disguise, and answering thy brain!
O, I will be a sharp disease unto 'em.
   Mosca. Sir, you must look for curses—
   Volpone.   Till they burst;
The fox fares ever best when he is cursed. [*Exeunt.*]

95. obstreperous—noisy. 96. Conceive . . . fee—I'll pay the standard rates.
101. costive—constipated. 102. lettuce—a laxative. 108. doubt—fear.
116. answering—appropriate to. 119. fox . . . cursed—the more the hunters curse, the better off the fox is.

ACT V
SCENE IV

                                        [*Sir Politic's house.*]
                    [*Enter Peregrine disguised, and three Merchants.*]
    Peregrine. Am I enough disguised?
    1st Merchant.   I warrant you.
    Peregrine. All my ambition is to fright him only.
    2nd Merchant. If you could ship him away, 'twere
                                                        [excellent.
      3rd Merchant. To Zant, or to Aleppo?
      Peregrine.   Yes, and ha' his
Adventures put i' th' book of voyages,   5
And his gulled story registered for truth?
Well, gentlemen, when I am in a while,
And that you think us warm in our discourse,
Know your approaches.
        1st Merchant.   Trust it to our care. [*Exeunt
                                                        [*Merchants.*]
                                                        [*Enter Woman.*]
      Peregrine. Save you, fair lady. Is Sir Pol within?   10
      Woman. I do not know, sir.
      Peregrine.   Pray you say unto him,
Here is a merchant, upon earnest business,
Desires to speak with him.
        Woman.   I will see, sir.
        Peregrine.   Pray you. [*Exit Woman.*]
I see the family is all female here.

                                        [*Re-enter Woman.*]
      Woman. He says, sir, he has weighty affairs of state   15
That now require him whole; some other time
You may possess him.
        Peregrine.   Pray you, say again,
If those require him whole, these will exact him
Whereof I bring him tidings. [*Exit Woman.*] What might be
His grave affair of state now? How to make   20

---

1. warrant—assure.   5. book of voyages—any book of this common type.
9. Know your approaches—enter on cue.   16. require him whole—occupy
his entire attention.

Bolognian sausages here in Venice, sparing
One o' th' ingredients?

[*Re-enter Woman.*]

    Woman.   Sir, he says he knows
By your word "tidings" that you are no statesman,
And therefore wills you stay.
    Peregrine.   Sweet, pray you return him:
I have not read so many proclamations   25
And studied them for words, as he has done,
But—Here he deigns to come.

[*Enter Sir Politic.*]

    Sir Politic.   Sir, I must crave
Your courteous pardon. There hath chanced today
Unkind disaster 'twixt my lady and me,
And I was penning my apology   30
To give her satisfaction, as you came now.
    Peregrine. Sir, I am grieved I bring you worse disaster:
The gentleman you met at th' port today,
That told you he was newly arrived—
    Sir Politic.   Ay, was
A fugitive punk?
    Peregrine. No, sir, a spy set on you,   35
And he has made relation to the Senate
That you professed to him to have a plot
To sell the state of Venice to the Turk.
    Sir Politic. O me!
    Peregrine.   For which warrants are signed by this time
To apprehend you and to search your study   40
For papers—
    Sir Politic. Alas, sir, I have none but notes
Drawn out of play-books—
    Peregrine.   All the better, sir.
    Sir Politic. And some essays. What shall I do?
    Peregrine.   Sir, best
Convey yourself into a sugar-chest,
Or, if you could lie round, a frail were rare,   45

---

23. "tidings"—a statesman would say "intelligences."   24. stay—wait.
35. punk—whore.   42. play-books—printed plays. All the better—such extracts are liable to be interpreted as code.   45. lie round—curl up.   frail—rush basket.

And I could send you aboard.
    Sir Politic.   Sir, I but talked so
For discourse' sake merely.   *They knock without.*
    Peregrine.   Hark, they are there.
    Sir Politic. I am a wretch, a wretch!
    Peregrine.   What will you do, sir?
Ha' you ne'er a currant-butt to leap into?
They'll put you to the rack, you must be sudden.   50
    Sir Politic. Sir, I have an engine—
    3rd Merchant. [*Calling from off-stage.*] Sir Politic Wouldbe!
    2nd Merchant. Where is he?
    Sir Politic.   That I have thought upon beforetime.
    Peregrine. What is it?
    Sir Politic.   I shall ne'er endure the torture!
Marry, it is, sir, of a tortoise-shell,
Fitted for these extremities. Pray you, sir, help me.
                [*He gets into a large tortoise shell.*]
Here I've a place, sir, to put back my legs;
Please you to lay it on, sir. With this cap
And my black gloves, I'll lie, sir, like a tortoise,
Till they are gone.
    Peregrine.   And call you this an engine?
    Sir Politic. Mine own device—Good sir, bid my wife's
                       [women   60
To burn my papers.
               They [*The three Merchants*] *rush in.*
    1st Merchant. Where's he hid?
    3rd Merchant.   We must,
And will, sure, find him.
    2nd Merchant.   Which is his study?
    1st Merchant.   What
Are you, sir?
    Peregrine. I'm a merchant that came here
To look upon this tortoise.
    3rd Merchant.   How!
    1st Merchant.   St. Mark!
What beast is this?
    Peregrine.   It is a fish.
    2nd Merchant.   Come out here!   65

---

49. currant-butt—cask for currants.   51. engine—contrivance.

 Peregrine. Nay, you may strike him, sir, and tread upon
                [him.
He'll bear a cart.
 1st Merchant. What, to run over him?
 Peregrine.   Yes.
 3rd Merchant. Let's jump upon him.
 2nd Merchant.   Can he not go?
 Peregrine.   He creeps, sir.
 1st Merchant. Let's see him creep. [*Prodding him.*]
 Peregrine.   No, good sir, you will hurt him.
 2nd Merchant. Heart, I'll see him creep, or prick his guts. 70
 3rd Merchant. Come out here!
 Peregrine. [*Aside to Sir Politic.*] Pray you, sir, creep a
                [little.
 1st Merchant.   Forth!
 2nd Merchant. Yet further.
 Peregrine. [*Aside to Sir Politic.*] Good sir, creep.
 2nd Merchant.   We'll see his legs.
    They pull off the shell and discover him.
 3rd Merchant. Godso, he has garters!
 1st Merchant.   Ay, and gloves!
 2nd Merchant.   Is this
Your fearful tortoise?
 Peregrine.   Now, Sir Pol, we are even;
       [*Throwing off his disguise.*]
For your next project I shall be prepared. 75
I am sorry for the funeral of your notes, sir.
 1st Merchant. 'Twere a rare motion to be seen in Fleet
               [Street.
 2nd Merchant. Ay, i' the term.
 1st Merchant.   Or Smithfield, in the fair.
 3rd Merchant. Methinks 'tis but a melancholic sight.
 Peregrine. Farewell, most politic tortoise!
    [*Exeunt Peregrine and Merchants.*]
 Sir Politic.   Where's my lady? 80
Knows she of this?
 Woman. I know not, sir.

---

76. funeral—i.e., funeral pyre. 78. i' the term—when courts were in
session and the city more crowded. Smithfield . . . fair—Bartholomew Fair
was held in Smithfield.

Sir Politic.   Inquire.   [*Exit Woman.*]
O, I shall be the fable of all feasts,
The freight of the *gazetti*, ship-boy's tale,
And, which is worst, even talk for ordinaries.

                                        [*Re-enter Woman.*]
Woman. My lady's come most melancholic home,   85
And says, sir, she will straight to sea, for physic.
Sir Politic. And I, to shun this place and clime forever,
Creeping with house on back, and think it well
To shrink my poor head in my politic shell.   [*Exeunt.*]

83. freight . . . *gazetti*—subject of newssheets.   84. ordinaries—taverns.
86. physic—medical purposes.

ACT V

SCENE V

                                        [*Volpone's house.*]
                        [*Enter Volpone in the habit of a commendatore,
                                        Mosca of a clarissimo.*]
Volpone. Am I then like him?
Mosca.   O sir, you are he;
No man can sever you.
Volpone.   Good.
Mosca.   But what am I?
Volpone. 'Fore heav'n, a brave *clarissimo,* thou becom'st
                                                        [it!
Pity thou wert not born one.
Mosca.   If I hold
My made, 'twill be well.
Volpone.   I'll go and see   5
What news, first, at the court.   [*Exit.*]
Mosca.   Do so. My fox
Is out on his hole, and ere he shall re-enter,
I'll make him languish in his borrowed case,
Except he come to composition with me.

9. Except . . . composition—unless he makes a deal.

Androgyno, Castrone, Nano! [*Enter Androgyno, Castrone,*
                                                         [*and Nano.*]   10

    All.   Here.

    Mosca. Go recreate yourselves abroad, go sport.
                                              [*Exeunt the three.*]

So, now I have the keys and am possessed.
Since he will needs be dead afore his time,
I'll bury him, or gain by him. I'm his heir,
And so will keep me, till he share at least.   15
To cozen him of all were but a cheat
Well placed; no man would cónstrue it a sin.
Let his sport pay for 't. This is called the fox-trap.   [*Exit.*]

12. possessed—in possession.

ACT V
SCENE VI

                 [*A Venetian street.*]
         [*Enter Corbaccio and Corvino.*]

    Corbaccio. They say the court is set.

    Corvino.   We must maintain
Our first tale good, for both our reputations.

    Corbaccio. Why, mine's no tale! My son would there
                                              [have killed me.

    Corvino. That's true, I had forgot. Mine is, I am sure.
But for your will, sir.

    Corbaccio.   Ay, I'll come upon him   5
For that hereafter, now his patron's dead.

             [*Enter Volpone in disguise.*]

    Volpone. Signior Corvino! And Corbaccio! Sir,
Much joy unto you.

    Corvino.   Of what?

    Volpone.   The sudden good
Dropped down upon you—

    Corbaccio.   Where?

    Volpone.   And none knows how,
From old Volpone, sir.

5. come—be revenged.

Corbaccio.   Out, arrant knave!   10
Volpone. Let not your too much wealth, sir, make you
                                                    [furious.
Corbaccio. Away, thou varlet.
Volpone.   Why, sir?
Corbaccio.   Dost thou mock me?
Volpone. You mock the world, sir; did you not change
                                                    [wills?
Corbaccio. Out, harlot!
Volpone.   O! Belike you are the man,
Signior Corvino? Faith, you carry it well;   15
You grow not mad withal. I love your spirit.
You are not over-leavened with your fortune.
You should ha' some would swell now like a wine-fat
With such an autumn—Did he gi' you all, sir?
    Corvino. Avoid, you rascal.
    Volpone.   Troth, your wife has shown   20
Herself a very woman! But you are well,
You need not care, you have a good estate
To bear it out, sir, better by this chance.
Except Corbaccio have a share?
    Corbaccio.   Hence, varlet.
    Volpone. You will not be a'known, sir? Why, 'tis wise.   25
Thus do all gamesters, at all games, dissemble.
No man will seem to win. [*Exeunt Corvino and Corbaccio.*]
                                    [Here comes my vulture,
Heaving his beak up i' the air, and snuffing.

14. Belike—perhaps.   17. over-leavened—puffed up.   18. fat—vat.
20. Avoid—get out.   21. very—true.   25. a'known—"acknowledged
(the heir)" (Kernan).

ACT V
SCENE VII

[*Enter Voltore to Volpone.*]

Voltore. Outstripped thus, by a parasite! A slave,
Would run on errands, and make legs for crumbs?
Well, what I'll do—
    Volpone.   The court stays for your worship.
I e'en rejoice, sir, at your worship's happiness,
And that it fell into so learned hands,   5
That understand the fingering—
    Voltore.   What do you mean?
    Volpone. I mean to be a suitor to your worship
For the small tenement, out of reparations,
That at the end of your long row of houses,
By the *Pescheria*; it was, in Volpone's time,   10
Your predecessor, ere he grew diseased,
A handsome, pretty, customed bawdy-house
As any was in Venice—none dispraised—
But fell with him. His body and that house
Decayed together.
    Voltore.   Come, sir, leave your prating.   15
    Volpone. Why, if your worship give me but your hand,
That I may ha' the refusal, I have done.
'Tis a mere toy to you, sir, candle-rents.
As your learned worship knows—
    Voltore.   What do I know?
    Volpone. Marry, no end of your wealth, sir, God decrease
                                 [it.   20
    Voltore. Mistaking knave! What, mock'st thou my
                             [misfortune?
    Volpone. His blessing on your heart, sir; would 'twere
                             [more!
                    [*Exit Voltore.*]
Now, to my first again, at the next corner.

8. reparations—repair.   10. *Pescheria*—fish market.   12. customed—
filled with customers.   13. none dispraised—(1) criticized by no one,
(2) with no offense to the others.   16. hand—signature.   17. refusal—
option.   18. candle-rents—self-consuming because the property is de-
teriorating.

ACT V
SCENE VIII

[*Volpone walks aside. Corbaccio and Corvino enter.*]
          [*Mosca passes slowly across the stage.*]
  Corbaccio. See, in our habit! See the impudent varlet!
  Corvino. That I could shoot mine eyes at him, like
                        [gunstones!
                   [*Exit Mosca.*]
  Volpone. But is this true, sir, of the parasite?
  Corbaccio. Again t' afflict us? Monster!
  Volpone.   In good faith, sir,
I'm heartily grieved a beard of your grave length   5
Should be so over-reached. I never brooked
That parasite's hair; methought his nose should cozen.
There still was somewhat in his look did promise
The bane of a *clarissimo.*
    Corbaccio.   Knave—
  Volpone.   Methinks
Yet you, that are so traded i' the world,   10
A witty merchant, the fine bird Corvino,
That have such moral emblems on your name,
Should not have sung your shame, and dropped your cheese,
To let the fox laugh at your emptiness.
    Corvino. Sirrah, you think the privilege of the place,   15
And your red, saucy cap, that seems to me
Nailed to your jolt-head with those two chequins,
Can warrant your abuses. Come you hither:
You shall perceive, sir, I dare beat you. Approach.
    Volpone. No haste, sir. I do know your valor well,   20
Since you durst publish what you are, sir.
    Corvino.   Tarry,
I'd speak with you.
    Volpone.   Sir, sir, another time—   [*Backing away.*]
    Corvino. Nay, now.
    Volpone.   O God, sir! I were a wise man

1. our habit—i.e., the dress of a *clarissimo.* 2. gunstones—stone cannonballs.
6. brooked—could endure. 10. traded—experienced. 12–14. moral
emblems . . . emptiness—see I.ii.94n. 15. the place—your rank of *com-*
mendatore. 17. jolt-head—blockhead. two chequins—two bright buttons
on his cap.

Would stand the fury of a distracted cuckold. *Mosca walks by*
                                                                    [*'em.*

   Corbaccio. What, come again!

   Volpone. [*Aside.*]   Upon 'em, Mosca; save me.   25

   Corbaccio. The air's infected where he breathes.

   Corvino.   Let's fly him.

                [*Exeunt Corvino and Corbaccio.*]

   Volpone. Excellent basilisk! Turn upon the vulture.

27. basilisk—a monster believed able to kill with a glance.

ACT V

SCENE IX

                            [*Enter Voltore.*]

   Voltore. Well, flesh-fly, it is summer with you now;
Your winter will come on.

   Mosca.   Good advocate,
Pray thee not rail, nor threaten out of place thus;
Thou'lt make a solecism, as Madam says.
Get you a biggen more; your brain breaks loose.   [*Exit.*]   5

   Voltore. Well, sir.

   Volpone.   Would you ha' me beat the insolent slave?
Throw dirt upon his first good clothes?

   Voltore.   This same
Is doubtless some familiar!

   Volpone.   Sir, the court,
In troth, stays for you. I am mad; a mule
That never read Justinian, should get up   10
And ride an advocate! Had you no quirk
To avoid gullage, sir, by such a creature?
I hope you do but jest; he has not done 't;
This's but confederacy to blind the rest.
You are the heir?

1. flesh-fly—apparently Mosca's name means a particular kind of fly.
5. a biggen more—another biggen (lawyer's cap).   7. This same—i.e.,
Volpone.   8. familiar—a devil.   9. I am mad—I must be crazy to think
that a mule . . .   10. Justinian—emperor who had all Roman law codified
in the sixth century.

Voltore.   A strange, officious,   15
Troublesome knave! Thou dost torment me.
    Volpone. [*Aside.*]   —I know—
It cannot be, sir, that you should be cozened;
'Tis not within the wit of man to do it.
You are so wise, so prudent, and 'tis fit
That wealth and wisdom still should go together.   [*Exeunt.*]   20

ACT V
SCENE X

                                    [*The Scrutineo.*]
        [*Enter four Avocatori, Notario, Commendatori, Bonario,
                         Celia, Corbaccio, Corvino.*]
    1st Avocatore. Are all the parties here?
    Notario.   All but the advocate.
    2nd Avocatore. And here he comes.
                    [*Enter Voltore, Volpone following him.*]
    1st Avocatore.   Then bring 'em forth to sentence.
    Voltore. O my most honored fathers, let your mercy
Once win upon your justice, to forgive—
I am distracted—
    Volpone. [*Aside.*] What will he do now?
    Voltore.   O,   5
I know not which t' address myself to first,
Whether your fatherhoods, or these innocents—
    Corvino. [*Aside.*] Will he betray himself?
    Voltore.   Whom equally
I have abused, out of most covetous ends—
    Corvino. The man is mad!
    Corbaccio.   What's that?
    Corvino.   He is possessed.   10
    Voltore. For which, now struck in conscience, here I
                                    [*prostrate*
Myself at your offended feet, for pardon.   [*He kneels.*]
    1st, 2nd Avocatori. Arise.
    Celia.   O heav'n, how just thou art!

4. Once win upon—prevail, for once, over.   10. possessed—i.e., by a devil.

  Volpone. [*Aside.*]   I'm caught
I' mine own noose.
  Corvino. [*Aside to Corbaccio.*] Be constant, sir, nought
                [now
Can help but impudence.
  1st Avocatore.   Speak forward.
  Commendatore. [*To the Courtroom.*] Silence!   15
   Voltore. It is not passion in me, reverend fathers,
But only conscience, conscience, my good sires,
That makes me now tell truth. That parasite,
That knave, hath been the instrument of all.
  2nd Avocatore. Where is that knave? Fetch him.
  Volpone.   I go. [*Exit.*]
  Corvino.   Grave fathers, 20
This man's distracted; he confessed it now.
For, hoping to be old Volpone's heir,
Who now is dead—
  3rd Avocatore. How!
  2nd Avocatore.   Is Volpone dead?
  Corvino. Dead since, grave fathers—
  Bonario.   O sure vengeance!
  1st Avocatore.   Stay.
Then he was no deceiver?
  Voltore.   O, no, none;   25
The parasite, grave fathers.
  Corvino.   He does speak
Out of mere envy, 'cause the servant's made
The thing he gaped for. Please your fatherhoods,
This is the truth; though I'll not justify
The other, but he may be some-deal faulty.   30
  Voltore. Ay, to your hopes, as well as mine, Corvino.
But I'll use modesty. Pleaseth your wisdoms
To view these certain notes, and but confer them;
         [*Gives them notes.*]
As I hope favor, they shall speak clear truth.
  Corvino. The devil has entered him!
  Bonario.   Or bides in you. 35

---

21. distracted . . . now—he's mad, as he himself just confessed (see 1.5).
30. some-deal—somewhat. 32. modesty—restraint. 33. but confer—
just compare.

4th Avocatore. We have done ill, by a public officer
To send for him, if he be heir.
    2nd Avocatore.   For whom?
    4th Avocatore. Him that they call the parasite.
    3rd Avocatore.   'Tis true,
He is a man of great estate now left.
    4th Avocatore. Go you, and learn his name, and say the
                                       [court   40
Entreats his presence here, but to the clearing
Of some few doubts.   *[Exit Notario.]*
    2nd Avocatore. This same's a labyrinth!
    1st Avocatore. Stand you unto your first report?
    Corvino.   My state,
My life, my fame—
    Bonario.   Where is't?
    Corvino.   Are at the stake.
    1st Avocatore. Is yours so too?
    Corbaccio.   The advocate's a knave,   45
And has a forkèd tongue—
    2nd Avocatore.   Speak to the point.
    Corbaccio. So is the parasite too.
    1st Avocatore.   This is confusion.
    Voltore. I do beseech your fatherhoods, read but those.
    Corvino. And credit nothing the false spirit hath writ.
It cannot be but he is possessed, grave fathers.   50

ACT V

SCENE XI

                        [A street, Volpone alone.]
    Volpone. To make a snare for mine own neck! And run
My head into it wilfully, with laughter!
When I had newly 'scaped, was free and clear!
Out of mere wantonness! O, the dull devil
Was in this brain of mine when I devised it,   5
And Mosca gave it second; he must now
Help to sear up this vein, or we bleed dead.

6. gave it second—seconded it.   7. sear—cauterize.

[*Enter Nano, Androgyno, and Castrone.*]
How now! Who let you loose? Whither go you now?
What, to buy gingerbread, or to drown kitlings?
    Nano. Sir, Master Mosca called us out of doors,   10
And bid us all go play, and took the keys.
    Androgyno.   Yes.
    Volpone. Did Master Mosca take the keys? Why, so!
I am farther in. These are my fine conceits!
I must be merry, with a mischief to me!
What a vile wretch was I, that could not bear   15
My fortune soberly; I must ha' my crotchets
And my conundrums! Well, go you and seek him.
His meaning may be truer than my fear.
Bid him, he straight come to me to the court;
Thither will I, and if't be possible,   20
Unscrew my advocate, upon new hopes.
When I provoked him, then I lost myself.   [*Exeunt.*]

9. kitlings—kittens.   13. conceits—(1) notions, (2) schemes.
16. crotchets—whims.   17. conundrums—perverse whims, puzzles.
21. Unscrew—undo.   upon—by means of.

ACT V

SCENE XII

[*The Scrutineo.*]
[*Four Avocatori, Notario, Voltore, Bonario, Celia, Corbaccio,*
                               Corvino.]
    1st Avocatore.   [*Looking over Voltore's notes.*]
These things can ne'er be reconciled. He here
Professeth that the gentleman was wronged,
And that the gentlewoman was brought thither,
Forced by her husband, and there left.
    Voltore.   Most true.
    Celia. How ready is heav'n to those that pray!
    1st Avocatore.   But that   5
Volpone would have ravished her, he holds
Utterly false, knowing his impotence.
    Corvino. Grave fathers, he is possessed; again, I say,

Possessed. Nay, if there be possession
And obsession, he has both.

    3rd Avocatore.   Here comes our officer.   10

                [Enter Volpone, still disguised.]

    Volpone. The parasite will straight be here, grave fathers.

    4th Avocatore. You might invent some other name, sir

                                     [varlet.

    3rd Avocatore. Did not the notary meet him?

    Volpone.   Not that I know.

    4th Avocatore. His coming will clear all.

    2nd Avocatore.   Yet, it is misty.

    Voltore. May't please your fatherhoods—

    Volpone.   Sir, the parasite   15

            Volpone whispers [to] the Advocate.

Willed me to tell you that his master lives;
That you are still the man; your hopes the same;
And this was only a jest—

    Voltore.   How?

    Volpone.   Sir, to try

If you were firm, and how you stood affected.

    Voltore. Art sure he lives?

    Volpone.   Do I live, sir?

    Voltore.   O me!   20

I was too violent.

    Volpone.   Sir, you may redeem it:

They said you were possessed: fall down, and seem so.
I'll help to make it good. God bless the man!   *Voltore falls.*

                  [Aside to Voltore.]

—Stop your wind hard, and swell—See, see, see, see!
He vomits crooked pins! His eyes are set   25
Like a dead hare's hung in a poulter's shop!
His mouth's running away! Do you see, signior?
Now, 'tis in his belly.

    Corvino.   Ay, the devil!

    Volpone. Now, in his throat.

9–10. possession . . . obsession—possession was attack from within; obsession,
from without.   20. Do I live—Volpone probably reveals his identity to
Voltore here.   25–28. vomits . . . belly—symptoms described in contemporary accounts of witchcraft in England.   26. poulter's—poultry seller's.
27. running away—twisting violently.

  Corvino.   Ay, I perceive it plain.

  Volpone. 'Twill out, 'twill out! Stand clear. See where it

               [flies! 30

In shape of a blue toad, with a bat's wings! [*Pointing.*]

Do you not see it, sir?

  Corbaccio. What? I think I do.

  Corvino. 'Tis too manifest.

  Volpone.   Look! He comes t' himself!

  Voltore. Where am I?

  Volpone.   Take good heart, the worst is past, sir.

You are dispossessed.

  1st Avocatore. What accident is this?   35

  2nd Avocatore. Sudden, and full of wonder!

  3rd Avocatore.   If he were

Possessed, as it appears, all this is nothing. [*Waving notes.*]

  Corvino. He has been often subject to these fits.

  1st Avocatore. Show him that writing.—Do you know it,

                [sir?

  Volpone. [*Aside.*] Deny it sir, forswear it, know it not. 40

  Voltore. Yes, I do know it well, it is my hand;

But all that it contains is false.

  Bonario.   O practice!

  2nd Avocatore. What maze is this!

  1st Avocatore.   Is he not guilty then,

Whom you, there, name the parasite?

  Voltore.   Grave fathers,

No more than his good patron, old Volpone.   45

  4th Avocatore. Why, he is dead.

  Voltore.   O, no, my honored fathers.

He lives—

  1st Avocatore. How! Lives?

  Voltore.   Lives.

  2nd Avocatore.   This is subtler yet!

  3rd Avocatore. You said he was dead.

  Voltore.   Never.

  3rd Avocatore.   You said so!

  Corvino.   I heard so.

  4th Avocatore. Here comes the gentleman, make him way.

            [*Enter Mosca.*]

42. practice—intrigue.

3rd Avocatore.   A stool!

4th Avocatore. A proper man and, were Volpone dead,   50
A fit match for my daughter.

    3rd Avocatore.   Give him way.

    Volpone. [*Aside to Mosca.*] Mosca, I was almost lost; the
                                          [advocate
Had betrayed all; but now it is recovered.
All's o' the hinge again. Say I am living.

    Mosca. What busy knave is this? Most reverend fathers,   55
I sooner had attended your grave pleasures,
But that my order for the funeral
Of my dear patron did require me—

    Volpone. [*Aside.*]   Mosca!

    Mosca. Whom I intend to bury like a gentleman.

    Volpone. [*Aside.*] Ay, quick, and cozen me of all.

    2nd Avocatore.   Still stranger!   60
More intricate!

    1st Avocatore. And come about again!

    4th Avocatore. [*Aside.*] It is a match, my daughter is
                                    [bestowed.

    Mosca. [*Aside to Volpone.*] Will you gi' me half?

    Volpone. [*Half aloud.*]   First I'll be hanged.

    Mosca. [*Aside.*]   I know
Your voice is good, cry not so loud.

    1st Avocatore.   Demand
The advocate. Sir, did not you affirm   65
Volpone was alive?

    Volpone.   Yes, and he is;
This gent'man told me so. [*Aside to Mosca.*] Thou shalt have
                                          [half.

    Mosca. Whose drunkard is this same? Speak, some that
                                        [know him.
I never saw his face. [*Aside to Volpone.*] I cannot now
Afford it you so cheap.

    Volpone. [*Aside.*] No?

    1st Avocatore. [*To Voltore.*] What say you?   70

    Voltore. The officer told me.

    Volpone.   I did, grave fathers,

---

50. proper—handsome.   55. busy—meddling.   60. quick—alive.
64. Demand—ask.

And will maintain he lives with mine own life,
And that this creature told me. [*Aside.*] I was born
With all good stars my enemies!
    Mosca.   Most grave fathers,
If such an insolence as this must pass   75
Upon me, I am silent; 'twas not this
For which you sent, I hope.
    2nd Avocatore.   Take him away.
    Volpone. [*Aside.*] Mosca!
    3rd Avocatore.   Let him be whipped.
    Volpone. [*Aside.*]   Wilt thou betray me?
Cozen me?
    3rd Avocatore. And taught to bear himself
Toward a person of his rank.
    4th Avocatore. [*The Officers seize Volpone.*] Away.   80
    Mosca. I humbly thank your fatherhoods.
    Volpone. [*Aside.*]   Soft, soft. Whipped?
And lose all that I have? If I confess,
It cannot be much more.
    4th Avocatore. [*To Mosca.*] Sir, are you married?
    Volpone. [*Aside.*] They'll be allied anon; I must be
                                      [resolute:
The fox shall here uncase.   *He puts off*
    Mosca. [*Aside.*]   Patron!   *his disguise.*
    Volpone.   Nay, now   85
My ruins shall not come alone; your match
I'll hinder sure. My substance shall not glue you,
Nor screw you, into a family.
    Mosca. [*In one last attempt, aside.*] Why, patron!
    Volpone. I am Volpone, and this is my knave;
This, his own knave; this, avarice's fool;   90
This, a chimera of wittol, fool, and knave.
And, reverend fathers, since we all can hope
Nought but a sentence, let's not now despair it.
You hear me brief.
    Corvino.   May it please your fatherhoods—
    Commendatore.   Silence.
    1st Avocatore. The knot is now undone by miracle!   95

89–91. this . . . this—points in turn to Mosca, Voltore, Corbaccio, and Corvino.   91. chimera—mythical monster, part lion, goat and serpent.

 2nd Avocatore. Nothing can be more clear.

 3rd Avocatore.   Or can more prove
These innocent.

 1st Avocatore. Give 'em their liberty.

 Bonario. Heaven could not long let such gross crimes be
               [hid.

 2nd Avocatore. If this be held the highway to get riches,
May I be poor!

 3rd Avocatore. This's not the gain, but torment.   100

 1st Avocatore. These possess wealth as sick men possess
               [fevers,
Which trulier may be said to possess them.

 2nd Avocatore. Disrobe that parasite.

 Corvino, Mosca.   Most honored fathers—

 1st Avocatore. Can you plead aught to stay the course of
              [justice?
If you can, speak.

 Corvino, Voltore. We beg favor.

 Celia.   And mercy.   105

 1st Avocatore. You hurt your innocence, suing for the
              [guilty.

Stand forth; and first the parasite. You appear
T'have been the chiefest minister, if not plotter,
In all these lewd impostures; and now, lastly,
Have with your impudence abused the court,   110
And habit of a gentleman of Venice,
Being a fellow of no birth or blood:
For which our sentence is, first thou be whipped;
Then live perpetual prisoner in our galleys.

 Volpone. I thank you for him.

 Mosca.   Bane to thy wolfish nature.   115

 1st Avocatore. Deliver him to the *Saffi*. [*Mosca is taken*
              [*out.*]

         Thou, Volpone,
By blood and rank a gentleman, canst not fall
Under like censure; but our judgment on thee
Is that thy substance all be straight confiscate
To the hospital of the *Incurabili*.   120

115. I thank you—revenge on Mosca, who had thanked the court at line 81.
119. straight confiscate—immediately confiscated.   120. *Incurabili*—
"Incurables," a hospital for treatment of venereal disease.

And since the most was gotten by imposture,
By feigning lame, gout, palsy, and such diseases,
Thou art to lie in prison, cramped with irons,
Till thou be'st sick and lame indeed. Remove him.
    Volpone. This is called mortifying of a fox.   125
    1st Avocatore. Thou, Voltore, to take away the scandal
Thou hast giv'n all worthy men of thy profession,
Art banished from their fellowship, and our state.
Corbaccio, bring him near! We here possess
Thy son of all thy state, and confine thee   130
To the monastery of *San' Spirito*;
Where, since thou knew'st not how to live well here,
Thou shalt be learned to die well.
    Corbaccio. [*Cupping his ear.*] Ha! What said he?
    Commendatore. You shall know anon, sir.
    1st Avocatore.   Thou, Corvino, shalt
Be straight embarked from thine own house, and rowed   135
Round about Venice, through the Grand Canal,
Wearing a cap with fair long ass's ears
Instead of horns; and so to mount, a paper
Pinned on thy breast, to the *Berlina*—
    Corvino.   Yes,
And have mine eyes beat out with stinking fish,   140
Bruised fruit, and rotten eggs—'Tis well. I'm glad
I shall not see my shame yet.
    1st Avocatore.   And to expiate
Thy wrongs done to thy wife, thou art to send her
Home to her father, with her dowry trebled.
And these are all your judgments.
    All.   Honored fathers!   145
    1st Avocatore. Which may not be revoked. Now you
                               [begin,
When crimes are done and past, and to be punished,
To think what your crimes are. Away with them!
Let all that see these vices thus rewarded
Take heart, and love to study 'em. Mischiefs feed   150
Like beasts, till they be fat, and then they bleed.   [*Exeunt.*]
                     [*Volpone comes forward.*]

---

125. mortifying—(1) hanging up of meat, (2) spiritual humbling.   131. *San'*
Spirito—Monastery of the Holy Spirit.   139. *Berlina*—pillory.

Volpone. The seasoning of a play is the applause.
Now, though the fox be punished by the laws,
He yet doth hope there is no suff'ring due
For any fact which he hath done 'gainst you.   155
If there be, censure him; here he doubtful stands.
If not, fare jovially, and clap your hands.

THE END

155. fact—crime.

BARTHOLOMEW FAIR

INTRODUCTION

The ending of *Bartholomew Fair* differs strikingly from the ending of *Volpone*. Instead of a judge sentencing the guilty, a judge is himself exposed; instead of harsh punishments, there is forgiveness; instead of fragmentation of the play's society as each person goes to his separate doom, the play's society is integrated as all go off together for a feast at the home of the repentant judge.

How can we account for these differences? Between 1606 and 1614 did Jonson give up his goal of reforming society? Is he in *Bartholomew Fair* cynically pandering to the audience's desire for pleasure and disregarding his self-imposed obligation to provide moral profit along with the pleasure? One begins to wonder. In the Induction the bookholder, Jonson's spokesman, reads a mock contract between the author and the spectators in which the author, in return for certain considerations, promises to provide both the "favoring and judicious" and the "grounded judgments" with "a new sufficient play called *Barthol'mew Fair*, merry, and as full of noise as sport, made to delight all, and to offend none" (77–78). There is no mention of profit.

Jonson certainly fulfills his promise to provide pleasure. The taste of the ignorant stage-keeper in the Induction runs toward "a fine pump upon the stage" with "a punk [whore] set under upon her head, with her stern upward, ... soused by my witty young masters o' the Inns o' Court" (30–32). Jonson ridicules the stage-keeper's tastes; yet he himself provides some marvelous scenes of low farce such as Ursula scalding herself (II.v), Wasp beating

137

Overdo (II.vi), Zeal-of-the-Land Busy overthrowing the gingerbread
(III.vi), and Bartholomew Cokes picking up the pears (IV.ii). In a
recent production by the Royal Shakespeare Company, the puppet
show got more laughs from the audience than any other scene. The
visual comedy made the lines obscenely funny rather than merely
vulgar.

Despite the extraordinary amount of physical comedy, however,
the play contains plenty of material for the "favoring and judicious"
spectator. I suggest that the main theme is judgment. The Induction
concerns only judgment of art, but Jonson demonstrates throughout
the play that one's judgment of art is a crucial indication of one's
judgment in general. Character after character exhibits some major
flaw in both kinds of judgment.

Zeal-of-the-Land Busy, the "superlunatical hypocrite," is clearly
Jonson's favorite object of satire. Quarlous sums up this Puritan's
character: "[He] derides all antiquity; defies any other learning than
inspiration; and what discretion soever years should afford him, it is
all prevented in his original ignorance" (I.iii.138–40). His ignorance
leads him to abuse language violently with his pretentious repetition
("Very likely, exceeding likely, very exceeding likely" [I.vi.100]).
In the jargon of Biblical prophecy he inveighs against the wickedness
of the fair; he is silent only when his mouth is full of roast pig. He is
also a confidence man; we learn from Dame Purecraft that he has
been practicing legal trickery on his coreligionists for years. He is
therefore not only ignorant but hypocritical and gluttonous.

It is no coincidence that Busy, the worst enemy of true moral
judgment, is also the bitterest enemy of art and festivity. He
combines in ludicrous fashion the Puritan objection to statues in the
churches, which they regarded as popish idols, and their objection to
"fairs and May-games, wakes and Whitsun-ales" (IV.vi.87–88), which
they regarded as frivolous pursuits designed to take one's mind off
God. The result is his furious rage against the carnival Kewpie dolls
in Littlewit's booth: "See you not Goldylocks, the purple strumpet,
there, in her yellow gown and green sleeves? the profane pipes, the
tinkling timbrels? A shop of relics!" (III.vi.89–91). Busy is equally
vehement in denouncing the puppet Dionysus as "that idol, that
heathenish idol" (V.v.4–5). He connects puppets with other forms
of art "such as are your stage-players, rhymers, and morris dancers,
who have walked hand in hand in contempt of the brethren and the
cause" (V.v.9–11).

Humphrey Wasp is a kind of secular Puritan. He talks in staccato waspish buzzes rather than in the language of Biblical prophecy, but his comic flaw is similar to Busy's: he tries to reform others (specifically Cokes) when he himself is ignorant. He proudly announces at his first entrance that he cannot read: "I am no clerk, I scorn to be saved by my book" (I.iv.7–8). Yet he officiously accuses Cokes of "errors, diseases of youth, which he will mend when he comes to judgment and knowledge of matters" (I.v.42–44). Wasp, like Busy, is an enemy of the fair and by implication of all art and festivity. He objects to Cokes' singing ballads: "He has learned nothing but to sing catches and repeat *Rattle bladder rattle* and *O Madge*" (I.iv.72–74). Even when he is drunk Wasp is angry rather than festive. His alcoholic judgment on himself is more appropriate than he knows: "I have no reason, nor will I hear of no reason, nor will I look for no reason, and he is an ass that either knows any or looks for't from me" (IV.iv.43–45). Buzz! Buzz! Buzz! Buzz! Buzz!

Adam Overdo is not such an indiscriminate enemy of art as Busy and Wasp; he typifies the Renaissance statesman who tolerates and even quotes Latin poetry if the tag teaches a sound moral, but who has no conception of the delight in poetry. He fails to understand the importance of not being earnest. Thus, while he alludes to "my Quintus Horace" (II.i.5) and quotes "my friend Ovid" (II.iv.73), Virgil (III.iii.31–32), and Juvenal (V.vi.22), in Latin, he also suspects Ezekiel Edgworth "of a terrible taint, poetry! with which idle disease if he be infected, there's no hope of him in a state-course" [i.e., as a statesman] (III.v.6–7). When Overdo hears "The Ballad of the Cutpurse," he exclaims, "It doth discover enormity, I'll mark it more; I ha' not liked a paltry piece of poetry so well, a good while" (III.v.134–36). When he is exposing the "enormities" of the fair in the last scene, he addresses Lantern Leatherhead as "thou other extremity, thou profane professor of puppetry, little better than poetry" (V.vi.40–42).

Overdo is ignorant not of books but of life. He quotes the classics, but he mistakes a cutpurse for a "civil young man." He jumps to this amazing conclusion because of his own naïve intuitions, which are unfortunately confirmed by Mooncalf's jocular remark (II.iv.30). Overdo needs to heed the admonition that Jonson put in *Discoveries*: "For to all the observations of the Ancients we have our own experience, which, if we will use, and apply, we have better means to pronounce" (*Discoveries*, 134–37).

Busy, Wasp, and Overdo, then are all meddling reformers; they are enemies of the fair, of festivity, and of art itself. If the comic poet is to imitate justice, as Jonson believed he should,[1] these impostors must be brought to judgment in both the legal sense and the moral sense. Each of them is arrested, and as they appear together in the stocks (IV.vi) we see a hilarious metaphor of their essential kinship. But this judgment is temporary; they get away physically, and they are morally unreconstructed: Busy turns up at the puppet show to denounce it and Overdo turns up there to denounce everybody.

Wasp too is unrepentant when he leaves the stocks. He undergoes a sudden change of heart, however, when Cokes reveals that he knows about his little old governor's humiliation. "Sententious Numps" ruefully says, "I must think no longer to reign. ... He that will correct another must want fault in himself" (V.iv.102–104). Significantly, Wasp's first act is to watch the puppet show and enjoy it; "well acted, with all my heart," he says (V.iv.283).

Busy's conversion is also symbolized by his change of attitude toward the puppet show. When he charges the puppets with disobeying the Biblical injunction against one sex wearing the clothing of the other, the puppet replies, "It is your old stale argument against the players, but it will not hold against the puppets; for we have neither male nor female amongst us (*The Puppet takes up his garment*)" (V.v.102–5). Busy, the archenemy of art, is confuted by a puppet. Suddenly, like Saul on the road to Damascus, he is struck with a blinding realization: "The cause hath failed me" (line 112). Instead of stomping out, Malvolio-style, he remains in the group. He drops his hostility to art, and when he is admonished to let the puppet play go on, he replies, "Let it go on. For I am changed, and will become a beholder with you" (lines 116–117).

Overdo's oration in the last scene (the Last "Judgment") shows that at this point he has lost none of his comic *hubris*: "Look upon me, O London! and see me, O Smithfield! the example of justice and mirror of magistrates" (V.vi.33–35). When his wife turns up, drunk, as one of Whit's twelve-penny ladies, he is silenced. When his "innocent young man" is revealed as a cutpurse, he is crushed. Like

---

[1] See my Introduction to *Volpone*.

Busy and Wasp, however, he repents. Quarlous' lecture has its effect: "This pleasant conceited gentleman hath wrought upon my judgment, and prevailed" (V.vi.108–9). Far from sulking, he invites the entire company to supper. Even against the three enemies of the fair and of art Jonson's judgment is exposure rather than expulsion.

In Jonson's view, art often suffers as much damage from its supposed friends as from its enemies. Another set of characters in the play enjoy art and understand festivity, but their debased judgment and profiteering motives show up in their flawed sense of social decorum and their attitudes toward art. John Littlewit is the worst offender in this regard. Ever since *Poetaster* (1601) Jonson had been inveighing against dabblers with no dedication to profit or to pleasure but merely to their own egos. Littlewit's little wit shows up in his obsessive punning. Quarlous identifies him with Justice Overdo: "You grow so insolent with it, and overdoing, John" (I.v.72–73). Littlewit excuses his appalling vulgarization of the classical story in the puppet play: "I have only made it a little easy and modern for the times, sir, that's all" (V.iii.121–22). But in the process he has turned it into pornography. The puppet show is funny in the theater, but we laugh at the dialogue rather than with it.

Littlewit's lack of artistic taste in sexual matters—so apparent in the language of the puppet play—is of a piece with his curious attitude toward his wife's sexual conduct. Either he is incredibly stupid or he is pandering his wife. He insists that she kiss Quarlous repeatedly, and leaves her with such "gentlemen" as Whit and Knockem. One is reminded of a story that Jonson told Drummond of an "accident strange" in which "a man made his own wife to court him, whom he [Jonson] enjoyed two years ere he [the husband] knew of it, and one day finding them by chance, was passingly delighted with it."

The people of the fair do not have the position in society that Littlewit does; therefore, Jonson does not expect as much of them. Nevertheless, he satirizes them as commercializers of art. Lantern Leatherhead, for instance, resembles Philip Henslowe, the theatrical manager for whom Jonson had worked; Leatherhead is frankly interested in money. Recalling a certain puppet play fondly, he sighs, "There was a get-penny!" (V.i.11–12). He considers *Hero and Leander* "too learned and poetical for our audience" (V.iii.111–12) in its unaltered form. Leatherhead's artistic laxity is accompanied, as usual in *Bartholomew Fair*, by moral laxity. The puppeteer schemes to slip away with all his merchandise even though he has already sold it to Cokes.

Cokes himself is destructive of true art because he has no discrimination whatever. Whereas Busy does not like any art, Cokes likes everything. Jonson is out to show that one must exercise some judgment; enjoying art is not enough. Cokes buys Leatherhead's whole shop rather than try to decide which hobbyhorses he wants most; he loves the puppet show but cannot tell life from art ("Between you and I, sir," says Leatherhead, "we do but make show" [V.iv.297]). In life, as in art, he has no judgment. As a substantial landowner, he should be acting with the decorum befitting his position. Instead, he wanders about the fair losing one by one the symbols of his social position—purses, hat, cloak, sword. Because he has acted like a perpetual child, his fate is to wander about the fair followed by a crowd of jeering children. But he bounds back from this humiliation with the resilience of a child, and at the end of the play he is just as exuberant as ever. The comic judgment on him is less severe than that on Busy, Wasp, Overdo, and Littlewit; his crimes are evidently less serious than theirs.

Quarlous is an important character who does not fit neatly into either of the categories I have created. Among other things he is a professional satirist who gets off some fine diatribes, such as his Juvenalian attack on widows and widow-hunting (I.iii.55–98) and his prose "character" of Busy as a typical Puritan (lines 129–42). He and Winwife tell us what to think of the characters as we meet them ("What pity 'tis yonder wench should marry such a cokes" [I.v.50–51]). Quarlous is eager to expose Wasp not because he will profit but because "of all beasts I love the serious ass" (III.v.300), and so he gets Edgworth to steal the license. Quarlous plays the satirist in the last scene, exposing Overdo mercilessly.

But Quarlous' attacks on others do not sound self-righteous and pompous because he readily admits his own complicity in human folly: *Facinus quos inquinat, aequat* ("Crime levels those whom it pollutes" [IV.vi.29–30]). Although a gentleman by rank, he is listed in the *dramatis personae* as a "gamester." In 1614 this word could have meant one who plays any game, an actor, a jokester, or a rake, and Quarlous is all these. He goes to the fair to have sport, and he wins the widow with his acting skill. As jokester, actor, and con artist he has a supply of false beards with him. He is sexually licentious and utterly unprincipled in his financial dealings with Dame Purecraft, Overdo, and Grace. He is constantly quarreling with someone. Yet while he scorns the people of the fair, he realizes that "our very being here makes us fit to be demanded, as well as others" (II.v.16–17). At the end he admonishes Adam Overdo and symbolically all of us: "Remember you are but Adam, flesh and blood! You have your frailty; forget your other name of Overdo and invite us all to supper" (V.vi.98–100). Quarlous can see the fair for what it is—a Saturnalian holiday that should promote celebration rather than punishment.

Through Quarlous Jonson laughs at his own quarrelsomeness and lack of moral perfection and at the severity of the satire in his early comedies. He never ceased to believe that crusading is the most valuable activity in life—indeed, *Bartholomew Fair* is a crusade against bad moral and artistic judgment—but he also says through this play that crusading must not be Overdone. Jonson, who is often portrayed as merciless in his hatred of vice, demonstrates here a genuine sympathy for human weakness and a grudging recognition that in the real world even the best examples of virtue fall short of the ideal.

FACTS AND REFERENCES

FIRST PERFORMANCE

All evidence indicates that the date given in the Induction (October 31, 1614) is real rather than fictional; there was a performance at court the next day (November 1). The company was the Lady Elizabeth's Men; the theater the Hope.

SELECTED BIBLIOGRAPHY

Early Editions

My modernized text is based on the only early edition, printed in 1631 and distributed as a part of the 1640 folio.

Modern Editions (other than H&S)

Horsman, E. A., ed. The Revels Plays. London: Methuen & Co., Ltd., 1960.

Hussey, Maurice, ed. The New Mermaids. London: Ernest Benn, Ltd., 1964.

Partridge, Edward, ed. Regents Renaissance Drama. Lincoln: University of Nebraska Press, 1964.

Waith, Eugene, ed. The Yale Ben Jonson.[1] New Haven, Conn.: Yale University Press, 1963.

Other Scholarship and Criticism[2]

Barish, Jonas A. "*Bartholomew Fair* and Its Puppets." *MLQ* 20 (1959): 3–17.

Cope, Jackson. "*Bartholomew Fair* as Blasphemy." *Renaissance Drama* 8 (1965): 127–52.

Potter, John M. "Old Comedy in *Bartholomew Fair*." *Criticism* 10 (1968): 290–99.

Robinson, James E. "*Bartholomew Fair*: Comedy of Vapors." *SEL* 1 (1961): 65–80.

Targan, Barry. "The Moral Structure of *Bartholomew Fair*." *Discourse* 8 (1965): 276–84.

Waith, Eugene M. "The Staging of *Bartholomew Fair*." *SEL* 2 (1962): 181–95.

---

[1] My text and notes are often indebted to this excellent edition.

[2] Many books listed in the Selected Bibliography following the General Introduction include discussions of *Bartholomew Fair*.

BARTHOLOMEW FAIR

Your Majesty is welcome to a Fair;
Such place, such men, such language and such ware
You must expect; with these the zealous noise
Of your land's faction, scandalized at toys,
As babies, hobbyhorses, puppet plays,   5
And such like rage, whereof the petulant ways
Yourself have known, and have been vexed with long.
These for your sport, without particular wrong,
Or just complaint of any private man
Who of himself or shall think well or can,   10
The maker doth present, and hopes tonight
To give you for a fairing true delight.

4. faction—the Puritans.   5. babies—dolls.   10. or . . . or—either . . . or.

THE PERSONS OF THE PLAY

JOHN LITTLEWIT, *a proctor*
[SOLOMON, *his man*]
WIN LITTLEWIT, *his wife*
DAME PURECRAFT, *her mother and a widow*
ZEAL-OF-THE-LAND BUSY, *her suitor, a Banbury man*
WINWIFE, *his rival, a gentleman*

proctor—agent, attorney.   Banbury—town near Oxford, noted for Puritans.

QUARLOUS, *his companion, a gamester*
BARTHOLOMEW COKES, *an esquire of Harrow*
HUMPHREY WASP, *his man*
ADAM OVERDO, *a justice of peace*
DAME OVERDO, *his wife*
GRACE WELLBORN, *his ward*
LANTERN LEATHERHEAD, *a hobbyhorse-seller*
JOAN TRASH, *a gingerbread-woman*
EZEKIEL EDGWORTH, *a cutpurse*
NIGHTINGALE, *a ballad-singer*
URSULA, *a pig-woman*
MOONCALF, *her tapster*
JORDAN KNOCKEM, *a horse-courser and ranger o' Turnbull*
VAL CUTTING, *a roarer*
CAPTAIN WHIT, *a bawd*
PUNK ALICE, *mistress o' the game*
TROUBLE-ALL, *a madman*
WATCHMEN, three [HAGGIS, BRISTLE, and POACHER, *a beadle*]
COSTERMONGER
[PASSENGERS]
[CORNCUTTER]
[TINDERBOX-MAN]
CLOTHIER, [NORTHERN]
WRESTLER [PUPPY]
DOORKEEPERS [FILCHER and SHARKWELL]
PUPPETS

gamester—a word with many meanings, including a player at any game, actor, gambler, merry person, one addicted to amorous sport. Any one or even all of these senses could be intended here.   Cokes—a cokes was a sucker, a fool. pig-woman—literally, seller of roast pig.   Mooncalf—deformed at birth by the moon.   Jordan ... Turnbull—a good example of Jonson's ability to pack many meanings into his comic names.   A *jordan* was a chamber-pot; *knock,* slang for copulate;   *horse-courser,* a dealer in used horses and whores; *ranger,* keeper of a park (read brothel);   *Turnbull,* an infamous red-light district.   roarer—swaggerer.   the game—prostitution.   beadle—messenger for the authorities; deputy.   Costermonger—fruit-peddler.   [Passengers]— passersby.   [Tinderbox-man] —seller of tinderboxes; later called mousetrap man.

THE INDUCTION ON THE STAGE

[*Enter Stage-keeper.*]

[*Stage-keeper.*] Gentlemen, have a little patience, they are
e'en upon coming, instantly. He that should begin the play,
Master Littlewit, the proctor, has a stitch new fall'n in his
black silk stocking; 'twill be drawn up ere you can tell twenty.
He plays one o' the Arches, that dwells about the hospital, and   5
he has a very pretty part. But for the whole play, will you ha'
the truth on't? (I am looking, lest the poet hear me, or his
man, Master Brome, behind the arras) it is like to be a very
conceited scurvy one, in plain English. When't comes to the
Fair once, you were e'en as good go to Virginia, for anything   10
there is of Smithfield. He has not hit the humors, he does not
know 'em; he has not conversed with the Barthol'mew-birds,
as they say; he has ne'er a sword-and-buckler man in his Fair,
nor a little Davy to take toll o' the bawds there, as in my time,
nor a Kindheart, if anybody's teeth should chance to ache in   15
his play. Nor a juggler with a well-educated ape to come over
the chain for the King of England and back again for the
Prince, and sit still on his arse for the Pope and the King of
Spain! None o' these fine sights! Nor has he the canvas-cut i'
the night for a hobbyhorse-man to creep in to his she-neighbor   20
and take his leap there! Nothing! No, an' some writer (that I
know) had had but the penning o' this matter, he would ha'
made you such a jig-a-jog i' the booths, you should ha' thought
an earthquake had been i' the Fair! But these master-poets,
they will ha' their own absurd courses; they will be informed   25
of nothing! He has, sir-reverence, kicked me three or four
times about the tiring-house, I thank him, for but offering to

[*Enter Stage-keeper*] —perhaps carrying a broom as an indication of how
menial his job is.   5. Arches—an ecclesiastical court.   about the hospital—near St. Bartholomew Hospital.   8. Brome—Richard Brome later became a famous writer of comedy himself.   arras—cloth hanging at rear of
stage.   9. conceited—witty. Presumably the stage-keeper disapproves
because he is thinking of verbal wit (e.g., puns), whereas he prefers his own
"conceit" (line 27) based on physical comedy. (The word is related to
concept, i.e., idea, notion.)   11. Smithfield—district of the (real) Bartholomew Fair.   humors—eccentricities.   13. sword-and-buckler man—
ruffian who came to the fair to fight.   14. little Davy—swordsman and
bully.   15. Kindheart—famous tooth-drawer.   21. an'—if.   26. sir-
reverence—short for "saving your reverence," expression used to preface
vulgar language.   27. tiring-house—dressing room area (attire).

put in, with my experience. I'll be judged by you, gentlemen,
now, but for one conceit of mine! Would not a fine pump
upon the stage ha' done well for a property now? And a punk   30
set under upon her head, with her stern upward, and ha' been
soused by my witty young masters o' the Inns o' Court? What
think you o' this for a show, now? He will not hear o' this! I
am an ass, I! And yet I kept the stage in Master Tarlton's time,
I thank my stars. Ho! an' that man had lived to have played in   35
Barthol'mew Fair, you should ha' seen him ha' come in, and
ha' been cozened i' the cloth-quarter, so finely! And Adams,
the rogue, ha' leaped and capered upon him, and ha' dealt his
vermin about as though they had cost him nothing. And then a
substantial watch to ha' stol'n in upon 'em, and taken 'em   40
away with mistaking words, as the fashion is in the stage-
practice.

                    [*Enter Book-holder, Scrivener.*]
     Book-holder. How now? What rare discourse are you fall'n
upon, ha? Ha' you found any familiars here, that you are so
free? What's the business?   45
     Stage-keeper. Nothing, but the understanding gentlemen o'
the ground here asked my judgment.
     Book-holder. Your judgment, rascal? For what? Sweeping
the stage? Or gathering up the broken apples for the bears
within? Away, rogue, it's come to a fine degree in these   50
spectacles when such a youth as you pretend to a judgment.
[*Exit Stage-keeper.*] And yet he may, i' the most o' this
matter i' faith; for the author hath writ it just to his meridian,

---

30. punk—whore.   32. Inns o'Court—the law schools.   34. Tarleton—
star comedian of the previous generation.   cloth-quarter—one of Tarleton's
Jests (1611) was of his being cheated of his clothes. Jonson appropriately
places the event in the cloth section of the fair.   37–39. Adams . . .
vermin—evidently some kind of slapstick routine performed by Tarleton and
a fellow actor named Adams. Perhaps it included Adams picking imaginary
vermin off Tarleton.   41. with mistaking words—like the watch in Shakespeare's *Much Ado About Nothing.*   43. *Book-holder*—prompter.
46–47. understanding gentlemen o' the ground—the groundlings, who paid
a low admission fee, stood in the pit between the seats and the jutting stage.
They are gentlemen in no sense and understanding in the punning sense that
they stand under (by the side of) the raised stage, looking up.   49. the
bears—the trestle stage at the Hope was removed for bearbaiting on Tuesdays
and Thursdays. In bearbaiting the audience watches a pack of dogs kill a bear.
53. meridian—"to the height of his understanding" (Waith).

and the scale of the grounded judgments here, his play-fellows
in wit. Gentlemen, not for want of a prologue, but by way of a   55
new one, I am sent out to you here with a scrivener and
certain articles drawn out in haste between our author and
you; which if you please to hear, and as they appear
reasonable, to approve of, the play will follow presently. Read,
scribe; gi' me the counterpane.   60

 Scrivener. Articles of Agreement indented between the
spectators or hearers at the Hope on the Bankside, in the
county of Surrey, on the one party, and the author of
Barthol'mew Fair in the said place and county, on the other
party, the one and thirtieth day of October, 1614, and in the   65
twelfth year of the reign of our Sovereign Lord, James, by the
grace of God King of England, France, and Ireland, Defender
of the Faith; and of Scotland the seven and fortieth.

 INPRIMIS, It is covenanted and agreed by and between
the parties above-said and the said spectators and hearers, as   70
well the curious and envious as the favoring and judicious, as
also the grounded judgments and under-standings do for
themselves severally covenant and agree, to remain in the
places their money or friends have put them in, with patience,
for the space of two hours and an half and somewhat more. In   75
which time the author promiseth to present them, by us, with
a new sufficient play called *Barthol'mew Fair*, merry, and as
full of noise as sport, made to delight all, and to offend none;
provided they have either the wit or the honesty to think well
of themselves.   80

 It is further agreed that every person here have his or their
free-will of censure, to like or dislike at their own charge, the
author having now departed with his right: it shall be lawful
for any man to judge his six pen'orth, his twelve pen'orth, so
to his eighteen pence, two shillings, half a crown, to the value   85
of his place; provided always his place get not above his wit.
And if he pay for half a dozen, he may censure for all them
too, so that he will undertake that they shall be silent. He shall
put in for censures here as they do for lots at the lottery;
marry, if he drop but sixpence at the door, and will censure a   90

---

60. counterpane—matching half; legal documents were torn in parts and each
party given a piece; authenticity was checked by matching. 82. censure—
judgment, favorable or unfavorable.

crown's worth, it is thought there is no conscience or justice in
that.

It is also agreed that every man here exercise his own
judgment, and not censure by contagion, or upon trust, from
another's voice or face that sits by him, be he never so first in   95
the commission of wit; as also, that he be fixed and settled in
his censure, that what he approves or not approves today, he
will do the same tomorrow, and if tomorrow, the next day,
and so the next week (if need be), and not to be brought
about by any that sits on the bench with him, though they   100
indict and arraign plays daily. He that will swear *Jeronimo* or
Andronicus are the best plays yet, shall pass unexcepted at
here as a man whose judgment shows it is constant, and hath
stood still these five and twenty, or thirty years. Though it be
an ignorance, it is a virtuous and staid ignorance, and next to   105
truth, a confirmed error does well; such a one the author
knows where to find him.

It is further covenanted, concluded, and agreed that how
great soever the expectation be, no person here is to expect
more than he knows, or better ware than a Fair will afford;   110
neither to look back to the sword-and-buckler age of
Smithfield, but content himself with the present. Instead of a
little Davy to take toll o' the bawds, the author doth promise a
strutting horse-courser with a leer drunkard, two or three to
attend him in as good equipage as you would wish. And then   115
for Kindheart, the tooth-drawer, a fine oily pig-woman with
her tapster to bid you welcome, and a consort of roarers for
music. A wise justice of peace *meditant,* instead of a juggler
with an ape. A civil cutpurse *searchant.* A sweet singer of new
ballads *allurant*; and as fresh an hypocrite as ever was broached   120
rampant. If there be never a servant-monster i' the Fair, who
can help it? he says; nor a nest of antics? He is loth to make
nature afraid in his plays, like those that beget Tales,

---

101. *Jeronimo*—Kyd's *Spanish Tragedy.*   102. *Andronicus*—Shakespeare's
Titus Andronicus.   unexcepted at—unchallenged.   111. sword-and-
buckler—swashbuckling (see *I Henry IV* I.iii.230 and *OED* 6d).   114. leer—
useless companion. "A leer horse was one without rider or load, hence often
a led horse" (Waith).   118–21. *meditant . . . rampant*—a parody of heral-
dic terms.   121–24. servant-monster . . . Tempests—a slam at Shakespeare's *Winter's Tale* (c. 1610) with its antics (grotesque dancers) such as the
satyrs (IV.iv) and *The Tempest* (c. 1611) with its servant-monster Caliban
(see III.ii).

Tempests, and such like drolleries, to mix his head with other
men's heels, let the concupiscence of jigs and dances reign as   125
strong as it will amongst you; yet if the puppets will please
anybody, they shall be entreated to come in.

   In consideration of which, it is finally agreed by the
foresaid hearers and spectators that they neither in themselves
conceal, nor suffer by them to be concealed, any state-   130
decipherer, or politic picklock of the scene, so solemnly
ridiculous as to search out who was meant by the gingerbread-
woman, who by the hobbyhorse-man, who by the costermonger, nay, who by their wares. Or that will pretend to affirm, on
his own inspired ignorance, what mirror of magistrates is   135
meant by the Justice, what great lady by the pig-woman, what
concealed statesman by the seller of mousetraps, and so of the
rest. But that such person or persons, so found, be left
discovered to the mercy of the author, as a forfeiture to the
stage and your laughter aforesaid. As also, such as shall so   140
desperately or ambitiously play the fool by his place aforesaid,
to challenge the author of scurrility because the language
somewhere savors of Smithfield, the booth, and the pig-broth;
or of profaneness because a madman cries, "God quit you," or
"bless you." In witness whereof, as you have preposterously   145
put to your seals already (which is your money), you will now
add the other part of suffrage, your hands. The play shall
presently begin. And though the Fair be not kept in the same
region that some here, perhaps, would have it, yet think that
therein the author hath observed a special decorum, the place   150
being as dirty as Smithfield, and as stinking every whit.

   Howsoever, he prays you to believe his ware is still the
same; else you will make him justly suspect that he that is so
loth to look on a baby or an hobbyhorse here, would be glad
to take up a commodity of them, at any laughter, or loss, in   155
another place.   [*Exeunt.*]

---

145. preposterously—in reverse order.   150. the place—i.e., the Hope
Theatre, stinking because of the bearbaiting.   155. commodity—quantity, alluding to a swindle in which the loan-shark forces the borrower to
accept part of the loan in overpriced merchandise and later buys it back,
through an agent, at a reduced price. Jonson means that anyone who prefers
another's wares to his is a sucker and may find himself forced to sell the overpriced merchandise at a loss.

ACT I
SCENE I

[*Littlewit's house.*]
[*Enter Littlewit holding a license.*]

Littlewit. A pretty conceit, and worth the finding! I ha'
such luck to spin out these fine things still, and like a
silk-worm, out of myself. Here's Master Barthol'mew Cokes, of
Harrow o' th' Hill, i' th' County of Middlesex, Esquire, takes   5
forth his license to marry Mistress Grace Wellborn of the said
place and county. And when does he take it forth? Today!
The four and twentieth of August! Barthol'mew Day!
Barthol'mew upon Barthol'mew! There's the device! Who
would have marked such a leap-frog chance now? A very less   10
than ames-ace on two dice! Well, go thy ways, John Littlewit,
Proctor John Littlewit—one o' the pretty wits o' Paul's, the
"Little-wit of London" (so thou art called) and something
beside. When a quirk or a quiblin does 'scape thee, and thou
dost not watch, and apprehend it, and bring it afore the   15
constable of conceit (there now, I speak quib too), let 'em
carry thee out o' the archdeacon's court into his kitchen, and
make a Jack of thee, instead of a John. (There I am again, la!)
[*Enter Win.*]
Win, good morrow, Win. Aye marry, Win! Now you look
finely indeed, Win! This cap does convince! You'd not ha'   20
worn it, Win, nor ha' had it velvet, but a rough country beaver
with a copper band, like the coney-skin woman of Budge
Row! Sweet Win, let me kiss it! And her fine high shoes, like
the Spanish lady! Good Win, go a little; I would fain see thee
pace, pretty Win! By this fine cap, I could never leave kissing   25
on't.

Win. Come, indeed la, you are such a fool, still!

Littlewit. No, but half a one, Win; you are the tother half:
man and wife make one fool, Win. (Good!) Is there the
proctor, or doctor indeed, i' the diocese, that ever had the   30

---

11. ames-ace—double ace.   12. Paul's—St. Paul's Cathedral, a favorite social
gathering place.   14. quirk, quiblin—pun.   15. apprehend—(1) seize
physically, (2) perceive, understand. This word is a favorite of Littlewit's; he
uses it five times in the first act.   18. Jack—servant.   22–23. Budge
Row—street with many fur and skin sellers.

fortune to win him such a Win! (There I am again!) I do feel
conceits coming upon me, more than I am able to turn tongue
to. A pox o' these pretenders to wit! your Three Cranes, Mitre,
and Mermaid men! Not a corn of true salt nor a grain of right
mustard amongst them all. They may stand for places or so,   35
again' the next witfall, and pay twopence in a quart more for
their canary than other men. But gi' me the man can start up a
justice of wit out of six-shillings beer, and give the law to all
the poets and poet-suckers i' town, because they are the
players' gossips! 'Slid, other men have wives as fine as the   40
players, and as well dressed. Come hither, Win.

> [*He kisses her.*]

33. Three Cranes . . . Mermaid—taverns that Jonson and his friends frequent-
ed.   34. corn—grain.   36. again'—against, in anticipation of.
37. canary—a relatively expensive wine.   38. six-shillings—cheap.
39. poet-suckers—young (suckling) poets.   40. gossips—close friends. because . . . gossips!—possibly: the Mermaid men (poets) consider themselves
superior because they are close friends of the players. If this is the meaning,
Littlewit is displaying his little wit, since Jonson elsewhere expresses scorn for
players.   'Slid—by God's eyelid.

ACT I
SCENE II

> [*Enter Winwife.*]

Winwife. Why, how now, Master Littlewit! Measuring of
lips or moulding of kisses? Which is it?

Littlewit. Troth, I am a little taken with my Win's dressing
here! Does't not fine, Master Winwife? How do you apprehend, sir? She would not ha' worn this habit. I challenge all   5
Cheapside to show such another—Moorfields, Pimlico path, or
the Exchange, in a summer evening—with a lace to boot, as
this has. Dear Win, let Master Winwife kiss you. He comes
a-wooing to our mother, Win, and may be our father perhaps,
Win. There's no harm in him, Win.   10

4–5. how . . . apprehend—what do you think?   6. Cheapside—cloth district. Moorfields—a park. Pimlico—a tavern near London.   7. Exchange—
a shopping area.

Winwife. None i' the earth, Master Littlewit.   [*He kisses*
                                                     [*her.*]

Littlewit. I envy no man my delicates, sir.

Winwife. Alas, you ha' the garden where they grow still! A
wife here with a strawberry-breath, cherry-lips, apricot-cheeks,
and a soft velvet head, like a melicotton.   15

Littlewit. Good i' faith! Now dullness upon me, that I had
not that before him, that I should not light on't as well as he!
Velvet head!

Winwife. But my taste, Master Littlewit, tends to fruit of
a later kind: the sober matron, you wife's mother.   20

Littlewit. Aye! we know you are a suitor, sir. Win and I
both wish you well; by this license here, would you had her,
that your two names were as fast in it, as here are a couple.
Win would fain have a fine young father i' law with a feather,
that her mother might hood it and chain it with Mistress   25
Overdo. But you do not take the right course, Master Winwife.

Winwife. No, Master Littlewit? Why?

Littlewit. You are not mad enough.

Winwife. How? Is madness a right course?

Littlewit. I say nothing, but I wink upon Win. You have a   30
friend, one Master Quarlous, comes here sometimes?

Winwife. Why? he makes no love to her, does he?

Littlewit. Not a tokenworth that ever I saw, I assure you,
but—

Winwife. What?   35

Littlewit. He is the more madcap o' the two. You do not
apprehend me.

Win. You have a hot coal i' your mouth now, you cannot
hold.

Littlewit. Let me out with it, dear Win.   40

Win. I'll tell him myself.

Littlewit. Do, and take all the thanks, and much good do
thy pretty heart, Win.

Win. Sir, my mother has had her nativity-water cast lately
by the cunning men in Cow-lane, and they ha' told her her   45

---

15. velvet head—she is wearing a velvet cap (I.i.20–21).   melicotton—cross
between a peach and a quince.   24. with a feather—i.e., a gentleman.
25. hood, chain—insignia of civic office.   44. nativity-water—horoscope
made by urinalysis.

fortune, and do ensure her she shall never have happy hour, unless she marry within this sen'night, and when it is, it must be a madman, they say.

　　Littlewit. Aye, but it must be a gentleman madman.

　　Win. Yes, so the tother man of Moorfields says.　　　　　　50

　　Winwife. But does she believe 'em?

　　Littlewit. Yes, and has been at Bedlam twice since, every day, to inquire if any gentleman be there, or to come there, mad!

　　Winwife. Why, this is a confederacy, a mere piece of　　55
practice upon her, by these imposters!

　　Littlewit. I tell her so; or else say I that they mean some young madcap-gentleman (for the devil can equivocate as well as a shopkeeper) and therefore would I advise you to be a little madder than Master Quarlous, hereafter.　　　　　　60

　　Winwife. Where is she? Stirring yet?

　　Littlewit. Stirring! Yes, and studying an old elder, come from Banbury, a suitor that puts in here at meal-tide, to praise the painful brethren, or pray that the sweet singers may be restored; says a grace as long as his breath lasts him! Sometime　　65
the spirit is so strong with him, it gets quite out of him, and then my mother, or Win, are fain to fetch it again with malmsey, or *aqua coelestis.*

　　Win. Yes indeed, we have such a tedious life with him for his diet, and his clothes too; he breaks his buttons and cracks　　70
seams at every saying he sobs out.

　　Littlewit. He cannot abide my vocation, he says.

　　Win. No, he told my mother a proctor was a claw of the Beast, and that she had little less than committed abomination in marrying me so as she has done.　　　　　　75

　　Littlewit. Every line, he says, that a proctor writes, when it comes to be read in the Bishop's court, is a long black hair, kembed out of the tail of Antichrist.

　　Winwife. When came this proselyte?

　　Littlewit. Some three days since.　　　　　　80

---

47. sen'night—week.　　52. Bedlam—the London insane asylum.
64. painful—full of pain, suffering.　　66. spirit—etymologically, *spirit*
means *breath.*　　68. malmsey—sweet wine.　*aqua coelestis*—brandy (literally, celestial water).　　73–74. claw of the Beast—agent of the church
courts, which the Puritans hated.　The Puritans interpreted the Beast of Revelation 13 as the established church.　　78. kembed—combed (cf. unkempt).

ACT I
SCENE III

[*Enter Quarlous.*]

Quarlous. O sir, ha' you ta'en soil here? It's well a man
may reach you after three hours running, yet! What an
unmerciful companion art thou, to quit thy lodging at such
ungentlemanly hours! None but a scattered covey of fiddlers,
or one of these rag-rakers in dunghills, or some marrow-bone   5
man at most, would have been up when thou wert gone
abroad, by all description. I pray thee what ailest thou, thou
canst not sleep? Hast thou thorns i' thy eyelids, or thistles i'
thy bed?

Winwife. I cannot tell. It seems you had neither i' your   10
feet, that took this pain to find me.

Quarlous. No, an' I had, all the lyam-hounds o' the City
should have drawn after you by the scent rather. Master John
Littlewit! God save you, sir. 'Twas a hot night with some of
us, last night, John. Shall we pluck a hair o' the same wolf   15
today, Proctor John?

Littlewit. Do you remember, Master Quarlous, what we
discoursed on last night?

Quarlous. Not I, John. Nothing that I either discourse or
do; at those times I forfeit all to forgetfulness.   20

Littlewit. No? not concerning Win? Look you, there she
is, and dressed as I told you she should be. Hark you, sir, had
you forgot?   [*Whispers to Quarlous.*]

Quarlous. By this head, I'll beware how I keep you
company, John, when I am drunk, an' you have this dangerous   25
memory! That's certain.

Littlewit. Why sir?

Quarlous. Why? [*Turning to Winwife.*] We were all a little
stained last night, sprinkled with a cup or two, and I agreed
with Proctor John here to come and do somewhat with Win (I   30
know not what 'twas) today; and he puts me in mind on't,
now; he says he was coming to fetch me.—Before truth, if you
have that fearful quality, John, to remember, when you are

---

12. lyam-hounds—hounds on leash.   15. hair . . . wolf—hair of the dog that
bit you.

sober, John, what you promise drunk, John, I shall take heed
of you, John. For this once, I am content to wink at you.   35
Where's your wife? Come hither, Win.   *He kisseth her.*

    Win. Why, John! do you see this, John? Look you! help
me, John.

    Littlewit. O Win, fie, what do you mean, Win! Be
womanly, Win; make an outcry to your mother, Win? Master   40
Quarlous is an honest gentleman, and our worshipful good
friend, Win; and he is Master Winwife's friend, too. And Master
Winwife comes a suitor to your mother, Win, as I told you
before, Win, and may perhaps be our father, Win. They'll do
you no harm, Win; they are both our worshipful good friends.   45
Master Quarlous! You must know Master Quarlous, Win; you
must not quarrel with Master Quarlous, Win.

    Quarlous. No, we'll kiss again and fall in.

    Littlewit. Yes, do, good Win.

    Win. I' faith you are a fool, John.   50

                      [*They kiss again, ardently.*]

    Littlewit. A fool-John she calls me, do you mark that,
gentlemen? Pretty littlewit of velvet! A fool-John!

    Quarlous. She may call you an apple-John, if you use this.

    Winwife. Pray thee forbear, for my respect somewhat.

    Quarlous. Hoy-day! How respective you are become o' the   55
sudden! I fear this family will turn you reformed too; pray
you come about again. Because she is in possibility to be your
daughter-in-law, and may ask you blessing hereafter, when she
courts it to Tottenham to eat cream—well, I will forbear, sir;
but i' faith, would thou wouldst leave thy exercise of   60
widow-hunting once, this drawing after an old reverend smock
by the splay-foot! There cannot be an ancient tripe or trillibub
i' the town, but thou art straight nosing it; and 'tis a fine

---

46. know—Littlewit is forgetting that *know* can mean have carnal knowledge
of.   48. fall in—patch the quarrel, with obvious sexual innuendo (cf.
Triolus and Cressida, "Falling in, after falling out, may make them three"
[III.i.114]).   53. apple-John—shriveled apple, with suggestion of the slang
apple-squire, pander. use—make a habit of.   56. reformed—Puritan.
57. come about—reverse your direction, a nautical term.   59. courts . . .
cream—Tottenham court, known for cakes and sweetened cream, the ice cream
of the day.   61. drawing after—tracking by the scent.   62. tripe,
trillibub—entrails.

occupation thou'lt confine thyself to, when thou hast got
one—scrubbing a piece of buff, as if thou hadst the perpetuity   65
of Pannyer Alley to stink in; or perhaps, worse, currying a
carcass that thou hast bound thyself to alive. I'll be sworn,
some of them, that thou art or hast been a suitor to, are so old
as no chaste or married pleasure can ever become 'em. The
honest instrument of procreation has, forty years since, left to   70
belong to 'em. Thou must visit 'em, as thou wouldst do a
tomb, with a torch, or three handfuls of link, flaming hot, and
so thou mayst hap to make 'em feel thee, and after, come to
inherit according to thy inches. A sweet course for a man to
waste the brand of life for, to be still raking himself a fortune   75
in an old woman's embers; we shall ha' thee, after thou hast
been but a month married to one of 'em, look like the quartan
ague and the black jaundice met in a face, and walk as if thou
hadst borrowed legs of a spinner, and voice of a cricket. I
would endure to hear fifteen sermons a week for her, and such   80
coarse and loud ones as some of 'em must be; I would e'en
desire of Fate I might dwell in a drum, and take in my
sustenance with an old broken tobacco-pipe and a straw. Dost
thou ever think to bring thine ears or stomach to the patience
of a dry grace as long as thy tablecloth, and droned out by thy   85
son here, that might be thy father, till all the meat o' thy
board has forgot it was that day i' the kitchen? Or to brook
the noise made in a question of predestination, by the good
laborers and painful eaters assembled together, put to 'em by
the matron, your spouse, who moderates with a cup of wine,   90
ever and anon, and a sentence out of Knox between? Or the
perpetual spitting, before and after a sober drawn exhortation
of six hours, whose better part was the hum-ha-hum? Or to
hear prayers groaned out over thy iron-chests, as if they were
charms to break 'em? And all this, for the hope of two   95

---

64. occupation—Partridge suggests a pun on *occupy,* have sexual intercourse.
65. buff—(1) leather, (2) slang for nude human skin.   66. Pannyer Alley—
probably a leather district.   72. link—tow and pitch for torches (from
Martial III.xciii.18–27).   74. inherit . . . inches—from Juvenal I.40–41.
77–78. quartan ague—fever that wracks the victim every fourth day.
79. spinner—spider.   80. for—instead of.   91. sentence . . . Knox—
moral maxim from the works of John Knox, Scottish Presbyterian leader
revered by English Puritans.   94. iron-chests—strong-boxes.   95. break
'em—elicit contributions.

apostle-spoons, to suffer! And a cup to eat a caudle in! For
that will be thy legacy. She'll ha' conveyed her state, safe
enough from thee, an' she be a right widow.

    Winwife. Alas, I am quite off that scent now.

    Quarlous. How so?   100

    Winwife. Put off by a brother of Banbury, one that, they
say, is come here and governs all, already.

    Quarlous. What do you call him? I knew divers of those
Banburians when I was in Oxford.

    Winwife. Master Littlewit can tell us.   105

    Littlewit. Sir! Good Win, go in, and if Master Barthol'mew
Cokes his man come for the license (the little old fellow), let
him speak with me. What say you, gentlemen?   [*Exit Win.*]

    Winwife. What call you the reverend elder you told me
of—your Banbury man?   110

    Littlewit. Rabbi Busy, sir. He is more than an elder, he is a
prophet, sir.

    Quarlous. O, I know him! A baker, is he not?

    Littlewit. He was a baker, sir, but he does dream now, and
see visions; he has given over his trade.   115

    Quarlous. I remember that too—out of a scruple he took,
that (in spiced conscience) those cakes he made were served to
bridals, maypoles, morrises, and such profane feasts and
meetings. His Christian name is Zeal-of-the-land.

    Littlewit. Yes, sir, Zeal-of-the-land Busy.   120

    Winwife. How, what a name's there!

    Littlewit. O, they have all such names, sir. He was witness
for Win here (they will not be called godfathers), and named
her Win-the-fight. You thought her name had been Winifred,
did you not?   125

    Winwife. I did indeed.

    Littlewit. He would ha' thought himself a stark reprobate,
if it had.

    Quarlous. Aye, for there was a blue-starch-woman o' the
name, at the same time. A notable hypocritical vermin it is; I   130
know him. One that stands upon his face more than his faith,

---

96. apostle-spoons—silver, with the Apostles' images carved at the handle's
end.   caudle—warm potion for invalids; wine, spices, sugar.   97. state—
estate; made her will to another before the marriage.   118. morrises—
morris-dances, performed at rustic festivals.   129. blue-starch-woman—
starch made ruffs stiff, and the Puritans regarded ruffs as badges of pride.

at all times; ever in seditious motion, and reproving for
vain-glory; of a most lunatic conscience and spleen, and affects
the violence of singularity in all he does (he has undone a
grocer here, in Newgate-market, that broke with him, trusted   135
him with currants, as arrant a zeal as he, that's by the way). By
his profession he will ever be i' the state of innocence, though,
and childhood; derides all antiquity; defies any other learning
than inspiration; and what discretion soever years should
afford him, it is all prevented in his original ignorance. Ha' not   140
to do with him; for he is a fellow of a most arrogant and
invincible dullness, I assure you. Who is this?

134–36. (undone . . . by the way)—he has caused the bankruptcy of a grocer
that dealt with him for currants, who, by the way, is as puritanical as Busy
himself.   On the "spasmodic quality" of this passage see Jonas Barish, *Ben
Jonson and the Language of Prose Comedy*, (Cambridge, Mass.: Harvard University Press, 1960), pp. 190–93.   136–38. By . . . childhood—some Puritans believed that once a person had professed his faith, he became a child of
God and would never sin again.

ACT I
SCENE IV

[*Enter Wasp, Win.*]

Wasp. By your leave, gentlemen, with all my heart to you,
and God you good morrow. Master Littlewit, my business is to
you. Is this license ready?

Littlewit. Here, I ha' it for you in my hand, Master
Humphrey.   5

Wasp. That's well. Nay, never open or read it to me; it's
labor in vain, you know. I am no clerk, I scorn to be saved by
my book, i' faith I'll hang first. Fold it up o' your word and gi'
it me. What must you ha' for't?

Littlewit. We'll talk of that anon, Master Humphrey.   10

Wasp. Now, or not at all, good Master Proctor; I am for no
anons, I assure you.

2. God you—God give you.   7. clerk—strictly, member of clergy; actually,
any educated man. Jonson himself once escaped hanging by pleading benefit
of clergy.

Littlewit. Sweet Win, bid Solomon send me the little black box within, in my study.

Wasp. Aye, quickly, good mistress, I pray you; for I have   15
both eggs o' the spit, and iron i' the fire. Say what you must
have, good Master Littlewit.   [*Exit Win.*]

Littlewit. Why, you know the price, Master Numps.

Wasp. I know? I know nothing, I. What tell you me of
knowing? Now I am in haste, sir, I do not know, and I will not   20
know, and I scorn to know, and yet (now I think on't) I will
and do know as well as another; you must have a mark for
your thing here, and eightpence for the box. I could ha' saved
twopence i' that, an' I had brought it myself, but here's
fourteen shillings for you. Good Lord, how long your little   25
wife stays! Pray God, Solomon, your clerk, be not looking i'
the wrong box, Master Proctor.

Littlewit. Good i' faith! No. I warrant you, Solomon is
wiser than so, sir.

Wasp. Fie, fie, fie, by your leave, Master Littlewit, this is   30
scurvy, idle, foolish, and abominable; with all my heart, I do
not like it.

Winwife. Do you hear, Jack Littlewit? What business does
thy pretty head think this fellow may have, that he keeps such
a coil with?   35

Quarlous. More than buying of gingerbread i' the Cloister,
here (for that we allow him), or a gilt pouch i' the Fair?

Littlewit. Master Quarlous, do not mistake him. He is his
master's both-hands, I assure you.

Quarlous. What? to pull on his boots, a-mornings, or his   40
stockings, does he?

Littlewit. Sir, if you have a mind to mock him, mock him
softly, and look tother way; for if he apprehend you flout him
once, he will fly at you presently. A terrible testy old fellow,
and his name is Wasp too.   45

Quarlous. Pretty insect! make much on him.

Wasp. A plague o' this box, and the pox too, and on him
that made it, and her that went for't, and all that should ha'
sought it, sent it, or brought it! Do you see, sir?

Littlewit. Nay, good Master Wasp.   50

22. mark—13s. 4d.   34–35. keeps . . . coil—makes a fuss.   36. Cloister—
a shopping district, near the fair.   39. both-hands—a Jonson coinage apparently meaning even more vital than a right-hand man.

Wasp. Good Master Hornet, turd i' your teeth, hold you
your tongue! Do not I know you? Your father was a
'pothecary, and sold glisters, more than he gave, I wusse. And
turd i' your little wife's teeth too—here she comes—'twill make
her spit, as fine as she is, for all her velvet-custard on her head,   55
sir.

[*Re-enter Win.*]

Littlewit. O! be civil, Master Numps.

Wasp. Why, say I have a humor not to be civil; how then?
Who shall compel me? You?

Littlewit. Here is the box now.   60

Wasp. Why a pox o' your box, once again. Let your little
wife stale in it, an' she will. Sir, I would have you to
understand, and these gentlemen too, if they please—

Winwife. With all our hearts, sir.

Wasp. That I have a charge, gentlemen.   65

Littlewit. They do apprehend, sir.

Wasp. Pardon me, sir, neither they nor you can apprehend
me yet. (You are an ass.) I have a young master, he is now
upon his making and marring; the whole care of his well-doing
is now mine. His foolish schoolmasters have done nothing but   70
run up and down the country with him to beg puddings and
cake-bread of his tenants, and almost spoiled him; he has
learned nothing but to sing catches and repeat *Rattle bladder
rattle* and *O Madge*. I dare not let him walk alone for fear of
learning of vile tunes, which he will sing at supper and in the   75
sermon-times! If he meet but a carman i' the street, and I find
him not talk to keep him off on him, he will whistle him and
all his tunes over at night in his sleep! He has a head full of
bees! I am fain now, for this little time I am absent, to leave
him in charge with a gentlewoman. 'Tis true, she's a justice of   80
peace his wife, and a gentlewoman o' the hood, and his natural
sister; but what may happen under a woman's government,
there's the doubt. Gentlemen, you do not know him. He is
another manner of piece than you think for! But nineteen year
old, and yet he is taller than either of you, by the head, God   85
bless him.

53. glisters—enema tubes. I wusse—indeed.   62. stale—urinate (of live-
stock).   71. puddings—sausages.   73–74. *Rattle bladder rattle*—a
tongue twister.   *O Madge*—a ballad.   76. carman—carrier; they were noted
whistlers.   79. fain—obliged.   81. peace his—peace's.

Quarlous. [*To Winwife.*] Well, methinks this is a fine fellow!

Winwife. He has made his master a finer by this description, I should think. 90

Quarlous. 'Faith, much about one; it's cross and pile whether, for a new farthing.

Wasp. I'll tell you, gentlemen—

Littlewit. Will't please you drink, Master Wasp?

Wasp. Why, I ha' not talked so long to be dry, sir. You see 95 no dust or cobwebs come out o' my mouth, do you? You'd ha' me gone, would you?

Littlewit. No, but you were in haste e'en now, Master Numps.

Wasp. What an' I were? So I am still, and yet I will stay 100 too. Meddle you with your match, your Win, there; she has as little wit as her husband, it seems. I have others to talk to.

Littlewit. She's my match indeed, and as little wit as I, good!

Wasp. We ha' been but a day and a half in town, 105 gentlemen, 'tis true; and yesterday i' the afternoon we walked London to show the city to the gentlewoman he shall marry, Mistress Grace; but afore I will endure such another half day with him I'll be drawn with a good gib-cat through the great pond at home, as his uncle Hodge was! Why, we could not 110 meet that heathen thing all day, but stayed him. He would name you all the signs over, as he went, aloud; and where he spied a parrot or a monkey, there he was pitched with all the little long-coats about him, male and female; no getting him away! I thought he would ha' run mad o' the black boy in 115 Bucklersbury that takes the scurvy, roguy tobacco there.

Littlewit. You say true, Master Numps; there's such a one indeed.

Wasp. It's no matter whether there be or no. What's that to you? 120

Quarlous. He will not allow of John's reading at any hand.

---

91. one—the same.   cross and pile—heads or tails.   92. whether—which (of the two).   109. gib-cat—a tomcat; the reference is to a practical joke in which a yokel is bet that a cat can draw him across a pond with a rope. Once the rope is tied to both, the jokesters help the cat and the victim get a ducking.   114. long-coats—children.

ACT I
SCENE V

[*Enter Cokes, Mistress Overdo, Grace.*]

Cokes. O Numps! are you here, Numps? Look where I am,
Numps! And Mistress Grace, too! Nay, do not look angerly,
Numps. My sister is here, and all. I do not come without her.

Wasp. What the mischief, do you come with her? Or she
with you?   5

Cokes. We came all to seek you, Numps.

Wasp. To seek me? Why, did you all think I was lost? Or
run away with your fourteen shillings worth of small ware
here? Or that I had changed it i' the Fair for hobbyhorses?
'Sprecious—to seek me!   10

Mistress Overdo. Nay, good Master Numps, do you show
discretion, though he be exorbitant, as Master Overdo says,
an't be but for conservation of the peace.

Wasp. Marry gip, goody she-justice, Mistress French-hood!
Turd i' your teeth; and turd i' your French-hood's teeth, too,   15
to do you service, do you see? Must you quote your Adam to
me? You think you are Madam Regent still, Mistress Overdo,
when I am in place? No such matter, I assure you; your reign is
out when I am in, dame.

Mistress Overdo. I am content to be in abeyance, sir, and   20
be governed by you; so should he too, if he did well; but 'twill
be expected you should also govern your passions.

Wasp. Will't so forsooth? Good Lord! How sharp you are!
With being at Bedlam yesterday? Whetstone has set an edge
upon you, has he?   25

Mistress Overdo. Nay, if you know not what belongs to
your dignity, I do, yet, to mine.

Wasp. Very well, then.

Cokes. Is this the license, Numps? For love's sake, let me
see't. I never saw a license.   30

Wasp. Did you not so? Why, you shall not see't, then.

Cokes. An' you love me, good Numps.

Wasp. Sir, I love you, and yet I do not love you, i' these

10. 'Sprecious—by God's precious blood.   14. Marry gip—an oath, by St.
Mary of Egypt.   24. Whetstone—a keeper at Bedlam Hospital whose name
was used for the sake of the pun (?).

fooleries; set your heart at rest; there's nothing in't but hard
words; and what would you see't for?   35

Cokes. I would see the length and the breadth on't, that's
all; and I will see't now, so I will.

Wasp. You sha' not see it here.

Cokes. Then I'll see't at home, and I'll look upo' the case
here.   40

Wasp. Why, do so; [*Shows the box.*] a man must give way
to him a little in trifles, gentlemen: these are errors, diseases of
youth, which he will mend when he comes to judgment and
knowledge of matters. I pray you conceive so, and I thank
you. And I pray you pardon him, and I thank you again.   45

Quarlous. Well, this dry nurse, I say still, is a delicate man.

Winwife. And I am for the cosset, his charge! Did you ever
see a fellow's face more accuse him for an ass?

Quarlous. Accuse him? It confesses him one without
accusing. What pity 'tis yonder wench should marry such a   50
cokes!

Winwife. 'Tis true.

Quarlous. She seems to be discreet, and as sober as she is
handsome.

Winwife. Aye, and if you mark her, what a restrained   55
scorn she casts upon all his behavior and speeches!

Cokes. Well, Numps, I am now for another piece of
business more, the Fair, Numps, and then—

Wasp. Bless me! deliver me, help, hold me! the Fair!

Cokes. Nay, never fidge up and down, Numps, and vex   60
itself. I am resolute Barthol'mew, in this; I'll make no suit on't
to you; 'twas all the end of my journey, indeed, to show
Mistress Grace my Fair. I call't my Fair because of
Barthol'mew: you know my name is Barthol'mew, and
Barthol'mew Fair.   65

Littlewit. That was mine afore, gentlemen—this morning. I
had that i' faith, upon his license; believe me, there he comes
after me.

Quarlous. Come, John, this ambitious wit of yours, I am
afraid, will do you no good i' the end.   70

Littlewit. No? Why, sir?

Quarlous. You grow so insolent with it, and overdoing,

47. cosset—spoiled child.

John, that if you look not to it, and tie it up, it will bring you
to some obscure place in time, and there 'twill leave you.

    Winwife. Do not trust it too much, John; be more sparing,   75
and use it but now and then. A wit is a dangerous thing in this
age; do not overbuy it.

    Littlewit. Think you so, gentlemen? I'll take heed on't
hereafter.

    Win. Yes, do, John.   80

    Cokes. A pretty little soul, this same Mistress Littlewit!
Would I might marry her.

    Grace. [*Aside.*] So would I, or anybody else, so I might
'scape you.

    Cokes. Numps, I will see it, Numps, 'tis decreed. Never be   85
melancholy for the matter.

    Wasp. Why, see it, sir, do see it! Who hinders you? Why do
you not go see it? 'Slid, see it.

    Cokes. The Fair, Numps, the Fair.

    Wasp. Would the Fair and all the drums and rattles in't   90
were i' your belly for me! They are already i' your brain; he
that had the means to travel your head, now, should meet
finer sights than any are i' the Fair, and make a finer voyage
on't, to see it all hung with cockle-shells, pebbles, fine
wheat-straws, and here and there a chicken's feather and a   95
cobweb.

    Quarlous. Good faith, he looks, methinks, an' you mark
him, like one that were made to catch flies, with his Sir
Cranion legs.

    Winwife. And his Numps to flap 'em away.   100

    Wasp. God be w'you, sir. There's your bee in a box, and
much good do't you.   [*Gives him the box and starts to leave.*]

    Cokes. Why, your friend, and Barthol'mew, an' you be so
contumacious.

    Quarlous. What mean you, Numps?   105

    Wasp. I'll not be guilty, I, gentlemen.

    Mistress Overdo. You will not let him go, brother, and
lose him?

    Cokes. Who can hold that will away? I had rather lose him
than the Fair, I wusse.   110

    Wasp. You do not know the inconvenience, gentlemen,

---

77. overbuy—pay too much for.   98–99. Sir Cranion legs—daddy longlegs.

you persuade to; nor what trouble I have with him in these
humors. If he go to the Fair, he will buy of everything to a
baby there; and household-stuff for that too. If a leg or an arm
on him did not grow on, he would lose it i' the press. Pray   115
heaven I bring him off with one stone! And then he is such a
ravener after fruit! You will not believe what a coil I had
t'other day to compound a business between a Cather'ne-pear-
woman and him about snatching! 'Tis intolerable, gentlemen.
    Winwife. O! but you must not leave him now to these   120
hazards, Numps.
    Wasp. Nay, he knows too well I will not leave him, and
that makes him presume. Well, sir, will you go now? If you
have such an itch i' your feet to foot it to the Fair, why do
you stop? Am I your tarriers? Go, will you go, sir? Why do   125
you not go?
    Cokes. O Numps! have I brought you about? Come,
Mistress Grace, and sister, I am resolute Bat, i' faith, still.
    Grace. Truly, I have no such fancy to the Fair, nor
ambition to see it; there's none goes thither of any quality or   130
fashion.
    Cokes. O Lord, sir! You shall pardon me, Mistress Grace,
we are enow of ourselves to make it a fashion; and for
qualities, let Numps alone, he'll find qualities.
              [*Exeunt Cokes, Wasp, Grace, Mistress Overdo.*]
    Quarlous. What a rogue in apprehension is this, to   135
understand her language no better!
    Winwife. Aye, and offer to marry to her! Well, I will leave
the chase of my widow for today, and directly to the Fair.
These flies cannot, this hot season, but engender us excellent
creeping sport.   140
    Quarlous. A man that has but a spoonful of brain would
think so. Farewell, John.   [*Exeunt Quarlous, Winwife.*]
    Littlewit. Win, you see 'tis in fashion to go to the Fair,
Win. We must to the Fair too, you and I, Win. I have an affair
i' the Fair, Win, a puppet play of mine own making—say   145
nothing—that I writ for the motion-man, which you must see,
Win.

116. stone—testicle.   125. Am . . . tarriers?—am I holding you back?
130. quality—high social rank.   134. qualities—attributes of worth or the
lack of it (see III.iv.106–108).   146. motion-man—puppet-master.

Win. I would I might, John, but my mother will never consent to such a "profane motion," she will call it.

Littlewit. Tut, we'll have a device, a dainty one (now, 150 Wit, help at a pinch, good Wit come, come, good Wit, an't be thy will). I have it, Win, I have it i' faith, and 'tis a fine one. Win, long to eat of a pig, sweet Win, i' the Fair; do you see? I' the heart o' the Fair; not at Pie-corner. Your mother will do anything, Win, to satisfy your longing, you know; pray thee 155 long, presently, and be sick o' the sudden, good Win. I'll go in and tell her. Cut thy lace i' the meantime, and play the hypocrite, sweet Win.

Win. No, I'll not make me unready for it. I can be hypocrite enough, though I were never so strait-laced. 160

Littlewit. You say true. You have been bred i' the family, and brought up to't. Our mother is a most elect hypocrite, and has maintained us all this seven year with it, like gentlefolks.

Win. Aye, let her alone, John; she is not a wise wilful widow for nothing, nor a sanctified sister for a song. And let 165 me alone too; I ha' somewhat o' the mother in me, you shall see. Fetch her, fetch her. Ah ah!

> [*Exit Littlewit.*]

159. make me unready—undress.   160. strait-laced—(1) laced tightly, (2) puritanical.   166. the mother—(1) she is in fact pregnant, (2) she can imitate her own hypocritical mother, (3) the mother was the common name for a diseased swelling of the womb called hysteria.

ACT I
SCENE VI

> [*Enter Purecraft, Littlewit.*]

Purecraft. Now the blaze of the beauteous discipline fright away this evil from our house! How now, Win-the-fight, child, how do you? Sweet child, speak to me.

Win. Yes, forsooth.

Purecraft. Look up, sweet Win-the-fight, and suffer not 5 the enemy to enter you at this door; remember that your education has been with the purest. What polluted one was it that named first the unclean beast, pig, to you, child?

Win. Uh, uh!

Littlewit. Not I, o' my sincerity, mother. She longed   10
above three hours ere she would let me know it. Who was it,
Win?

Win. A profane black thing with a beard, John.

Purecraft. O! resist it, Win-the-fight, it is the Tempter, the
wicked Tempter; you may know it by the fleshly motion of   15
pig. Be strong against it, and its foul temptations, in these
assaults, whereby it broacheth flesh and blood, as it were, on
the weaker side; and pray against its carnal provocations, good
child, sweet child, pray.

Littlewit. Good mother, I pray you that she may eat some   20
pig, and her belly full, too; and do not you cast away your
own child, and perhaps one of mine, with your tale of the
Tempter. How do you, Win? Are you not sick?

Win. Yes, a great deal, John. Uh, uh!

Purecraft. What shall we do? Call our zealous brother   25
Busy hither, for his faithful fortification in this charge of the
adversary; child, my dear child, you shall eat pig, be
comforted, my sweet child.   [*Exit Littlewit.*]

Win. Aye, but i' the Fair, mother.

Purecraft. I mean i' the Fair, if it can be any way made or   30
found lawful. Where is our brother Busy? Will he not come?
Look up, child.

[*Re-enter Littlewit.*]

Littlewit. Presently, mother, as soon as he has cleansed his
beard. I found him fast by the teeth i' the cold turkey-pie i'
the cupboard, with a great white loaf on his left hand, and a   35
glass of malmsey on his right.

Purecraft. Slander not the brethren, wicked one.

Littlewit. Here he is now, purified, mother.

[*Enter Busy.*]

Purecraft. O Brother Busy! your help here to edify and
raise us up in a scruple. My daughter Win-the-fight is visited   40
with a natural disease of woman, called "A longing to eat pig."

Littlewit. Aye sir, a Barthol'mew-pig, and in the Fair.

Purecraft. And I would be satisfied from you, religiously-
wise, whether a widow of the sanctified assembly, or a
widow's daughter, may commit the act without offence to the   45
weaker sisters.

Busy. Verily, for the disease of longing, it is a disease, a

carnal disease, or appetite, incident to woman; and as it is
carnal, and incident, it is natural, very natural. Now pig, it is a
meat, and a meat that is nourishing, and may be longed for,   50
and so consequently eaten; it may be eaten; very exceeding
well eaten. But in the Fair, and as a Barthol'mew-pig, it cannot
be eaten, for the very calling it a Barthol'mew-pig, and to eat it
so, is a spice of idolatry, and you make the Fair no better than
one of the high places. This, I take it, is the state of the   55
question. A high place.

    Littlewit. Aye, but in state of necessity, place should give
place, Master Busy. (I have a conceit left, yet.)

    Purecraft. Good Brother Zeal-of-the-land, think to make it
as lawful as you can.   60

    Littlewit. Yes sir, and as soon as you can; for it must be,
sir; you see the danger my little wife is in, sir.

    Purecraft. Truly, I do love my child dearly, and I would
not have her miscarry, or hazard his first fruits, if it might be
otherwise.   65

    Busy. Surely it may be otherwise, but it is subject to
construction, subject, and hath a face of offence with the
weak, a great face, a foul face, but that face may have a veil
put over it, and be shadowed, as it were. It may be eaten, and
in the Fair, I take it, in a booth, the tents of the wicked. The   70
place is not much, not very much; we may be religious in
midst of the profane, so it be eaten with a reformed mouth,
with sobriety, and humbleness; not gorged in with gluttony or
greediness; there's the fear: for, should she go there, as taking
pride in the place, or delight in the unclean dressing, to feed   75
the vanity of the eye or the lust of the palate, it were not well,
it were not fit, it were abominable, and not good.

    Littlewit. Nay, I knew that afore, and told her on't; but
courage, Win, we'll be humble enough; we'll seek out the
homeliest booth i' the Fair, that's certain. Rather than fail,   80
we'll eat it o' the ground.

    Purecraft. Aye, and I'll go with you myself, Win-the-fight,
and my brother Zeal-of-the-land shall go with us too, for our
better consolation.

54. spice—touch, trace, dash (*OED*) idolatry—"because of the use of saint's
name" (Waith).   55. high places—site of heathen idols in the Old Testament
(e.g., *Lev.* 26:30).

Win. Uh, uh! 85

Littlewit. Aye, and Solomon, too, Win; the more the merrier, Win; [*Aside to Win.*] we'll leave Rabbi Busy in a booth—Solomon, my cloak.

[*Enter Solomon.*]

Solomon. Here, sir.

Busy. In the way of comfort to the weak, I will go and 90 eat. I will eat exceedingly and prophesy; there may be a good use made of it, too, now I think on't: by the public eating of swine's flesh, to profess our hate and loathing of Judaism, whereof the brethren stand taxed. I will therefore eat, yea, I will eat exceedingly. 95

Littlewit. Good, i' faith, I will eat heartily too, because I will be no Jew; I could never away with that stiff-necked generation. And truly, I hope my little one will be like me, that cries for pig so, i' the mother's belly.

Busy. Very likely, exceeding likely, very exceeding likely. 100

[*Exeunt.*]

94. stand taxed—on account of their emphasis on the Old Testament.
97. away with—bear, tolerate.

ACT II

SCENE I

[*The Fair.*]

[*Enter Justice Overdo, disguised as mad Arthur of Bradley.*]

Overdo. Well, in justice' name, and the King's, and for the commonwealth! defy all the world, Adam Overdo, for a disguise, and all story; for thou hast fitted thyself, I swear. Fain would I meet the Lynceus now, that eagle's eye, that

S.D. Waith argues persuasively that during this soliloquy Leatherhead and Trash probably enter and set up their stands (see Yale *Bartholomew Fair*, p. 211). The 1969 Royal Shakespeare production had Overdo speak his lines while donning his disguise, but the text implies that he has already donned it (lines 3–7). 4. Lynceus—argonaut famed for keen sight.

piercing Epidaurian serpent (as my Quintus Horace calls him),   5
that could discover a justice of peace (and lately of the
quorum) under this covering. They may have seen many a fool
in the habit of a justice; but never till now a justice in the
habit of a fool. Thus must we do, though, that wake for the
public good; and thus hath the wise magistrate done in all ages.   10
There is a doing of right out of wrong, if the way be found.
Never shall I enough commend a worthy worshipful man,
sometime a capital member of this city, for his high wisdom in
this point, who would take you, now the habit of a porter,
now of a carman, now of the dog-killer, in this month of   15
August; and in the winter of a seller of tinder-boxes. And what
would he do in all these shapes? Marry, go you into every
ale-house, and down into every cellar; measure the length of
puddings, take the gauge of black pots and cans, aye, and
custards, with a stick; and their circumference, with a thread;   20
weigh the loaves of bread on his middle-finger; then would he
send for 'em, home; give the puddings to the poor, the bread
to the hungry, the custards to his children; break the pots and
burn the cans himself; he would not trust his corrupt officers;
he would do't himself. Would all men in authority would   25
follow this worthy precedent! For alas, as we are public
persons, what do we know? Nay, what can we know? We hear
with other men's ears; we see with other men's eyes. A foolish
constable or a sleepy watchman is all our information; he
slanders a gentleman by the virtue of his place, as he calls it,   30
and we, by the vice of ours, must believe him. As, a while
gone, they made me, yea me, to mistake an honest zealous

---

5. Epidaurian serpent—from Horace, *Satires*, I.iii. where the context is rele-
vant to Overdo's character: "When you look over your own sins, your eyes
are rheumy and daubed with ointment; why, when you view the failings of
your friends, are you as keen of sight as an eagle or as a serpent of Epidaurus?
But, on the other hand, the result for you is that they, too, in turn peer into
your faults" (lines 25–28, trans. H. R. Fairclough).   7. quorum—justices
whose presence was required because of their learning or ability.   13. capital—head, chief; possibly a reference to Sir Thomas Hayes, Lord Mayor of London in 1614, who disguised himself to discover wrongdoing in alehouses.
15. dog-killer . . . August—strays were killed to inhibit plague, especially in
summer.   22. 'em—the culprits.   home—hit 'em where they live.
26. precedent—spelled *president* in folio as it often was at this time; the context would admit a pun: (1) precedent, (2) president, i.e., magistrate.

pursuivant for a seminary, and a proper young Bachelor of
Music for a bawd. This we are subject to, that live in high
place; all our intelligence is idle, and most of our intelligencers   35
knaves; and, by your leave, ourselves thought little better, if
not arrant fools, for believing 'em. I, Adam Overdo, am
resolved therefore to spare spy-money hereafter, and make
mine own discoveries. Many are the yearly enormities of this
Fair, in whose courts of Pie-powders I have had the honor   40
during the three days sometimes to sit as judge. But this is the
special day for detection of those foresaid enormities. Here is
my black book for the purpose; this the cloud that hides me;
under this covert I shall see and not be seen. On, Junius
Brutus! And as I began so I'll end: in justice' name, and the   45
King's; and for the commonwealth!

33. pursuivant—warrant-server for ecclesiastical courts.   seminary—Catholic
priests trained on the Continent, who were often accused of being spies.
40. Pie-powders—temporary court specifically for the fair.   44–45. Junius
Brutus—ancient Roman who once disguised himself as an idiot, and who,
by sentencing his own sons to death, gained a reputation as a severe judge.

ACT II

SCENE II

[*Leatherhead and Joan Trash at their booths.*]
Leatherhead. The Fair's pest'lence dead, methinks; people
come not abroad today, whatever the matter is. Do you hear,
Sister Trash, Lady o' the Basket? Sit farther with your
gingerbread-progeny there, and hinder not the prospect of my
shop, or I'll ha' it proclaimed i' the Fair what stuff they are   5
made on.
    Trash. Why, what stuff are they made on, Brother
Leatherhead? Nothing but what's wholesome, I assure you.
    Leatherhead. Yes, stale bread, rotten eggs, musty ginger,
and dead honey, you know.   10

S.D. *at their booths*—see note to stage direction at beginning of II.i.
1. pest'lence dead—dead because of the plague, which had actually caused the
closing of the fair in 1603.

Overdo. [*Aside.*] Aye! have I met with enormity so soon?

Leatherhead. I shall mar your market, old Joan.

Trash. Mar my market, thou too-proud pedlar? Do thy
worst; I defy thee, I, and thy stable of hobbyhorses. I pay for
my ground as well as thou dost; an' thou wrong'st me, for all   15
thou art parcel-poet and an inginer, I'll find a friend shall right
me and make a ballad of thee and thy cattel all over. Are you
puffed up with the pride of your wares? Your arsedine?

Leatherhead. Go to, old Joan, I'll talk with you anon; and
take you down too afore Justice Overdo; he is the man must   20
charm you. I'll ha' you i' the Pie-powders.

Trash. Charm me? I'll meet thee face to face afore his
worship when thou dar'st; and though I be a little crooked o'
my body, I'll be found as upright in my dealing as any woman
in Smithfield, I; charm me?   25

Overdo. [*Aside.*] I am glad to hear my name is their
terror, yet; this is doing of justice.

[*Enter Passengers.*]

Leatherhead. What do you lack? What is't you buy? What
do you lack? Rattles, drums, halberts, horses, babies o' the
best? Fiddles o' th' finest?   30

[*Enter Costermonger (and Nightingale).*]

Costermonger. Buy any pears, pears, fine, very fine pears!

Trash. Buy any gingerbread, gilt gingerbread.

Nightingale.   *Hey, now the Fair's a filling!*
          O, for a tune to startle
          The birds o' the booths here billing   35
          Yearly with old Saint Bartle!
          The drunkards they are wading,
          The punks and chapmen trading;
          Who'd see the Fair without his lading?
Buy any ballads; new ballads?   40

[*Exeunt Passengers, Costermonger.*]
[*Enter Ursula from the back part of her booth.*]

Ursula. Fie upon't: who would wear out their youth and
prime thus in roasting of pigs, that had any cooler vocation?
Hell's a kind of cold cellar to't, a very fine vault, o' my
conscience! What, Mooncalf!

16. parcel-poet—part-time poet.   inginer—puppeteer.   17. cattel—chattle,
property.   18. arsedine—imitation goldleaf, used to ornament toys.
32. gilt—"gold leaf was used to decorate ginger bread" (Horsman).

Mooncalf. [*Within.*] Here, Mistress.   45

Nightingale. How now, Urs'la? In a heat, in a heat?

Ursula. [*To Mooncalf.*] My chair, you false faucet you;
and my morning's draught, quickly, a bottle of ale to quench
me, rascal. I am all fire and fat, Nightingale; I shall e'en melt
away to the first woman, a rib again, I am afraid. I do water   50
the ground in knots as I go, like a great garden-pot; you may
follow me by the S's I make.

Nightingale. Alas, good Urs; was 'Zekiel here this
morning?

Ursula. 'Zekiel? what 'Zekiel?   55

Nightingale. 'Zekiel Edgworth, the civil cutpurse; you
know him well enough: he that talks bawdy to you still. I call
him my secretary.

Ursula. He promised to be here this morning, I remember.

Nightingale. When he comes, bid him stay. I'll be back   60
again presently.

Ursula. Best take your morning's dew in your belly,
Nightingale. (*Mooncalf brings in the chair.*) Come, sir, set it
here. Did not I bid you should get this chair let out o' the sides
for me, that my hips might play? You'll never think of   65
anything till your dame be rump-galled. 'Tis well, changeling;
because it can take in your grasshopper's thighs you care for
no more. Now you look as you had been i' the corner o' the
booth, fleaing your breech with a candle's end, and set fire o'
the Fair. Fill, stote, fill.   70

Overdo. [*Aside.*] This pig-woman do I know, and I will
put her in for my second enormity; she hath been before me,
punk, pinnace, and bawd, any time these two and twenty
years, upon record i' the Pie-powders.

Ursula. Fill again, you unlucky vermin.   75

Mooncalf. Pray you be not angry, mistress; I'll ha' it
widened anon.

---

47. faucet—so called because he is a tapster and because he is as thin as a tap
(for a barrel).   51. knots—lines crisscrossing each other.   garden-pot—
sprinkling can.   58. secretary—confidant.   66. galled—chafed. changeling—"a child (usually stupid or ugly) supposed to have been left by fairies to
exchange for one stolen" (*OED*).   69. fleaing—driving out fleas with a
burning candle (?).   breech—rump, buttocks.   70. stote—stupid person or
perhaps stoat, a weasel, alluding to Mooncalf's thinness.   73. pinnace—a
fast ship; hence, go-between, bawd.

Ursula. No, no, I shall e'en dwindle away to't, ere the Fair be done, you think, now you ha' heated me! A poor vexed thing I am. I feel myself dropping already, as fast as I can; two   80
stone o' suet a day is my proportion. I can but hold life and soul together with this (here's to you, Nightingale) and a whiff of tobacco, at most. Where's my pipe now? Not filled? Thou arrant incubee!

Nightingale. Nay, Urs'la, thou'lt gall between the tongue   85
and the teeth with fretting, now.

Ursula. How can I hope that ever he'll discharge his place of trust—tapster, a man of reckoning under me—that remembers nothing I say to him? [*Exit Nightingale.*] But look to't, sirrah, you were best; threepence a pipeful I will ha' made of   90
all my whole half-pound of tobacco, and a quarter of a pound of coltsfoot mixed with it too, to itch it out. I that have dealt so long in the fire will not be to seek in smoke, now. Then, six and twenty shillings a barrel I will advance o' my beer, and fifty shillings a hundred o' my bottle-ale; I ha' told you the   95
ways how to raise it. Froth your cans well i' the filling, at length, rogue, and jog your bottles o' the buttock, sirrah, then skink out the first glass, ever, and drink with all companies, though you be sure to be drunk; you'll misreckon the better, and be less ashamed on't. But your true trick, rascal, must be   100
to be ever busy, and mis-take away the bottles and cans in haste before they be half drunk off, and never hear anybody call (if they should chance to mark you) till you ha' brought fresh, and be able to forswear 'em. Give me a drink of ale.

Overdo. [*Aside.*] This is the very womb and bed of   105
enormity! gross as herself! This must all down for enormity, all, every whit on't.   *One knocks.*

Ursula. Look who's there, sirrah! Five shillings a pig is my price, at least; if it be a sow-pig, sixpence more; if she be a great-bellied wife, and long for't, sixpence more for that.   110

80–81. two stone . . . proportion—I'm losing twenty-eight pounds of fat per day.   84. incubee—small incubus, "little devil."   88. man of reckoning—(1) one who totals up the customers' bills, (2) man to be reckoned with.   92. coltsfoot—an herb used to adulterate tobacco.   itch—"to augment, increase" (*OED*).   93. to seek—"wanting or deficient" (*OED*).   94. advance—hike the price.   98. skink—pour.   107. *One knocks*—Overdo, who must have been lurking at the side of the booth's opening, out of Ursula's view.

Overdo. [*Aside.*] *O tempora! O mores!* I would not ha'
lost my discovery of this one grievance for my place and
worship o' the bench. How is the poor subject abused here!
Well, I will fall in with her, and with her Mooncalf, and win
out wonders of enormity. [*To Ursula.*] By thy leave, goodly   115
woman, and the fatness of the Fair, oily as the King's
constable's lamp, and shining as his shoeing-horn! Hath thy ale
virtue, or thy beer strength? that the tongue of man may be
tickled? and his palate pleased in the morning? Let thy pretty
nephew here go search and see.   120

Ursula. What new roarer is this?

Mooncalf. O Lord! do you not know him, mistress? 'Tis
mad Arthur of Bradley, that makes the orations. Brave master,
old Arthur of Bradley, how do you? Welcome to the Fair!
When shall we hear you again, to handle your matters? With   125
your back again a booth, ha? I ha' been one o' your little
disciples i' my days!

Overdo. Let me drink, boy, with my love, thy aunt, here,
that I may be eloquent; but of thy best, lest it be bitter in my
mouth, and my words fall foul on the Fair.   130

Ursula. Why dost thou not fetch him drink? And offer
him to sit?

Mooncalf. Is't ale or beer, Master Arthur?

Overdo. Thy best, pretty stripling, thy best; the same thy
dove drinketh and thou drawest on holy days.   135

Ursula. Bring him a sixpenny bottle of ale; they say a
fool's handsel is lucky.

Overdo. Bring both, child. Ale for Arthur and beer for
Bradley. Ale for thy aunt, boy. [*Exit Mooncalf.*] [*Aside.*] My
disguise takes to the very wish and reach of it. I shall, by the   140
benefit of this, discover enough and more, and yet get off with
the reputation of what I would be: a certain middling thing
between a fool and a madman.

---

111. *O tempora! O mores!*—"Oh the times and the customs!" (Cicero,
"against Catiline," I.i.2; Jonson had dramatized this speech in all seriousness
in *Catiline*, IV.i.190).   126. again—against.   137. handsel—first
money received each day.

ACT II
SCENE III

[*Enter Knockem.*]

Knockem. What! my little lean Urs'la! my she-bear! art thou alive yet, with thy litter of pigs, to grunt out another Barthol'mew Fair, ha?

Ursula. Yes, and to amble afoot, when the Fair is done, to hear you groan out of a cart, up the heavy hill.   5

Knockem. Of Holborn, Urs'la, meanst thou so? For what? For what, pretty Urs?

Ursula. For cutting halfpenny purses, or stealing little penny dogs out o' the Fair.

Knockem. O! good words, good words, Urs.   10

Overdo. [*Aside.*] Another special enormity. A cutpurse of the sword, the boot, and the feather! Those are his marks.

[*Re-enter Mooncalf.*]

Ursula. You are one of those horse-leeches that gave out I was dead in Turnbull Street of a surfeit of bottle-ale and tripes?   15

Knockem. No, 'twas better meat, Urs: cow's udders, cow's udders!

Ursula. Well, I shall be meet with your mumbling mouth one day.

Knockem. What? Thou'lt poison me with a newt in a   20
bottle of ale, wilt thou? Or a spider in a tobacco-pipe, Urs? Come, there's no malice in these fat folks. I never fear thee, an' I can 'scape thy lean Mooncalf here. Let's drink it out, good Urs, and no vapors!   [*Exit Ursula.*]

Overdo. Dost thou hear, boy? (There's for thy ale, and the   25
remnant for thee.) Speak in thy faith of a faucet, now; is this goodly person before us here, this vapors, a knight of the knife?

---

1. she-bear—Latin *ursa*, "bear"; Ursula is a diminutive.   5. heavy hill—
Holborn hill, part of the route from Newgate Prison to Tyburn gallows.
13. horse-leeches—(1) horse-doctors, (2) bloodsuckers.   18. meet—even.
22. fat folks—Jonson described himself as fat in 1619.   27. vapors—a key
word. In general it seems to mean a spirit that leads one to contradict or
otherwise insult another, but Knockem uses it to mean almost anything he
chooses (e.g., "good vapors" at the end of this scene).

    Mooncalf. What mean you by that, Master Arthur?

    Overdo. I mean a child of the horn-thumb, a babe of   30
booty, boy; a cutpurse.

    Mooncalf. O Lord, sir! far from it. This is Master Dan
Knockem—Jordan, the ranger of Turnbull. He is a horse-
courser, sir.

    Overdo. Thy dainty dame, though, called him a cutpurse.   35

    Mooncalf. Like enough, sir. She'll do forty such things in
an hour (an' you listen to her) for her recreation, if the toy
take her i' the greasy kerchief. It makes her fat, you see. She
battens with it.

    Overdo. [*Aside.*] Here might I ha' been deceived, now,   40
and ha' put a fool's blot upon myself, if I had not played an
after-game o' discretion.

                         Ursula comes in again dropping.

    Knockem. Alas, poor Urs, this's an ill season for thee.

    Ursula. Hang yourself, hackney-man.

    Knockem. How, how, Urs? vapors? motion breed vapors?   45

    Ursula. Vapors? Never tusk nor twirl your dibble, good
Jordan; I know what you'll take to a very drop. Though you
be captain o' the roarers, and fight well at the case of piss-pots,
you shall not fright me with your lion-chap, sir, nor your
tusks. You angry? You are hungry. Come, a pig's head will   50
stop your mouth and stay your stomach at all times.

    Knockem. Thou art such another mad merry Urs still!
Troth, I do make conscience of vexing thee now i' the
dog-days, this hot weather, for fear of found'ring thee i' the
body, and melting down a pillar of the Fair. Pray thee take thy   55
chair again, and keep state; and let's have a fresh bottle of ale
and a pipe of tobacco; and no vapors. I'll ha' this belly o' thine
taken up and thy grass scoured, wench. Look! here's Ezekiel
Edgworth, a fine boy of his inches as any is i' the Fair! Has
still money in his purse, and will pay all with a kind heart; and   60
good vapors.

---

30. horn-thumb—horn thimble to protect the thumb while cutting a purse.
46. tusk . . . dibble—stroke your beard into a sharp point (a fashion affected
by toughs).   49. chap—jaw.   54. found'ring—of a horse, allowing it to
drink too much when overheated.   56. keep state—like a queen on the
throne, holding formal audience.   58. grass scoured—purging the belly of
grass, a veterinary term.

ACT II

SCENE IV

[*Enter Edgworth, Nightingale, Corncutter,
                              Tinderbox-man, Passengers.*]

Edgworth. That I will, indeed, willingly, Master Knockem;
[*To Mooncalf.*] fetch some ale and tobacco. [*Exit Mooncalf.*]

Leatherhead. What do you lack, gentlemen? Maid, see a
fine hobbyhorse for your young master; cost you but a token
a week his provender.   5

Corncutter. Ha' you any corns i' your feet and toes?

Tinderbox-man. Buy a mousetrap, a mousetrap, or a
tormentor for a flea.

Trash. Buy some gingerbread.

Nightingale.   *Ballads, ballads! fine new ballads:*   10
                  Hear for your love and buy for your money!
                  *A delicate ballad o' "The Ferret and the
                     Coney."*
                  "A Preservative again the Punks' Evil."
                  Another of "Goose-green Starch and the   15
                     Devil."
                  *"A Dozen of Divine Points" and "The
                     Godly Garters."*
                  *"The Fairing of Good Counsel," of an ell
                     and three quarters.*   20

What is't you buy?

                  *"The Windmill blown down by the witch's
                     fart!"*
                  *Or "Saint George, that O! did break the
                     dragon's heart!"*   25

[*Re-enter Mooncalf.*]

Edgworth. Master Nightingale, come hither, leave your
mart a little.

[*Exeunt Passengers, Corncutter, Tinderbox-man.*]

---

1. That I will—pay all, as Knockem has just suggested.   8. tormentor—
trap.   12,13. *Ferret, Coney*—swindler and dupe in thieves' jargon.
15. *Goose-green*—"yellowish green, a fashionable color, inelegantly called
goose-turd green" (Waith).   17. *Divine Points*—(1) moral maxims,
(2) heavenly suspenders (cf. "*Godly garters*").   19. *ell*—forty-five inches;
implying that its length makes it a good buy.

Nightingale. O my secretary! What says my secretary?

Overdo. Child o' the bottles, what's he? what's he?

Mooncalf. A civil young gentleman, Master Arthur, that 30
keeps company with the roarers and disburses all, still. He has
ever money in his purse; he pays for them, and they roar for
him: one does good offices for another. They call him the
secretary, but he serves nobody. A great friend of the
ballad-man's—they are never asunder. 35

Overdo. What pity 'tis so civil a young man should haunt
this debauched company! Here's the bane of the youth of our
time apparent. A proper penman, I see't in his countenance; he
has a good clerk's look with him, and I warrant him a quick
hand. 40

Mooncalf. A very quick hand, sir. [*Exit.*]

Edgworth. [*To Nightingale.*] All the purses *This*
and purchase I give you today by conveyance, *they*
bring hither to Urs'la's presently. Here we will *whisper,*
meet at night in her lodge, and share. Look you *that* 45
choose good places for your standing i' the Fair *Overdo*
when you sing, Nightingale. *hears*

Ursula. Aye, near the fullest passages; and *it*
shift em often. *not.*

Edgworth. And i' your singing you must use your hawk's 50
eye nimbly, and fly the purse to a mark still—where 'tis worn
and o' which side—that you may gi' me the sign with your
beak, or hang your head that way i' the tune.

Ursula. Enough, talk no more on't. Your friendship,
masters, is not now to begin. Drink your draught of indenture, 55
your sup of covenant, and away. The Fair fills apace, company
begins to come in, and I ha' ne'er a pig ready yet.

Knockem. Well said! Fill the cups and light the tobacco.
Let's give fire i' th' works and noble vapors.

Edgworth. And shall we ha' smocks, Urs'la, and good 60
whimsies, ha?

Ursula. Come, you are i' your bawdy vein! The best the
Fair will afford, 'Zekiel, if bawd Whit keep his word.

[*Re-enter Mooncalf.*]

How do the pigs, Mooncalf?

---

43. purchase—booty.   51. fly . . . mark—falconry term for a hawk's halting just where prey disappeared.   60–61. smocks, whimsies—whores.

Mooncalf. Very passionate, mistress; one on 'em has wept   65
out an eye. Master Arthur o' Bradley is melancholy, here;
nobody talks to him. Will you any tobacco, Master Arthur?

Overdo. No, boy, let my meditations alone.

Mooncalf. He's studying for an oration, now.

Overdo. [*Aside.*] If I can, with this day's travail, and all   70
my policy, but rescue this youth here out of the hands of the
lewd man and the strange woman, I will sit down at night and
say with my friend Ovid, *Iamque opus exegi, quod nec Iovis
ira, nec ignis, etc.*

Knockem. Here, 'Zekiel; here's a health to Urs'la, and a   75
kind vapor. Thou hast money i' thy purse still; and store! How
dost thou come by it? Pray thee vapor thy friends some in a
courteous vapor.   [*Exit Ursula.*]

Edgworth. Half I have, Master Dan Knockem, is always at
your service.   80

Overdo. [*Aside.*] Ha, sweet nature! What goshawk would
prey upon such a lamb?

Knockem. Let's see what 'tis, 'Zekiel! Count it, come, fill
him to pledge me.   [*Edgworth starts counting his money.*]

65–66. wept out an eye—sign that a roasting pig was almost done.
72. strange woman—biblical phrase for harlot.   73–74. *Iamque . . . etc.*—
does the *etc.* indicate that Overdo has forgotten the rest of the quotation?
The entire passage runs: "And now my work is done, which neither the wrath
of Jove, nor fire, nor sword, nor the gnawing tooth of time shall ever be able
to undo" (*Metamorphoses* XV, 871–72, trans. F. J. Miller).

ACT II

SCENE V

[*Enter Winwife, Quarlous.*]

Winwife. We are here before 'em, methinks.

Quarlous. All the better; we shall see 'em come in now.

Leatherhead. What do you lack, gentlemen, what is't you
lack? A fine horse? A lion? A bull? A bear? A dog, or a cat?
An excellent fine Barthol'mew-bird? Or an instrument? What   5
is't you lack?

Quarlous. 'Slid! here's Orpheus among the beasts, with his
fiddle and all!

Trash. Will you buy any comfortable bread, gentlemen?

Quarlous. And Ceres selling her daughter's picture in   10
ginger-work!

Winwife. That these people should be so ignorant to think
us chapmen for 'em! Do we look as if we would buy
gingerbread? Or hobbyhorses?

Quarlous. Why, they know no better ware than they have,   15
nor better customers than come. And our very being here
makes us fit to be demanded, as well as others. Would Cokes
would come! There were a true customer for 'em.

Knockem. [*To Edgworth.*] How much is't? Thirty shillings? Who's yonder? Ned Winwife? and Tom Quarlous, I   20
think! Yes. (Gi' me it all, gi' me it all.) Master Winwife! Master
Quarlous! Will you take a pipe of tobacco with us? (Do not
discredit me now, 'Zekiel.)

Winwife. Do not see him! He is the roaring horse-courser.
Pray thee let's avoid him; turn down this way.   25

Quarlous. 'Slood, I'll see him, and roar with him too, an'
he roared as loud as Neptune; pray thee go with me.

Winwife. You may draw me to as likely an inconvenience,
when you please, as this.

Quarlous. Go to then, come along. We ha' nothing to do,   30
man, but to see sights now.

Knockem. Welcome, Master Quarlous and Master
Winwife! Will you take any froth and smoke with us?

Quarlous. Yes, sir, but you'll pardon us if we knew not of
so much familiarity between us afore.   35

Knockem. As what, sir?

Quarlous. To be so lightly invited to smoke and froth.

Knockem. A good vapor! Will you sit down, sir? This is
old Urs'la's mansion. How like you her bower? Here you may
ha' your punk and your pig in state, sir, both piping hot.   40

Quarlous. I had rather ha' my punk cold, sir.

Overdo. [*Aside.*] There's for me; punk! and pig!

Ursula. (*She calls within.*) What, Mooncalf? You rogue.

Mooncalf. By and by; the bottle is almost off, mistress.
Here, Master Arthur.   45

9. comfortable—sustaining.   10. Ceres—goddess of grain harvest, mother
of Prosperine.   13. chapmen—buyers.   26. 'Slood—by God's
blood.   41. cold—i.e., without venereal disease.   44. off—emptied.

Ursula. [*Within.*] I'll part you and your play-fellow there
i' the guarded coat, an' you sunder not the sooner.

Knockem. Master Winwife, you are proud, methinks; you
do not talk nor drink; are you proud?

Winwife. Not of the company I am in, sir, nor the place, I   50
assure you.

Knockem. You do not except at the company! do you?
Are you in vapors, sir?

Mooncalf. Nay, good Master Dan Knockem, respect my
mistress' bower, as you call it; for the honor of our booth,   55
none o' your vapors here.

Ursula. (*She comes out with a firebrand.*) Why, you thin
lean polecat you, an' they have a mind to be i' their vapors,
must you hinder 'em? What did you know, vermin, if they
would ha' lost a cloak, or such a trifle? Must you be drawing   60
the air of pacification here, while I am tormented, within, i'
the fire, you weasel?

Mooncalf. Good mistress, 'twas in the behalf of your
booth's credit that I spoke.

Ursula. Why? Would my booth ha' broke if they had fall'n   65
out in't, sir? Or would their heat ha' fired it? In, you rogue,
and wipe the pigs, and mend the fire, that they fall not, or I'll
both baste and roast you till your eyes drop out like 'em.
(*Leave the bottle behind you, and be curst awhile.*)

[*Exit Mooncalf.*]

Quarlous. Body o' the Fair! what's this? Mother o' the   70
bawds?

Knockem. No, she's mother o' the pigs, sir, mother o' the
pigs!

Winwife. Mother o' the Furies, I think, by her firebrand.

Quarlous. No, she is too fat to be a Fury, sure some   75
walking sow of tallow!

Winwife. An inspired vessel of kitchen-stuff!

She drinks this while.

Quarlous. She'll make excellent gear for the coach-makers
here in Smithfield to anoint wheels and axle-trees with.

47. guarded—trimmed.   59–60. What . . . trifle—How did you know they
wouldn't take off their cloaks to fight (permitting us to steal them)? (see
IV.iv. 148, 204).   68. baste—(1) cooking term, (2) beat, thrash.   77. inspired—possessing the "breath of life" (Gen. 2:7), but with a suggestion that
Nature has overinflated her (Latin *spiro*, "to breathe, blow").   kitchen-
stuff—cooking grease.   78. gear—material.

Ursula. Aye, aye, gamesters, mock a plain plump soft   80
wench o' the suburbs, do, because she's juicy and wholesome.
You must ha' your thin pinched ware, pent up i' the compass
of a dog-collar (or 'twill not do), that looks like a long laced
conger, set upright, and a green feather, like fennel, i' the jowl
on't.   85

Knockem. Well said, Urs, my good Urs; to 'em, Urs.

Quarlous. Is she your quagmire, Dan Knockem? Is this
your bog?

Nightingale. We shall have a quarrel presently.

Knockem. How? Bog? Quagmire? Foul vapors! Hum'h!   90

Quarlous. Yes, he that would venture for't, I assure him,
might sink into her and be drowned a week ere any friend he
had could find where he were.

Winwife. And then he would be a fortnight weighing up
again.   95

Quarlous. 'Twere like falling into a whole shire of butter.
They had need be a team of Dutchmen, should draw him out.

Knockem. Answer 'em, Urs; where's thy Barthol'mew-wit,
now, Urs? thy Barthol'mew-wit?

Ursula. Hang 'em, rotten, roguy cheaters, I hope to see   100
'em plagued one day (poxed they are already, I am sure) with
lean playhouse poultry, that has the bony rump sticking out
like the ace of spades or the point of a partizan, that every rib
of 'em is like the tooth of a saw; and will so grate 'em with
their hips and shoulders, as (take 'em altogether) they were as   105
good lie with a hurdle.

Quarlous. Out upon her, how she drips! She's able to give
a man the sweating sickness with looking on her.

Ursula. Marry look off, with a patch o' your face and a
dozen i' your breech, though they be o' scarlet, sir. I ha' seen   110
as fine outsides as either o' yours bring lousy linings to the
brokers ere now, twice a week!

Quarlous. Do you think there may be a fine new

---

81. suburbs—red-light district.   83—84. laced conger—striped sea eel.
84. jowl—fishhead.   87. quagmire, bog—crooked horse dealers sometimes
kept a muddy corner of the lot, where horses with bad ankles were left,
bogged to their knees.   94. weighing up—raising a sunken ship. 103. partizan—sharp weapon.   109. patch—to cover sores caused by the pox (syphilis).   112. brokers—pawnbrokers.

cucking-stool i' the Fair to be purchased? One large enough, I
mean. I know there is a pond of capacity for her.   115

Ursula. For your mother, you rascal! Out, you rogue, you
hedge-bird, you pimp, you pannier-man's bastard, you!

Quarlous. Ha, ha, ha.

Ursula. Do you sneer, you dog's-head, you trendle-tail!
You look as you were begotten atop of a cart in harvest-time,   120
when the whelp was hot and eager. Go, snuff after your
brother's bitch, Mistress Commodity. That's the livery you
wear; 'twill be out at the elbows shortly. It's time you went
to't, for the tother remnant.

Knockem. Peace, Urs, peace, Urs. [*Aside.*] They'll kill the   125
poor whale and make oil of her.—Pray thee go in.

Ursula. I'll see 'em poxed first, and piled, and double
piled.

Winwife. Let's away; her language grows greasier than her
pigs.   130

Ursula. Does't so, snotty nose? Good Lord! are you
snivelling? You were engendered on a she-beggar in a barn
when the bald thrasher, your sire, was scarce warm.

Winwife. Pray thee, let's go.

Quarlous. No, faith; I'll stay the end of her, now; I know   135
she cannot last long; I find by her similes she wanes apace.

Ursula. Does she so? I'll set you gone. Gi' me my pig-pan
hither a little. I'll scald you hence, an' you will not go. [*Exit.*]

Knockem. Gentlemen, these are very strange vapors! And
very idle vapors, I assure you!   140

Quarlous. You are a very serious ass, we assure you.

Knockem. Hum'h! Ass? And serious? Nay, then pardon
me my vapor. I have a foolish vapor, gentlemen: any man that
does vapor me the ass, Master Quarlous—

Quarlous. What then, Master Jordan?   145

Knockem. I do vapor him the lie.

---

114. cucking-stool—stool connected to a pole able to swivel; bawds were
sometimes punished by binding them in the stool, swinging them out over a
pond and dunking them repeatedly.   117. hedge-bird—vagrant (sleeping
under hedges).   pannier-man's—peddler's.   119. trendle-tail—mongrel dog.
121–24. snuff . . . remnant—you're a commodity swindler, and its time you
bought back the remnant of goods from the unsuspecting victim (see Induction
153–56).   127. piled—(1) suffering from piles, (2) stripped of hair (by syphilis).   127–28. double piled—punning reference to the nap on expensive
cloth.

    Quarlous. Faith, and to any man that vapors me the lie, I
do vapor that.   [*Strikes him.*]
    Knockem. Nay, then, vapors upon vapors.
    Edgworth, Nightingale. 'Ware the pan, the pan, the pan;   150
she comes with the pan, gentlemen. (*Ursula comes in with the
scalding-pan. They fight. She falls with it.*) God bless the
woman!
    Ursula. Oh!   [*Exeunt Quarlous, Winwife.*]
    Trash. [*Running to Ursula's booth.*] What's the matter?   155
    Overdo. Goodly woman!
    Mooncalf. Mistress!
    Ursula. Curse of hell, that ever I saw these fiends! Oh! I
ha' scalded my leg, my leg, my leg! I ha' lost a limb in the
service! Run for some cream and salad oil, quickly! [*To*   160
Mooncalf.] Are you under-peering, you baboon? Rip off my
hose, an' you be men, men, men!
    Mooncalf. Run you for some cream, good mother Joan.
I'll look to your basket.   [*Exit Trash.*]
    Leatherhead. Best sit up i' your chair, Urs'la. Help,   165
gentlemen.   [*They lift her up.*]
    Knockem. Be of good cheer, Urs; thou hast hindered me
the currying of a couple of stallions here, that abused the good
race-bawd o' Smithfield; 'twas time for 'em to go.
    Nightingale. I'faith, when the pan came, they had made   170
you run else. [*To Edgworth.*] This had been a fine time for
purchase, if you had ventured.
    Edgworth. Not a whit; these fellows were too fine to carry
money.
    Knockem. Nightingale, get some help to carry her leg out   175
o' the air; take off her shoes; body o' me, she has the
mallanders, the scratches, the crown scab, and the quitter bone
i' the tother leg.
    Ursula. Oh! the pox, why do you put me in mind o' my
leg thus, to make it prick and shoot? Would you ha' me i' the   180
Hospital afore my time?
    Knockem. Patience, Urs. Take a good heart; 'tis but a
blister as big as a windgall. I'll take it away with the white of

---

167. hindered me the currying—prevented me from thrashing.   169. race-
bawd—as in race-mare, mare for breeding.   177. mallanders . . . bone—horse
diseases.   183. windgall—sore on horse's leg.

an egg, a little honey, and hog's grease; ha' thy pasterns well
rolled, and thou shalt pace again by tomorrow. I'll tend thy   185
booth and look to thy affairs the while; thou shalt sit i' thy
chair and give directions, and shine Ursa major.

> [*They carry Ursula in her chair into the back part of her
> booth.*]

187. Ursa major—the Great Bear (constellation).

ACT II
SCENE VI

[*Enter Cokes, Wasp, Mistress Overdo, Grace.*]

Overdo. These are the fruits of bottle-ale and tobacco! the
foam of the one and the fumes of the other! Stay, young man,
and despise not the wisdom of these few hairs that are grown
grey in care of thee.

   Edgworth. Nightingale, stay a little. Indeed I'll hear some   5
o' this!

   Cokes. Come, Numps, come, where are you? Welcome
into the Fair, Mistress Grace.

   Edgworth. [*To Nightingale.*] 'Slight, he will call company,
you shall see, and put us into doings presently.   10

   Overdo. Thirst not after that frothy liquor, ale; for who
knows, when he openeth the stopple, what may be in the
bottle? Hath not a snail, a spider, yea, a newt been found
there? Thirst not after it, youth; thirst not after it.

   Cokes. This is a brave fellow, Numps; let's hear him.   15

   Wasp. 'Sblood, how brave is he? In a guarded coat? You
were best truck with him; e'en strip and truck presently; it will
become you. Why will you hear him? Because he is an ass, and
may be akin to the Cokeses?

   Cokes. O, good Numps!   20

   Overdo. Neither do thou lust after that tawny weed,
tobacco.

   Cokes. Brave words!

16. brave—(1) fine, (2) richly dressed. Cokes means the former, Wasp the
latter.   17. truck—trade.

Overdo. Whose complexion is like the Indian's that vents   25
it!

    Cokes. Are they not brave words, sister?

    Overdo. And who can tell if, before the gathering and
making up thereof, the alligarta hath not pissed thereon?

    Wasp. 'Heart, let 'em be brave words, as brave as they will!
An' they were all the brave words in a country, how then? Will   30
you away yet? Ha' you enough on him? Mistress Grace, come
you away, I pray you, be not you accessory. If you do lose
your license, or somewhat else, sir, with list'ning to his fables,
say Numps is a witch, with all my heart, do, say so.

    Cokes. Avoid, i' your satin doublet, Numps.   35

    Overdo. The creeping venom of which subtle serpent, as
some late writers affirm, neither the cutting of the perilous
plant, nor the drying of it, nor the lighting or burning, can any
way persway or assuage.

    Cokes. Good, i' faith! is't not, sister?   40

    Overdo. Hence it is that the lungs of the tobacconist are
rotted, the liver spotted, the brain smoked like the backside of
the pig-woman's booth, here, and the whole body within,
black as her pan you saw e'en now, without.

    Cokes. A fine similitude, that, sir! Did you see the pan?   45
    Edgworth. Yes, sir.

    Overdo. Nay, the hole in the nose here, of some
tobacco-takers, or the third nostril (if I may so call it), which
makes that they can vent the tobacco out like the ace of clubs,
or rather the flower-de-lys, is caused from the tobacco, the   50
mere tobacco! when the poor innocent pox, having nothing to
do there, is miserably and most unconscionably slandered.

    Cokes. Who would ha' missed this, sister?

    Mistress Overdo. Not anybody but Numps.

    Cokes. He does not understand.   55

    Edgworth. Nor you feel.   *He picketh his purse.*

    Cokes. What would you have, sister, of a fellow that
knows nothing but a basket-hilt and an old fox in't? The best
music i' the Fair will not move a log.

28. alligarta—alligator, from Spanish *el lagarto,* "lizard."   34. witch—
i.e., can predict the future; males were often called witches.   35. Avoid—
go away.   36. serpent—the alligator mentioned above.   37. some
late writers—including King James, *A Counterblast to Tobacco* (1604).
39. persway—diminish.   58. basket-hilt—sword handle curved in the shape
of a basket.   an old fox—kind of sword.

Edgworth. In to Urs'la, Nightingale, and carry her   60
comfort; see it told [*Gives purse to Nightingale*]. This fellow
was sent to us by fortune for our first fairing.

[*Exit Nightingale.*]

Overdo. But what speak I of the diseases of the body,
children of the Fair?

Cokes. That's to us, sister. Brave i' faith!   65

Overdo. Hark, O you sons and daughters of Smithfield!
and hear what malady it doth the mind: it causeth swearing, it
causeth swaggering, it causeth snuffling, and snarling, and now
and then a hurt.

Mistress Overdo. He hath something of Master Overdo,   70
methinks, brother.

Cokes. So methought, sister, very much of my brother
Overdo; and 'tis when he speaks.

Overdo. Look into any angle o' the town—the Straits, or
the Bermudas—where the quarrelling lesson is read, and   75
how do they entertain the time but with bottle-ale and
tobacco? The lecturer is o' one side, and his pupils o' the
other; but the seconds are still bottle-ale and tobacco, for
which the lecturer reads and the novices pay. Thirty pound a
week in bottle-ale! forty in tobacco! and ten more in ale again.   80
Then for a suit to drink in, so much, and (that being slavered)
so much for another suit, and then a third suit, and a fourth
suit! and still the bottle-ale slavereth, and the tobacco
stinketh!

Wasp. Heart of a madman! are you rooted here? Will you   85
never away? What can any man find out in this bawling fellow
to grow here for? He is a full handful higher sin' he heard him.
Will you fix here? And set up a booth, sir?

Overdo. I will conclude briefly—

Wasp. Hold your peace, you roaring rascal! I'll run my   90
head i' your chaps else. [*To Cokes.*] You were best build a
booth and entertain him; make your will, an' you say the
word, and him your heir! Heart, I never knew one taken with a
mouth of a peck, afore. By this light, I'll carry you away o' my
back, an' you will not come.   95

61. told—counted.   74–75. Straits, Bermudas—disreputable areas (of London).   78. seconds—assistants.   81. slavered—soiled.   87. He is a full
handful higher—Cokes has been here so long that he has grown a hand's length.
94. of a peck—i.e., big as a peck (eight quarts).

He gets him up on pick-pack.

Cokes. Stay, Numps, stay, set me down. I ha' lost my purse, Numps, O my purse! One o' my fine purses is gone.

Mistress Overdo. Is't indeed, brother?

Cokes. Aye, as I am an honest man, would I were an arrant rogue, else! A plague of all roguy, damned cutpurses for me. 100

Wasp. Bless 'em with all my heart, with all my heart, do you see! Now, as I am no infidel, that I know of, I am glad on't. Aye, I am; here's my witness! do you see, sir? I did not tell you of his fables, I? No, no, I am a dull malt-horse, I, I 105 know nothing. Are you not justly served i' your conscience now? Speak i' your conscience. Much good do you with all my heart, and his good heart that has it, with all my heart again.

Edgworth. [*Aside.*] This fellow is very charitable; would he had a purse too! But I must not be too bold all at a time. 110

Cokes. Nay, Numps, it is not my best purse.

Wasp. Not your best! Death! why should it be your worst? Why should it be any, indeed, at all? Answer me to that; gi' me a reason from you, why it should be any.

Cokes. Nor my gold, Numps; I ha' that yet; look here else, 115 sister. [*Holds up his purse.*]

Wasp. Why so, there's all the feeling he has!

Mistress Overdo. I pray you, have a better care of that, brother.

Cokes. Nay, so I will, I warrant you; let him catch this, 120 that catch can. I would fain see him get this, look you here.

Wasp. So, so, so, so, so, so, so, so! Very good.

Cokes. I would ha' him come again, and but offer at it. Sister, will you take notice of a good jest? I will put it just where th'other was, and if we ha' good luck you shall see a 125 delicate fine trap to catch the cutpurse nibbling.

Edgworth. [*Aside.*] Faith, and he'll try ere you be out o' the Fair.

Cokes. Come, Mistress Grace, prithee be not melancholy for my mischance; sorrow wi' not keep it, sweetheart. 130

Grace. I do not think on't, sir.

104–05. I . . . fables—didn't I warn you that in listening to Mad Arthur's stories you might be the victim of theft? (see lines 32–34). 105. malt-horse—draft horse.

Cokes. 'Twas but a little scurvy white money, hang it; it
may hang the cutpurse one day. I ha' gold left to gi' thee a
fairing, yet, as hard as the world goes. Nothing angers me but
that nobody here looked like a cutpurse, unless 'twere Numps.   135

Wasp. How? I? I look like a cutpurse? Death! your sister's
a cutpurse! and your mother and father and all your kin were
cutpurses! And here is a rogue is the bawd o' the cutpurses,
whom I will beat to begin with.

> *They speak all together; and Wasp beats the Justice.*

Cokes. Numps, Numps!	*Overdo.* Hold thy hand, child 140
Mistress Overdo. Good	of wrath and heir of anger,
Master Humphrey.	make it not Childermass day in
Wasp. You are the	thy fury, or the feast of the
Patrico, are you? the patri-	French Barthol'mew, parent of
arch of the cutpurses? You	the Massacre. 145

share, sir, they say; let them share this with you. Are you i'
your hot fit of preaching again? I'll cool you.

Overdo. Murder, murder, murder!   [*Exeunt.*]

142. Childermass day—Feast of the Innocents, commemorating their slaughter.   144. Patrico—priest or parson (beggar's slang).   144–45. French . . .
Massacre—massacre in Paris of Protestants on Saint Bartholomew Day, 1572.

ACT III

SCENE I

> [*Enter Whit, Haggis, Bristle;*
> *Leatherhead and Joan at their booths.*]

Whit. Nay, 'tish all gone, now! Dish 'tish, phen tou vilt
not be phitin call, Mas[h] ter Offisher! Phat ish a man te better
to lishen out noishes for tee an' tou art in an oder 'orld—being
very shuffishient noishes and gallantsh too, one o' their
brabblesh would have fed ush all dish fortnight; but tou art so   5
bushy about beggersh still, tou hast no leshure to intend
shentlemen, an't be.

1. *Whit*—Whit's stage Irish is more easily understood if read aloud.   The beginning of the second sentence translates: This 'tis, when thou wilt not be
within call, Master Officer!   What is a man the better to listen out noises [be
an informer] for thee, an' [if] thou art in an other world . . . .   5. brabblesh—brabbles, brawls.   6. bushy—busy.   intend—pay attention to.

Haggis. Why, I told you, Davy Bristle.

Bristle. Come, come, you told me a pudding, Toby Haggis; a matter of nothing; I am sure it came to nothing! You said, 10 "Let's go to Urs'la's," indeed; but then you met the man with the monsters, and I could not get you from him. An old fool, not leave seeing yet?

Haggis. Why, who would ha' thought anybody would ha' quarrelled so early? Or that the ale o' the Fair would ha' been 15 up so soon?

Whit. Phy, phat o' clock tost tou tink it ish, man?

Haggis. I cannot tell.

Whit. Tou art a vishe vatchman, i' te mean teeme.

Haggis. Why, should the watch go by the clock, or the 20 clock by the watch, I pray?

Bristle. One should go by another, if they did well.

Whit. Tou art right now! Phen didst tou ever know or hear of a shuffishient vatchman but he did tell the clock, phat bushiness soever he had? 25

Bristle. Nay, that's most true, a sufficient watchman knows what o'clock it is.

Whit. Shleeping or vaking! ash well as te clock himshelf, or te jack dat shtrikes him!

Bristle. Let's inquire of Master Leatherhead, or Joan Trash 30 here. Master Leatherhead, do you hear, Master Leatherhead?

Whit. If it be a Ledderhead, tish a very tick Ledderhead, tat sho mush noish vill not piersh him.

Leatherhead. I have a little business now, good friends; do not trouble me. 35

Whit. Phat? Because o' ty wrought neet-cap and ty phelvet sherkin, man? Phy? I have sheen tee in ty ledder sherkin ere now, mashter o' de hobbyhorses, as bushy and as stately as tou sheem'st to be.

Trash. Why, what an' you have, Captain Whit? He has his 40 choice of jerkins, you may see by that, and his caps too, I assure you, when he pleases to be either sick or employed.

Leatherhead. God a mercy, Joan, answer for me.

Whit. Away, be not sheen i' my company; here be shentlemen, and men of vorship.   [*Exeunt Haggis, Bristle.*] 45

9. a pudding—(1) nothing, (2) Haggis, name for a kind of pudding.
12. monsters—the freak show.   29. jack—mechanical man that strikes the hour.   36. wrought neet-cap—embroidered nightcap.

ACT III
SCENE II

[*Enter Quarlous, Winwife.*]

Quarlous. We had wonderful ill luck to miss this prologue
o' the purse, but the best is we shall have five acts of him ere
night. He'll be spectacle enough! I'll answer for't.

Whit. O Creesh! Duke Quarlous, how dosht tou? Tou
dosht not know me, I fear? I am te vishest man, but Justice   5
Overdo, in all Barthol'mew Fair, now. Gi' me twelvepence
from tee, I vill help tee to a vife vorth forty marks for't, an't
be.

Quarlous. Away, rogue, pimp, away.

Whit. And she shall show tee as fine cut 'ork for't in her   10
shmock too, as tou cansht vish i' faith. Vilt tou have her,
vorshipful Vinvife? I vill help tee to her, here, be an't be, in te
pig-quarter, gi' me ty twel'pence from tee.

Winwife. Why, there's twel'pence; pray thee, wilt thou be
gone?   15

Whit. Tou art a vorthy man, and a vorshipful man still.

Quarlous. Get you gone, rascal.

Whit. I do mean it, man. Prinsh Quarlous, if tou hasht
need on me, tou shalt find me here at Urs'la's. I vill see phat
ale and punk ish i' te pigshty for tee, bless ty good vorship.   20

[*Exit.*]

Quarlous. Look! who comes here! John Littlewit!

Winwife. And his wife and my widow, her mother; the
whole family.

[*Enter Busy, Purecraft, Littlewit, Win.*]

Quarlous. 'Slight, you must gi' em all fairings, now!

Winwife. Not I, I'll not see 'em.   25

Quarlous. They are going a-feasting. What school-master's
that is with 'em?

Winwife. That's my rival, I believe, the baker!

Busy. So, walk on in the middle way, fore-right; turn
neither to the right hand nor to the left. Let not your eyes be   30
drawn aside with vanity, nor your ear with noises.

Quarlous. O, I know him by that start!

---

4. Creesh—Christ.   10. cut 'ork—cutwork, embroidery.   29. fore-right—
straight ahead.

Leatherhead. What do you lack? What do you buy, pretty Mistress? [*To Win Littlewit.*] a fine hobbyhorse, to make your son a tilter? a drum to make him a soldier? a fiddle to make   35
him a reveller? What is't you lack? Little dogs for your daughters? or babies, male or female?

Busy. Look not toward them, hearken not! The place is Smithfield, or the field of smiths, the grove of hobbyhorses and trinkets. The wares are the wares of devils; and the whole   40
Fair is the shop of Satan! They are hooks and baits, very baits, that are hung out on every side to catch you, and to hold you as it were, by the gills and by the nostrils, as the fisher doth; therefore, you must not look, nor turn toward them. The heathen man could stop his ears with wax against the harlot o'   45
the sea; do you the like, with your fingers, against the bells of the Beast.

Winwife. What flashes comes from him!

Quarlous. O, he has those of his oven! A notable hot baker 'twas, when he plied the peel. He is leading his flock into   50
the Fair, now.

Winwife. Rather driving 'em to the pens; for he will let 'em look upon nothing.

[*Enter Knockem, Whit, from back part of Ursula's booth.*]

Knockem. Gentlewomen, the weath-   *Littlewit is*
er's hot! Whither walk you? Have a care o'   *gazing at the*   55
your fine velvet caps; the Fair is dusty.   *sign; which is*
Take a sweet delicate booth with boughs,   *the pig's head*
here, i' the way, and cool yourselves i' the   *with a large*
shade, you and your friends. The best pig   *writing under it.*
and bottle-ale i' the Fair, sir. Old Urs'la is cook, there you may   60
read: the pig's head speaks it. Poor soul, she has had a stringhalt, the maryhinchco; but she's prettily amended.

Whit. A delicate show-pig, little mistress, with shweet sauce, and crackling like de bay leaf i' de fire, la! Tou shalt ha'

---

35. tilter—jouster.   39. grove of hobbyhorses—a grove is the usual site for idols in the Old Testament.   Jonson parodies the Puritan belief that all statues (e.g., of the Virgin) constitute idols.   45–46. heathen . . . sea—Ulysses evading the Sirens had his crew stop their ears, but he was lashed to the mast. Busy did not learn the classics very well in his bakery.   46. bells—hobbyhorses usually had cheap little bells attached, as they do now.   48. comes—good grammar in 1614.   50. peel—shovel for handling hot loaves.
62. stringhalt, maryhinchco—more horse diseases.

de clean side o' de table-clot and dy glass vashed with phatersh   65
of Dame Annessh Cleare.

Littlewit. This's fine, verily: "Here be the best pigs, and
she does roast 'em as well as ever she did," the pig's head says.

Knockem. Excellent, excellent, mistress, with fire o'
juniper and rosemary branches! The oracle of the pig's head,   70
that, sir.

Purecraft. Son, were you not warned of the vanity of the
eye? Have you forgot the wholesome admonition so soon?

Littlewit. Good mother, how shall we find a pig if we do
not look about for't? Will it run off o' the spit into our   75
mouths, think you? as in Lubberland? and cry, "We, we"?

Busy. No, but your mother, religiously wise, conceiveth it
may offer itself by other means to the sense, as by way of
steam, which I think it doth here in this place. (Huh, huh) yes,
it doth. (*Busy scents after it like a hound.*) And it were a sin of   80
obstinacy, great obstinacy, high and horrible obstinacy, to
decline or resist the good titillation of the famelic sense, which
is the smell. Therefore be bold (huh, huh, huh); follow the
scent. Enter the tents of the unclean for once, and satisfy your
wife's frailty. Let your frail wife be satisfied; your zealous   85
mother and my suffering self will also be satisfied.

Littlewit. Come, Win, as good winny here as go farther
and see nothing.

Busy. We 'scape so much of the other vanities by our early
en'tring.   90

Purecraft. It is an edifying consideration.

Win. This is scurvy, that we must come into the Fair and
not look on't.

Littlewit. Win, have patience, Win, I'll tell you more anon.

Knockem. Mooncalf, entertain within there; the best pig i'   95
the booth, a pork-like pig. These are Banbury-bloods, o' the
sincere stud, come a pig-hunting. Whit, wait, Whit, look to
your charge.

Busy. A pig prepare presently; let a pig be prepared to us.

---

66. Annessh Cleare—Annis Clare, a spring.   76. Lubberland—where work is
unnecessary and delicious food everywhere, as in the Land of Cockayne or (in
American folksong) the Big Rock Candy Mountain.   82. famelic—pertaining
to hunger.   87. winny—a nonsense word that Littlewit creates for the sake
of a pun.   96–97. o' the sincere stud—from genuine (Puritan) stock.

[*Exeunt Busy, Purecraft, Win, Littlewit, Whit into back part of booth while Mooncalf and Ursula, arriving, look on.*]

Mooncalf. 'Slight, who be these?   100

Ursula. Is this the good service, Jordan, you'd do me?

Knockem. Why, Urs? Why, Urs? Thou'lt ha' vapors i' thy leg again presently; pray thee go in; 't may turn to the scratches else.

Ursula. Hang your vapors, they are stale, and stink like   105
you. Are these the guests o' the game you promised to fill my pit withal, today?

Knockem. Aye, what ail they, Urs?

Ursula. Ail they? They are all sippers, sippers o' the city. They look as they would not drink off two pen'orth of   110
bottle-ale amongst 'em.

Mooncalf. A body may read that i' their small printed ruffs.

Knockem. Away, thou art a fool, Urs, and thy Mooncalf too, i' your ignorant vapors, now! hence! Good guests, I say,   115
right hypocrites, good gluttons. In, and set a couple o' pigs o' the board, and half a dozen of the biggest bottles afore 'em, and call Whit. I do not love to hear innocents abused. Fine ambling hypocrites! and a stone-puritan with a sorrel head and beard, good mouthed gluttons: two to a pig. Away!   120

[*Exit Mooncalf.*]

Ursula. Are you sure they are such?

Knockem. O' the right breed; thou shalt try 'em by the teeth, Urs. Where's this Whit?

[*Re-enter Whit.*]

Whit. Behold, man, and see, what a worthy man am ee!
With the fury of my sword, and the shaking of my   125
beard,
I will make ten thousand men afeared.

Knockem. Well said, brave Whit; in, and fear the ale out o' the bottles into the bellies of the brethren and the sisters; drink to the cause, and pure vapors.   130

[*Exeunt Knockem, Whit, Ursula.*]

Quarlous. My roarer is turned tapster, methinks. Now

108. what ail they—what's wrong with them?   112–13. small printed ruffs—
Puritans wore ruffs in small or Geneva print.   119. stone-puritan—male Puritan, as in stone-horse, stallion.

were a fine time for thee, Winwife, to lay aboard thy widow;
thou'lt never be master of a better season or place; she that
will venture herself into the Fair and a pig-box will admit any
assault, be assured of that.   135

    Winwife. I love not enterprises of that suddenness,
though.

    Quarlous. I'll warrant thee, then, no wife out o' the
widow's hundred. If I had but as much title to her as to have
breathed once on that strait stomacher of hers, I would now   140
assure myself to carry her yet, ere she went out of Smithfield.
Or she should carry me, which were the fitter sight, I confess.
But you are a modest undertaker, by circumstances and
degrees; come, 'tis disease in thee, not judgment; I should offer
at all together. Look, here's the poor fool again that was stung   145
by the wasp, erewhile.

132. lay aboard—attack (nautical term).   139. hundred—class, group.
140. strait stomacher—stiff garment covering abdomen and chest.
144–45. offer at all together—risk everything.

ACT III
SCENE III

                                                                     [Enter Overdo.]
    Overdo. I will made no more orations shall draw on these
tragical conclusions. And I begin now to think that, by a spice
of collateral justice, Adam Overdo deserved this beating; for I,
the said Adam, was one cause (a by-cause) why the purse was
lost; and my wife's brother's purse too, which they know not   5
of yet. But I shall make very good mirth with it at supper (that
will be the sport), and put my little friend Master Humphrey
Wasp's choler quite out of countenance. When, sitting at the
upper end o' my table, as I use, and drinking to my brother
Cokes and Mistress Alice Overdo, as I will, my wife, for their   10
good affection to old Bradley, I deliver to 'em it was I that was
cudgelled, and show 'em the marks. To see what bad events
may peep out o' the tail of good purposes! The care I had of

3. collateral—indirect.   4. by-cause—incidental cause.   13. peep . . .
tail—be born from.

that civil young man I took fancy to this morning (and have
not left it yet) drew me to that exhortation, which drew the   15
company, indeed, which drew the cutpurse; which drew the
money; which drew my brother Cokes his loss; which drew on
Wasp's anger; which drew on my beating: a pretty gradation!
And they shall ha' it i' their dish, i' faith, at night for fruit; I
love to be merry at my table. I had thought once, at one   20
special blow he ga' me, to have revealed myself; but then (I
thank thee, fortitude) I remembered that a wise man (and who
is ever so great a part o' the commonwealth in himself) for no
particular disaster ought to abandon a public good design. The
husbandman ought not, for one unthankful year, to forsake   25
the plough; the shepherd ought not, for one scabbed sheep, to
throw by his tar-box; the pilot ought not, for one leak i' the
poop, to quit the helm; nor the alderman ought not, for one
custard more at a meal, to give up his cloak; the constable
ought not to break his staff and forswear the watch, for one   30
roaring night; nor the piper o' the parish (*ut parvis componere
magna solebam*) to put up his pipes, for one rainy Sunday.
These are certain knocking conclusions; out of which I am
resolved, come what come can—come beating, come imprison-
ment, come infamy, come banishment, nay, come the rack,   35
come the hurdle, welcome all—I will not discover who I am till
my due time; and yet still all shall be, as I said ever, in justice'
name, and the King's and for the commonwealth!

    Winwife. What does he talk to himself, and act so
seriously? Poor fool!   [*Exit Overdo.*]   40

    Quarlous. No matter what. Here's fresher argument,
intend that.

31–32. *ut parvis componere magna solebam*—"as I used to compare great
things with small" (Virgil, *Eclogues* I.23, trans. H. R. Fairclough).
36. hurdle—"a kind of frame . . . on which traitors used to be drawn through
the streets to execution" (*OED*).   41. argument—theme.

ACT III
SCENE IV

[*Enter Cokes, Mistress Overdo, Grace, followed by
                              Wasp, loaded with toys, etc.*]

Cokes. Come, Mistress Grace, come sister, here's more fine
sights yet, i' faith. God's lid, where's Numps?

Leatherhead. What do you lack, gentlemen? What is't you
buy? Fine rattles? drums? babies? little dogs? and birds for
ladies? What do you lack?   5

Cokes. Good honest Numps, keep afore. I am so afraid
thou'lt lose somewhat; my heart was at my mouth when I
missed thee.

Wasp. You were best buy a whip i' your hand to drive me.

Cokes. Nay, do not mistake, Numps, thou art so apt to   10
mistake; I would but watch the goods. Look you now, the
treble fiddle was e'en almost like to be lost.

Wasp. Pray you take heed you lose not yourself. Your
best way were e'en get up and ride for more surety. Buy a
token's worth of great pins to fasten yourself to my shoulder.   15

Leatherhead. What do you lack, gentlemen? Fine purses,
pouches, pincases, pipes? What is't you lack? A pair o' smiths
to wake you i' the morning? or a fine whistling bird?

Cokes. Numps, here be finer things than any we ha'
bought, by odds! And more delicate horses, a great deal! Good   20
Numps, stay, and come hither.

Wasp. Will you scourse with him? You are in Smithfield;
you may fit yourself with a fine easy-going street-nag for your
saddle again' Michaelmas term, do. Has he ne'er a little odd
cart for you, to make a caroche on, i' the country, with four   25
pied hobbyhorses? Why the measles should you stand here
with your train, cheaping of dogs, birds, and babies? You ha'
no children to bestow 'em on, ha' you?

Cokes. No, but again' I ha' children, Numps, that's all one.

Wasp. Do, do, do, do. How many shall you have, think   30
you? An' I were as you, I'd buy for all my tenants, too. They

---

17. pair o' smiths—perhaps a mechanical toy.   22. scourse—barter.
24. again' Michaelmas term—in anticipation of the fall court term, during
which many country gentlemen stayed in the city.   25. caroche—
elegant coach.   27. cheaping of—bargaining for.

are a kind o' civil savages that will part with their children for
rattles, pipes, and knives. You were best buy a hatchet or two
and truck with 'em.

Cokes. Good Numps, hold that little tongue o' thine, and   35
save it a labor. I am resolute Bat, thou know'st.

Wasp. A resolute fool you are, I know, and a very
sufficient coxcomb, with all my heart; nay, you have it, sir, an'
you be angry, turd i' your teeth, twice (if I said it not once
afore); and much good do you.   40

Winwife. Was there ever such a self-affliction? And so
impertinent?

Quarlous. Alas! his care will go near to crack him; let's in
and comfort him.

Wasp. Would I had been set i' the ground, all but the head   45
on me, and had my brains bowled at, or threshed out, when
first I underwent this plague of a charge!

Quarlous. How now, Numps! Almost tired i' your
protectorship? Overparted? Overparted?

Wasp. Why, I cannot tell, sir; it may be I am; does't grieve   50
you?

Quarlous. No, I swear dos't not, Numps, to satisfy you.

Wasp. Numps? 'Sblood, you are fine and familiar! How
long ha' we been acquainted, I pray you?

Quarlous. I think it may be remembered, Numps, that?   55
'Twas since morning sure.

Wasp. Why, I hope I know't well enough, sir; I did not ask
to be told.

Quarlous. No? Why then?

Wasp. It's no matter why; you see with your eyes, now,   60
what I said to you today? You'll believe me another time?

Quarlous. Are you removing the Fair, Numps?

Wasp. A pretty question! and a very civil one! Yes faith, I
ha' my lading you see, or shall have anon; you may know
whose beast I am by my burthen. If the pannier-man's jack   65
were ever better known by his loins of mutton, I'll be flayed
and feed dogs for him, when his time comes.

Winwife. How melancholy Mistress Grace is yonder! Pray
thee let's go enter ourselves in grace with her.

49. Overparted—given too hard a part.   65. pannier-man's Jack—servant who carried provisions for the Inns of Court.

Cokes. Those six horses, friend, I'll have—   70
Wasp. How!
Cokes. And the three Jew's trumps; and a half dozen o'
birds, and that drum (I have one drum already) and your
smiths (I like that device o' your smiths very pretty well) and
four halberts—and (le'me see) that fine painted great lady, and   75
her three women for state, I'll have.
Wasp. No, the shop; buy the whole shop, it will be best,
the shop, the shop!
Leatherhead. If his worship please.
Wasp. Yes, and keep it during the Fair, bobchin.   80
Cokes. Peace, Numps. Friend, do not meddle with him,
an' you be wise, and would show your head above board. He
will sting thorough your wrought nightcap, believe me. A set
of these violins I would buy too, for a delicate young noise I
have i' the country, that are every one a size less than another,   85
just like your fiddles. I would fain have a fine young masque at
my marriage, now I think on't; but I do want such a number o'
things. And Numps will not help me now, and I dare not speak
to him.
Trash. Will your worship buy any gingerbread, very good   90
bread, comfortable bread?
Cokes. Gingerbread! Yes, let's see.   *He runs to her shop.*
Wasp. There's the tother springe!
Leatherhead. Is this well, goody Joan? to interrupt my
market? in the midst? and call away my customers? Can you   95
answer this at the Pie-powders?
Trash. Why, if his mastership have a mind to buy, I hope
my ware lies as open as another's; I may show my ware as well
as you yours.
Cokes. Hold your peace; I'll content you both: I'll buy up   100
his shop and thy basket.
Wasp. Will you i' faith?
Leatherhead. Why should you put him from it, friend?
Wasp. Cry you mercy! you'd be sold too, would you?

---

72. Jew's trumps—Jew's harps.   76. state—stateliness.   80. bobchin—
apparently, fool whose chin jerks up and down.   84. noise—band of musicians.   93. springe—trap.

What's the price on you? Jerkin and all, as you stand? Ha' you   105
any qualities?

 Trash. Yes, goodman angry-man, you shall find he has
qualities, if you cheapen him.

 Wasp. Godso, you ha' the selling of him! What are they?
Will they be bought for love or money?   110

 Trash. No indeed, sir.

 Wasp. For what then? Victuals?

 Trash. He scorns victuals, sir; he has bread and butter at
home, thanks be to God! And yet he will do more for a good
meal, if the toy take him i' the belly; marry then they must   115
not set him at lower end; if they do, he'll go away, though he
fast. But put him atop o' the table, where his place is, and he'll
do you forty fine things. He has not been sent for, and sought
out, for nothing, at your great city-suppers, to put down
Coriat and Cokely, and been laughed at for his labor. He'll   120
play you all the puppets i' the town over, and the players,
every company, and his own company too; he spares nobody!

 Cokes. I' faith?

 Trash. He was the first, sir, that ever baited the fellow i'
the bear's skin, an't like your worship. No dog ever came near   125
him since. And for fine motions!

 Cokes. Is he good at those too? Can he set out a masque,
trow?

 Trash. O Lord, master! sought to, far and near, for his
inventions; and he engrosses all, he makes all the puppets i' the 130
Fair.

 Cokes. Dost thou, in troth, old velvet jerkin? Give me thy
hand.

 Trash. Nay, sir, you shall see him in his velvet jerkin, and a
scarf too, at night, when you hear him interpret Master   135
Littlewit's motion.

 Cokes. Speak no more, but shut up shop presently, friend.
I'll buy both it and thee too, to carry down with me, and her

---

106, 108. qualities—attributes of worth (see I.v.130, 134). 109. Godso—
euphemistic alteration of catso, common exclamation (from Italian, *cazzo*,
"penis"). 116. lower end—i.e., of the table. 120. Coriat, Cokely—
famous jesters. 121. play you—mimic. 124–25. baited . . .skin—
one actor plays the bear, others the dogs. 126. motions—puppet shows.
128. trow—I wonder. 130. inventions—the plays and masques he invents,
i.e., thinks up. engrosses—gains monopoly of.

hamper beside. Thy shop shall furnish out the masque, and
hers the banquet. I cannot go less, to set out anything with   140
credit. What's the price, at a word, o' thy whole shop, case and
all as it stands?

    Leatherhead. Sir, it stands me in six and twenty shillings
sevenpence halfpenny, besides three shillings for my ground.

    Cokes. Well, thirty shillings will do all, then! And what   145
comes yours to?

    Trash. Four shillings and elevenpence, sir, ground and all,
an't like your worship.

    Cokes. Yes, it does like my worship very well, poor
woman; that's five shillings more. What a masque shall I   150
furnish out for forty shillings (twenty pound Scotch). And a
banquet of gingerbread! There's a stately thing! Numps!
Sister! And my wedding gloves too! (That I never thought on
afore.) All my wedding gloves gingerbread! O me! what a
device will there be to make 'em eat their fingers' ends! And   155
delicate brooches for the bridemen and all! And then I'll ha'
this posy put to 'em: "For the best grace," meaning Mistress
Grace, my wedding posy.

    Grace. I am beholden to you, sir, and to your
Barthol'mew-wit.   160

    Wasp. You do not mean this, do you? Is this your first
purchase?

    Cokes. Yes, faith, and I do not think, Numps, but thou'lt
say, it was the wisest act that ever I did in my wardship.

    Wasp. Like enough! I shall say anything, I!   165

140. banquet—dessert.   143. it stands me in—I have invested.
158. posy—motto.

ACT III
SCENE V

        [*Enter Overdo, Edgworth, Nightingale.*]

    Overdo. [*Aside.*] I cannot beget a project, with all my
political brain, yet; my project is how to fetch off this proper
young man from his debauched company. I have followed him

2. political—shrewd.

all the Fair over, and still I find him with this songster; and I
begin shrewdly to suspect their familiarity; and the young man   5
of a terrible taint, poetry! with which idle disease if he be
infected, there's no hope of him in a state-course. *Actum est*
of him for a commonwealth's-man if he go to't in rhyme once.

    Edgworth. [*To Nightingale.*] Yonder he is buying o'
gingerbread. Set in quickly, before he part with too much on   10
his money.

    Nightingale. My masters and friends and good people,
draw near, etc.

    Cokes. Ballads! hark, hark! Pray thee, fellow, stay a little;
good Numps, look to the goods. What ballads hast thou? Let   15
me see, let me see myself.

                          He runs to the ballad-man.

    Wasp. Why so! He's flown to another lime-bush; there he
will flutter as long more, till he ha' ne'er a feather left. Is there
a vexation like this, gentlemen? Will you believe me now?
Hereafter shall I have credit with you?   20

    Quarlous. Yes faith, shalt thou, Numps, an' thou art
worthy on't, for thou sweatest for't. I never saw a young pimp
errant and his squire better matched.

    Winwife. Faith, the sister comes after 'em well, too.

    Grace. Nay, if you saw the justice her husband, my   25
guardian, you were fitted for the mess; he is such a wise one
his way—

    Winwife. I wonder we see him not here.

    Grace. O! he is too serious for this place, and yet better
sport than the other three, I assure you, gentlemen, wher'er he   30
is, though't be o' the bench.

    Cokes. How dost thou call it? *A Caveat Against Cut-
purses!* A good jest, i' faith; I would fain see that demon, your
cutpurse, you talk of; that delicate-handed devil; they say he
walks hereabout. I would see him walk, now. Look you, sister,   35
here, here, let him come, sister, and welcome. (*He shows his
purse boastingly.*) Balladman, does any cutpurses haunt

7. in a state-course—as a statesman. *Actum est*—it is finished (not a biblical
reference, however, since the Latin of John 19:30 is *Consummatum est.*)
17. lime-bush—bird-lime made a bird's feet stick to the bough, trapping it.
22–23. pimp errant—like knight errant, but errant could mean erring as well
as wandering.   26. mess—a group, usually of four, into which banqueters
were divided.

hereabout? Pray thee raise me one or two; begin and show me
one.

    Nightingale. Sir, this is a spell against 'em, spick and span   40
new; and 'tis made as 'twere in mine own person, and I sing it
in mine own defence. But 'twill cost a penny alone, if you buy
it.

    Cokes. No matter for the price; thou dost not know me, I
see; I am an odd Barthol'mew.   45

    Mistress Overdo. Ha'st a fine picture, brother?

    Cokes. O sister, do you remember the ballads over the
nursery-chimney at home o' my own pasting up? There be
brave pictures! Other manner of pictures than these, friend.

    Wasp. Yet these will serve to pick the pictures out o' your   50
pockets, you shall see.

    Cokes. So I heard 'em say. Pray thee mind him not,
fellow; he'll have an oar in everything.

    Nightingale. It was intended, sir, as if a purse should
chance to be cut in my presence, now, I may be blameless,   55
though; as by the sequel will more plainly appear.

    Cokes. We shall find that i' the matter. Pray thee begin.

    Nightingale. To the tune of *Paggington's Pound,* sir.

    Cokes. Fa, la la la, la la la, fa la la la. Nay, I'll put thee in
tune, and all! Mine own country dance! Pray thee begin.   60

    Nightingale. It is a gentle admonition, you must know, sir,
both to the purse-cutter and the purse-bearer.

    Cokes. Not a word more, out o' the tune, an' thou lov'st
me. Fa, la la la, la la la, fa la la la. Come, when?

    Nightingale. My masters and friends   65
       and good people draw near,
       And look to your purses, for that I
         do say;

    Cokes. Ha, ha, this chimes! Good counsel at first dash.

    Nightingale. And though little money   70
       in them you do bear,
       It cost more to get than to lose in a   *Cokes.* Good!
         day.
       You oft have been told,
       Both the young and the old,   75

50–51. pictures . . . pockets—images on his money.

And bidden beware of the cutpurse
  so bold
Then if you take heed not, free me
  from the curse,
Who both give you warning for and
  the cutpurse.

Cokes. Well said! He were to blame that would not, i' faith.   80

Youth, youth, thou hadst better
  been starved by thy nurse,
Than to live to be hangèd for
  cutting a purse.   85

Cokes. Good i' faith, how say you, Numps? Is there any harm i' this?

Nightingale. It hath been upbraided
  to men of my trade
That oftentimes we are the cause
  of this crime.

Cokes. The more coxcombs they that did it, I wusse.   90

Alack and for pity, why should it
  be said?
As if they regarded or places or
  time.   95

Examples have been
Of some that were seen
In Westminster Hall, yea the
  pleaders between;

Cokes. God a mercy for that! Why should they be more free indeed?   100

Then why should the judges be free
  from this curse,
More than my poor self, for cutting
  the purse?
Youth, youth, thou hadst better
  been starved by thy nurse,

He sings the burden with him.   105

Than live to be hangèd for cutting
  a purse.

Cokes. That again, good ballad-man, that again. O rare! I would fain rub mine elbow now, but I dare not pull out my hand. On, I pray thee; he that made this ballad shall be poet to   110 my masque.

Nightingale. At Worcester 'tis known
  well, and even i' the jail,

---

80. *for and*—and moreover.   98. *Westminster Hall*—where high courts sat.
109. rub mine elbow—an indication of pleasure.

> *A knight of good worship did there*
>   *show his face,*   115
> *Against the foul sinners, in zeal for*
>   *to rail,*
> *And lost* (ipso facto) *his purse in*   *Cokes.* Is
>   *the place.*   it possible?
> *Nay, once from the seat*   120
> *Of judgment so great*
> *A judge there did lose a fair pouch*   *Cokes.* I' faith?
>   *of velvet.*
> *O Lord for thy mercy, how wicked*
>   *or worse*   125
> *Are those that so venture their*
>   *necks for a purse!*
> *Youth, youth, etc.*

Cokes. Youth, youth, etc. [*Sings with him again.*] Pray thee stay a little, friend. Yet o' thy conscience, Numps, speak, is there any harm i' this?

Wasp. To tell you true, 'tis too good for you, 'less you had grace to follow it.

Overdo. [*Aside.*] It doth discover enormity, I'll mark it more; I ha' not liked a paltry piece of poetry so well, a good while.

Cokes. Youth, youth, etc. Where's this youth, now? A man must call upon him, for his own good, and yet he will not appear. Look here, here's for him; handy-dandy, which hand will he have? (*He shows his purse.*) On, I pray thee, with the rest; I do hear of him, but I cannot see him, this Master Youth, the cutpurse.

> *Nightingale. At plays and at sermons,*
>   *and at the sessions,*
> *'Tis daily their practice such booty*   145
>   *to make:*
> *Yea, under the gallows, at execu-*
>   *tions,*
> *They stick not the stare-abouts'*
>   *purses to take.*   150
> *Nay, one without grace,*   *Cokes.* That
> *At a better place,*   was a fine

---

139. handy-dandy—children's game of guessing in which hand an object is concealed.

At court, and in Christmas, before
  the King's face.
Alack then for pity, must I bear
  the curse   fellow! I would have him, now.   155
That only belongs to the cunning
  cutpurse?

Cokes. But where's their cunning now, when they should use it? They are all chained now, I warrant you. *Youth, youth,* 160 *thou hadst better, etc.* The rat-catcher's charm[s] are all fools and asses to this! A pox on 'em, that they will not come! that a man should have such a desire to a thing and want it!

Quarlous. 'Fore God, I'd give half the Fair, an' 'twere mine, for a cutpurse for him, to save his longing. 165

Cokes. Look you, sister, here, here, where is't now? which pocket is't in, for a wager?   *He shows his purse again.*

Wasp. I beseech you leave your wagers and let him end his matter, an't may be.

Cokes. O, are you edified, Numps? 170

Overdo. [*Aside.*] Indeed he does interrupt him too much; there Numps spoke to purpose.

Cokes. Sister, I am an ass, I cannot keep my purse. On, on, I pray thee, friend.   [*He shows it*] *again.*

    Edgworth gets up to him and tickles him in the ear with
       a straw twice to draw his hand out of his pocket.

Nightingale. But O, you vile nation   Winwife. Will 175
  of cutpurses all,   you see sport?
Relent and repent, and amend and   Look, there's
  be sound,   a fellow
And know that you ought not, by   gathers up
  honest men's fall,   to him, 180
Advance your own fortunes, to die   mark.
  above ground;   Quarlous.
And though you go gay   Good, i'
In silks as you may,   faith! O, he
It is not the highway to heaven (as   has lighted 185
  they say).   on the
Repent then, repent you, for   wrong pocket.
  better, for worse: Winwife. He

---

161. rat-catcher's charm[s] —it was believed that rats in Ireland were killed or driven away by rhymes.   163. want—lack.

> *And kiss not the gallows for cut-*   has it, 'fore
> *ting a purse.*   God he is a   190
> *Youth, youth thou hadst better*   brave fellow;
> *been starved by thy nurse,*   pity he should
> *Than live to be hangèd for cutting*   be detected.
> *a purse.*

All. An excellent ballad! an excellent ballad!   195

Edgworth. Friend, let me ha' the first, let me ha' the first,
I pray you.

Cokes. Pardon me, sir. First come, first served; and I'll
buy the whole bundle too.

     [*Edgworth slips the purse to Nightingale.*]

Winwife. That conveyance was better than all, did you   200
see't? He has given the purse to the ballad-singer.

Quarlous. Has he?

Edgworth. Sir, I cry you mercy; I'll not hinder the poor
man's profit; pray you, mistake me not.

Cokes. Sir, I take you for an honest gentleman, if that be   205
mistaking; I met you today afore. Ha! humh! O God! my
purse is gone, my purse, my purse, etc.

Wasp. Come, do not make a stir and cry yourself an ass
thorough the Fair afore your time.

Cokes. Why, hast thou it, Numps? Good Numps, how   210
came you by it? I mar'l!

Wasp. I pray you seek some other gamester to play the
fool with. You may lose it time enough, for all your Fair-wit.

Cokes. By this good hand, glove and all, I ha' lost it
already, if thou hast it not; feel else, and Mistress Grace's   215
handkercher, too, out o' the tother pocket.

Wasp. Why, 'tis well; very well, exceeding pretty, and well.

Edgworth. Are you sure you ha' lost it, sir?

Cokes. O God! yes; as I am an honest man, I had it but
e'en now, at *Youth, youth.*   220

Nightingale. I hope you suspect not me, sir.

Edgworth. Thee? That were a jest indeed! Dost thou think
the gentleman is foolish? Where hadst thou hands, I pray thee?
[*To Nightingale.*] Away, ass, away.

---

209. thorough—through. 211. mar'l—marvel. 217. *Wasp.* Why, 'tis
well; very well, exceedingly pretty, and well—cf. Busy, "Very likely, exceeding
likely, very exceeding likely" (I.vi.100).

[*Exit Nightingale into back part of Ursula's booth.*]

Overdo. [*Aside.*] I shall be beaten again if I be spied.   225

Edgworth. Sir, I suspect an odd fellow, yonder, is stealing away.

Mistress Overdo. Brother, it is the preaching fellow! You shall suspect him. He was at your tother purse, you know! Nay, stay, sir, and view the work you ha' done; an' you   230
beneficed at the gallows and preach there, thank your own handiwork.

Cokes. Sir, you shall take no pride in your preferment; you shall be silenced quickly.

Overdo. What do you mean, sweet buds of gentility?   235

Cokes. To ha' my pennyworths out on you, bud. No less than two purses a day serve you? I thought you a simple fellow when my man Numps beat you i' the morning, and pitied you—

Mistress Overdo. So did I, I'll be sworn, brother; but now   240
I see he is a lewd and pernicious enormity (as Master Overdo calls him).

Overdo. [*Aside.*] Mine own words turned upon me like swords.

Cokes. Cannot a man's purse be at quiet for you i' the   245
master's pocket, but you must entice it forth and debauch it?

Wasp. Sir, sir, keep your debauch and your fine Barthol'mew-terms to yourself, and make as much on 'em as you please. But gi' me this from you i' the meantime; I beseech you, see if I can look to this. [*Tries to take the box.*]   250

Cokes. Why, Numps?

Wasp. Why? Because you are an ass, sir; there's a reason the shortest way, an' you will needs ha' it. Now you ha' got the trick of losing, you'd lose your breech, an't 'twere loose. I know you, sir; come, deliver. (*Wasp takes the license from*   255
him.) You'll go and crack the vermin you breed now, will you? 'Tis very fine, will you ha' the truth on't? They are such retchless flies as you are, that blow cutpurses abroad in every corner; your foolish having of money makes 'em. An' there were no wiser than I, sir, the trade should lie open for you, sir;   260

231. beneficed—given a position in the church.   254. breech—rump.
256. crack—smash.   258. retchless—careless.   blow—deposit eggs for
hatching.   260. the trade . . . you—you would learn a trade (?).

it should i' faith, sir. I would teach your wit to come to your
head, sir, as well as your land to come into your hand, I assure
you, sir.

    Winwife. Alack, good Numps.

    Wasp. Nay, gentlemen, never pity me; I am not worth it.   265
Lord send me at home once, to Harrow o' the Hill again; if I
travel any more, call me Coriat, with all my heart.

    [*Exeunt Wasp, Cokes, and Mistress Overdo with Overdo in
                                       custody.*]

    Quarlous. Stay, sir, I must have a word with you in
private. Do you hear?

    Edgworth. With me, sir? What's your pleasure, good sir?   270

    Quarlous. Do not deny it. You are a cutpurse, sir; this
gentleman here, and I, saw you, nor do we mean to detect you
(though we can sufficiently inform ourselves toward the
danger of concealing you), but you must do us a piece of
service.   275

    Edgworth. Good gentlemen, do not undo me; I am a civil
young man, and but a beginner, indeed.

    Quarlous. Sir, your beginning shall bring on your ending,
for us. We are no catchpoles nor constables. That you are to
undertake is this; you saw the old fellow with the black box   280
here?

    Edgworth. The little old governor, sir?

    Quarlous. That same. I see you have flown him to a mark
already. I would ha' you get away that box from him, and
bring it us.   285

    Edgworth. Would you ha' the box and all, sir? or only
that that is in't? I'll get you that, and leave him the box to
play with still (which will be the harder o' the two), because I
would gain your worships' good opinion of me.

    Winwife. He says well; 'tis the greater mastery, and 'twill   290
make the more sport when 'tis missed.

    Edgworth. Aye, and 'twill be the longer a-missing, to draw
on the sport.

---

  267. Coriat—this jester was also a famous traveler.   272. detect—inform on.
278–79. beginning . . . us—you can continue to the end as a cutpurse, as far as
we're concerned; or—since you've begun this way, you must end by doing service for us.   279. catchpoles—minor officers who could make arrests.
282. governor—tutor.

Quarlous. But look you do it now, sirrah, and keep your
word, or— 295

Edgworth. Sir, if ever I break my word with a gentleman,
may I never read word at my need. Where shall I find you?

Quarlous. Somewhere i' the Fair, hereabouts. Dispatch it
quickly. [*Exit Edgworth.*] I would fain see the careful fool
deluded! Of all beasts I love the serious ass—he that takes pains 300
to be one, and plays the fool with the greatest diligence that
can be.

Grace. Then you would not choose, sir, but love my
guardian, Justice Overdo, who is answerable to that description in every hair of him. 305

Quarlous. So I have heard. But how came you, Mistress
Wellborn, to be his ward, or have relation to him, at first?

Grace. Faith, through a common calamity; he bought me,
sir; and now he will marry me to his wife's brother, this wise
gentlemen that you see, or else I must pay value o' my land. 310

Quarlous. 'Slid, is there no device of disparagement, or so?
Talk with some crafty fellow, some picklock o' the law! Would
I had studied a year longer i' the Inns of Court, an't had been
but i' your case.

Winwife. [*Aside.*] Aye, Master Quarlous, are you 315
proffering?

Grace. You'd bring but little aid, sir.

Winwife. [*Aside.*] I'll look to you i' faith, gamester—An
unfortunate foolish tribe you are fall'n into, lady; I wonder
you can endure 'em. 320

Grace. Sir, they that cannot work their fetters off must
wear 'em.

Winwife. You see what care they have on you, to leave
you thus.

Grace. Faith, the same they have of themselves, sir. I 325
cannot greatly complain if this were all the plea I had against
'em.

Winwife. 'Tis true! but will you please to withdraw with
us a little, and make them think they have lost you? I hope

---

297. read . . . need—referring to his neck verse.   308. bought me—many
tenants technically held their land from the king; he could therefore sell the
guardianship of their minor heirs.   311. disparagement—marriage to an
inferior in rank; a guardian could not legally enforce such a marriage.

our manners ha' been such hitherto, and our language, as will   330
give you no cause to doubt yourself in our company.

    Grace. Sir, I will give myself no cause; I am so secure of
mine own manners as I suspect not yours.

    Quarlous. Look where John Littlewit comes.

    Winwife. Away, I'll not be seen by him.   335

    Quarlous. No, you were not best, he'd tell his mother, the
widow.

    Winwife. Heart, what do you mean?

    Quarlous. Cry you mercy, is the wind there? Must not the
widow be named?   [*Exeunt Grace, Winwife, Quarlous.*]   340

ACT III
SCENE VI

    [*Enter from back part of Ursula's booth Littlewit, Win.*]

Littlewit. Do you hear, Win, Win?

Win. What say you, John?

Littlewit. While they are paying the reckoning, Win, I'll
tell you a thing, Win: we shall never see any sights i' the Fair,
Win, except you long still, Win. Good Win, sweet Win, long to   5
see some hobbyhorses and some drums and rattles and dogs
and fine devices, Win. The bull with the five legs, Win, and the
great hog. Now you ha' begun with pig, you may long for
anything, Win, and so for my motion, Win.

    Win. But we sha' not eat o' the bull and the hog, John;   10
how shall I long then?

    Littlewit. O yes, Win! you may long to see as well as to
taste, Win. How did the 'pothecary's wife, Win, that longed to
see the anatomy, Win? Or the lady, Win, that desired to spit i'
the great lawyer's mouth after an eloquent pleading? I assure   15
you they longed, Win; good Win, go in, and long.

                               [*Exeunt Littlewit, Win.*]

    Trash. I think we are rid of our new customer,   *They*
Brother Leatherhead; we shall hear no more of him.   *plot*

    Leatherhead. All the better; let's pack up all and   *to be*
be gone before he find us.   *gone.*   20

9. my motion—see I.v.145–46.   14. anatomy—dissection.

Trash. Stay a little, yonder comes a company; it may be
we may take some more money.

[Enter Knockem, Busy.]

Knockem. Sir, I will take your counsel and cut my hair
and leave vapors. I see that tobacco and bottle-ale and pig and
Whit and very Urs'la herself is all vanity.   25

Busy. Only pig was not comprehended in my admonition;
the rest were. For long hair, it is an ensign of pride, a banner,
and the world is full of those banners, very full of banners.
And bottle-ale is a drink of Satan's, a diet-drink of Satan's,
devised to puff us up and make us swell in this latter age of   30
vanity, as the smoke of tobacco to keep us in mist and error;
but the fleshy woman, which you call Urs'la, is above all to be
avoided, having the marks upon her of the three enemies of
man: the world, as being in the Fair; the devil, as being in the
fire; and the flesh, as being herself.   35

[Enter Purecraft.]

Purecraft. Brother Zeal-of-the-land! what shall we do? My
daughter, Win-the-fight, is fall'n into her fit of longing again.

Busy. For more pig? There is no more, is there?

Purecraft. To see some sights i' the Fair.

Busy. Sister, let her fly the impurity of the place swiftly,   40
lest she partake of the pitch thereof. Thou art the seat of the
Beast, O Smithfield, and I will leave thee. Idolatry peepeth out
on every side of thee.

Knockem. [*Aside.*] An excellent right hypocrite! Now his
belly is full, he falls a-railing and kicking, the jade. A very good 45
vapor! I'll in and joy Urs'la with telling how her pig works;
two and a half he eat to his share. And he has drunk a pailfull.
He eats with his eyes as well as his teeth.   [*Exit.*]

Leatherhead. What do you lack, gentlemen? What is't you
buy? Rattles, drums, babies—   50

Busy. Peace with thy apocryphal wares, thou profane
publican—thy bells, thy dragons, and thy Toby's dogs. Thy

29. diet-drink—medicine.   41–42. the Beast—Revelation 13.   45. jade—
worthless horse.   47. eat—the past tense, pronounced *et*.   51. apocryphal—sham; the Puritans vehemently excluded the books called the Apocrypha
from the biblical canon.   52. publican—a tax collector in the New Testament, hated by the Jews. The irony here is that Jesus, unlike Busy, showed
charity for publicans (e.g., Luke 15: 1–2).   bells . . . dogs—punning allusions
to the stories in the Apocrypha of Bel and the Dragon and Tobias (Toby), who
was followed by a faithful dog.

hobbyhorse is an idol, a very idol, a fierce and rank idol; and thou the Nebuchadnezzar, the proud Nebuchadnezzar of the Fair, that sett'st it up for children to fall down to and worship.   55

Leatherhead. Cry you mercy, sir, will you buy a fiddle to fill up your noise?

[*Re-enter Littlewit, Win.*]

Littlewit. Look, Win; do look o' God's name, and save your longing. Here be fine sights.

Purecraft. Aye, child, so you hate 'em, as our brother Zeal   60 does, you may look on 'em.

Leatherhead. Or what do you say to a drum, sir?

Busy. It is the broken belly of the Beast, and thy bellows there are his lungs, and these pipes are his throat, those feathers are of his tail, and thy rattles the gnashing of his   65 teeth.

Trash. And what's my gingerbread, I pray you?

Busy. The provender that pricks him up. Hence with thy basket of popery, thy nest of images, and whole legend of ginger-work.   70

Leatherhead. Sir, if you be not quiet the quicklier, I'll ha' you clapped fairly by the heels for disturbing the Fair.

Busy. The sin of the Fair provokes me; I cannot be silent.

Purecraft. Good Brother Zeal!

Leatherhead. Sir, I'll make you silent, believe it.   75

Littlewit. [*Aside to Leatherhead.*] I'd give a shilling you could, i' faith, friend.

Leatherhead. Sir, give me your shilling; I'll give you my shop if I do not, and I'll leave it in pawn with you i' the meantime.   80

Littlewit. A match i' faith, but do it quickly, then.

[*Exit Leatherhead.*]

Busy. (*He speaks to the widow.*) Hinder me not, woman. I was moved in spirit to be here this day in this Fair, this wicked and foul Fair—and fitter may it be called a foul than a Fair—to protest against the abuses of it, the foul abuses of it, in regard   85 of the afflicted saints, that are troubled, very much troubled,

---

54. Nebuchadnezzar—Chaldean king who required idol worship of the captive Jews (Daniel 3).   68. pricks him up—stimulates him.   69. images— gingerbread men.   legend—collection of saints' lives, regarded by the Puritans as "rags of Rome."   72. clapped . . . heels—put in the stocks.

exceedingly troubled, with the opening of the merchandise of
Babylon again, and the peeping of popery upon the stalls,
here, here, in the high places. See you not Goldylocks, the
purple strumpet, there, in her yellow gown and green sleeves?   90
the profane pipes, the tinkling timbrels? A shop of relics!

    Littlewit. Pray you forbear, I am put in trust with 'em.

    Busy. And this idolatrous grove of images, this flasket of
idols! which I will pull down—

                  Overthrows the gingerbread.

    Trash. O my ware, my ware, God bless it.   95

    Busy. —in my zeal, and glory to be thus exercised.

                 Leatherhead enters with officers.

    Leatherhead. Here he is. Pray you lay hold on his zeal; we
cannot sell a whistle, for him, in tune. Stop his noise first!

    Busy. Thou canst not; 'tis a sanctified noise. I will make a
loud and most strong noise, till I have daunted the profane   100
enemy. And for this cause—

    Leatherhead. Sir, here's no man afraid of you or your
cause. You shall swear it i' the stocks, sir.

    Busy. I will thrust myself into the stocks, upon the pikes
of the land.   105

    Leatherhead. Carry him away.

    Purecraft. What do you mean, wicked men?

    Busy. Let them alone; I fear them not.

       [*Exeunt officers with Busy, followed by Purecraft.*]

    Littlewit. Was not this shilling well ventured, Win, for our
liberty? Now we may go play, and see over the Fair, where we   110
list, ourselves; my mother is gone after him, and let her e'en go
and loose us.

    Win. Yes, John, but I know not what to do.

    Littlewit. For what, Win?

    Win. For a thing I am ashamed to tell you, i' faith, and 'tis   115
too far to go home.

    Littlewit. I pray thee be not ashamed, Win. Come, i' faith
thou shall not be ashamed; is it anything about the
hobbyhorse-man? An't be, speak freely.

    Win. Hang him, base bobchin, I scorn him; no, I have very   120
great what sha' call 'um, John.

---

91. relics—another "popish" concept the Puritans hated.   93. flasket—a long
basket.

Littlewit. O! is that all, Win? We'll go back to Captain Jordan; to the pig-woman's, Win. He'll help us, or she with a dripping pan, or an old kettle, or something. The poor greasy soul loves you, Win, and after we'll visit the Fair all over, Win,   125 and see my puppet play, Win; you know it's a fine matter, Win.

[*Exeunt Littlewit, Win into Ursula's booth.*]

Leatherhead. Let's away; I counselled you to pack up afore, Joan.

Trash. A pox of his Bedlam purity. He has spoiled half my   130 ware; but the best is, we lose nothing if we miss our first merchant.

Leatherhead. It shall be hard for him to find or know us when we are translated, Joan.

[*They pack up their wares, take down their stands,*
and exeunt.]

132. merchant—customer.   134. translated—metamorphosed, i.e., disguised. See *Midsummer Night's Dream* III.i.122.

ACT IV
SCENE I

[*Enter Trouble-all, Bristle, Haggis, Cokes, Overdo.*]

Trouble-all. My Masters, I do make no doubt but you are officers.

Bristle. What then, sir?

Trouble-all. And the King's loving and obedient subjects.

Bristle. Obedient, friend? Take heed what you speak, I   5 advise you; Oliver Bristle advises you. His loving subjects, we grant you; but not his obedient, at this time, by your leave; we know ourselves a little better than so; we are to command, sir, and such as you are to be obedient. Here's one of his obedient subjects going to the stocks, and we'll make you such another,   10 if you talk.

Trouble-all. You are all wise enough i' your places, I know.

Bristle. If you know it, sir, why do you bring it in question?   15

Trouble-all. I question nothing, pardon me. I do only hope you have warrant for what you do, and so, quit you, and so, multiply you.   *He goes away.*

Haggis. What's he? Bring him up to the stocks there. Why bring you him not up?   [*Trouble-all*] *comes again.*   20

Trouble-all. If you have Justice Overdo's warrant, 'tis well; you are safe. This is the warrant of warrants. I'll not give this button for any man's warrant else.

Bristle. Like enough, sir; but let me tell you, an' you play away your buttons thus, you will want 'em ere night, for any   25
store I see about you. You might keep 'em, and save pins, I wusse.   [*Trouble-all*] *goes away.*

Overdo. [*Aside.*] What should he be, that doth so esteem and advance my warrant? He seems a sober and discreet person! It is a comfort to a good conscience to be followed   30
with a good fame in his sufferings. The world will have a pretty taste by this, how I can bear adversity; and it will beget a kind of reverence toward me hereafter, even from mine enemies, when they shall see I carry my calamity nobly, and that it doth neither break me nor bend me.   35

Haggis. Come, sir, here's a place for you to preach in. Will you put in your leg?   *They put him in the stocks.*

Overdo. That I will, cheerfully.

Bristle. O' my conscience, a seminary! He kisses the stocks.   40

Cokes. Well, my masters, I'll leave him with you; now I see him bestowed, I'll go look for my goods and Numps.

Haggis. You may, sir, I warrant you; where's the tother bawler? Fetch him too, you shall find 'em both fast enough.

[*Exit Cokes.*]

Overdo. [*Aside.*] In the midst of this tumult I will yet be   45
the author of mine own rest, and, not minding their fury, sit in the stocks in that calm as shall be able to trouble a triumph.

[*Trouble-all*] *comes again.*

Trouble-all. Do you assure me upon your words? May I undertake for you, if I be asked the question, that you have this warrant?   50

Haggis. What's this fellow, for God's sake?

17. quit—God requite, reward.   18. multiply you—God increase your family.   47. triumph—Roman victory celebration that included a procession of captives.

Trouble-all. Do but show me Adam Overdo, and I am satisfied.   *Goes out.*

Bristle. He is a fellow that is distracted, they say—one Trouble-all. He was an officer in the court of Pie-powders here   55
last year, and put out on his place by Justice Overdo.

Overdo. Ha!

Bristle. Upon which he took an idle conceit, and's run mad upon't. So that ever since, he will do nothing but by Justice Overdo's warrant; he will not eat a crust, nor drink a   60
little, nor make him in his apparel ready. His wife, sir-reverence, cannot get him make his water or shift his shirt without his warrant.

Overdo. [*Aside.*] If this be true, this is my greatest disaster! How am I bound to satisfy this poor man, that is of   65
so good a nature to me, out of his wits, where there is no room left for dissembling!

                                   [*Trouble-all*] *comes in.*

Trouble-all. If you cannot show me Adam Overdo, I am in doubt of you. I am afraid you cannot answer it.

                                                    Goes again.

Haggis. Before me, neighbor Bristle, (and now I think on't   70
better) Justice Overdo is a very peremptory person.

Bristle. O! are you advised of that? And a severe justicer, by your leave.

Overdo. [*Aside.*] Do I hear ill o' that side, too?

Bristle. He will sit as upright o' the bench, an' you mark   75
him, as a candle i' the socket, and give light to the whole court in every business.

Haggis. But he will burn blue and swell like a boil (God bless us!) an' he be angry.

Bristle. Aye, and he will be angry too, when him list,   80
that's more; and when he is angry, be it right or wrong, he has the law on's side ever. I mark that too.

Overdo. [*Aside.*] I will be more tender hereafter. I see compassion may become a justice, though it be a weakness, I confess, and nearer a vice than a virtue.   85

Haggis. Well, take him out o' the stocks again. We'll go a

---

58. idle—foolish.   78. blue—pale, an ill omen.   80. him list—it pleases him.

sure way to work; we'll ha' the ace of hearts of our side, if we can.

    They take the Justice out. [*Enter Poacher, Busy, Purecraft.*]

    Poacher. Come, bring him away to his fellow, there. Master Busy, we shall rule your legs, I hope, though we cannot   90
rule your tongue.

    Busy. No, minister of darkness, no, thou canst not rule my tongue; my tongue it is mine own, and with it I will both knock and mock down your Barthol'mew-abominations, till you be made a hissing to the neighbor parishes round about.   95

    Haggis. Let him alone; we have devised better upon't.

    Purecraft. And shall he not into the stocks then?

    Bristle. No, mistress, we'll have 'em both to Justice Overdo, and let him do over 'em as is fitting. Then I and my gossip Haggis and my beadle Poacher are discharged.   100

    Purecraft. O, I thank you, blessed, honest men!

    Bristle. Nay, never thank us, but thank this madman that comes here. He put it in our heads.

                      [*Trouble-all*] *comes again.*

    Purecraft. Is he mad? Now heaven increase his madness, and bless it, and thank it; sir, your poor handmaid thanks you.   105

    Trouble-all. Have you a warrant? An' you have a warrant, show it.

    Purecraft. Yes, I have a warrant out of the Word, to give thanks for removing any scorn intended to the brethren.

    Trouble-all. It is Justice Overdo's warrant that I look for.   110
If you have not that, keep your word, I'll keep mine. Quit ye, and multiply ye.   [*Exeunt all but Trouble-all.*]

87. ace of hearts—a high card, i.e., Justice Overdo's warrant. They have decided to take the culprit to court immediately.

ACT IV
SCENE II

                    [*Enter Edgworth, Nightingale.*]

    Edgworth. Come away, Nightingale, I pray thee.

    Trouble-all. Whither go you? Where's your warrant?

    Edgworth. Warrant, for what, sir?

Trouble-all. For what you go about; you know how fit it
is; an' you have no warrant, bless you, I'll pray for you, that's   5
all I can do.   *Goes out.*

Edgworth. What means he?

Nightingale. A madman that haunts the Fair; do you not
know him? It's marvel he has not more followers after his
ragged heels.   10

Edgworth. Beshrew him, he startled me. I thought he had
known of our plot. Guilt's a terrible thing! Ha' you prepared
the costermonger?

Nightingale. Yes, and agreed for his basket of pears. He is
at the corner here, ready. [*Enter Costermonger.*] And your   15
prize, he comes down, sailing that way, all alone, without his
protector; he is rid of him, it seems.

Edgworth. Aye, I know; I should ha' followed his
protectorship for a feat I am to do upon him; but this offered
itself so i' the way, I could not let it 'scape. Here he comes;   20
whistle. Be this sport called "Dorring the Dottrel."

[*Enter Cokes.*]

Nightingale. (*Whistles.*) Wh, wh, wh, wh, etc.

Cokes. By this light, I cannot find my gingerbread-wife
nor my hobbyhorse-man in all the Fair, now, to ha' my money
again. And I do not know the way out on't, to go home for   25
more, do you hear, friend, you that whistle? what tune is that
you whistle?

Nightingale. A new tune I am practising, sir.

Cokes. Dost thou know where I dwell, I pray thee? Nay,
on with thy tune, I ha' no such haste for an answer. I'll   30
practise with thee.

Costermonger. Buy any pears, very fine pears, pears fine.

*Nightingale sets his foot afore him, and he falls with
his basket.*

Cokes. Godso! a muss, a muss, a muss, a muss.

[*He starts picking up the pears.*]

Costermonger. Good gentleman, my ware, my ware! I am
a poor man. Good sir, my ware.   35

Nightingale. [*To Cokes.*] Let me hold your sword, sir, it
troubles you.

16. prize—ship victimized by pirate or privateer.   21. "Dorring the
Dottrel"—fleecing the fool (*dor*, trick; *dottrell*, bird easily caught).
33. muss—scramble.

Cokes. Do, and my cloak, an' thou wilt; and my hat too.
Cokes falls a-scrambling whilst they run away with his things.
    Edgworth. A delicate great boy! methinks he out-
scrambles 'em all. I cannot persuade myself but he goes to   40
grammar-school yet, and plays the truant today.
    Nightingale. Would he had another purse to cut, 'Zekiel.
    Edgworth. Purse? a man might cut out his kidneys, I
think, and he never feel 'em, he is so earnest at the sport.
    Nightingale. His soul is half-way out on's body at the   45
game.
    Edgworth. Away, Nightingale; that way.
           [*Exit Nightingale with sword, cloak, and hat.*]
    Cokes. I think I am furnished for Cather'ne pears for one
undermeal. Gi' me my cloak.
    Costermonger. Good gentleman, give me my ware.   50
    Cokes. Where's the fellow I ga' my cloak to? My cloak?
and my hat? Ha! God's lid, is he gone? Thieves, thieves! Help
me to cry, gentlemen.   *He runs out.*
    Edgworth. Away, costermonger, come to us to Urs'la's.
[*Exit Costermonger.*] Talk of him to have a soul? 'Heart, if he   55
have any more than a thing given him instead of salt, only to
keep him from stinking, I'll be hanged afore my time,
presently. Where should it be, trow? In his blood? He has not
so much toward it in his whole body as will maintain a good
flea. And if he take this course, he will not ha' so much land   60
left as to rear a calf within this twelvemonth. Was there ever
green plover so pulled! That his little overseer had been here
now, and been but tall enough, to see him steal pears in
exchange for his beaver-hat and his cloak thus! I must go find
him out next, for his black box and his patent (it seems) he   65
has of his place; which I think the gentleman would have a
reversion of, that spoke to me for it so earnestly.   [*Exit.*]
                           He [*Cokes*] *comes again.*
    Cokes. Would I might lose my doublet, and hose too, as I
am an honest man, and never stir, if I think there be anything
but thieving and coz'ning i' this whole Fair. Barthol'mew Fair,   70

49. undermeal—afternoon meal.   62. plover . . . pulled—stupid bird
plucked. The dottrell was a species of plover.   65–67. patent . . . reversion of—Edgworth thinks the paper to be stolen is Wasp's patent or grant of
office (place) and that Quarlous wants the job next (a reversion).   68. hose—
trousers.

quoth he; an' ever any Barthol'mew had that luck in't that I
have had, I'll be martyred for him, and in Smithfield too. I ha'
paid for my pears, a rot on 'em, I'll keep 'em no longer.
(*Throws away his pears.*) You were choke-pears to me; I had
been better ha' gone to mum-chance for you, I wusse.   75
Methinks the Fair should not have used me thus, an' 'twere
but for my name's sake; I would not ha' used a dog o' the
name so. O, Numps will triumph now! (*Trouble-all comes
again.*) Friend, do you know who I am? Or where I lie? I do
not myself, I'll be sworn. Do but carry me home, and I'll   80
please thee; I ha' money enough there. I ha' lost myself, and
my cloak and my hat; and my fine sword and my sister and
Numps and Mistress Grace (a gentlewoman that I should ha'
married) and a cut-work handkercher she ga' me and two
purses, today. And my bargain o' hobbyhorses and ginger-   85
bread, which grieves me worst of all.

    Trouble-all. By whose warrant, sir, have you done all this?

    Cokes. Warrant? thou art a wise fellow, indeed—as if a
man need a warrant to lose anything with.

    Trouble-all. Yes, Justice Overdo's warrant, a man may get   90
and lose with, I'll stand to't.

    Cokes. Justice Overdo? Dost thou know him? I lie there,
he is my brother-in-law, he married my sister. Pray thee show
me the way, dost thou know the house?

    Trouble-all. Sir, show me your warrant; I know nothing   95
without a warrant, pardon me.

    Cokes. Why, I warrant thee, come along. Thou shalt see I
have wrought pillows there, and cambric sheets, and sweet
bags too. Pray thee guide me to the house.

    Trouble-all. Sir, I'll tell you: go you thither yourself, first,   100
alone; tell your worshipful brother your mind; and but bring
me three lines of his hand, or his clerk's, with "Adam Overdo"
underneath. Here I'll stay you; I'll obey you, and I'll guide you
presently.

    Cokes. [*Aside.*] 'Slid, this is an ass; I ha' found him. Pox   105
upon me, what do I talking to such a dull fool?—Farewell. You
are a very coxcomb, do you hear?

    Trouble-all. I think I am; if Justice Overdo sign to it, I am,
and so we are all; he'll quit us all, multiply us all.   [*Exeunt.*]

---

74. choke-pears—coarse kind of pears.   75. mum-chance—a dice game.
98–99. sweet bags—bags of fragrant herbs to perfume the bed-clothes.

ACT IV
SCENE III

[*Enter Grace, Quarlous, Winwife.*]
They [*Quarlous, Winwife*] *enter with their swords drawn.*

Grace. Gentlemen, this is no way that you take. You do but breed one another trouble and offence, and give me no contentment at all. I am no she that affects to be quarrelled for, or have my name or fortune made the question of men's swords.   5

Quarlous. 'Slood, we love you.

Grace. If you both love me, as you pretend, your own reason will tell you but one can enjoy me; and to that point there leads a directer line than by my infamy, which must follow if you fight. 'Tis true, I have professed it to you   10
ingenuously, that rather than be yoked with this bridegroom is appointed me, I would take up any husband, almost upon any trust. Though subtlety would say to me (I know) he is a fool, and has an estate, and I might govern him and enjoy a friend beside. But these are not my aims. I must have a husband I   15
must love, or I cannot live with him. I shall ill make one of these politic wives!

Winwife. Why, if you can like either of us, lady, say which is he, and the other shall swear instantly to desist.

Quarlous. Content; I accord to that willingly.   20

Grace. Sure you think me a woman of an extreme levity, gentlemen, or a strange fancy, that (meeting you by chance in such a place as this, both at one instant, and not yet of two hours' acquaintance, neither of you deserving afore the other of me) I should so forsake my modesty (though I might affect   25
one more particularly) as to say, "This is he," and name him.

Quarlous. Why, wherefore should you not? What should hinder you?

Grace. If you would not give it to my modesty, allow it yet to my wit; give me so much of woman and cunning as not   30
to betray myself impertinently. How can I judge of you so far as to a choice without knowing you more? You are both equal and alike to me yet; and so indifferently affected by me as each of you might be the man if the other were away. For you are reasonable creatures; you have understanding and dis-   35
course. And if fate send me an understanding husband, I have

no fear at all but mine own manners shall make him a good one.

    Quarlous. Would I were put forth to making for you, then.   40

    Grace. It may be you are; you know not what's toward you. Will you consent to a motion of mine, gentlemen?

    Winwife. Whatever it be, we'll presume reasonableness, coming from you.

    Quarlous. And fitness too.   45

    Grace. I saw one of you buy a pair of tables, e'en now.

    Winwife. Yes, here they be, and maiden ones too, unwritten in.

    Grace. The fitter for what they may be employed in. You shall write, either of you, here, a word or a name—what you   50 like best—but of two or three syllables at most; and the next person that comes this way (because destiny has a high hand in business of this nature) I'll demand which of the two words he or she doth approve; and according to that sentence fix my resolution and affection without change.   55

    Quarlous. Agreed. My word is conceived already.

    Winwife. And mine shall not be long creating after.

    Grace. But you shall promise, gentlemen, not to be curious to know which of it is, [is] taken; but give me leave to conceal that till you have brought me either home, or where I   60 may safely tender myself.

    Winwife. Why, that's but equal.

    Quarlous. We are pleased.

    Grace. Because I will bind both your endeavors to work together, friendly and jointly, each to the other's fortune, and   65 have myself fitted with some means to make him that is forsaken a part of amends.

    Quarlous. These conditions are very courteous. Well, my word is out of the *Arcadia,* then: "Argalus."

    Winwife. And mine out of the play, "Palamon."   70

                          Trouble-all comes again.

39. to making for you—to be trained by you.   41. toward—in store for.
46. pair of tables—tablet for writing.   61. tender—entrust, take care of.
62. equal—just, fair.   67. a part of amends—partial compensation, i.e., give part of her estate.   69. Argalus—lover in Sidney's *Arcadia.*
70. Palamon—probably from a play, *The Two Noble Kinsmen,* 1613. Its original was Chaucer's *Knight's Tale.*

Trouble-all. Have you any warrant for this, gentlemen?

Quarlous, Winwife. Ha!

Trouble-all. There must be a warrant had, believe it.

Winwife. For what?

Trouble-all. For whatsoever it is, anything indeed, no   75
matter what.

Quarlous. 'Slight, here's a fine ragged prophet, dropped
down i' the nick!

Trouble-all. Heaven quit you, gentlemen.

Quarlous. Nay, stay a little. Good lady, put him to the   80
question.

Grace. You are content, then?

Winwife, Quarlous. Yes, yes.

Grace. Sir, here are two names written—

Trouble-all. Is Justice Overdo one?   85

Grace. How, sir? I pray you read 'em to yourself—it is for
a wager between these gentlemen—and with a stroke or any
difference, mark which you approve best.

Trouble-all. They may be both worshipful names for
ought I know, mistress, but Adam Overdo had been worth   90
three of 'em, I assure you, in this place; that's in plain English.

Grace. This man amazes me! I pray you, like one of 'em,
sir.

Trouble-all. I do like him there, that has the best warrant.
Mistress, to save your longing (and multiply him), it may be   95
this. [*Marks the book.*] But I am aye still for Justice Overdo,
that's my conscience. And quit you.   [*Exit.*]

Winwife. Is't done, lady?

Grace. Aye, and strangely as ever I saw! What fellow is
this, trow?   100

Quarlous. No matter what, a fortune-teller we ha' made
him. Which is't, which is't?

Grace. Nay, did you not promise not to inquire?

          [*Enter Edgworth.*]

Quarlous. 'Slid, I forgot that, pray you pardon me. Look,
here's our Mercury come. The license arrives i' the finest time,   105
too! 'Tis but scraping out Cokes his name, and 'tis done.

Winwife. How now, lime-twig? Hast thou touched?

---

88. difference—differentiating mark. 105. Mercury—because of his speed,
god of thieves.

Edgworth. Not yet, sir; except you would go with me and
see't, it's not worth speaking on. The act is nothing without a
witness. Yonder he is, your man with the box, fall'n into the   110
finest company, and so transported with vapors; they ha' got
in a northern clothier and one Puppy, a western man, that's
come to wrestle before my Lord Mayor anon, and Captain
Whit, and one Val Cutting, that helps Captain Jordan to roar, a
circling boy; with whom your Numps is so taken that you may   115
strip him of his clothes, if you will. I'll undertake to geld him
for you, if you had but a surgeon, ready, to sear him. And
Mistress Justice, there, is the goodest woman! She does so love
'em all over, in terms of justice and the style of authority, with
her hood upright—that I beseech you come away, gentlemen,   120
and see't.

Quarlous. 'Slight, I would not lose it for the Fair; what'll
you do, Ned?

Winwife. Why, stay here about for you; Mistress Wellborn
must not be seen.   125

Quarlous. Do so, and find out a priest i' the meantime; I'll
bring the license. [*To Edgworth.*] Lead, which way is't?
                                        [*Exeunt Winwife, Grace.*]

Edgworth. Here, sir, you are o' the backside o' the booth
already; you may hear the noise.

115. circling boy—see IV.iv.137–46.

ACT IV

SCENE IV

[*Knockem, Northern, Puppy, Cutting, Whit, Wasp,
            Mistress Overdo revealed in Ursula's booth.*]

Knockem. Whit, bid Val Cutting continue the vapors for a
lift, Whit, for a lift.

Northern. I'll ne mare, I'll ne mare, the eale's too
meeghty.

Knockem. How now! my Galloway Nag, the staggers? Ha!   5
Whit, gi' him a slit i' the forehead. Cheer up, man; a needle and

2. lift—trick.   5. Galloway Nag—Scottish breed.   6. slit—supposed
cure for the staggers (dizziness); other remedies follow.

thread to stitch his ears. I'd cure him now, an' I had it, with a little butter and garlic, long-pepper, and grains. Where's my horn? I'll gi' him a mash, presently, shall take away this dizziness.   10

Puppy. Why, where are you, zurs? Do you vlinch and leave us i' the zuds, now?

Northern. I'll ne mare, I is e'en as vull as a paiper's bag, by my troth, I.

Puppy. Do my northern cloth zhrink i' the wetting, ha?   15

Knockem. Why, well said, old flea-bitten, thou'lt never tire, I see.

> *They fall to their vapors again.*

Cutting. No, sir, but he may tire, if it please him.

Whit. Who told dee sho? that he vuld never teer, man?

Cutting. No matter who told him so, so long as he knows.   20

Knockem. Nay, I know nothing, sir, pardon me there.

Edgworth. [*To Quarlous.*] They are at it still, sir; this they call vapors.

Whit. He shall not pardon dee, Captain, dou shalt not be pardoned. Pre'de shweetheart, do not pardon him.   25

Cutting. 'Slight, I'll pardon him, an' I list, whosoever says nay to't.

Quarlous. Where's Numps? I miss him.

Wasp. Why, I say nay to't.

Quarlous. O there he is!   30

Knockem. To what do you say nay, sir?

> *Here they continue their game of vapors, which is*
> *nonsense: every man to oppose the last man that spoke,*
> *whether it concerned him or no.*

Wasp. To anything, whatsoever it is, so long as I do not like it.

Whit. Pardon me, little man, dou musht like it a little.

Cutting. No, he must not like it at all, sir; there you are i'   35
the wrong.

Whit. I tink I be; he musht not like it, indeed.

Cutting. Nay, then he both must and will like it, sir, for all you.

Knockem. If he have reason, he may like it, sir.   40

---

9. horn—vessel used in giving medicine to horses.   12. i' the zuds—(1) in the ale, (2) in trouble.   13. paiper's bag—the Northern man naturally refers to bagpipes.   16. flea-bitten—spotted horse (not a term of abuse).

Whit. By no meansh, Captain, upon reason; he may like nothing upon reason.

Wasp. I have no reason, nor I will hear of no reason, nor I will look for no reason, and he is an ass that either knows any or looks for't from me.   45

Cutting. Yes, in some sense you may have reason, sir.

Wasp. Aye, in some sense, I care not if I grant you.

Whit. Pardon me, thou oughsht to grant him nothing, in no shensh, if dou do love dyshelf, angry man.

Wasp. Why then, I do grant him nothing; and I have no   50
sense.

Cutting. 'Tis true, thou hast no sense indeed.

Wasp. 'Slid, but I have sense, now I think on't better, and I will grant him anything, do you see?

Knockem. He is i' the right, and does utter a sufficient   55
vapor.

Cutting. Nay, it is no sufficient vapor, neither; I deny that.

Knockem. Then it is a sweet vapor.

Cutting. It may be a sweet vapor.   60

Wasp. Nay, it is no sweet vapor, neither, sir; it stinks, and I'll stand to't.

Whit. Yes, I tink it doesh shtink, Captain. All vapor doesh shtink.

Wasp. Nay, then it does not stink sir, and it shall not   65
stink.

Cutting. By your leave, it may, sir.

Wasp. Aye, by my leave, it may stink; I know that.

Whit. Pardon me, thou knowesht nothing; it cannot by thy leave, angry man.   70

Wasp. How can it not?

Knockem. Nay, never question him, for he is i' the right.

Whit. Yesh, I am i' de right, I confesh it; so ish de little man too.

Wasp. I'll have nothing confessed that concerns me. I am   75
not i' the right, nor never was i' the right, nor never will be i' the right, while I am in my right mind.

Cutting. Mind? Why, here's no man minds you, sir, nor anything else.

                                        They drink again.

Puppy. Vriend, will you mind this that we do?   80

Quarlous. [*To Edgworth.*] Call you this vapors? This is
such belching of quarrel as I never heard. Will you mind your
business, sir?

Edgworth. You shall see, sir.

Northern. I'll ne mair, my waimb warks too mickle with   85
this aiready.

Edgworth. Will you take that, Master Wasp, that nobody
should mind you?

Wasp. Why? What ha' you to do? Is't any matter to you?

Edgworth. No, but methinks you should not be un-   90
minded, though.

Wasp. Nor I wu' not be, now I think on't; do you hear,
new acquaintance, does no man mind me, say you?

Cutting. Yes, sir, every man here minds you, but how?

Wasp. Nay, I care as little how as you do; that was not my 95
question.

Whit. No, noting was ty question; tou art a learned man,
and I am a valiant man; i' faith la, tou shalt speak for me, and I
vill fight for tee.

Knockem. Fight for him, Whit? A gross vapor; he can   100
fight for himself.

Wasp. It may be I can, but it may be I wu' not, how then?

Cutting. Why, then you may choose.

Wasp. Why, and I'll choose whether I'll choose or no.

Knockem. I think you may, and 'tis true; and I allow it   105
for a resolute vapor.

Wasp. Nay, then, I do think you do not think and it is no
resolute vapor.

Cutting. Yes, in some sort he may allow you.

Knockem. In no sort, sir, pardon me, I can allow him   110
nothing. You mistake the vapor.

Wasp. He mistakes nothing, sir, in no sort.

Whit. Yes, I pre dee now, let him mistake.

Wasp. A turd i' your teeth, never pre dee me, for I will
have nothing mistaken.   115

Knockem. Turd, ha, turd? A noisome vapor; strike, Whit.
      They fall by the ears. [*As they are fighting, Edgworth
            steals the license out of the box and exits.*]

Mistress Overdo. Why gentlemen, why gentlemen, I charge
you upon my authority, conserve the peace. In the King's

85. waimb . . . mickle—womb (stomach) churns too much.

name, and my husband's, put up your weapons; I shall be
driven to commit you myself, else.   120

    Quarlous. Ha, ha, ha.

    Wasp. Why do you laugh, sir?

    Quarlous. Sir, you'll allow me my Christian liberty. I may
laugh, I hope.

    Cutting. In some sort you may, and in some sort you may   125
not, sir.

    Knockem. Nay, in some sort, sir, he may neither laugh nor
hope in this company.

    Wasp. Yes, then he may both laugh and hope in any sort,
an't please him.   130

    Quarlous. Faith, and I will then, for it doth please me
exceedingly.

    Wasp. No exceeding neither, sir.

    Knockem. No, that vapor is too lofty.

    Quarlous. Gentlemen, I do not play well at your game of   135
vapors; I am not very good at it, but—

    Cutting. Do you hear, sir? I would speak with you in
circle!

                             He draws a circle on the ground.

    Quarlous. In circle, sir? What would you with me in
circle?   140

    Cutting. Can you lend me a piece, a jacobus, in circle?

    Quarlous. 'Slid, your circle will prove more costly than
your vapors, then. Sir, no, I lend you none.

    Cutting. Your beard's not well turned up, sir.

                       [Handles Quarlous' beard.]

    Quarlous. How, rascal? Are you playing with my beard?   145
I'll break circle with you.

                     They draw all, and fight.

    Puppy. Northern. Gentlemen, gentlemen.

    Knockem. Gather up, Whit, gather up, Whit, Good vapors!

                           [Exit.]

      [Whit gathers up cloaks and conceals them.]

    Mistress Overdo. What mean you? are you rebels, gentle-
men? Shall I send out a sergeant-at-arms or a writ o' rebellion   150

---

120. commit—place in custody, but the word was also slang for fornicate.
125. sort—(1) kind, fashion, (2) group, company.   141. jacobus—gold
coin.

against you? I'll commit you, upon my womanhood, for a riot, upon my justice-hood, if you persist.

                         [Exeunt Quarlous, Cutting.]

    Wasp. Upon your justice-hood? Marry, shit o' your hood; you'll commit? Spoke like a true justice of peace's wife, indeed, and a fine female lawyer! Turd i' your teeth for a fee,   155
now.

    Mistress Overdo. Why, Numps, in Master Overdo's name, I charge you.

    Wasp. Good Mistress Underdo, hold your tongue.

    Mistress Overdo. Alas! poor Numps.   160

    Wasp. Alas! And why alas from you, I beseech you? Or why poor Numps, Goody Rich? Am I come to be pitied by your tuft taffeta now? Why mistress, I knew Adam, the clerk, your husband, when he was Adam scrivener, and writ for twopence a sheet, as high as he bears his head now, or you   165
your hood, dame. *(The watch comes in.)* What are you, sir?

    Bristle. We be men, and no infidels. What is the matter here, and the noises? Can you tell?

    Wasp. Heart, what ha' you to do? Cannot a man quarrel in quietness, but he must be put out on't by you? What are you?   170

    Bristle. Why, we be His Majesty's Watch, sir.

    Wasp. Watch? 'Sblood, you are a sweet watch, indeed. A body would think, an' you watched well a-nights, you should be contented to sleep at this time a-day. Get you to your fleas and your flock-beds, you rogues, your kennels, and lie down   175
close.

    Bristle. Down? Yes, we will down, I warrant you; down with him in His Majesty's name, down, down with him, and carry him away to the pigeon-holes.

                    [Bristle and Poacher seize Wasp.]

    Mistress Overdo. I thank you, honest friends, in the behalf   180
o' the Crown and the peace, and in Master Overdo's name, for suppressing enormities.

    Whit. Stay, Bristle, here ish a noder brash o' drunkards, but very quiet, special drunkards, will pay dee five shillings very well. Take 'em to dee, in de graish o' God. One of 'em   185

---

159. Underdo—possible sexual meanings abound here.   163. tuft taffeta—
a rich cloth.   175. flock-beds—beds made of flock, a coarse stuffing.
179. pigeon-holes—stocks.

does change cloth for ale in the Fair here, te toder ish a strong
man, a mighty man, my Lord Mayor's man, and a wrestler. He
has wreshled so long with the bottle, here, that the man with
the beard hash almost streek up hish heelsh.

 Bristle. 'Slid, the Clerk o' the Market has been to cry him 190
all the Fair over, here, for my Lord's service.

 Whit. Tere he ish, pre de taik him hensh and make ty best
on him. [*Exit watch with Wasp, Northern, Puppy.*] How now,
woman o' shilk, vat ailsh ty shweet faish? Art tou melancholy?

 Mistress Overdo. A little distempered with these enormi- 195
ties; shall I entreat a courtesy of you, Captain?

 Whit. Entreat a hundred, velvet voman, I vill do it; shpeak
out.

 Mistress Overdo. I cannot with modesty speak it out,
but—   200

 Whit. I vill do it, and more, and more, for dee. What,
Urs'la, an't be bitch, an't be bawd, an't be!

               [*Enter Ursula.*]

 Ursula. How now, rascal? What roar you for, old pimp?

 Whit. [*To Ursula.*] Here, put up de cloaks, Ursh; de
purchase; pre dee now, shweet Ursh, help dis good brave 205
voman to a jordan, an't be.

 Ursula. 'Slid, call your Captain Jordan to her, can you
not?

 Whit. Nay, pre dee leave dy consheits, and bring the velvet
woman to de—   210

 Ursula. I bring her! Hang her! Heart, must I find a
common pot for every punk i' your purlieus?

 Whit. O good voordsh, Ursh; it ish a guest o' velvet, i' fait
la.

 Ursula. Let her sell her hood and buy a sponge, with a pox 215
to her. My vessel is employed, sir. I have but one, and 'tis the
bottom of an old bottle. An honest proctor and his wife are at
it, within; if she'll stay her time, so.

 Whit. As soon ash tou cansht, shweet Ursh. Of a valiant
man I tink I am the patientsh man i' the world, or in 220
Smithfield.

            [*Re-enter Knockem.*]

188–89. man with the beard—"jug with a face on it" (Waith). 190. cry—
page.

Knockem. How now, Whit? Close vapors, stealing your leaps? Covering in corners, ha?

Whit. No, fait, Captain, dough tou beesht a vishe man, dy vit is a mile hence, now. I vas procuring a shmall courtesy for a woman of fashion here. 225

Mistress Overdo. Yes, Captain, though I am justice of peace's wife, I do love men of war and the sons of the sword, when they come before my husband.

Knockem. Say'st thou so, filly? Thou shalt have a leap 230 presently; I'll horse thee myself, else.

Ursula. Come, will you bring her in now? and let her take her turn?

Whit. Gramercy, good Ursh, I tank dee.

Mistress Overdo. Master Overdo shall thank her.   [*Exit.*] 235

223. Covering—copulating (of horses).

ACT IV
SCENE V

[*Enter Littlewit, Win.*]

Littlewit. Good Gammer Urs, Win and I are exceedingly beholden to you, and to Captain Jordan and Captain Whit. Win, I'll be bold to leave you i' this good company, Win, for half an hour or so, Win, while I go and see how my matter goes forward, and if the puppets be perfect; and then I'll come and 5 fetch you, Win.

Win. Will you leave me alone with two men, John?

Littlewit. Aye, they are honest gentlemen, Win, Captain Jordan and Captain Whit; they'll use you very civilly, Win; God b' w' you, Win. 10

Ursula. [*To Knockem and Whit.*] What, is her husband gone?

Knockem. On his false gallop, Urs, away.

Ursula. An' you be right Barthol'mew-birds, now show yourselves so; we are undone for want of fowl i' the Fair, here. 15 Here will be 'Zekiel Edgworth and three or four gallants with

11. What, is—Gifford emendation; folio reads, "What's."

him at night, and I ha' neither plover nor quail for 'em.
Persuade this between you two to become a bird o' the game,
while I work the velvet woman within (as you call her).

Knockem. I conceive thee, Urs! go thy ways. [*Exit*   20
Ursula.] Dost thou hear, Whit? is't not pity my delicate dark
chestnut here—with the fine lean head, large forehead, round
eyes, even mouth, sharp ears, long neck, thin crest, close
withers, plain back, deep sides, short fillets, and full flanks;
with a round belly, a plump buttock, large thighs, knit knees,   25
straight legs, short pasterns, smooth hoofs, and short heels—
should lead a dull honest woman's life, that might live the life
of a lady?

Whit. Yes, by my fait and trot it is, Captain. De honesht
woman's life is a scurvy dull life, indeed la.   30

Win. How, sir? Is an honest woman's life a scurvy life?

Whit. Yes, fait, shweetheart, believe him, de leef of a
bondwoman! But if dou vilt harken to me, I vill make tee a
freewoman and a lady. Dou shalt live like a lady, as te captain
saish.   35

Knockem. Aye, and be honest too, sometimes; have her
wires and her tires, her green gowns and velvet petticoats.

Whit. Aye, and ride to Ware and Rumford i' dy coash,
shee de players, be in love vit 'em; sup vit gallantsh, be drunk,
and cost de noting.   40

Knockem. Brave vapors!

Whit. And lie by twenty on 'em, if dou pleash,
shweetheart.

Win. What, and be honest still? That were fine sport.

Whit. Tish common, shweetheart; tou may'st do it, by my   45
hand. It shall be justified to ty husband's faish, now; tou shalt
be as honesht as the skin between his hornsh, la!

Knockem. Yes, and wear a dressing, top and top-gallant,
to compare with e'er a husband on 'em all, for a fore-top. It is
the vapor of spirit in the wife to cuckold, nowadays, as it is   50
the vapor of fashion in the husband not to suspect. Your
prying cat-eyed-citizen is an abominable vapor.

---

17. plover, quail—loose women.   37. wires—used to stiffen ruffs.   tires—
dresses.   green gowns—green from having tumbled in the grass.   38. Ware
and Rumford—villages in which assignations were often kept.   48. top and
top-gallant—sails.   48–49. dressing . . . husband—"high coiffure to match
her husband's horns" (Waith).

Win. Lord, what a fool have I been!

Whit. Mend, then, and do everyting like a lady hereafter; never know ty husband from another man.   55

Knockem. Nor any one man from another, but i' the dark.

Whit. Aye, and then it ish no dishgrash to know any man.

                                                 [*Re-enter Ursula.*]

Ursula. Help, help here.

Knockem. How now? What vapor's there?

Ursula. O, you are a sweet ranger! and look well to your   60
walks! Yonder is your punk of Turnbull, Ramping Alice, has fall'n upon the poor gentlewoman within, and pulled her hood over her ears, and her hair through it.

                         Alice enters, beating the Justice's wife.

Mistress Overdo. Help, help, i' the King's name.

Alice. A mischief on you, they are such as you are that   65
undo us, and take our trade from us, with your tuft taffeta haunches.

Knockem. How now, Alice!

Alice. The poor common whores can ha' no traffic for the privy rich ones; your caps and hoods of velvet call away our   70
customers and lick the fat from us.

Ursula. Peace, you foul ramping jade, you—

Alice. Od's foot, you bawd in grease, are you talking?

Knockem. Why, Alice, I say.

Alice. Thou sow of Smithfield, thou.   75

Ursula. Thou tripe of Turnbull.

Knockem. Catamountain vapors! ha!

Ursula. You know where you were tawed lately, both lashed and slashed you were in Bridewell.

Alice. Aye, by the same token, you rid that week, and   80
broke out the bottom o' the cart, night-tub.

Knockem. Why, lion face! ha! do you know who I am? Shall I tear ruff, slit waistcoat, make rags of petticoat? Ha! go to, vanish, for fear of vapors. Whit, a kick, Whit, in the parting vapor. [*They kick Alice out.*] Come, brave woman, take a   85
good heart, thou shalt be a lady, too.

Whit. Yes, fait, dey shall all both be ladies and write

---

55. know—pun, have carnal knowledge of.   61. Ramping—raging (of beasts).   73. in grease—fat, ready for killing (of animals).   78. tawed—beaten.   79. Bridewell—prison for bawds, whores, etc.   81. the cart—bawds rode a cart in public humiliation.   night-tub—chamber pot.

Madam. I vill do't myself for dem. Do is the vord, and D is the middle letter of Madam. DD, put 'em together and make deeds, without which all words are alike, la.   90

    Knockem. 'Tis true. Urs'la, take 'em in, open thy wardrobe, and fit 'em to their calling. Green gowns, crimson petticoats, green women! My Lord Mayor's green women! guests o' the game, true bred. I'll provide you a coach to take the air in.   95

    Win. But do you think you can get one?

    Knockem. O, they are as common as wheelbarrows where there are great dunghills. Every pettifogger's wife has 'em; for first he buys a coach, that he may marry, and then he marries that he may be made cuckold in't. For if their wives ride not   100 to their cuckolding, they do 'em no credit. Hide and be hidden; ride and be ridden, says the vapor of experience.

               [*Exeunt Ursula, Win, Mistress Overdo.*]

98. pettifogger's—cheap lawyer's.

ACT IV
SCENE VI

                             Enter Trouble-all.

    Trouble-all. By what warrant does it say so?

    Knockem. Ha! mad child o' the Pie-powders, art thou there? Fill us a fresh can, Urs; we may drink together.

    Trouble-all. I may not drink without a warrant, Captain.

    Knockem. 'Slood, thou'll not stale without a warrant,   5 shortly. Whit, give me pen, ink, and paper. I'll draw him a warrant presently.

    Trouble-all. It must be Justice Overdo's.

    Knockem. I know, man. Fetch the drink, Whit.

    Whit. I pre dee now, be very brief, Captain; for de new   10 ladies stay for dee.

    Knockem. O, as brief as can be; here 'tis already. "Adam Overdo."

    Trouble-all. Why, now I'll pledge you, Captain.

    Knockem. Drink it off. I'll come to thee, anon, again.   15

[*Exit Knockem into back part of Ursula's booth, Trouble-all
at a door. At the other enter Quarlous, Edgworth.*]

Quarlous. (*To the cutpurse.*) Well, sir, you are now
discharged; beware of being spied, hereafter.

Edgworth. Sir, will it please you enter in here at Urs'la's
and take part of a silken gown, a velvet petticoat, or a wrought
smock? I am promised such, and I can spare any gentleman a   20
moiety.

Quarlous. Keep it for your companions in beastliness; I
am none of 'em, sir. If I had not already forgiven you a greater
trespass, or thought you yet worth my beating, I would
instruct your manners, to whom you made your offers. But go   25
your ways, talk not to me, the hangman is only fit to discourse
with you; the hand of beadle is too merciful a punishment for
your trade of life. [*Exit Edgworth.*] I am sorry I employed
this fellow; for he thinks me such: *Facinus quos inquinat,
aequat.* But it was for sport. And would I make it serious, the   30
getting of this license is nothing to me, without other
circumstances concur. I do think how impertinently I labor, if
the word be not mine that the ragged fellow marked; and what
advantage I have given Ned Winwife in this time now, of
working her, though it be mine. He'll go near to form to her   35
what a debauched rascal I am, and fright her out of all good
conceit of me. I should do so by him, I am sure, if I had the
opportunity. But my hope is in her temper, yet; and it must
needs be next to despair, that is grounded on any part of a
woman's discretion. I would give, by my troth, now, all I   40
could spare (to my clothes and my sword) to meet my tattered
soothsayer again, who was my judge i' the question, to know
certainly whose word he has damned or saved. For till then I
live but under a reprieve. I must seek him. Who be these?

Enter Wasp with the officers, [*Bristle and Poacher.*]

Wasp. Sir, you are a Welsh cuckold, and a prating runt,   45
and no constable.

Bristle. You say very well. Come put in his leg in the
middle roundel, and let him hole there.

---

21. moiety—share.   30–31. *Facinus . . . aequat*—"Crime levels those
whom it pollutes" (Lucan, *The Civil War* V.290, trans. J. D. Duff).   32. impertinently—uselessly.   35. form—formulate.   45. runt—ignorant fellow.

Wasp. You stink of leeks, metheglin, and cheese, you rogue.   50

Bristle. Why, what is that to you, if you sit sweetly in the stocks in the meantime? If you have a mind to stink too, your breeches sit close enough to your bum. Sit you merry, sir.

Quarlous. How now, Numps?

Wasp. It is no matter how; pray you look off.   55

Quarlous. Nay, I'll not offend you, Numps. I thought you had sat there to be seen.

Wasp. And to be sold, did you not? Pray you mind your business, an' you have any.

Quarlous. Cry you mercy, Numps. Does your leg lie high   60
enough?

[*Enter Haggis with Overdo and Busy.*]

Bristle. How now, neighbor Haggis, what says Justice Overdo's worship to the other offenders?

Haggis. Why, he says just nothing; what should he say? Or where should he say? He is not to be found, man. He ha' not   65
been seen i' the Fair, here, all this live-long day, never since seven o'clock i' the morning. His clerks know not what to think on't. There is no court of Pie-powders yet. Here they be returned.

Bristle. What shall be done with 'em, then, in your   70
discretion?

Haggis. I think we were best put 'em in the stocks, in discretion (there they will be safe in discretion) for the valor of an hour or such a thing, till his worship come.

Bristle. It is but a hole matter if we do, Neighbor Haggis.   75
[*To Wasp.*] Come, sir, here is company for you. Heave up the stocks.

Wasp. [*Aside.*] I shall put a trick upon your Welsh diligence, perhaps.

> As they open the stocks, Wasp puts his shoe on his hand,
> and slips it in for his leg. They bring Busy and put him
> in.

Bristle. Put in your leg, sir.   80

Quarlous. What, Rabbi Busy! Is he come?

Busy. I do obey thee; the lion may roar, but he cannot

49. metheglin—Welsh mead.   73. valor—value, amount.   80. your leg—
the singular indicates that the offenders were fastened by one leg only with
hands free.

bite. I am glad to be thus separated from the heathen of the
land, and put apart in the stocks for the holy cause.

Wasp. What are you, sir?   85

Busy. One that rejoiceth in his affliction and sitteth here
to prophesy the destruction of fairs and May-games, wakes and
Whitsun-ales, and doth sigh and groan for the reformation of
these abuses.

[*They put Overdo in and walk to one side with their backs to
                                            the stocks.*]

Wasp. [*To Overdo.*] And do you sigh and groan too, or   90
rejoice in your affliction?

Overdo. I do not feel it, I do not think of it, it is a thing
without me. Adam, thou art above these batt'ries, these
contumelies. *In te manca ruit fortuna*, as thy friend Horace
says; thou art one, *Quem neque pauperies, neque mors, neque*   95
vincula terrent. And therefore, as another friend of thine says
(I think it be thy friend Persius), *Non te quaesiveris extra.*

Quarlous. What's here? A stoic i' the stocks? The fool is
turned philosopher.

Busy. Friend, I will leave to communicate my spirit with   100
you if I hear any more of those superstitious relics, those lists
of Latin, the very rags of Rome and patches of Popery.

Wasp. Nay, an' you begin to quarrel, gentlemen, I'll leave
you. I ha' paid for quarrelling too lately. Look you, a device,
but shifting in a hand for a foot. God b' w' you.   105

                                            He gets out.

Busy. Wilt thou then leave thy brethren in tribulation?

Wasp. For this once, sir.   [*Exit.*]

Busy. Thou art a halting neutral—[*Shouts.*] stay him
there, stop him—that will not endure the heat of persecution.

Bristle. How, now, what's the matter?   110

---

88. Whitsun-ales—parish festivals at Whitsuntide (Pentecost), a summer holiday.   93. without—outside; the Stoics distinguished between things under
our control and not under our control.   94. *In te . . . fortuna*—"against thee
Fortune in her onset is ever maimed." Adapted from Horace (*Satires*
II.vii.88). Overdo has characteristically applied the compliment to himself,
whereas Horace's subject is "the wise man [*sapiens*], against whom [*in
quem* . . .]."   95–96. *Quem . . . terrent*—"whom neither poverty nor death
nor bonds affright" (Ibid. line 84, trans. H. R. Fairclough).   97. *Non . . .*
extra—"look to no one outside yourself" (Persius, *Satires* I.7, trans. G. G.
Ramsay).   98. stoic i' the stocks—cf. *The Taming of the Shrew* I.i.31.
101. lists—cloth strips.

Busy. He is fled, he is fled, and dares not sit it out.

Bristle. What, has he made an escape? Which way? Follow, neighbor Haggis.   [*Exeunt Bristle, Haggis.*]
                                                [*Enter Purecraft.*]

Purecraft. O me! In the stocks! Have the wicked prevailed?   115

Busy. Peace, religious sister; it is my calling, comfort yourself, an extraordinary calling, and done for my better standing, my surer standing hereafter.

                                        The madman enters.

Trouble-all. By whose warrant, by whose warrant, this?

Quarlous. O, here's my man dropped in, I looked for.   120

Overdo. Ha!

Purecraft. O good sir, they have set the faithful here to be wondered at; and provided holes for the holy of the land.

Trouble-all. Had they warrant for it? Showed they Justice Overdo's hand? If they had no warrant, they shall answer it.   125

                                     [*Re-enter Bristle, Haggis.*]

Bristle. Sure you did not lock the stocks sufficiently, neighbor Toby!

Haggis. No? See if you can lock 'em better.

Bristle. [*Tries the lock.*] They are very sufficiently locked, and truly, yet something is in the matter.   130

Trouble-all. True, your warrant is the matter that is in question; by what warrant?

Bristle. Madman, hold your peace; I will put you in his room else, in the very same hole, do you see?

Quarlous. How? Is he a madman?   135

Trouble-all. Show me Justice Overdo's warrant, I obey you.

Haggis. You are a mad fool; hold your tongue.

Trouble-all. In Justice Overdo's name I drink to you, and here's my warrant.   140

   Shows his can. [*Exeunt Bristle and Haggis looking for Wasp.*]

Overdo. [*Aside.*] Alas, poor wretch! How it earns my heart for him!

Quarlous. [*Aside.*] If he be mad, it is in vain to question him. I'll try, though. [*To him.*] Friend, there was a gentlewoman showed you two names, some hour since, Argalus and   145

141. earns—grieves.

Palamon, to mark in a book. Which of 'em was it you marked?

Trouble-all. I mark no name but Adam Overdo; that is the name of names; he only is the sufficient magistrate; and that name I reverence; show it me.

Quarlous. [*Aside.*] This fellow's mad indeed. I am further 150
off now than afore.

Overdo. [*Aside.*] I shall not breathe in peace till I have made him some amends.

Quarlous. [*Aside.*] Well, I will make another use of him, is come in my head: I have a nest of beards in my trunk, one 155
something like his.   [*Exit.*]

                          The watchmen come back again.

Bristle. This mad fool has made me that I know not whether I have locked the stocks or no; I think I locked 'em.

Trouble-all. Take Adam Overdo in your mind and fear nothing.   160

Bristle. 'Slid, madness itself, hold thy peace, and take that.   [*Strikes him.*]

Trouble-all. Strikest thou without a warrant? Take thou that.

The madman fights with 'em, and they leave open the stocks.

Busy. We are delivered by miracle; fellow in fetters, let us 165
not refuse the means; this madness was of the spirit. The malice of the enemy hath mocked itself.

                          [*Exeunt Busy and Overdo.*]

Purecraft. Mad, do they call him! The world is mad in error, but he is mad in truth. I love him o' the sudden (the cunning man said all true), and shall love him more and more. 170
How well it becomes a man to be mad in truth! O, that I might be his yoke-fellow and be mad with him! What a many should we draw to madness in truth with us!

          [*Exit.*] *The watch, missing them, are affrighted.*

Bristle. How now! All 'scaped? Where's the woman? It is witchcraft! Her velvet hat is a witch, o' my conscience, or my 175
key, t'one! The madman was a devil and I am an ass; so bless me, my place, and mine office.   [*Exeunt.*]

---

148. name of names—epithet for God.   155. trunk—trunk-hose, "full bag-like breeches" (*OED*).   176. t'one—one or the other.

ACT V
SCENE I

[*Enter Leatherhead, Filcher, Sharkwell.*]

Leatherhead. Well, luck and Saint Barthol'mew! Out with
the sign of our invention, in the name of wit, and do you beat
the drum, the while. All the fowl i' the Fair, I mean all the dirt
in Smithfield (that's one of Master Littlewit's carwitchets
now), will be thrown at our banner today if the matter does   5
not please the people. O the motions that I, Lantern
Leatherhead, have given light to i' my time, since my Master
Pod died! *Jerusalem* was a stately thing; and so was *Nineveh,*
and *The City of Norwich;* and *Sodom and Gomorrah,* with the
rising o' the prentices and pulling down the bawdy houses   10
there, upon Shrove Tuesday; but *The Gunpowder Plot,* there
was a get-penny! I have presented that to an eighteen- or
twenty-pence audience nine times in an afternoon. Your
home-born projects prove ever the best, they are so easy and
familiar. They put too much learning i' their things nowadays,   15
and that I fear will be the spoil o' this. Littlewit? I say
Micklewit! if not too mickle! Look to your gathering there,
goodman Filcher.

Filcher. I warrant you, sir.

Leatherhead. An' there come any gentlefolks, take two-   20
pence a piece, Sharkwell.

Sharkwell. I warrant you, sir, threepence an' we can.

---

2. sign of our invention—sign advertising our puppet show.   4. carwitchets—
quibbles.   8. Pod—"Pod was a Master of motions before him" (marginal
note by Jonson), perhaps referring to a real person.   8–9. *Jerusalem* . . .
Gomorrah—between the two sets of biblical cities, all four of which were destroyed, is the homely English Norwich.   10. rising . . . Shrove Tuesday—
apprentices traditionally rioted on Mardi Gras and vandalized bawdyhouses
and theaters.   11. *Gunpowder Plot*—the unsuccessful attempt in 1605
to blow up Parliament with barrels of gunpowder in the building's cellar.
17. Micklewit—great wit.   gathering—collecting admission fees.

ACT V
SCENE II

> *The Justice comes in like a porter.*

Overdo. This later disguise, I have borrowed of a porter, shall carry me out to all my great and good ends; which, however interrupted, were never destroyed in me. Neither is the hour of my severity yet come, to reveal myself, wherein, cloud-like, I will break out in rain and hail, lightning and   5 thunder, upon the head of enormity. Two main works I have to prosecute: first, one is to invent some satisfaction for the poor kind wretch who is out of his wits for my sake; and yonder I see him coming. I will walk aside and project for it.
> *[Enter Winwife, Grace.]*

Winwife. I wonder where Tom Quarlous is, that he returns   10 not; it may be he is struck in here to seek us.

Grace. See, here's our madman again.

> *[Enter Quarlous, Purecraft.] Quarlous in the habit of the madman is mistaken by Mistress Purecraft.*

Quarlous. [*Aside.*] I have made myself as like him as his gown and cap will give me leave.

Purecraft. Sir, I love you and would be glad to be mad   15 with you in truth.

Winwife. How? my widow in love with a madman?

Purecraft. Verily, I can be as mad in spirit as you.

Quarlous. By whose warrant? Leave your canting. [*To Grace.*] Gentlewoman, have I found you? (Save ye, quit ye,   20 and multiply ye.) Where's your book? 'Twas a sufficient name I marked, let me see't, be not afraid to show't me.

> *He desires to see the book of Mistress Grace.*

Grace. What would you with it, sir?

Quarlous. Mark it again, and again, at your service.

Grace. Here it is, sir; this was it you marked.   25

Quarlous. Palamon? Fare you well, fare you well.

Winwife. How, Palamon!

Grace. Yes, faith, he has discovered it to you now, and therefore 'twere vain to disguise it longer; I am yours, sir, by the benefit of your fortune.   30

---

9. project—plan.   11. struck—gone.   19. canting—Puritan preaching.

    Winwife. And you have him, Mistress, believe it, that shall never give you cause to repent her benefit, but make you rather to think that, in this choice, she had both her eyes.

    Grace. I desire to put it to no danger of protestation.

                              [*Exeunt Winwife, Grace.*]

    Quarlous. Palamon the word and Winwife the man?   35

    Purecraft. Good sir, vouchsafe a yoke-fellow in your madness; shun not one of the sanctified sisters, that would draw with you in truth.

    Quarlous. Away! You are a herd of hypocritical proud ignorants, rather wild than mad. Fitter for woods and the   40 society of beasts than houses and the congregation of men. You are the second part of the society of canters, outlaws to order and discipline, and the only privileged church-robbers of Christendom. Let me alone. Palamon the word and Winwife the man?   45

    Purecraft. [*Aside.*] I must uncover myself unto him or I shall never enjoy him, for all the cunning men's promises.— Good sir, hear me, I am worth six thousand pound; my love to you is become my rack; I'll tell you all, and the truth, since you hate the hypocrisy of the party-colored brotherhood.   50 These seven years I have been a wilful holy widow only to draw feasts and gifts from my entangled suitors. I am also by office an assisting sister of the deacons and a devourer, instead of a distributor, of the alms. I am a special maker of marriages for our decayed brethren with our rich widows, for a third   55 part of their wealth, when they are married, for the relief of the poor elect; as also our poor handsome young virgins with our wealthy bachelors or widowers, to make them steal from their husbands when I have confirmed them in the faith and got all put into their custodies. And if I ha' not my bargain,   60 they may sooner turn a scolding drab into a silent minister than make me leave pronouncing reprobation and damnation unto them. Our elder, Zeal-of-the-land, would have had me, but I know him to be the capital knave of the land, making himself rich by being made feoffee in trust to deceased   65 brethren, and coz'ning their heirs by swearing the absolute gift

---

36–38. yoke-fellow . . . draw—like a team of oxen.   50. party-colored— meant figuratively, perhaps (1) inconsistent, (2) given to party, faction. 65. feoffee in trust—trustee of a freehold estate.

of their inheritance. And thus, having eased my conscience and uttered my heart with the tongue of my love, enjoy all my deceits together, I beseech you. I should not have revealed this to you but that in time I think you are mad; and I hope you'll   70
think me so too, sir?

    Quarlous. Stand aside, I'll answer you presently. (*He considers with himself of it.*) Why should not I marry this six thousand pound, now I think on't? And a good trade too, that she has beside, ha? The tother wench Winwife is sure of;   75
there's no expectation for me there! Here I may make myself some saver yet, if she continue mad—there's the question. It is money that I want; why should I not marry the money, when 'tis offered me? I have a license and all; it is but razing out one name and putting in another. There's no playing with a man's   80
fortune! I am resolved! I were truly mad an' I would not! [*To her.*] Well, come your ways, follow me an' you will be mad, I'll show you a warrant.

                               He takes her along with him.

    Purecraft. Most zealously; it is that I zealously desire.

                               The Justice calls him.

    Overdo. Sir, let me speak with you.   85

    Quarlous. By whose warrant?

    Overdo. The warrant that you tender and respect so: Justice Overdo's! I am the man, friend Trouble-all, though thus disguised (as the careful magistrate ought) for the good of the republic, in the Fair, and the weeding out of enormity. Do   90
you want a house or meat or drink or clothes? Speak whatsoever it is, it shall be supplied you. What want you?

    Quarlous. Nothing but your warrant.

    Overdo. My warrant? For what?

    Quarlous. To be gone, sir.   95

    Overdo. Nay, I pray thee stay. I am serious, and have not many words nor much time to exchange with thee; think what may do thee good.

    Quarlous. Your hand and seal will do me a great deal of good; nothing else in the whole Fair, that I know.   100

    Overdo. If it were to any end, thou should'st have it willingly.

---

70. in time . . . mad—just when I needed a madman you came along.
76–77. make myself some saver—make up a loss (a gambling term).

Quarlous. Why, it will satisfy me; that's end enough to look on. An' you will not gi' it me, let me go.

Overdo. Alas! thou shalt ha' it presently. I'll but step into   105
the scrivener's hereby and bring it. Do not go away.

                                        The Justice goes out.

Quarlous. [*Aside.*] Why, this madman's shape will prove a very fortunate one, I think! Can a ragged robe produce these effects? If this be the wise Justice, and he bring me his hand, I shall go near to make some use on't. [*Overdo*] *returns.* He is   110
come already!

Overdo. Look thee! here is my hand and seal, Adam Overdo; if there be anything to be written above in the paper, that thou want'st now or at any time hereafter, think on't; it is my deed, I deliver it so; can your friend write?   115

Quarlous. Her hand for a witness, and all is well.

Overdo. With all my heart.   *He urgeth Mistress Purecraft.*

Quarlous. [*Aside.*] Why should not I ha' the conscience to make this a bond of a thousand pound, now? or what I would else?   120

Overdo. Look you, there it is; and I deliver it as my deed again.

Quarlous. Let us now proceed in madness.

                                        He takes her in with him.

Overdo. Well, my conscience is much eased; I ha' done my part; though it doth him no good, yet Adam hath offered   125
satisfaction! The sting is removed from hence. Poor man, he is much altered with his affliction; it has brought him low! Now, for my other work, reducing the young man I have followed so long in love from the brink of his bane to the center of safety. Here, or in some such like vain place, I shall be sure to find   130
him. I will wait the good time.

128. reducing—leading back.

ACT V
SCENE III

[*Enter Cokes, followed by boys.*]

Cokes. How now? What's here to do? Friend, art thou the master of the monuments?

Sharkwell. 'Tis a motion, an't please your worship.

Overdo. [*Aside.*] My fantastical brother-in-law, Master Barthol'mew Cokes!   5

Cokes. A motion? What's that? (*He reads the bill.*) "The ancient modern history of *Hero and Leander*, otherwise called *The Touchstone of True Love*, with as true a trial of friendship between Damon and Pythias, two faithful friends o' the Bankside." Pretty i' faith; what's the meaning on't? Is't an   10 interlude? or what is't?

Filcher. Yes, sir; please you come near, we'll take your money within.

Cokes. Back with these children; they do   *The boys o'* so follow me up and down.   *the Fair*   15
                                follow him.
                      [*Enter Littlewit.*]

Littlewit. By your leave, friend.

Filcher. You must pay, sir, an' you go in.

Littlewit. Who, I? I perceive thou know'st not me. Call the master o' the motion.

Sharkwell. What, do you not know the author, fellow   20 Filcher? You must take no money of him; he must come in *gratis*. Master Littlewit is a voluntary; he is the author.

Littlewit. Peace, speak not too loud; I would not have any notice taken that I am the author till we see how it passes.

Cokes. Master Littlewit, how dost thou?   25

Littlewit. Master Cokes! you are exceeding well met; what, in your doublet and hose, without a cloak or a hat?

Cokes. I would I might never stir, as I am an honest man, and by that fire; I have lost all i' the Fair, and all my acquaintance too. Didst thou meet anybody that I know,   30 Master Littlewit? my man Numps, or my sister Overdo, or

---

11. interlude—stage play.   14. Back . . . children—get these children back from me.   29. by that fire—pointing to the fire in Ursula's booth.

Mistress Grace? Pray thee, Master Littlewit, lend me some
money to see the interlude, here. I'll pay thee again, as I am a
gentleman. If thou'lt but carry me home, I have money
enough there.   35

    Littlewit. O, sir, you shall command it; what, will a crown
serve you?

    Cokes. I think it will. What do we pay for coming in,
fellows?

    Filcher. Twopence, sir.   40

    Cokes. Twopence? there's twelvepence, friend. Nay, I am
a gallant, as simple as I look now, if you see me with my man
about me and my artillery again.

    Littlewit. You man was i' the stocks e'en now, sir.

    Cokes. Who, Numps?   45

    Littlewit. Yes, faith.

    Cokes. For what, i' faith? I am glad o' that; remember to
tell me on't anon; I have enough now! What manner of matter
is this, Master Littlewit? What kind of actors ha' you? Are
they good actors?   50

    Littlewit. Pretty youths, sir, all children, both old and
young; here's the master of 'em—

                            [Enter Leatherhead.]

    Leatherhead. (*Whispers to Littlewit.*) Call me not Leather-
head, but Lantern.

    Littlewit. —Master Lantern, that gives light to the   55
business.

    Cokes. In good time, sir, I would fain see 'em; I would be
glad [to] drink with the young company. Which is the
tiring-house?

    Leatherhead. Troth, sir, our tiring-house is somewhat   60
little; we are but beginners, yet, pray pardon us; you cannot
go upright in't.

    Cokes. No? Not now my hat is off? What would you have
done with me if you had had me, feather and all, as I was once
today? Ha' you none of your pretty impudent boys, now, to   65
bring stools, fill tobacco, fetch ale, and beg money, as they
have at other houses? Let me see some o' your actors.

---

42. simple—(1) unadorned, (2) foolish.   43. artillery—implements of war;
he has lost his sword.   53–54. Call . . . Lantern—he and Joan are "translated" to avoid Cokes.   66–67. bring stools . . . other houses—a description
of actual practices at the indoor and rather exclusive "private" theaters.

Littlewit. Show him 'em, show him 'em. Master Lantern, this is a gentleman that is a favorer of the quality.

[*Leatherhead goes behind puppet-booth.*]

Overdo. [*Aside.*] Aye, the favoring of this licentious 70
quality is the consumption of many a young gentleman; a
pernicious enormity.

He [*Leatherhead*] *brings them out in a basket.*

Cokes. What, do they live in baskets?

Leatherhead. They do lie in a basket, sir; they are o' the
small players.   75

Cokes. These be players minors, indeed. Do you call these
players?

Leatherhead. They are actors, sir, and as good as any,
none dispraised, for dumb shows; indeed I am the mouth of
'em all!   80

Cokes. Thy mouth will hold 'em all. I think one Taylor
would go near to beat all this company, with a hand bound
behind him.

Littlewit. Aye, and eat 'em all, too, an' they were in
cake-bread.   85

Cokes. I thank you for that, Master Littlewit, a good jest!
Which is your Burbage now?

Leatherhead. What mean you by that, sir?

Cokes. Your best actor, your Field?

Littlewit. Good, i' faith! You are even with me, sir.   90

Leatherhead. This is he that acts young Leander, sir. He is
extremely beloved of womenkind, they do so affect his action,
the green gamesters that come here; and this is lovely Hero;
this with the beard, Damon; and this, pretty Pythias. This is
the ghost of King Dionysius in the habit of a scrivener, as you 95
shall see anon, at large.

Cokes. Well, they are a civil company. I like 'em for that;

---

69. the quality—the profession (of acting).   81. Taylor—a minor poet who
had recently entertained an audience at the Hope until the regular company of
players arrived. Also a possible allusion to the actor Joseph Taylor, who was
perhaps in the cast of this play.   84–85. in cake-bread—made of cake, like
Joan's gingerbread images. Tailors were proverbially great eaters of bread,
hence Littlewit's pun.   87. Burbage—leading actor in Shakespeare's company,
the King's Men.   89. Field—leading actor in the company performing
Bartholomew Fair; he had studied classics under Jonson's direction.   96. at
large—in full.

they offer not to fleer nor jeer nor break jests, as the great
players do. And then there goes not so much charge to the
feasting of 'em or making 'em drunk, as to the other, by   100
reason of their littleness. Do they use to play perfect? Are
they never flustered?

Leatherhead. No, sir, I thank my industry and policy for
it; they are as well-governed a company, though I say it—And
here is young Leander, is as proper an actor of his inches; and   105
shakes his head like an ostler.

Cokes. But do you play it according to the printed book?
I have read that.

Leatherhead. By no means, sir.

Cokes. No? How then?   110

Leatherhead. A better way, sir; that is too learned and
poetical for our audience. What do they know what Hellespont
is? "Guilty of true love's blood"? Or what Abydos is? Or "the
other Sestos hight"?

Cokes. Th' art i' the right. I do not know myself.   115

Leatherhead. No, I have entreated Master Littlewit to take
a little pains to reduce it to a more familiar strain for our
people.

Cokes. How, I pray thee, good Master Littlewit?

Littlewit. It pleases him to make a matter of it, sir. But   120
there is no such matter I assure you. I have only made it a
little easy and modern for the times, sir, that's all; as, for the
Hellespont, I imagine our Thames here; and then Leander I
make a dyer's son, about Puddle Wharf; and Hero a wench o'
the Bankside, who going over one morning to Old Fish Street,   125
Leander spies her land at Trig Stairs, and falls in love with her.
Now do I introduce Cupid, having metamorphosed himself
into a drawer, and he strikes Hero in love with a pint of sherry;
and other pretty passages there are o' the friendship, that will
delight you, sir, and please you of judgment.   130

Cokes. I'll be sworn they shall. I am in love with the

---

106. ostler—probably an allusion to the actor William Ostler.   112–14. Hellespont . . . Sestos hight—Marlowe's opening lines run:

> On Hellespont, guilty of true love's blood,
> In view and opposite two cities stood,
> Sea-borderers, disjoin'd by Neptune's might;
> The one Abydos, the other Sestos hight.

actors already, and I'll be allied to them presently. (They respect gentlemen, these fellows.) Hero shall be my fairing; but which of my fairings? Le'me see—i' faith, my fiddle! and Leander my fiddlestick; then Damon my drum, and Pythias   135 my pipe, and the ghost of Dionysius my hobbyhorse. All fitted.

132. allied—he associates each puppet with one of his toys.

ACT V

SCENE IV

[*Enter Winwife, Grace.*]

Winwife. Look, yonder's your Cokes gotten in among his playfellows; I thought we could not miss him at such a spectacle.

Grace. Let him alone. He is so busy, he will never spy us.

Leatherhead. Nay, good sir.   5

Cokes. I warrant thee, I will not hurt her,   *Cokes is*
fellow; what, dost think me uncivil? I pray   *handling the*
thee be not jealous; I am toward a wife.   *puppets.*

Littlewit. Well, good Master Lantern, make ready to begin, that I may fetch my wife, and look you be perfect; you   10 undo me else i' my reputation.

Leatherhead. I warrant you, sir. Do not you breed too great an expectation of it among your friends. That's the only hurter of these things.

Littlewit. No, no, no.   [*Exit.*]   15

Cokes. I'll stay here and see; pray thee let me see.

Winwife. How diligent and troublesome he is!

Grace. The place becomes him, methinks.

Overdo. [*Aside.*] My ward, Mistress Grace, in the company of a stranger? I doubt I shall be compelled to   20 discover myself before my time!

[*Enter Knockem, Edgworth, Win, Whit, Mistress Overdo, the
ladies masked.*]

8. toward—about to get.   20. doubt—wonder if.

Filcher. Twopence apiece, gentlemen, an   *The door-*
excellent motion.   *keepers speak.*

Knockem. Shall we have fine fireworks and good vapors?

Sharkwell. Yes, Captain, and waterworks too.   25

Whit. I pree dee, take a care o' dy shmall lady, there,
Edgworth; I will look to dish tall lady myself.

Leatherhead. Welcome, gentlemen; welcome, gentlemen.

Whit. Predee, mashter o' de monshtersh, help a very sick
lady here to a chair to shit in.   30

Leatherhead. Presently, sir.

                            They bring Mistress Overdo a chair.

Whit. Good fait now, Urs'la's ale and *aqua vitae* ish to
blame for't; shit down, shweetheart, shit down and shleep a
little.   [*She sits down and goes to sleep.*]

Edgworth. [*To Win.*] Madam, you are very welcome   35
hither.

Knockem. Yes, and you shall see very   [*Overdo is*]
good vapors.   *by*

Overdo. [*Aside.*] Here is my care come! I   *Edgworth.*
like to see him in so good company; and yet I wonder that   40
persons of such fashion should resort hither!

Edgworth. This is a very private house,   *The cutpurse*
madam.   *courts Mistress*

Leatherhead. Will it please your lady-   *Littlewit.*
ship sit, madam?   45

Win. Yes, good-man. They do so all-to-be-madam me, I
think they think me a very lady!

Edgworth. What else, madam?

Win. Must I put off my mask to him?

Edgworth. O, by no means.   50

Win. How should my husband know me, then?

Knockem. Husband? an idle vapor; he must not know
you, nor you him; there's the true vapor.

Overdo. [*Aside.*] Yea, I will observe more of this. [*To
Whit.*] Is this a lady, friend?   55

Whit. Aye, and dat is anoder lady, shweetheart; if dou
hasht a mind to 'em, give me twelvepence from tee, and dou
shalt have eder-oder on 'em!

---

25. waterworks—imitation tapestry, painted in watercolors; cheap stagehang-
ings.

Overdo. [*Aside*.] Aye? This will prove my chiefest
enormity. I will follow this.   60

Edgworth. Is not this a finer life, lady, than to be clogged
with a husband?

Win. Yes, a great deal. When will they begin, trow, in the
name o' the motion?

Edgworth. By and by, madam; they stay but for   65
company.

Knockem. Do you hear, puppet-master, these are tedious
vapors; when begin you?

Leatherhead. We stay but for Master Littlewit, the author,
who is gone for his wife; and we begin presently.   70

Win. That's I, that's I.

Edgworth. That was you, lady; but now you are no such
poor thing.

Knockem. Hang the author's wife, a running vapor! Here
be ladies will stay for ne'er a Delia o' em all.   75

Whit. But hear me now, here ish one o' de ladish ashleep;
stay till she but vake, man.

                              [*Enter Wasp*.]

Wasp. How now, friends? What's here to do?

                    The doorkeepers [*take their places*] *again*.

Filcher. Twopence apiece, sir, the best motion in the Fair.

Wasp. I believe you lie; if you do, I'll have my money   80
again and beat you.

Winwife. Numps is come!

Wasp. Did you see a master of mine come in here, a tall
young squire of Harrow o' the Hill, Master Barthol'mew
Cokes?   85

Filcher. I think there be such a one within.

Wasp. Look he be, you were best; but it is very likely; I
wonder I found him not at all the rest. I ha' been at the eagle,
and the black wolf, and the bull with the five legs and two
pizzles (he was a calf at Uxbridge Fair, two years agone), and   90
at the dogs that dance the morris, and the hare o' the tabor,
and missed him at all these! Sure this must needs be some fine
sight that holds him so, if it have him.

Cokes. Come, come, are you ready now?

75. Delia—the heroine of Samuel Daniel's sonnet sequence *Delia* (1592).
91. hare o' the tabor—drum-playing rabbit.

Leatherhead. Presently, sir.   95

Wasp. Hoyday, he's at work in his doublet and hose. Do you hear, sir? are you employed, that you are bare-headed and so busy?

Cokes. Hold your peace, Numps; you ha' been i' the stocks, I hear.   100

Wasp. Does he know that? Nay, then the date of my authority is out; I must think no longer to reign, my government is at an end. He that will correct another must want fault in himself.

Winwife. Sententious Numps! I never heard so much from   105
him before.

Leatherhead. Sure, Master Littlewit will not come; please you take your place, sir, we'll begin.

Cokes. I pray thee do; mine ears long to be at it, and my eyes too. O Numps, i' the stocks, Numps? Where's your sword, 110
Numps?

Wasp. I pray you intend your game, sir; let me alone.

Cokes. Well then, we are quit for all. Come, sit down, Numps; I'll interpret to thee. Did you see Mistress Grace? It's no matter, neither, now I think on't, tell me anon.   115

Winwife. A great deal of love and care he expresses.

Grace. Alas! would you have him to express more than he has? That were tyranny.

> [*The curtain of the puppet booth is drawn.*]

Cokes. Peace, ho; now, now.

Leatherhead. *Gentles, that no longer your expectations*   120
    may wander,
Behold our chief actor, amorous Leander,
With a great deal of cloth lapped about him like a scarf,
For he yet serves his father, a dyer at Puddle Wharf,
Which place we'll make bold with, to call it our Abydos,   125
As the Bankside is our Sestos, and let it not be denied us.
Now, as he is beating, to make the dye take the fuller,
Who chances to come by but fair Hero in a sculler;
And seeing Leander's naked leg and goodly calf,
Cast at him, from the boat, a sheep's eye and a half.   130

120–21. *Gentles . . . amorous Leander*—the puppet play parodies the rhythm of Richard Edwardes' *Damon and Pithias* (1571).   127. *fuller*—a pun (1) more thoroughly, (2) a fuller was one whose occupation was to beat cloth for the purpose of thickening it.   128. *sculler*—rowboat.

Now she is landed, and the sculler come back;
By and by you shall see what Leander doth lack.

Pup. Leander. *Cole, Cole, old Cole.*

Leatherhead.   *That is the sculler's name*
    without control.   135

Pup. Leander. *Cole, Cole, I say, Cole.*

Leatherhead.   *We do hear you.*

Pup. Leander.   *Old Cole.*

Leatherhead. *Old Cole? Is the dyer turned collier? How*
    do you sell?   140

Pup. Leander. *A pox o' your manners, kiss my hole here*
    and smell.

Leatherhead. *Kiss your hole and smell? There's manners*
    indeed.

Pup. Leander. *Why, Cole, I say, Cole.*   145

Leatherhead.   *It's the sculler you need!*

Pup. Leander. *Aye, and be hanged.*

Leatherhead.   *Be hanged! Look you yonder,*
Old Cole, you must go hang with Master Leander.

Pup. Cole. *Where is he?*   150

Pup. Leander.   *Here, Cole. What fairest of fairs*
Was that fare that thou landedst but now a' Trig Stairs?

Cokes. What was that, fellow? Pray thee tell me; I scarce
understand 'em.

Leatherhead. *Leander does ask, sir, what fairest of fairs*   155
Was the fare that he landed but now at Trig Stairs.

Pup. Cole. *It is lovely Hero.*

Pup. Leander. *Nero?*

Pup. Cole. *No, Hero.*

Leatherhead. *It is Hero.*   160
Of the Bankside, he saith, to tell you truth without erring,
Is come over into Fish Street to eat some fresh herring.
Leander says no more, but as fast as he can,
Gets on all his best clothes, and will after to the Swan.

Cokes. Most admirable good, is't not?   165

---

133. *old Cole*—pander (slang).   139. *collier*—coal seller. Colliers had the
reputation of cheating customers.

Leatherhead. *Stay, sculler.*
Pup. Cole.   *What say you?*
Leatherhead.   *You must stay for Leander,*
And carry him to the wench.
Pup. Cole.   *You rogue, I am no pander.*   170

Cokes. He says he is no pander. 'Tis a fine language;
I understand it now.

Leatherhead. *Are you no pander, Goodman Cole? Here's*
    no man says you are.
You'll grow a hot Cole, it seems; pray you stay for your fare.   175
Pup. Cole. *Will he come away?*
Leatherhead.   *What do you say?*
Pup. Cole.   *I'd ha' him come*
    away.
Leatherhead. *Would you ha' Leander come away? Why*   180
    pray, sir, stay.
You are angry, Goodman Cole; I believe the fair maid
Came over w' you o' trust. Tell us, sculler, are you paid?
Pup. Cole. *Yes, Goodman Hogrubber o' Pickt-hatch.*
Leatherhead. *How, Hogrubber o' Pickt-hatch?*   185
Pup. Cole.   *Aye, Hogrubber o'*
    Pickt-hatch.
Take you that.   The puppet
Leatherhead. *O, my head!*   strikes him
Pup. Cole.   *Harm watch, harm catch.*   over the pate.   190

Cokes. Harm watch, harm catch, he says. Very good i'
faith; the sculler had like to ha' knocked you, sirrah.
Leatherhead. Yes, but that his fare called him away.

Pup. Leander. *Row apace, row apace, row, row, row, row,*
    row.   195
Leatherhead. *You are knavishly loaden, sculler, take heed*
    where you go.
Pup. Cole. *Knave i' your face, Goodman rogue.*
Pup. Leander.   *Row, row, row, row, row, row.*

---

184. *Hogrubber*—swineherd.   *Pickt-hatch*—brothel area.   190. *Harm*
watch, harm catch—if you seek trouble you'll get it.

 Cokes. He said knave i' your face, friend.   200

 Leatherhead. Aye, sir, I heard him. But there's no talking
to these watermen; they will ha' the last word.

 Cokes. God's my life! I am not allied to the sculler yet; he
shall be Dauphin my boy. But my fiddle-stick does fiddle in
and out too much; I pray you speak to him on't; tell him, I   205
would have him tarry in my sight more.

 Leatherhead. I pray you be content; you'll have enough
on him, sir.

Now gentles, I take it, here is none of you so stupid,
But that you have heard of a little god of love, called Cupid.   210
Who out of kindness to Leander, hearing he but saw her
This present day and hour, doth turn himself to a drawer.
And because he would have their first meeting to be merry,
He strikes Hero in love to him with a pint of sherry.

Which he tells her from amorous Leander is sent her,	Puppet Leander goes into 215
Who after him into the room of Hero doth venter.	Mistress Hero's room.

 Pup. Jonas. *A pint of sack, score a pint*
of sack i' the Coney.   220

 Cokes. Sack? You said but e'en now it should be sherry.

 Pup. Jonas. *Why so it is: sherry, sherry, sherry.*

 Cokes. Sherry, sherry, sherry. By my troth he makes me
merry. I must have a name for Cupid too. Let me see, thou
mightst help me now, an' thou wouldst, Numps, at a dead lift,   225
but thou art dreaming o' the stocks still! Do not think on't, I
have forgot it. 'Tis but a nine days' wonder, man; let it not
trouble thee.

 Wasp. I would the stocks were about your neck, sir;
condition I hung by the heels in them till the wonder were off   230
from you, with all my heart.

---

204. Dauphin my boy—my heir presumptive, alluding to a lost ballad.   fiddle-stick—Leander.   219–20. *score . . . Coney*—put on the bill of those in
the "Coney Room" of the Inn.   221–22. Sack . . . sherry—Cokes shows
his ignorance, since sack was a general term for Spanish white wines including
sherry.   225. at a dead lift—in an emergency.   230. condition—on condition that.

Cokes. Well said, resolute Numps. But hark you, friend,
where is the friendship, all this while, between my drum,
Damon, and my pipe, Pythias?

Leatherhead. You shall see by and by, sir.   235

Cokes. You think my hobbyhorse is forgotten, too. No,
I'll see 'em all enact before I go; I shall not know which to
love best, else.

Knockem. This gallant has interrupting vapors, troublesome vapors, Whit; puff with him.   240

Whit. No, I pre dee, Captain, let him alone. He is a child i'
faith, la.

Leatherhead. *Now, gentles, to the friends, who in number
        are two,*
And lodged in that ale-house in which fair Hero does do.   245
Damon (for some kindness done him the last week)
Is come fair Hero in Fish Street this morning to seek.
Pythias does smell the knavery of the meeting,
And now you shall see their true friendly greeting.
Pup. Pythias. *You whoremasterly slave, you.*   250

Cokes. Whoremasterly slave you? Very friendly and
familiar, that!

Pup. Damon.   *Whoremaster i' thy face,*
Thou hast lien with her thyself, I'll prove't i' this place.

Cokes. Damon says Pythias has lien with her himself; he'll 255
prove't in this place.

Leatherhead. *They are whoremasters both, sir, that's a
        plain case.*
Pup. Pythias. *You lie like a rogue.*
Leatherhead.   *Do I lie like a rogue?* 260
Pup. Pythias. *A pimp and a scab.*
Leatherhead.   *A pimp and a scab?*
I say between you, you have both but one drab.
Pup. Damon. *You lie again.*
Leatherhead. *Do I lie again?*   265

245. *does do*—does her thing, i.e., prostitution.

Pup. Damon. *Like a rogue again.*
Leatherhead. *Like a rogue again?*
Pup. Pythias. *And you are a pimp again.*

Cokes. And you are a pimp again, he says.

Pup. Damon. *And a scab again.*   270

Cokes. And a scab again, he says.

Leatherhead. *And I say again you are both whoremasters*
   again,
And you have both but one drab again.   They fight.
   Pup. Damon and Pythias. *Dost thou, dost thou, dost thou?* 275
   Leatherhead. *What, both at once?*
   Pup. Pythias. *Down with him, Damon.*
   Pup. Damon. *Pink his guts, Pythias.*
   Leatherhead. *What, so malicious?*
Will ye murder me, masters both, i' mine own house?   280

Cokes. Ho! well acted, my drum, well acted, my pipe,
well acted still.
   Wasp. Well acted, with all my heart.

Leatherhead. *Hold, hold your hands.*

Cokes. Aye, both your hands, for my sake! for you ha'   285
both done well.

Pup. Damon. *Gramercy, pure Pythias.*
Pup. Pythias. *Gramercy, dear Damon.*

Cokes. Gramercy to you both, my pipe and my drum.

Pup. Damon and Pythias. *Come now we'll together to*   290
breakfast to Hero.
   Leatherhead. *'Tis well, you can now go to breakfast to*
   Hero,
You have given me my breakfast, with a'hone and 'honero.

278. Pink—stab.   294. *'hone and 'honero*—"alas (Scots: ochone, ochon-
arie)" (Waith).

    Cokes. How is't, friend, ha' they hurt thee?   295
    Leatherhead.   O no!
Between you and I, sir, we do but make show.

Thus, gentles, you perceive, without any denial,
'Twixt Damon and Pythias here, friendship's true trial.
Though hourly they quarrel thus and roar each with other,   300
They fight you no more than does brother with brother.
But friendly together, at the next man they meet.
They let fly their anger, as here you might see't.

    Cokes. Well, we have seen't, and thou hast felt it, what-
soever thou sayest. What's next? What's next?   305

    Leatherhead. *This while young Leander with fair Hero is*
    drinking,
And Hero grown drunk, to any man's thinking!
Yet was it not three pints of sherry could flaw her,
Till Cupid, distinguished like Jonas the drawer,   310
From under his apron, where his lechery lurks,
Put love in her sack. Now mark how it works.
    Pup. Hero. *O Leander, Leander, my dear, my dear Leander,*
I'll forever be thy goose, so thou'lt be my gander.

    Cokes. Excellently well said, fiddle! She'll ever be his 315
goose, so he'll be her gander: was't not so?
    Leatherhead. Yes, sir, but mark his answer, now.

    Pup. Leander. *And sweetest of geese, before I go to bed,*
I'll swim o'er the Thames, my goose, thee to tread.

    Cokes. Brave! he will swim o'er the Thames and tread his 320
goose tonight, he says.
    Leatherhead. Aye, peace, sir, they'll be angry if they hear
you eavesdropping, now they are setting their match.

    Pup. Leander. *But lest the Thames should be dark, my*
    goose, my dear friend,   325
Let thy window be provided of a candle's end.
    Pup. Hero. *Fear not, my gander, I protest I should handle*
My matters very ill, if I had not a whole candle.

Pup. Leander. *Well then, look to't, and kiss me to boot.*

Leatherhead. *Now here come the friends*   Damon and   330
    again, Pythias and Damon,   Pythias
And under their cloaks they have of bacon a   enter.
gammon.

Pup. Pythias. *Drawer, fill some wine here.*

Leatherhead.   *How, some wine there?*   335
There's company already, sir, pray forbear!

Pup. Damon. *'Tis Hero.*

Leatherhead.   *Yes, but she will not be taken,*
After sack and fresh herring, with your Dunmow-bacon.

Pup. Pythias. *You lie, it's Westfabian.*   340

Leatherhead.   *Westphalian, you should say.*

Pup. Damon. *If you hold not your*   Leander and
    peace, you are a coxcomb, I would   Hero are kissing.
say.

Pup. Pythias. *What's here? What's here? Kiss, kiss*   345
    upon kiss.

Leatherhead. *Aye, wherefore should they not? What harm*
    is in this?
'Tis Mistress Hero.

Pup. Damon. *Mistress Hero's a whore.*   350

Leatherhead. *Is she a whore? Keep you quiet, or sir*
    knave out of door.

Pup. Damon. *Knave out of door?*   Here the puppets
Pup. Hero.   *Yes, knave*   quarrel and fall
    out of door.   together by the   355
Pup. Damon. *Whore out of door.*   ears.
Pup. Hero.   *I say knave out of door.*
Pup. Damon. *I say whore out of door.*
Pup. Pythias.   *Yea, so say I too.*
Pup. Hero. *Kiss the whore o' the arse.*   360

Leatherhead.   *Now you ha' something to do:*
You must kiss her o' the arse, she says.

Pup. Damon and Pythias. *So we will, so we will.*

                      [They kick her.]

Pup. Hero. *O my haunches, o my haunches, hold, hold.*

339. *Dunmow-bacon*—in Little Dunmow, Essex, any couple who could persuade a jury that their first year of marriage had been free of quarrel was presented a free flitch of bacon.   341. *Westphalian*—German province famous
for ham.

Leatherhead.   *Stand'st thou still?*   365
Leander, where art thou? Stand'st thou still like a sot,
And not offer'st to break both their heads with a pot?
See who's at thine elbow there! Puppet Jonas and Cupid.
    Pup. Jonas. *Upon 'em, Leander, be not so stupid.*   They
    Pup. Leander. *You goat-bearded slave!*   fight. 370
    Pup. Damon.   *You whoremaster knave!*
    Pup. Leander. *Thou art a whoremaster.*
    Pup. Jonas.   *Whoremasters all.*
    Leatherhead. *See, Cupid with a word has ta'en up the*
brawl.   375

    Knockem. These be fine vapors!
    Cokes. By this good day they fight bravely, do they not,
Numps?
    Wasp. Yes, they lacked but you to be their second, all this
while.   380

    Leatherhead. *This tragical encounter, falling out thus to*
        busy us,
It raises up the ghost of their friend Dionysius,
Not like a monarch, but the master of a school,
In a scrivener's furred gown, which shows he is no fool.   385
For therein he hath wit enough to keep himself warm.
"O Damon," he cries, "and Pythias, what harm
Hath poor Dionysius done you in his grave,
That after his death you should fall out thus, and rave,
And call amorous Leander whoremaster knave?"   390
    Pup. Dionysius. *I cannot, I will not, I promise you,*
        endure it.

---

367. *pot*—drinking pot, stein.   384. *master of a school*—not the God Dionysius but Dionysius the younger, tyrant of Syracuse 367–43 B.C. He was
said to have taught school after his exile from Syracuse.

ACT V

SCENE V

[*Enter Busy.*]

Busy. Down with Dagon, down with Dagon! 'Tis I will no longer endure your profanations.

Leatherhead. What mean you, sir?

Busy. I will remove Dagon there, I say, that idol, that heathenish idol, that remains, as I may say, a beam, a very 5
beam, not a beam of the sun, nor a beam of the moon, nor a beam of a balance, neither a house-beam nor a weaver's beam, but a beam in the eye, in the eye of the brethren; a very great beam, an exceeding great beam; such as are your stage-players, rhymers, and morris-dancers, who have walked hand 10
in hand in contempt of the brethren and the cause, and been borne out by instruments of no mean countenance.

Leatherhead. Sir, I present nothing but what is licensed by authority.

Busy. Thou art all license, even licentiousness itself, 15
Shimei!

Leatherhead. I have the Master of the Revels' hand for it, sir.

Busy. The master of rebels' hand thou hast—Satan's! Hold thy peace, thy scurrility, shut up thy mouth; thy profession is 20
damnable, and in pleading for it thou dost plead for Baal. I have long opened my mouth wide and gaped, I have gaped as the oyster for the tide, after thy destruction; but cannot compass it by suit or dispute; so that I look for a bickering ere long, and then a battle. 25

Knockem. Good Banbury-vapors.

Cokes. Friend, you'd have an ill match on't if you bicker with him here; though he be no man o' the fist, he has friends that will go to cuffs for him. Numps, will not you take our side? 30

---

1. Dagon—chief idol of the Philistines (1 Samuel 5).   5–9. beam—cf.
Matt. 7:3–4, modern translations of which use log or plank in place of beam.
12. countenance—repute.   16. Shimei—who cursed King David and threw
stones at him (2 Sam. 16:5–13). The relevance of the allusion is clear only to
Busy.   17. Master of the Revels—licenser of plays at this time.
21. Baal—a prominent Old Testament idol, associated with licentiousness.

Edgworth. Sir, it shall not need; in my mind, he offers
him a fairer course, to end it by disputation! Hast thou
nothing to say for thyself, in defence of thy quality?

Leatherhead. Faith, sir, I am not well studied in these
controversies between the hypocrites and us. But here's one of   35
my motion, Puppet Dionysius, shall undertake him, and I'll
venture the cause on't.

Cokes. Who? My hobbyhorse? Will he dispute with him?

Leatherhead. Yes, sir, and make a hobby-ass of him, I
hope.   40

Cokes. That's excellent! Indeed he looks like the best
scholar of 'em all. Come, sir, you must be as good as your
word, now.

Busy. I will not fear to make my spirit and gifts known!
Assist me, zeal; fill me, fill me, that is, make me full.   45

Winwife. What a desperate, profane wretch is this! Is there
any ignorance or impudence like his? To call his zeal to fill
him against a puppet?

Grace. I know no fitter match than a puppet to commit
with an hypocrite!   50

Busy. First, I say unto thee, idol, thou hast no calling.

Pup. Dionysius. You lie; I am called Dionysius.

Leatherhead. The motion says you lie, he is called
Dionysius i' the matter, and to that calling he answers.

Busy. I mean no vocation, idol, no present lawful calling.   55

Pup. Dionysius. Is yours a lawful calling?

Leatherhead. The motion asketh if yours be a lawful
calling.

Busy. Yes, mine is of the spirit.

Pup. Dionysius. Then idol is a lawful calling.   60

Leatherhead. He says, then idol is a lawful calling! For
you called him idol, and your calling is of the spirit.

Cokes. Well disputed, hobbyhorse!

Busy. Take not part with the wicked, young gallant. He
neigheth and hinnyeth; all is but hinnying sophistry. I call him 65
idol again. Yet, I say, his calling, his profession is profane, it is
profane, idol.

49. *Grace*—the folio gives this speech to Quarlous, who is not on stage. Waith
(p. 199) argues plausibly that it belongs to Grace.   49–50. commit with—
join battle with.   50. hypocrite—alluding to the etymological meaning of
hypocrite, stage actor.

Pup. Dionysius. It is not profane!

Leatherhead. It is not profane, he says.

Busy. It is profane.   70

Pup. Dionysius. It is not profane.

Busy. It is profane.

Pup. Dionysius. It is not profane.

Leatherhead. Well said, confute him with "not," still. You cannot bear him down with your base noise, sir.   75

Busy. Nor he me with his treble creaking, though he creak like the chariot wheels of Satan. I am zealous for the cause—

Leatherhead. As a dog for a bone.

Busy. And I say it is profane, as being the page of pride and the waiting-woman of vanity.   80

Pup. Dionysius. Yea? What say you to your tire-women, then?

Leatherhead. Good.

Pup. Dionysius. Or feather-makers i' the Friars, that are o' your faction of faith? Are not they with their perukes and   85 their puffs, their fans and their huffs, as much pages of pride and waiters upon vanity? What say you? What say you? What say you?

Busy. I will not answer for them.

Pup. Dionysius. Because you cannot, because you cannot.   90 Is a bugle-maker a lawful calling? or the confect-maker's? such you have there; or your French fashioner? You'd have all the sin within yourselves, would you not? would you not?

Busy. No, Dagon.

Pup. Dionysius. What then, Dagonet? Is a puppet worse   95 than these?

Busy. Yes, and my main argument against you is that you are an abomination; for the male among you putteth on the apparel of the female, and the female of the male.

Pup. Dionysius. You lie, you lie, you lie abominably.   100

Cokes. Good, by my troth, he has given him the lie thrice.

Pup. Dionysius. It is your old stale argument against the

---

84. feather-makers i' the Friars—makers of feather ornaments in the Black-friars district.   86. puffs . . . huffs—padding for fashionable clothing. 91. bugle-maker—maker of the tube-shaped glass beads used to ornament clothing. confect—confectionery, candy.   95. Dagonet—King Arthur's legendary fool.   98–99. male . . . female—cf. Deut. 22:5.

players, but it will not hold against the puppets; for we have
neither male nor female amongst us. And that thou may'st see,
if thou wilt, like a malicious purblind zeal as thou art!   105
                              The puppet takes up his garment.

Edgworth. By my faith, there he has answered you,
friend; by plain demonstration.

Pup. Dionysius. Nay, I'll prove, against e'er a rabbin of
'em all, that my standing is as lawful as his; that I speak by
inspiration as well as he; that I have as little to do with   110
learning as he; and do scorn her helps as much as he.

Busy. I am confuted; the cause hath failed me.

Pup. Dionysius. Then be converted, be converted.

Leatherhead. Be converted, I pray you, and let the play go
on!   115

Busy. Let it go on. For I am changed, and will become a
beholder with you!

Cokes. That's brave i' faith. Thou hast carried it away,
hobbyhorse; on with the play!
                              The Justice discovers himself.

Overdo. Stay, now do I forbid, I, Adam Overdo! Sit still, I   120
charge you.

Cokes. What, my brother-i'-law!

Grace. My wise guardian!

Edgworth. Justice Overdo!

Overdo. It is time to take enormity by the forehead, and   125
brand it; for I have discovered enough.

118. carried it away—brought it off, won the contest.

ACT V
SCENE VI

          Enter Quarlous (like the madman) with Purecraft.

Quarlous. Nay, come, Mistress bride. You must do as I do,
now. You must be mad with me in truth. I have here Justice
Overdo for it.

Overdo. [*To Quarlous.*] Peace, good Trouble-all; come
hither, and you shall trouble none. I will take the charge of   5
you and your friend too. (*To the cutpurse and Mistress
Littlewit.*) You also, young man, shall be my care; stand there.

Edgworth. Now, mercy upon me.

Knockem. Would we were away, Whit;   *The rest are*
these are dangerous vapors; best fall off with   *stealing away.*   10
our birds, for fear o' the cage.

Overdo. Stay, is not my name your terror?

Whit. Yesh, faith, man, and it ish for tat we would be
gone, man.

                                        [*Enter Littlewit.*]

Littlewit. O gentlemen, did you not see a wife of mine? I   15
ha' lost my little wife, as I shall be trusted, my little pretty
Win; I left her at the great woman's house in trust yonder, the
pig-woman's, with Captain Jordan and Captain Whit, very
good men, and I cannot hear of her. Poor fool, I fear she's
stepped aside. Mother, did you not see Win?   20

Overdo. If this grave matron be your mother, sir, stand by
her, *et digito compesce labellum*; I may perhaps spring a wife
for you anon. Brother Barthol'mew, I am sadly sorry to see
you so lightly given, and such a disciple of enormity, with
your grave governor Humphrey; but stand you both there in   25
the middle-place; I will reprehend you in your course. Mistress
Grace, let me rescue you out of the hands of the stranger.

Winwife. Pardon me, sir, I am a kinsman of hers.

Overdo. Are you so? Of what name, sir?

Winwife. Winwife, Sir.   30

Overdo. Master Winwife? I hope you have won no wife of
her, sir. If you have, I will examine the possibility of it at fit
leisure. Now to my enormities: look upon me, O London! and
see me, O Smithfield! the example of justice and mirror of
magistrates, the true top of formality and scourge of enormity.   35
Hearken unto my labors and but observe my discoveries, and
compare Hercules with me, if thou dar'st, of old; or Columbus,
Magellan, or our countryman Drake of later times. Stand forth,
you weeds of enormity, and spread. (*To Busy.*) First, Rabbi
Busy, thou super-lunatical hypocrite. (*To Lantern.*) Next, thou   40
other extremity, thou profane professor of puppetry, little
better than poetry. (*To the horse-courser and cutpurse.*) Then
thou strong debaucher and seducer of youth; witness this easy
and honest young man. (*Then Captain Whit and Mistress*

---

22. *et digito compesce labellum*—"keep your mouth shut!" (a free translation
of Juvenal I.160 used by the Royal Shakespeare Company production of *Bartholomew Fair*, 1969).

Littlewit.) Now thou esquire of dames, madams, and twelve-   45
penny ladies. Now my green madam herself, of the price. Let
me unmask your ladyship.

    Littlewit. O my wife, my wife, my wife!

    Overdo. Is she your wife? *Redde te Harpocratem!*

      Enter Trouble-all [followed by Ursula and Nightingale.]

    Trouble-all. By your leave, stand by, my masters; be   50
uncovered.

    Ursula. O stay him, stay him, help to cry, Nightingale; my
pan, my pan.

    Overdo. What's the matter?

    Nightingale. He has stol'n Gammer Urs'la's pan.   55

    Trouble-all. Yes, and I fear no man but Justice Overdo.

    Overdo. Urs'la? Where is she? O the sow of enormity, this!
(*To Ursula and Nightingale.*) Welcome, stand you there; you
songster, there.

    Ursula. An' please your worship, I am in no fault. A   60
gentleman stripped him in my booth, and borrowed his gown
and his hat; and he ran away with my goods, here, for it.

    Overdo. [*To Quarlous.*] Then this is the true madman,
and you are the enormity!

    Quarlous. You are i' the right, I am mad but from the   65
gown outward.

    Overdo. Stand you there.

    Quarlous. Where you please, sir.

              *Mistress Overdo [waking up] is sick, and her
                      husband is silenced.*

    Mistress Overdo. O lend me a basin, I am sick, I am sick.
Where's Master Overdo? Bridget, call hither my Adam.   70

    Overdo. How?

    Whit. Dy very own wife, i' fait, worshipful Adam.

    Mistress Overdo. Will not my Adam come at me? Shall I
see him no more then?

    Quarlous. Sir, why do you not go on with the enormity?   75
Are you oppressed with it? I'll help you, sir, i' your ear? your
"innocent young man," you have ta'en such care of all this
day, is a cutpurse, that hath got all your brother Cokes his
things, and helped you to your beating and the stocks; if you
have a mind to hang him now and show him your magistrate's   80

---

49. *Redde te Harpocratem*—"make yourself Harpocrates" (god of silence).
50–51. be uncovered—remove your hat in respect.

wit, you may; but I should think it were better recovering the
goods, and to save your estimation in him. I thank you, sir, for
the gift of your ward, Mistress Grace; look you, here is your
hand and seal, by the way. Master Winwife, give you joy, you
are Palamon; you are possessed of the gentlewoman, but she   85
must pay me value, here's warrant for it. And honest madman,
there's thy gown and cap again; I thank thee for my wife. (*To
the widow.*) Nay, I can be mad, sweetheart, when I please,
still; never fear me. And careful Numps, where's he? I thank
him for my license.   90

    Wasp. How!

    Quarlous. 'Tis true, Numps.

    Wasp. I'll be hanged then.

    Quarlous. Look i' your box, Numps. (*Wasp misseth the
license.*) [*To Overdo.*] Nay, sir, stand not you fixed here, like   95
a stake in Finsbury to be shot at, or the whipping post i' the
Fair, but get your wife out o' the air; it will make her worse
else; and remember you are but Adam, flesh and blood! You
have your frailty; forget your other name of Overdo and invite
us all to supper. There you and I will compare our discoveries,   100
and drown the memory of all enormity in your bigg'st bowl at
home.

    Cokes. How now, Numps, ha' you lost it? I warrant 'twas
when thou wert i' the stocks. Why dost not speak?

    Wasp. I will never speak while I live, again, for aught I   105
know.

    Overdo. Nay, Humphrey, if I be patient, you must be so
too; this pleasant conceited gentleman hath wrought upon my
judgment, and prevailed. I pray you take care of your sick
friend. Mistress Alice, and my good friends all—   110

    Quarlous. And no enormities.

    Overdo. I invite you home with me to my house, to
supper. I will have none fear to go along, for my intents are *ad
correctionem, non ad destructionem; ad aedificandum, non ad
diruendum.* So lead on.   115

    Cokes. Yes, and bring the actors along, we'll ha' the rest o'
the play at home.   [*Exeunt.*]

THE END

82. estimation in—reputation with.   96. stake in Finsbury—archery target.
113–15. *ad . . . diruendum*—"for correction, not destruction; for building up,
not tearing down."

THE
EPILOGUE

Your Majesty hath seen the play, and you
   Can best allow it from your ear and view.
You know the scope of writers, and what store
   Of leave is given them, if they take not more,
And turn it into license. You can tell   5
   If we have used that leave you gave us well;
Or whether we to rage or license break,
   Or be profane, or make profane men speak.
This is your power to judge, great sir, and not
   The envy of a few. Which if we have got,   10
We value less what their dislike can bring,
   If it so happy be, t' have pleased the King.

THE MASQUE OF QUEENS[1]

INTRODUCTION

The court masque was in vogue for only half a century, but it brought modern stagecraft to England and ushered in the island's first opera. The masque was neither play, poem, dance, nor concert, yet it borrowed features from all of these. It was an entertainment that depended even more than drama on the spectacle and music associated with it. It was like a play in that actors impersonated characters in a fictional story, but the narrative was much less important than in most plays. Like the Elizabethan court pageant, which was its immediate ancestor, the masque featured characters who did not interact with each other as much as they simply appeared, in magnificent and symbolic costume, as representatives of the abstract qualities (e.g., vices, virtues) for which they were named.

The purpose of the fiction was to provide a noble and symbolically plausible setting for the dances performed by prominent members of the court, whose active participation was an especially important distinguishing characteristic of the masque. The speaking parts were performed by professional actors, but the main dances were always performed by courtiers, i.e., by a part of the audience. King James himself did not dance, but he enjoyed watching this part of the evening, and Queen Anne was not only the instigator and sponsor but also the chief dancer of several masques, including *The Masque of Queens.*

[1] Jonson's footnotes abridged.

Because of such intense interest from the royal family, the expenditures for these entertainments were enormous even by modern standards. Stephen Orgel observes, "It was not uncommon for the king to spend £3,000 (the equivalent of several hundred thousand dollars today) on a production that would be performed once or twice, and witnessed by a thousand people."[2] It is no wonder that Puritan critics of the king complained and that the Puritan revolution put an end to this art form forever.

The court did not engage in this conspicuous consumption merely to outrage the Puritans, of course; the masque was an embodiment of the treasured ideals of the court. The dances in the masque were not designed to provide the courtiers with recreation so much as they were thought to reaffirm such values as order, harmony, and the beneficent influence of ceremony. Foreign ambassadors always described masques in detail for their governments at home, because the magnificence of such ceremonies was regarded as a significant index of a monarch's power and character.

Ben Jonson is by far the greatest writer of masques. As a poet he naturally insisted that the spectacle was ephemeral whereas the text could be read by posterity. Therefore, Jonson argued, poetry is the soul of the masque, the spectacle merely the body: "This it is hath made the most royal princes and greatest persons, who are commonly the personators of these actions, not only studious of riches and magnificence in the outward celebration or show, which rightly becomes them, but curious after the most high and hearty inventions to furnish the inward parts, and those grounded upon antiquity and solid learnings; which, though their voice be taught to sound to present occasions, their sense or [i.e., either] doth or should always lay hold on more removed mysteries" (*Hymenaei*, H&S 10–19).

For Jonson the "more removed mysteries" were Platonic conceptions of the Ideal symbolized in the Greek myths, especially as those myths were elaborately interpreted by Renaissance Platonists. The mythological character Perseus, for example, appears in *The Masque of Queens* as Heroic Virtue and is so named. Jonson says he found this symbolic equation in Hesiod and Apollodorus the Grammarian,[3] but his most immediate source was probably Caesare

---

[2] S. Orgel, ed., *Ben Jonson: The Complete Masques* (New Haven, Conn.: Yale University Press, 1969), p. 3.

[3] See Orgel, p. 542.

Ripa's *Iconologia* (1593). Sometimes the characters are not mytho-logical but simply allegorical like Fama Bona (Good Fame), whom Jonson also found described in Ripa.

At first Jonson's masques contained only the "more removed mysteries." But in the preface to *The Masque of Queens* he tells how he began writing, at the queen's request, an "anti-masque" to serve as a "foil, or false masque" (1.13). In the hands of a great writer of comedy like Jonson this presentation of evil or folly rapidly turned into a kind of satiric comedy. The antimasques, to Jonson's chagrin, became more popular than the serious "high and hearty inventions."

To his greater chagrin, it became clear that the spectacular stage effects and costumes designed by Inigo Jones were more highly prized by the court than Jonson's inventions. The passage quoted from *Hymenaei* was an early shot in a long battle between Jonson and Jones over whether the designer or the poet should have the place of honor and power in the creation of a masque. This issue was in part obscured by the sheer personal bitterness that developed between the two men.[4] Jones was victorious when Charles replaced James on the throne in 1625. Jonson was not asked to write the most important court masques for several years, whereas Jones was kept at work and given high honors.

Wherever our sympathies lie in the quarrel, there is no denying Inigo Jones' brilliance. Many of his designs survive and give us some idea of their beauty. The sets were among the first in England to create an elaborate illusion of reality; that is, in *The Masque of Queens* the House of Fame looked to the audience like a real palace. Jones achieved this effect by painting flats in perspective to give a three-dimensional appearance. Even more radical was his use of machines to move sets. In *The Masque of Queens* the sharp contrast between the world of evil and the world of good is strongly emphasized by the use of these machines: "In the heat of their dance on the sudden was heard a sound of loud music, ... with which not only the hags themselves but the hell into which they ran quite vanished, and the whole face of the scene altered, scarce suffering the memory of such a thing. But in the place of it appeared a glorious and magnificent building figuring the House of Fame, in the top of which were discovered the twelve masquers sitting upon a throne triumphal" (lines 350–58).

[4] See Jonson's satire of Jones in *A Tale of a Tub* and "An Expostulation with Inigo Jones," H&S VIII.402.

As the "sound of loud music" indicates, the music was necessary not only for the dances but for sound effects, like the musical score of a movie. There was also singing, only a few solos in *The Masque of Queens*, but a little later, in *Lovers Made Men* (1617), there is a chorus, and the whole masque was sung "after the Italian manner, *stilo recitativo*" (H&S 26–27). Clearly this was the first opera in England.

Despite the magnificence of the spectacle and the music, however, Jonson's poetry is clearly vital to *The Masque of Queens*. His witches, for example, are convincing because he draws not only on the learned sources he cites but on the folklore and the rhythms of his childhood. He admits at one point that an idea is based "on no other ground (to confess ingenuously) than a vulgar fable. ... It was a tale when I went to school" [p. 281 (note)]. All his written sources, either ancient or modern, were in Latin, but no amount of reading about the witches in Horace or Seneca could have given him the wonderful rhythm of incantation he attains in English. As in "Double, double, toil and trouble," we find a great deal of repetition, simple tetrameter, stark monosyllables, and heavy rhyming:

> Not yet? My rage begins to swell;
> Darkness, devils, night and hell
> Do not thus delay my spell!

> > (296–98)

But one also finds more complex and yet incantatory rhythms encased in the basic tetrameter line:

> When we have set the elements at wars,
> Made midnight see the sun, and day the stars;
> When the winged lightning in the course hath stayed,
> And swiftest rivers have run back, afraid

> > (230–33)

The most powerful incantatory verses achieve their effects by the perfect marriage of weird rhythm with nightmarish content:

> The dogs they do bay and the timbrels play,
>   The spindle is now a-turning;
> The moon it is red and the stars are fled,
>   But all the sky is a-burning

> > (74–77)

In contrast to the witches, Heroic Virtue and Good Fame speak only in pentameter couplets, which Dryden and Pope later took to be the only language Heroic Virtue could or should ever speak.

FACTS AND REFERENCES

FIRST PERFORMANCE

February 2, 1609 (modern reckoning), is given in many court records and the title pages themselves. Names of the masquers, designer, choreographer, and musicians are given in the text.

SELECTED BIBLIOGRAPHY

Early Editions

Holograph manuscript, 1609. In British Museum. Facsimile, King's Printers, 1930.

Quarto, 1609.

Folio, 1616 (basis for this edition).

Folio, 1640.

Modern Editions (other than H&S)

Orgel, Stephen, ed., *Ben Jonson: The Complete Masques.*[1] The Yale Ben Jonson. New Haven, Conn.: Yale University Press, 1969.

Other Scholarship and Criticism

Allen, Don Cameron. "Ben Jonson and the Hieroglyphics." *PQ* 18 (1939): 290–300.

Cunningham, Dolora. "The Jonsonian Masque as a Literary Form." *ELH* 22 (1955): 108–24.

Furniss, W. Todd. "The Annotation of Ben Jonson's *Masque of Queenes.*" *RES* 5 (1954): 344–60.

_____. "Jonson's Antimasques." *Renaissance News* 7 (1954): 21–2.

_____. "Ben Jonson's Masques." In *Three Studies in the Renaissance: Sidney, Jonson, Milton.* Yale Studies in English, no. 138. New Haven, Conn.: Yale University Press, 1958.

[1] My text and notes are often indebted to this excellent edition.

Gilbert, Allan H. *The Symbolic Persons in the Masques of Ben Jonson.* Durham, N. C.: Duke University Press, 1948.

Meagher, John C. *Method and Meaning in Jonson's Masques.* South Bend, Ind.: Notre Dame University Press, 1966.

Orgel, Stephen. *The Jonsonian Masque.* Cambridge, Mass.: Harvard University Press, 1965.

Talbert, Ernest W. "The Interpretation of Jonson's Courtly Spectacles." *PMLA* 61 (1946): 454–73.

_____. "New Light on Ben Jonson's Workmanship." *SP* 40 (1943): 154–85.

THE MASQUE OF QUEENS

Celebrated from the House of Fame, by the queen of Great Britain with her ladies. At Whitehall, February 2, 1609.

It increasing now to the third time of my being used in these services to her majesty's personal presentations, with the ladies whom she pleaseth to honor, it was my first and special regard to see that the nobility of the invention should be answerable to the dignity of their persons. For which reason I   5 chose the argument to be a celebration of honorable and true fame bred out of virtue, observing that rule of the best artist, to suffer no object of delight to pass without his mixture of profit and example.

And because her majesty (best knowing that a principal   10 part of life in these spectacles lay in their variety) had commanded me to think on some dance or show that might precede hers and have the place of a foil or false masque, I was careful to decline not only from others', but mine own steps in that kind, since the last year I had an anti-masque of boys; and   15 therefore now devised that twelve women in the habit of hags or witches, sustaining the persons of Ignorance, Suspicion, Credulity, etc., the opposites to good Fame, should fill that part—not as a masque but a spectacle of strangeness, producing multiplicity of gesture, and not unaptly sorting with the   20 current and whole fall of the device.

His majesty, then, being set, and the whole company in full expectation, the part of the scene which first presented itself was an ugly hell, which flaming beneath, smoked unto the top of the roof. And in respect all evils are, morally, said   25

7. best artist—"Horace, in *Ars Poetica*" (Jonson).   14. decline—deviate, turn aside.   15. last year—"In the Masque at my Lord Haddington's wedding" (Jonson).

*to come from hell, as also from that observation of Torrentius
upon Horace his Canidia,* quae tot instructa venenis, ex Orci
faucibus profecta videri possit, *these witches, with a kind of
hollow and infernal music, came forth from thence. First one,
then two, and three, and more, till their number increased to*   30
*eleven, all differently attired—some with rats on their head,
some on their shoulders; others with ointment pots at their
girdles; all with spindles, timbrels, rattles or other venefical
instruments, making a confused noise, with strange gestures.
The device of their attire was Master Jones his, with the*   35
*invention and architecture of the whole scene and machine.
Only I prescribed them their properties of vipers, snakes,
bones, herbs, roots and other ensigns of their magic, out of the
authority of ancient and late writers; wherein the faults are
mine, if there be any found, and for that cause I confess them.*   40

    *These eleven witches beginning to dance (which is an
usual ceremony at their convents, or meetings, where sometimes also they are vizarded and masked) on the sudden one of
them missed their chief, and interrupted the rest with this
speech:*   45

        Sisters, stay: we want our Dame;
        Call upon her by her name,
        And the charm we use to say,
        That she quickly anoint and come away.

                  CHARM 1

        Dame, Dame, the watch is set;   50
        Quickly come, we are all met.
        From the lakes and from the fens,
        From the rocks and from the dens,
        From the woods and from the caves,
        From the churchyards, from the graves,   55
        From the dungeon, from the tree
        That they die on, here are we.

27–28. quae . . . possit—"who, provided with so many poisons, might seem to
have issued out of the mouth of hell."   33. *venefical*—pertaining to
witchcraft.   35. *Master Jones*—Inigo Jones (1573–1652), architect and designer, Jonson's rival for preeminence in masque-making.   49. anoint—
"When they are to be transported from place to place they use to anoint themselves, and sometimes the things they ride on" (Jonson).

Comes she not yet?
Strike another heat.

CHARM 2

The weather is fair, the wind is good;   60
Up, Dame, o' your horse of wood;
Or else tuck up your gray frock,
And saddle your goat or your green cock,
And make his bridle a bottom of thread
To roll up how many miles you have rid.   65
Quickly come away,
For we all stay.
Nor yet? Nay, then,
We'll try her again.

CHARM 3

The owl is abroad, the bat and the toad,   70
    And so is the cat-a-mountain;
The ant and the mole sit both in a hole,
    And frog peeps out o' the fountain;
The dogs they do bay and the timbrels play,
    The spindle is now a-turning;   75
The moon it is red and the stars are fled,
    But all the sky is a-burning;
The ditch is made, and our nails the spade,
With pictures full, of wax and of wool;
Their livers I stick with needles quick;   80

59. strike . . . heat—try again.   63. goat—"The goat is the devil himself, upon whom they ride often to their solemnities" (Jonson).   green cock—"Of the green cock we have no other ground (to confess ingenuously) than a vulgar fable of a witch that with a cock of that color and a bottom [spool] of blue thread would transport herself through the air, and so escaped, at the time of her being brought to execution, from the hand of justice. It was a tale when I went to school" (Jonson).   64. bottom—spool.   71. cat-a-mountain—wildcat.   75. spindle—"All this is but a periphrasis of the night in their charm, and their applying themselves to it with their instruments, whereof the spindle in antiquity was the chief, and . . . was of special act to the troubling of the moon. . . . " (Jonson).   78. ditch—"This rite of making a ditch with their nails is frequent with our witches" (Jonson).   79. pictures . . . wax—After citing many ancient authorities for voodoo dolls, Jonson cites a recent book concerning "certain pictures of wax found in a dunghill near Islington, of our late queen's; which rumor I myself (being then very young) can yet remember to have been current."

There lacks but the blood to make up the flood.
    Quickly, Dame, then, bring your part in,
    Spur, spur upon little Martin,
    Merrily, merrily make him sail,
    A worm in his mouth and a thorn in's tail,   85
    Fire above and fire below,
    With a whip i' your hand to make him go.
      O, now she's come!
      Let all be dumb.

At this the Dame entered to them, naked armed,   90
barefooted, her frock tucked, her hair knotted and folded with
vipers; in her hand a torch made of a dead man's arm, lighted;
girded with a snake. To whom they all did reverence, and she
spake, uttering by way of question the end wherefore they
came—which, if it had been done either before or otherwise,   95
had not been so natural. For to have made themselves their
own decipherers, and each one to have told upon their
entrance what they were and whether they would, had been a
most piteous hearing, and utterly unworthy any quality of a
poem; wherein a writer should always trust somewhat to the   100
capacity of the spectator, especially at these spectacles, where
men, beside inquiring eyes, are understood to bring quick ears,
and not those sluggish ones of porters and mechanics that
must be bored through at every act with narrations.

Dame.
    Well done, my hags. And come we, fraught with spite,   105
    To overthrow the glory of this night?
    Holds our great purpose?
Hag.
                      Yes.
Dame.
                            But wants there none
    Of our just number?   110

---

83. little Martin—"Their little Martin is he that calls them to their conventi-
cles, which is done in a human voice; but coming forth, they find him in the
shape of a great buck-goat, upon whom they ride to their meetings" (Jonson).
90. *Dame*—"This Dame I make to bear the person of Ate, or mischief (for so
I interpret it) out of Homer's description of her, *Iliad* IX [505—12] . . . and
XIX [91—94]" (Jonson).   98. *whether they would*—what they desired.

Hag.

                              Call us one by one,
        And then our Dame shall see.
Dame.

                                    First, then, advance,
        My drowsy servant, stupid Ignorance,
        Known by thy scaly vesture; and bring on   115
        Thy fearful sister, wild Suspicion,
        Whose eyes do never sleep; let her knit hands
        With quick Credulity, that next her stands,
        Who hath but one ear, and that always ope;
        Two-facèd Falsehood follow in the rope;   120
        And lead on Murmur, with the cheeks deep hung;
        She Malice, whetting of her forkèd tongue;
        And Malice Impudence, whose forehead's lost;
        Let Impudence lead Slander on, to boast
        Her oblique look; and, to her subtle side,   125
        Thou, black-mouthed Execration, stand applied;
        Draw to thee Bitterness, whose pores sweat gall;
        She flame-eyed Rage; Rage, Mischief.
Hag.

                                    Here we are all.
Dame.

        Join now our hearts, we faithful opposites   130
        To Fame and Glory. Let not these bright nights
        Of honor blaze thus to offend our eyes.
        Show ourselves truly envious, and let rise
        Our wonted rages; do what may beseem
        Such names and natures. Virtue else will deem   135
        Our powers decreased, and think us banished earth,

113. First—"In the chaining of these vices, I make as if one link produced another, and the Dame were born out of them all. . . . Nor will it appear much
violenced if their series be considered, when the opposition to all virtue begins
out of Ignorance. That Ignorance begets Suspicion (for knowledge is ever open
and charitable), that Suspicion Credulity, as it is a vice; for being a virtue, and
free, it is opposite to it; but such as are jealous of themselves do easily credit
anything of others, whom they hate. Out of this Credulity springs Falsehood,
which begets Murmur; and that Murmur presently grows Malice, which begets
Impudence; that Impudence Slander, that Slander Execration, Execration
Bitterness, Bitterness Fury, and Fury Mischief. Now for the personal [i.e., al-
legorical] presentation of them, the authority in poetry is universal. But in the
absolute [i.e., perfect] Claudian there is a particular and eminent place where
the poet not only produceth such persons, but almost to a like purpose: *In
Rufinum* I [25–34] . . . " (Jonson).

No less than heaven. All her antique birth,
As Justice, Faith, she will restore; and, bold
Upon our sloth, retrieve her Age of Gold.
We must not let our native manners thus   140
Corrupt with ease. Ill lives not but in us.
I hate to see these fruits of a soft peace,
And curse the piety gives it such increase.
Let us disturb it then, and blast the light;
Mix hell with heaven, and make Nature fight   145
Within herself; loose the whole hinge of things,
And cause the ends run back into their springs.

Hag.

What our Dame bids us do
We are ready for.

Dame.

                    Then fall to.
But first relate me what you have sought,   150
Where you have been, and what you have brought.

1st Hag.

I have been all day looking after
A raven feeding upon a quarter,
And soon as she turned her beak to the south,
I snatched this morsel out of her mouth.   155

2nd Hag.

I have been gathering wolves' hairs,
The mad dogs' foam and the adders' ears;
The spurging of a dead man's eyes,
And all since the evening star did rise.

3rd Hag.

I last night lay all alone   160
O' the ground to hear the mandrake groan,

---

150. But first—"This is also solemn in their witchcraft, to be examined either
by the devil or their Dame at their meetings, of what mischief they have done,
and what they can confer to a future hurt . . ." (Jonson). After citing authorities for this point, Jonson mentions his effort at "reconciling (as near as we
can) the practice of antiquity to the neoteric, and making it familiar with our
popular witchcraft."   153. quarter—i.e., of a corpse.   154. the south—
associated with storms.   158. spurging—excretion.   161. mandrake—
plant used in medicine and potions; the belief that it groaned when pulled up
perhaps arose because its forked root bears a distant resemblance to the two
legs of a human trunk. Jonson cites Pliny and adds, "But we have later tradition, that the forcing of it up is so fatally dangerous, as the groan kills, and
therefore they do it with dogs."

> And plucked him up, though he grew full low,
> And as I had done, the cock did crow.

4th Hag.

> And I ha' been choosing out this skull
> From charnel houses that were full; 165
> From private grots and public pits,
> And frighted a sexton out of his wits.

5th Hag.

> Under a cradle I did creep
> By day, and when the child was asleep
> At night I sucked the breath, and rose 170
> And plucked the nodding nurse by the nose.

6th Hag.

> I had a dagger; what did I with that?
> Killed an infant to have his fat.
> A piper it got, at a church-ale;
> I bade him again blow wind i' the tail. 175

7th Hag.

> A murderer yonder was hung in chains,
> The sun and the wind had shrunk his veins;
> I bit off a sinew, I clipped his hair,
> I brought off his rags that danced i' the air.

8th Hag.

> The scritch-owl's eggs and the feathers black, 180
> The blood of the frog and the bone in his back
> I have been getting, and made of his skin
> A purset to keep Sir Cranion in.

9th Hag.

> And I ha' been plucking, plants among,
> Hemlock, henbane, adder's tongue, 185
> Nightshade, moonwort, libbard's bane,
> And twice by the dogs was like to be ta'en.

---

174. piper . . . got—a bagpiper begot the infant.   church-ale—a kind of alcoholic festivity sponsored by some parish churches; moralists were outraged by the practice.   175. blow . . . tail—impregnate another wench.   183. Sir Cranion—properly, a kind of fly. But *fly* was also the term for a familiar spirit such as Dapper wanted in *The Alchemist.* Thus Jonson, on the present passage, notes, "That of the skin (to make a purse for her fly) was meant ridiculous, to mock the keeping of their familiars."   186. libbard's—leopard's.
187. dogs . . . ta'en—"The common venefical ingredients . . . which I make her to have gathered, as about a castle, church, or some such vast building, kept by dogs among ruins, and wild heaps" (Jonson).

10th Hag.
    I from the jaws of a gard'ner's bitch
    Did snatch these bones, and then leaped the ditch;
    Yet went I back to the house again,   190
    Killed the black cat, and here's the brain.
11th Hag.
    I went to the toad breeds under the wall,
    I charmed him out and he came at my call;
    I scratched out the eyes of the owl, before;
    I tore the bat's wing; what would you have more?   195
Dame.
    Yes, I have brought, to help our vows,
    Hornèd poppy, cypress boughs,
    The fig-tree wild that grows on tombs,
    And juice that from the larch tree comes,
    The basilisk's blood and the viper's skin.   200
    And now, our orgies let's begin.

*Here the Dame put herself in the midst of them and began
her following invocation; wherein she took occasion to boast
all the power attributed to witches by the ancients, of which
every poet (or the most) do give some: Homer to Circe, in the*   205
Odyssey; *Theocritus to Simatha, in* Pharmaceutria; *Virgil to
Alphesiboeus in his; Ovid to Dipsas, in* Amores; *to Medea and
Circe, in* Metamorphoses; *Tibullus to saga; Horace to Canidia,
Sagana, Veia, Folia; Seneca to Medea, and the Nurse, in*
Hercules Oetaeus; *Petronius Arbiter to his saga, in* Fragmenta;   210
*and Claudian to Megaera, liber I, In Rufinum, who takes the
habit of a witch, as these do, and supplies that historical part
in the poem, beside her moral person of a fury. Confirming the
same drift in ours:*

    You fiends and furies, if yet any be   215
    Worse than ourselves, you that have quaked to see
    These knots untied, and shrunk when we have
                               [charmed;

---

188. gard'ner's—Jonson's manuscript uses a metrical apostrophe; the printers
omit it.   205–211. *Homer . . . Claudian*—for exact citations see Orgel
p. 479.   206–07. *Virgil . . . in his*—i.e., his *Pharmaceutria* (Eclogue VIII).
208. saga—sorceress.

You that to arm us have yourselves disarmed,
And to our powers resigned your whips and brands
When we went forth, the scourge of men and lands;   220
You that have seen me ride when Hecatè
Durst not take chariot, when the boisterous sea
Without a breath of wind hath knocked the sky,
And that hath thundered, Jove not knowing why;
When we have set the elements at wars,   225
Made midnight see the sun, and day the stars;
When the winged lightning in the course hath stayed,
And swiftest rivers have run back, afraid
To see the corn remove, the groves to range,
Whole places alter, and the seasons change;   230
When the pale moon at the first voice down fell
Poisoned, and durst not stay the second spell;
You that have oft been conscious of these sights,
And thou three-formèd star, that on these nights
Art only powerful, to whose triple name   235
Thus we incline: once, twice and thrice the same—
If now with rites profane and foul enough
We do invoke thee, darken all this roof
With present fogs. Exhale earth's rott'nest vapors,
And strike a blindness through these blazing tapers.   240
    Come, let a murmuring charm resound
    The whilst we bury all i' the ground.
    But first, see every foot be bare,
    And every knee.
Hag.

                    Yes, Dame, they are.   245

                    CHARM 4

Deep, O deep, we lay thee to sleep;
We leave thee drink by, if thou chance to be dry,
Both milk and blood, the dew and the flood.
We breathe in thy bed, at the foot and the head;
We cover thee warm, that thou take no harm;   250
And when thou dost wake,
    Dame earth shall quake,

---

234. three-formèd star—Hecate. Jonson quotes ancient writers who associated
the number three with this goddess of witchcraft.   239. present—immediate.

> And the houses shake,
> And her belly shall ache
> As her back were brake,   255
> Such a birth to make
> As is the blue drake,
> Whose form thou shalt take.

Dame.

> Never a star yet shot?
> Where be the ashes?   260

Hag.

>   Here i' the pot.

Dame.

> Cast them up, and the flintstone
> Over the left shoulder bone
> Into the west.

Hag.

>   It will be best.   265

CHARM 5

> The sticks are a-cross, there can be no loss,
> The sage is rotten, the sulfur is gotten
> Up to the sky that was i' the ground.
> Follow it then with our rattles, round,
> Under the bramble, over the briar;   270
> A little more heat will set it on fire;
> Put it in mind to do it kind,
> Flow water, and blow wind.
> Rouncy is over, Robble is under,
> A flash of light and a clap of thunder,   275
> A storm of rain, another of hail.
> We all must home i' the egg shell sail;
> The mast is made of a great pin,
> The tackle of cobweb, the sail as thin,

---

257. blue—"the color of plagues and things hurtful" (*OED*).   drake—dragon.
262. cast—Jonson, after quoting an authority who describes various superstitious acts by witches, comments: "And when they see the success, they are
more confirmed, as if the event followed their working. The like illusion is of
their fantasy, in sailing in egg shells, creeping through augur holes, and such
like, so vulgar in their confessions."   272. do . . . kind—do its kind, obey
its nature.   274. Rouncy, Robble—"onomatopoeia for thunder" (Orgel).

And if we go through and not fall in—   280

Dame.

Stay! All our charms do nothing win
Upon the night; our labor dies!
Our magic feature will not rise;
Nor yet the storm! We must repeat
More direful voices far, and beat   285
The ground with vipers till it sweat.

CHARM 6

Bark dogs, wolves howl,
Sea roar, woods roll,
Clouds crack, all be black
But the light our charms do make.   290

Dame.

Not yet? My rage begins to swell;
Darkness, devils, night and hell,
Do not thus delay my spell.
I call you once and I call you twice,
I beat you again if you stay me thrice;   295
Through these crannies where I peep
I'll let in the light to see your sleep,
And all the secrets of your sway
Shall lie as open to the day
As unto me. Still are you deaf?   300
Reach me a bough that ne'er bare leaf
To strike the air, and aconite
To hurl upon this glaring light;
A rusty knife to wound mine arm,
And as it drops I'll speak a charm   305
Shall cleave the ground as low as lies
Old shrunk up Chaos, and let rise
Once more his dark and reeking head
To strike the world and nature dead
Until my magic birth be bred.   310

---

281. Stay—"This stop, or interruption, showed the better by causing that general silence which made all the following noises . . . more direful" (Jonson).
295. stay me thrice—the manuscript reading; printed versions read "my."
302. aconite—"A deadly poisonous herb" (Jonson).

CHARM 7

Black go in and blacker come out;
At thy going down we give thee a shout.
   Hoo!
At thy rising again thou shalt have two,
And if thou dost what we would have thee do,   315
Thou shalt have three, thou shalt have four,
Thou shalt have ten, thou shalt have a score.
     Hoo! Har! Har! Hoo!

CHARM 8

A cloud of pitch, a spur and a switch
To haste him away, and a whirlwind play   320
Before and after, with thunder for laughter
And storms for joy of the roaring boy,
His head of a drake, his tail of a snake.

CHARM 9

About, about and about,
Till the mist arise and the lights fly out;   325
The images neither be seen nor felt;
The woolen burn and the waxen melt;
Sprinkle your liquors upon the ground
And into the air, around, around.
    Around, around,   330
    Around, around,
    Till a music sound
    And the pace be found
    To which we may dance
    And our charms advance.   335

*At which, with a strange and sudden music they fell into a
magical dance full of preposterous change and gesticulation,
but most applying to their property, who at their meetings do
all things contrary to the custom of men, dancing back to back
and hip to hip, their hands joined, and making their circles* 340
*backward, to the left hand, with strange fantastic motions of
their heads and bodies. All which were excellently imitated by
the maker of the dance, Master Hierome Herne, whose right it
is here to be named.*

In the heat of their dance on the sudden was heard a 345
sound of loud music, as if many instruments had made one
blast; with which not only the hags themselves but the hell
into which they ran quite vanished, and the whole face of the
scene altered, scarce suffering the memory of such a thing. But
in the place of it appeared a glorious and magnificent building 350
figuring the House of Fame, in the top of which were
discovered the twelve masquers sitting upon a throne trium-
phal erected in form of a pyramid and circled with all store of
light. From whom a person, by this time descended, in the
furniture of Perseus, and expressing heroic and masculine 355
virtue, began to speak:

Heroic Virtue.
    So should, at Fame's loud sound and Virtue's sight,
    All dark and envious witchcraft fly the light.
    I did not borrow Hermes' wings, nor ask
    His crooked sword, nor put on Pluto's casque, 360
    Nor on my arm advanced wise Pallas' shield
    (By which, my face aversed, in open field
    I slew the Gorgon) for an empty name:
    When Virtue cut off Terror, he gat Fame.
    And if when Fame was gotten, Terror died, 365
    What black *Erinyes* or more hellish pride
    Durst arm these hags, now she is grown and great,
    To think they could her glories once defeat?
    I was her parent, and I am her strength.
    Heroic Virtue sinks not under length 370
    Of years or ages, but is still the same
    While he preserves, as when he got good Fame.
    My daughter, then, whose glorious house you see
    Built all of sounding brass, whose columns be
    Men-making poets, and those well made men 375
    Whose strife it was to have the happiest pen
    Renown them to an after-life, and not

355. *furniture*—costumes and accoutrements. 363. Gorgon—Perseus slew
the Gorgon Medusa, whose look turned men to stone. He was aided by wings
for his feet from Hermes, a helmet from Pluto that made the wearer invisible,
and a shiny shield from Pallas Athena that he used as a mirror and thus avoided looking directly at his foe. 364. gat—begat. 366. *Erinyes*—Furies.
375. Men-making poets—poets whose works make men famous.

With pride to scorn the Muse and die, forgot;
She that inquireth into all the world,
And hath about her vaulted palace hurled   380
All rumors and reports, or true, or vain,
What utmost lands or deepest seas contain,
But only hangs great actions on her file;
She to this lesser world and greatest isle
Tonight sounds Honor, which she would have seen   385
In yond' bright bevy, each of them a queen.
Eleven of them are of times long gone:
Penthesilea, the brave Amazon,
Swift-foot Camilla, queen of Volscia,
Victorious Thomyris of Scythia,   390
Chaste Artemisia, the Carian dame,
And fair-haired Berenicè, Egypt's fame,
Hypsicratea, glory of Asia,
Candacè, pride of Ethiopia,
The Britain honor, Voadicea,   395
The virtuous Palmyrene, Zenobia,
The wise and warlike Goth, Amalasunta,
And bold Valasca of Bohemia.
These in their lives, as fortunes, crowned the choice
Of womankind, and 'gainst all opposite voice,   400
Made good to Time, had after death the claim
To live eternised in the House of Fame.
Where hourly hearing (as, what there is old?)
The glories of Bel-Anna so well told,
Queen of the ocean; how that she alone   405
Possessed all virtues, for which one by one
They were so famed; and wanting then a head
To form that sweet and gracious pyramid
Wherein they sit, it being the sovereign place
Of all that palace, and reserved to grace   410
The worthiest queen; these without envy on her,
In life desired that honor to confer,
Which with their death no other should enjoy.

383. file—a string on which papers were hung for safekeeping and easy reference.   384. greatest isle—England.   386. bevy—the Queen and her ladies.   388. Penthesilea—Jonson himself identifies all of the queens in more
detail below, pages 294–297.

She this embracing with a virtuous joy,
Far from self-love, as humbling all her worth   415
To him that gave it, hath again brought forth
Their names to memory, and means this night
To make them once more visible to light,
And to that light from whence her truth of spirit
Confesseth all the luster of her merit: 420
To you, most royal and most happy king,
Of whom Fame's house in every part doth ring
For every virtue, but can give no increase,
Not though her loudest trumpet blaze your peace;
To you, that cherish every great example   425
Contracted in yourself, and being so ample
A field of honor, cannot but embrace
A spectacle so full of love and grace
Unto your court, where every princely dame
Contends to be as bounteous of her fame   430
To others as her life was good to her.
For by their lives they only did confer
Good on themselves; but by their fame, to yours
And every age, the benefit endures.

Here the throne wherein they sat, being machina versatilis,   435
suddenly changed, and in the place of it appeared Fama bona,
as she is described (in Iconologia di Cesare Ripa), *attired in
white, with white wings, having a collar of gold about her neck
and a heart hanging at it, which Orus Apollo in his*
Hieroglyphica *interprets the note of a good Fame. In her right*   440
*hand she bore a trumpet, in her left an olive branch; and for
her state, it was as Virgil describes her, at the full, her feet on
the ground and her head in the clouds. She, after the music
had done, which waited on the turning of the machine, called
from thence to Virtue, and spake this following speech:*   445

---

435. machina versatilis—turning machine, one of the first mechanically revolv-
ing sets in England.   436. Fama bona—Good Fame.   437. Iconologia
di Cesare Ripa—Ripa's *Iconologia* was a popular manual of symbolism first
published in 1593.   439. *Orus Apollo*—Horapollo's *Hieroglyphics* was an interpretation of Egyptian hermetic symbolism probably written in the fourth
century A.D.   442. *Virgil*—"*Aeneid* IV [176–77]" (Jonson).

Fame.

  Virtue, my father and my honor, thou
  That mad'st me good, as great, and dar'st avow
  No fame for thine but what is perfect: aid
  Tonight the triumphs of thy white-winged maid.
  Do those renownèd queens all utmost rites   450
  Their states can ask. This is a night of nights.
  In mine own chariots let them crownèd ride,
  And mine own birds and beasts in gears applied
  To draw them forth. Unto the first car tie
  Far-sighted eagles, to note Fame's sharp eye;   455
  Unto the second, griffins, that design
  Swiftness and strength, two other gifts of mine;
  Unto the last, our lions, that imply
  The top of graces, state and majesty.
  And let those hags be led as captives, bound   460
  Before their wheels whilst I my trumpet sound.

*At which the loud music sounded as before, to give the
masquers time of descending. And here we cannot but take the
opportunity to make some more particular description of their
scene, as also of the persons they presented; which, though 465
they were disposed rather by chance than election, yet it is my
part to justify them all virtuous; and then the lady that will
own her presentation, may.*

* To follow, therefore, the rule of chronology which we
have observed in our verse, the most upward in time was 470
Penthesilea. She was queen of the Amazons. ... She lived and
was present at the war of Troy, on their part against the
Greeks. ...*

* Next follows Camilla, queen of the Volscians, celebrated
by Virgil ... than whose verses nothing can be imagined more 475
exquisite, or more honoring the person they describe. ...*

* The third lived in the age of Cyrus, the great Persian
monarch, and made him leave to live: Thomyris, queen of the*

453. gears—harness.   456. griffins—mythological beast, half eagle and
half lion.   471. Amazons . . . —Dots here and through line 547, indicate
points at which Jonson's text has been abridged for this edition.
474–75. *celebrated by Virgil*— Jonson here quotes *Aeneid* VII.803–11 and
adds, "All which if the poet created out of himself, without nature, he did but
show how much so divine a soul could exceed her." 478. *made him leave
to live*—i.e., killed him.

Scythians, or Massagets, a heroine of a most invincible and
unbroken fortitude. Who, when Cyrus had invaded her, and,   480
taking her only son (rather by treachery than war, as she
objected), had slain him, not touched with the grief of so great
a loss, in the juster comfort she took of a greater revenge,
pursued not only the occasion and honor of conquering so
potent an enemy, with whom fell two hundred thousand   485
soldiers, but (what was right memorable in her victory) left
not a messenger surviving of his side to report the massacre. ...

    The fourth was honored to life in the time of Xerxes, and
present at his great expedition into Greece: Artemisia, the
queen of Caria, whose virtue Herodotus, not without some   490
wonder, records. ...

    The fifth was the fair-haired daughter of Ptolomaeus
Philadelphus by the elder Arsinoe, who (married to her
brother Ptolomaeus, surnamed Euergetes) was after queen of
Egypt. I find her written both Beronice and Berenice. This   495
lady, upon an expedition of her new-wedded lord into Assyria,
vowed to Venus, if he returned safe, and conqueror, the
offering of her hair; which vow of hers, exacted by the success,
she afterward performed. But her father missing it, and
therewith displeased, Conon, a mathematician who was then in   500
household with Ptolemy and knew well to flatter him,
persuaded the king that it was ta'en up to heaven and made a
constellation, showing him those seven stars ad caudam Leonis
which are since called Coma Berenices. ...

    The sixth, that famous wife of Mithridates, and queen of   505
Pontus, Hypsicratea, no less an example of virtue than the rest;
who so loved her husband as she was assistant to him in all
labors and hazards of the war, in a masculine habit. ...

    The seventh, that renown of Ethiopia, Candacè, from
whose excellency the succeeding queens of that nation were   510
ambitious to be called so. A woman of a most haughty spirit
against enemies, and a singular affection to her subjects. ...

    The eighth, our own honor, Voadicea, or Boodicea; by
some, Bunduica, and Bunduca; queen of the Iceni, a people
that inhabited that part of our island which was called East   515
Anglia, and comprehended Suffolk, Norfolk, Cambridge and
Huntingdon shires. Since she was born here at home, we will

503. ad caudam Leonis—near the tail of Leo.   504. Coma Berenices—
Berenice's hair.

*first honor her with a home-born testimony, from the grave
and diligent Spenser:*

> *Bunduca Britoness*   520
> *Bunduca, that victorious conqueress,*
> *That, lifting up her brave, heroic thought*
> *'Bove women's weakness, with the Romans fought;*
> *Fought, and in field against them thrice prevailed, etc.*

...She lived in the time of Nero.   525
   The ninth in time, but equal in fame and (the cause of it)
virtue, was the chaste Zenobia, queen of the Palmyrenes, who
after the death of her husband, Odenatus, had the name to be
reckoned among the thirty that usurped the Roman empire
from Gallienus. She continued a long and brave war against   530
several chiefs, and was at length triumphed on by Aurelian. ...
   The tenth succeeding was that learned and heroic
Amalasunta, queen of the Ostrogoths, daughter to Theodoric,
that obtained the principality of Ravenna, and almost all Italy.
She drave the Burgundians and Almains out of Liguria, and   535
appeared in her government rather an example than a second.
She was the most eloquent of her age, and cunning in all
languages of any nation that had commerce with the Roman
Empire. ...
   The eleventh was that brave Bohemian queen Valasca,   540
who for her courage had the surname of Bold. That to redeem
herself and her sex from the tyranny of men which they lived
in under Primislaus, on a night and an hour appointed led on
the women to the slaughter of their barbarous husbands and
lords; and possessing themselves of their horses, arms, treasure 545
and places of strength, not only ruled the rest, but lived many
years after with the liberty and fortitude of Amazons. ...
   The twelfth, and worthy sovereign of all, I make
Bel-Anna, royal queen of the Ocean, of whose dignity and
person the whole scope of the invention doth speak through-   550
out; which to offer you again here might but prove offense to
that sacred modesty, which hears any testimony of others
iterated with more delight than her own praise. She being
placed above the need of such ceremony, and safe in her
princely virtue against the good or ill of any witness. The name 555

519. *Spenser—Ruins of Time, lines 106–11.*

of Bel-Anna I devised to honor hers proper by, as adding to it, the attribute of fair, and is kept by me in all my poems wherein I mention her majesty with any shadow or figure. Of which some may come forth with a longer destiny than this age commonly gives the best births, if but helped to the light   560 by her gracious and ripening favor.

But here I discern a possible objection arising against me, to which I must turn, as, how can I bring persons of so different ages to appear properly together? Or why (which is more unnatural) with Virgil's Mezentius, I join the living with   565 the dead? I answer to both these at once, nothing is more proper, nothing more natural; for these all live, and together, in their fame, and so I present them. Besides, if I would fly to the all-daring power of poetry, where could I not take sanctuary? Or in whose poem? For other objections, let the   570 looks and noses of judges hover thick, so they bring the brains; or if they do not, I care not. When I suffered it to go abroad, I departed with my right; and now so secure an interpreter I am of my chance that neither praise nor dispraise shall affect me.

There rests only that we give the description we promised   575 of the scene which was the House of Fame. The structure and ornament of which (as is professed before) was entirely Master Jones his invention and design. First, for the lower columns, he chose the statues of the most excellent poets, as Homer, Virgil, Lucan, etc., as being the substantial supporters of   580 Fame. For the upper, Achilles, Aeneas, Caesar, and those great heroes which these poets had celebrated. All which stood as in massy gold. Between the pillars, underneath, were figured land battles, sea fights, triumphs, loves, sacrifices, and all magnificent subjects of honor, in brass, and heightened with silver. In   585 which he professed to follow that noble description made by Chaucer of the place. Above were sited the masquers, over whose heads he devised two eminent figures of Honor and Virtue for the arch. The friezes both below and above were filled with several-colored lights like emeralds, rubies,   590 sapphires, carbuncles, etc., the reflex of which, with other lights placed in the concave, upon the masquers' habits, was full of glory. These habits had in them the excellency of all

---

565. *Virgil's Mezentius—Aeneid* VIII.485–88.   587. *Chaucer—House of Fame,* lines 1184ff.   *sited*—placed.   591. *reflex*—reflection.

device and riches, and were worthily varied by his invention to
the nations whereof they were queens. Nor are these alone his   595
due, but divers other accessions to the strangeness and beauty
of the spectacle, as the hell, the going about of the chariots,
the binding of the witches, the turning machine with the
presentation of Fame. All which I willingly acknowledge for
him, since it is a virtue planted in good natures that what   600
respects they wish to obtain fruitfully from others they will
give ingenuously themselves.

By this time imagine the masquers descended, and again
mounted into three triumphant chariots ready to come forth.
The first four were drawn with eagles (whereof I gave the   605
reason, as of the rest, in Fame's speech), their four torch-
bearers attending on the chariot sides, and four of the hags
bound before them. Then followed the second, drawn by
griffins, with their torch-bearers and four other hags. Then the
last, which was drawn by lions, and more eminent, wherein her   610
majesty was, and had six torch-bearers more, peculiar to her,
with the like number of hags. After which a full triumphant
music, singing this song while they rode in state about the
stage:

SONG

Help, help, all tongues, to celebrate this wonder: 615
The voice of Fame should be as loud as thunder.
  Her house is all of echo made
   Where never dies the sound;
  And as her brows the clouds invade,
   Her feet do strike the ground.   620
Sing then good Fame that's out of Virtue born,
For who doth Fame neglect doth Virtue scorn.

Here they lighted from their chariots and danced forth
their first dance; then a second, immediately following it; both
right curious and full of subtile and excellent changes, and   625
seemed performed with no less spirits than of those they
personated. The first was to the cornets, the second to the
violins. After which they took out the men and danced the
measures, entertaining the time almost to the space of an hour

625. *curious*—intricate.

with singular variety; when, to give them rest, from the music 630
which attended the chariots, by that most excellent tenor
voice and exact singer her majesty's servant Master John Allin,
this ditty was sung:

SONG

When all the ages of the earth
Were crowned but in this famous birth, 635
And that, when they would boast their store
Of worthy queens, they knew no more—
How happier is that age, can give
A queen in whom all they do live!

After it, succeeded their third dance, than which a more 640
numerous composition could not be seen, graphically disposed
into letters, and honoring the name of the most sweet and
ingenious prince, Charles, Duke of York; wherein, beside that
principal grace of perspicuity, the motions were so even and
apt and their expression so just, as if mathematicians had lost 645
proportion they might there have found it. The author was
Master Thomas Giles. After this, they danced galliards and
corantos, and then their last dance, no less elegant in the place
than the rest; with which they took their chariots again, and
triumphing about the stage had their return to the House of 650
Fame celebrated with this last song, whose notes, as the
former, were the work and honor of my excellent friend
Alfonso Ferrabosco:

SONG

Who, Virtue, can thy power forget
That sees these live and triumph yet? 655
Th'Assyrian pomp, the Persian pride,
Greeks' glory, and the Romans', died;
   And who yet imitate
Their noises, tarry the same fate.
   Force greatness all the glorious ways 660
      You can, it soon decays;
   But so good Fame shall never:
Her triumphs, as their causes, are forever.

641. *numerous*—rhythmic.

To conclude which, I know no worthier way of epilogue
than the celebration of who were the celebrators.   665

The queen's majesty	Countess of Montgomery
Countess of Arundel	Viscountess Cranborne
Countess of Derby	Lady Elizabeth Guildford
Countess of Huntington	Lady Anne Winter
Countess of Bedford	Lady Windsor 670
Countess of Essex	Lady Anne Clifford

POEMS

INTRODUCTION

To say that Ben Jonson's poetry was deeply influenced by the Greek and Roman classics is not merely to describe one aspect of it. The proper kind of imitation of the Ancients was for Jonson a pervasive concern, almost an obsession. As a critic he calls for an imitation so powerful that one virtually becomes the poet of old. He requires that the poet "make choice of one excellent man above the rest, and so to follow him till he grow very he, or so like him as the copy may be mistaken for the principal." Yet this almost magical transformation is not to be accomplished blindly: "Not to imitate servilely, as Horace saith, and catch at vices for virtue; but to draw forth out of the best and choicest flowers, with the bee, and turn all into honey" (*Discoveries*, H&S 2469–78). Jonson succeeds brilliantly in following his own recommendations. He converts the riches of the ancient poets to his own use so thoroughly that his poems seem to be pure English in style and content even when they are taken directly from some Greek or Latin source.

This is true because Jonson follows his own advice "not to imitate servilely." In versification, for example, Jonson always uses rhyme, whereas Greek and Roman poetry did not; he jokes about this difference in the half-serious poem "A Fit of Rhyme Against Rhyme." He also rejected the siren call of other classically inclined poets of his time to write verse with a rhythm determined by the length of time a syllable is sounded, as in the Greek and Roman languages, rather than by spacing out the heavy accents, as English verse had always done.

These major differences aside, however, he follows his classical models closely. The favorite classical model of English poets just before Jonson was Ovid, a poet of sensual love and sensuous language. Jonson consciously turns away from Ovid; his principal models are Martial and Horace and, to a lesser extent, such lyric poets as Pindar, Anacreon, and Catullus. He imitates these poets, according to his own understanding of imitation, in his choice of subjects, themes, genres, and verse forms.

Like Martial and Horace, Jonson is primarily a poet of moral and social relationships. Although he has written some excellent poems on the subjects of love and religion, his main concern is with the proper relationship between the poet and society. His typical poem is not introspective; it is usually addressed to a specific person or group, real or fictional. He holds to social and ethical ideals that are, for the most part, similar to those stressed by Martial and Horace. Although Jonson left only a few translations of classical poems, we find Martial's famous epigram on the good life and Horace's second Epode, "The Praises of a Country Life." The translation from Martial I quote in full:

> The things that make the happier life are these,
> Most pleasant Martial: substance got with ease,
> Not labored for, but left thee by thy sire;
> A soil not barren, a continual fire;
> Never at law, seldom in office gowned;
> A quiet mind, free powers, and body sound;
> A wise simplicity, friends alike-stated;
> Thy table without art, and easy-rated.
> Thy night not drunken, but from cares laid waste;
> No sour or sullen bed-mate, yet a chaste;
> Sleep that will make the darkest hours swift-paced;
> Will to be what thou art, and nothing more;
> Nor fear thy latest day, nor wish therefor.

> *(Modernized from H&S VIII.295)*

The emphasis is on order, simplicity, conviviality, freedom from ambition and care, and moderate sensual pleasures. Horace, in the epode Jonson translates (H&S VIII.289–91), stresses the same values. The poem "To Penshurst" is Jonson's own praise of the country life. Like Horace, he presents for our admiration a fairly realistic rural estate rather than a conventional pastoral landscape. Penshurst is set up not as a place of escape from the city but as a model of order, social decorum, abundance, and generosity that the city should imitate. Jonson praises Penshurst not as a beautiful place per se, as a Romantic poet might have done, but as an embodiment of the virtues of the Sidney family, its owners, and ultimately of an orderly kingdom. The poet's function, as Jonson saw it, is not only to praise the people who hold society together but to blame those who disrupt it or make it ugly with their vanity and vice. Therefore his epigrams, like Martial's, not only praise but also blame individuals and types. He honors the virtuous by using their real names, but in the case of the vicious, we can never be sure whether the epigram is directed at a real individual, since he uses fictitious names such as "Gut."

In his choice of genres, as in his subjects and themes, Jonson considered the Ancients his guides, although not commanders. The genres he favored were the epigram, modeled on Martial; the verse epistle, modeled on Horace; the lyric, with songs modeled on Anacreon, Catullus, and others, and odes modeled on Horace and Pindar.

He called his epigrams "the ripest of my studies," and he means not only that he worked longer and harder on them than on other portions of his writings but also that he studied Martial intensively. He follows Martial closely. For example, both poets define *epigram* broadly. The word originally meant an inscription, which is perforce both short in length and concise in style. Martial and Jonson retain both of these qualities for the most part, but they sometimes take liberties. While most of Martial's poems are a dozen lines or less, he has one of thirty-two lines, for example, inviting a friend to supper (V.LXXVIII). Jonson has a similar poem (CI)—modeled on Martial's— which is forty-two lines. In rhetorical structure Jonson also follows Martial fairly closely. First, a specific person, real or fictional, is either spoken to or spoken of. The writer concludes with a witty comment or question to which the rest of the epigram usually leads. This sharp conclusion (called, as in modern parlance, the *point*) frequently employs surprise achieved by extreme compression, puns, unusual metaphors, or some other such rhetorical device. Jonson's satiric epigrams are more often pointed in this sense than his epigrams of praise, but the latter often have a point also, as in Epigram XXXVI, "To the Ghost of Martial":

> Martial, thou gav'st far nobler epigrams
>   To thy Domitian than I can my James;
> But in my royal subject I pass thee;
>   Thou flattered'st thine, mine cannot flattered be.

The balanced contrasting clauses reinforce the contrast being drawn.

To Jonson, such technical features as meter were extremely important, and on such matters he followed his models as closely as the differences in the languages would allow. Martial's meter, for example, is normally the elegaic couplet (roughly speaking, a hexameter line followed by a pentameter line); Jonson seems to have regarded the rhyming pentameter couplet as the nearest English equivalent. He told Drummond that "couplets be the bravest sort of verses," and almost all his epigrams are in that verse form.

Both in *The Forest*, part of the 1616 folio, and in *Underwood* (1640) we find several verse epistles in the manner of Horace. Herford and Simpson, Jonson's modern editors, see them as similar to Jonson's epigrams of praise except that they are longer, less concise, and less pointed. Like the epigrams, they are almost all in pentameter couplets. They are usually addressed to Jonson's noble patrons or patronesses, and they deal not only in praise but in generalized moral counsel. The voice speaking is friendly but dignified, not intimate or confessional; it is a public voice even when it deals with personal matters, as in the "Epistle answering to one that asked to be Sealed of the tribe of Ben" (*Underwood* XLVII).

Jonson is not primarily a lyric poet, yet he has produced many lyrics of great beauty. The two principal kinds he practiced were songs and odes. Like the Ancients, Jonson associated the term *lyric* with the lyre and with musical rhythms not found in conversational kinds of poetry, such as the epistle. It is significant that not one of his songs or odes is in pentameter couplets. The subject of his songs, in accordance with lyric conventions, is usually love, but he frequently treats it in satiric manner. "Still to be Neat," from the play *Epicoene,* is a clever indictment of a lady's cosmetics. "A Celebration of Charis in Ten Lyric Pieces" (*Underwood* II) fearlessly juxtaposes the most delicate admiration for the lady (number four) with a bawdy joke (number ten). Jonson is just that way. Classical borrowings are frequent in the songs; the famous "Drink to me only with thine eyes," for instance, is a weaving together of scattered phrases and ideas from the Greek *Epistles* of Philostratus.

In his odes Jonson sometimes borrows the verse form of the Greek poet Pindar. For example, the Pindaric ode "To the immortal memory, and friendship of that noble pair, Sir Lucius Cary and Sir H. Morrison (*Underwood* LXX) is divided into what Pindar called the strophe (Jonson's *turn*), antistrophe (the *counterturn*) and epode (*stand*). The strophe and antistrophe correspond in meter and rhyme scheme; the epodes are different, but they correspond to each other. By using Pindar's form Jonson was reminding his readers of the ancient tradition in which he was working; he thus helped to give to his own art the dignity that educated men of the time accorded Antiquity.

Jonson's outstanding quality as a poet is his mastery of the plain style. In *Discoveries* he writes, "Pure and neat language I love, yet plain and customary." He practiced what he preached; the song "Queen and Huntress," for example, is a model of purity and simplicity of language.[1] Yet anyone who imagines that such verse is easy to write has not tried it. The secret is probably in Jonson's insistence on untiring revision. His criticism of Shakespeare always tells us more about himself than about Shakespeare. Just as he urged Shakespeare toward dramatic rules that he himself needed but Shakespeare did not,[2] so in his famous poem praising Shakespeare he described his own secret of success rather than Shakespeare's:

> For though the poet's matter Nature be,
>   His art doth give the fashion; and that he
> Who casts to write a living line, must sweat—
>   Such as thine are—and strike the second heat
> Upon the Muse's anvil; turn the same,
>   And himself with it that he thinks to frame;
> Or, for the laurel, he may gain a scorn,
>   For a good poet's made, as well as born.
>
>   *(57–64)*

Jonson succeeded in his passionate desire to pour clear, moral, and manly content into classical forms and then revise and revise until the form appears simple and perfect. The fierce energy that blazes through the comedies is not so readily apparent in the poems, but it is there; without it, Jonson could never have produced the "well-turnèd and true-filèd lines" (1.68) that he untiringly "brandished at the eyes of Ignorance" (1.70).

---

[1] For a convincing explanation of why this poem succeeds, see Phyllis Rackin, "Poetry Without Paradox: Jonson's 'Hymne' to Cynthia," *Criticism* 4 (1962), 186–96.

[2] See the introduction to the Literary Criticism section.

FACTS AND REFERENCES

Early Editions

Epigrams, The Forest: Folio, 1616.

Ben Jonson's Execration Against Vulcan. With Diverse Epigrams by the Same Author ... Never Published Before [incomplete; apparently obtained surreptitiously] : Quarto, 1640.

Q. Horatius Flaccus His Art of Poetry. Englished by Ben Jonson. [a reissue of the above preceded by *Ars Poetica* and *Gypsies Metamorphosed*] : Duodecimo, 1640.

Underwood: Folio, 1640 (basis for this edition).

Songs and poems from the plays: first folio edition of the play in question.

Poem to Shakespeare: facsimiles of the 1623 Shakespeare folio.

Modern Editions (other than H&S)

Hunter, William B., Jr., ed. *The Complete Poetry of Ben Jonson.* The Norton Library. New York: W. W. Norton & Company, Inc., 1963.

Johnston, George Burke, ed. *Poems of Ben Jonson.* The Muses Library. Cambridge, Mass.: Harvard University Press, 1954.

Newdigate, B. H., ed. *The Poems of Ben Jonson.* Oxford: Shakespeare Head Press, 1936.

The reader is also referred to the selection of Jonson's poetry in *Seventeenth Century Poetry: The Schools of Donne and Jonson,* ed. Hugh Kenner. New York: Holt, Rinehart and Winston, Inc., 1964.

Other Scholarship and Criticism

Beaurline, L. A. "The Selective Principle in Jonson's Shorter Poems." *Criticism* 8 (1966): 64–74.

Cubeta, Paul M. " 'A Celebration of Charis': An Evaluation of Jonsonian Poetic Strategy." *ELH* 25 (1958): 163–80.

———. "A Jonsonian Ideal: 'To Penshurst.' " *PQ* 42 (1963): 14–24.

Hutchison, Barbara. "Ben Jonson's 'Let Me Be What I Am': An Apology in Disguise." *ELN* 2 (1965): 185–90.

Maclean, Hugh. "Ben Jonson's Poems: Notes on the Ordered Society." In *Essays in English Literature from the Renaissance to the Victorian Age,* edited by Millar MacLure and F. W. Watt, pp. 43–68. Toronto: University of Toronto Press, 1964.

Parfitt, G. A. E. "The Poetry of Ben Jonson." *EIC* 18 (1968): 18–31.

Rackin, Phyllis. "Poetry without Paradox: Jonson's 'Hymne' to Cynthia." *Criticism* 4 (1962): 186–96.

Spanos, William V. "The Real Toad in the Jonsonian Garden." *JEGP* 68 (1969): 1–23.

Trimpi, Wesley. *Ben Jonson's Poems: A Study of the Plain Style.* Stanford, Calif.: Stanford University Press, 1962.

Winters, Yvor. "The Sixteenth Century Lyric in England." *Poetry* 53 (1939): 258–72; 320–35; 54 (1939): 35–51.

POEMS

I. FROM *Epigrams* (1616)

II
To My Book

It will be looked for, book, when some but see
Thy title, *Epigrams*, and named of me,
Thou should'st be bold, licentious, full of gall,
Wormwood, and sulphur, sharp and toothed withall,
Become a petulant thing, hurl ink and wit,   5
As mad-men stones, not caring whom they hit.
Deceive their malice, who could wish it so.
And by thy wiser temper, let men know
Thou art not covetous of least self-fame,
Made from the hazard of another's shame,   10
Much less with lewd, profane, and beastly phrase,
To catch the world's loose laughter or vain gaze.
He that departs with his own honesty
For vulgar praise, doth it too dearly buy.

2. named of—written by.　　13. departs—parts.　　14. doth . . . buy—pays too much for it.

VI
To Alchemists

If all you boast of your great art be true,
Sure, willing poverty lives most in you.

1. art—changing base metals into gold.

X
To My Lord Ignorant

Thou call'st me *Poet* as a term of shame;
But I have my revenge made in thy name.

XIII
To Doctor Empiric

When men a dangerous disease did 'scape,
Of old, they gave a cock to Aesculape;
Let me give two, that doubly am got free
From my disease's danger, and from thee.

2. Aesculape—Greek god of medicine.

XIV
To William Camden*

Camden, most reverend head, to whom I owe
All that I am in arts, all that I know,—
How nothing's that?—to whom my country owes
The great renown and name wherewith she goes;
Than thee the age sees not that thing more grave,   5
More high, more holy, that she more would crave.
What name, what skill, what faith hast thou in things!
What sight in searching the most antique springs!
What weight and what authority in thy speech!
Man scarce can make that doubt, but thou canst teach.   10
Pardon free truth, and let thy modesty,
Which conquers all, be once overcome by thee.
Many of thine this better could than I,
But for their powers, accept my piety.

Camden—leading scholar and historian (1551–1623); Jonson's teacher at
Westminster School.   4. name . . . goes—Camden's works on ancient Britain popularized the name. His *Britannia,* for instance, had gone through six
editions before this poem was published.   13. Many . . . I—many of your
exstudents could write this poem better than I.   14. piety—filial love
(Latin *pietas*).

XV
On Court-Worm

All men are worms; but this no man. In silk
'Twas brought to court first wrapped, and white as
                                                    [milk;

Where, afterwards, it grew a butterfly,
Which was a caterpillar. So 'twill die.

1. this—this is.

XXI
On Reformed Gamester

Lord, how is Gamester changed! his hair close cut!
His neck fenced round with ruff! his eyes half shut!
His clothes two fashions off, and poor! his sword
Forbid his side! and nothing but the word
Quick in his lips! Who hath this wonder wrought?   5
The late tane bastinado. So I thought.
What several ways men to their calling have!
The body's stripes, I see, the soul may save.

1. close cut—Puritan style.   4. the word—Puritan term for the Bible.
6. late tane bastinado—late-taken (i.e., recent) beating.

XXII
On My First Daughter

Here lies to each her parent's ruth,
Mary, the daughter of their youth;
Yet, all heaven's gifts, being heaven's due,
It makes the father less to rue.
At six month's end she parted hence   5
With safety of her innocence;
Whose soul heaven's Queen (whose name she bears),
In comfort of her mother's tears,
Hath placed amongst her virgin-train;
Where, while that severed doth remain,   10
This grave partakes the fleshly birth.
Which cover lightly, gentle earth.

1. ruth—pity.   10–11. Where . . . birth—Perhaps: This is the spot where
(while her soul remains severed from her body) the grave has for its share the
body. Jonson alludes to the belief that at the Resurrection our souls and bodies will be reunited.

XXV
On Sir Voluptuous Beast

While Beast instructs his fair and innocent wife
In the past pleasures of his sensual life,
Telling the motions of each petticoat,

And how his *Ganymede* moved, and how his goat,
And now, her (hourly) her own cucqueane makes,   5
In varied shapes, which for his lust she takes—
What doth he else, but say, "Leave to be chaste,
Just wife, and, to change me, make woman's haste?"

4. *Ganymede*—Jove's beautiful young cupbearer; here, paid homosexual partner.   5. cucqueane—"female cuckold" (Hunter).   6. shapes—disguises;
see *Volpone* III.vii. 221–33.

XXXVI
To The Ghost of Martial*

Martial, thou gav'st far nobler *Epigrams*
To thy Domitian than I can my James.
But in my royal subject I pass thee;
Thou flattered'st thine, mine cannot flattered be.

*Martial—Roman poet (A.D. 40–104) whose epigrams Jonson studied assid-
uously.   2. Domitian—emperor A.D. 81–96, a patron of Martial's.

XLII
On Giles and Joan

Who says that Giles and Joan at discord be?
Th'observing neighbors no such mood can see.
Indeed, poor Giles repents he married ever.
But that his Joan doth too. And Giles would never,
By his free will, be in Joan's company.   5
No more would Joan he should. Giles riseth early,
And having got him out of doors is glad.
The like is Joan. But turning home, is sad.
And so is Joan. Oft-times, when Giles doth find
Harsh sights at home, Giles wisheth he were blind.   10
All this doth Joan. Or that his long-yarn'd life
Were quite out-spun. The like wish hath his wife.
The children that he keeps, Giles swears are none
Of his begetting. And so swears his Joan.
In all affections she concurreth still.   15

11. long-yarn'd—seemingly endless.

> If, now, with man and wife, to will and nill
> The self-same things, a note of concord be—
> I know no couple better can agree!

16. will and nill—desire and not desire.

XLV
On My First Son

> Farewell, thou child of my right hand and joy;
> My sin was too much hope of thee, loved boy;
> Seven years thou'wert lent to me, and I thee pay,
> Exacted by thy fate, on the just day.
> Oh, could I lose all father, now. For why   5
> Will man lament the state he should envy?
> To have so soon 'scaped world's and flesh's rage,
> And, if no other misery, yet age?
> Rest in soft peace, and, asked, say here doth lie
> Ben Jonson his best piece of poetry.   10
> For whose sake, henceforth, all his vows be such,
> As what he loves may never like too much.

1. child . . . hand—in Hebrew, the name Benjamin means fortunate or dexter-
ous. Apparently the boy's name was Ben.   3. thou 'wert—the apostrophe
means that the two words are to be pronounced almost—but not quite—as if
they were a single syllable.   11–12. These lines are open to several interpre-
tations. My own preference is to take *like* in the sense of "to be pleasing, be
liked, or approved" (*OED*), in which case Jonson may be alluding to Martial
VI.xxix.8. The Romans believed that excessive excellence or good fortune may
make the gods jealous and bring on their revenge.

XLIX
To Playwright

> Playwright me reads, and still my verses damns;
> He says I want the tongue of *Epigrams*;
> I have no salt. No bawdry he doth mean;
> For witty, in his language, is obscene.
> Playwright, I loathe to have thy manners known   5
> In my chaste book; profess them in thine own.

LIX
On Spies

Spies, you are lights in state, but of base stuff,
Who, when you've burnt yourselves down to the snuff,
Stink, and are thrown away. End fair enough.

2. snuff—candle end.

LXII
To Fine Lady Would-Be

Fine Madame Would-Be, wherefore should you fear,
That love to make so well, a child to bear?
The world reputes you barren; but I know
Your 'pothecarie, and his drug says no.
Is it the pain affrights? that's soon forgot.   5
Or your complexion's loss? you have a pot,
That can restore that. Will it hurt your feature?
To make amends, you're thought a wholesome
                                              [creature.
What should the cause be? Oh, you live at court:
And there's both loss of time and loss of sport   10
In a great belly. Write, then, on thy womb,
"Of the not born, yet buried, here's the tomb."

4. drug says no—she has taken drugs to bring on a miscarriage.   6. pot—
i.e., of cosmetics.

LXV
To My Muse

Away, and leave me, thou thing most abhorred,
That hast betrayed me to a worthless lord;
Made me commit most fierce idolatry
To a great image through thy luxury.
Be thy next master's more unlucky Muse,   5
And, as thou'hast mine, his hours and youth abuse.
Get him the time's long grudge, the court's ill will;

4. luxury—lust, whoredom.   6. thou'hast—see XLV.3 (footnote).

And, reconciled, keep him suspected still.
Make him lose all his friends; and, which is worse,
Almost all ways to any better course.   10
With me thou leav'st an happier Muse than thee,
And which thou brought'st me, welcome poverty.
She shall instruct my after-thoughts to write
Things manly, and not smelling parasite.
But I repent me; stay. Who e're is raised   15
For worth he has not, he is taxed, not praised.

LXXV
On Lippe,* The Teacher

I cannot think there's that antipathy
'Twixt Puritans and players, as some cry;
Though Lippe, at Paul's, ran from his text away,
T'inveigh 'gainst plays—what did he then but play?

*Lippe—not only one who blabs but also Latin *lippus*, "blear-eyed."
3. Paul's—St. Paul's Cathedral, London's principal church.

LXXVI
On Lucy Countess of Bedford

This morning, timely rapt with holy fire,
   I thought to form unto my zealous Muse
What kind of creature I could most desire
   To honor, serve, and love, as poets use.
I meant to make her fair and free and wise,   5
   Of greatest blood, and yet more good than great;
I meant the day-star should not brighter rise,
   Nor lend like influence from his lucent seat.
I meant she should be courteous, facile, sweet,
   Hating that solemn vice of greatness, pride;   10
I meant each softest virtue there should meet,
   Fit in that softer bosom to reside.
Only a learnèd and a manly soul

8. influence—a certain virtue or power was believed to flow from each star.
lucent—Jonson is punning on the lady's name and Latin *lux*, "light."

> I purposed her, that should with even powers
> The rock, the spindle, and the shears control   15
> Of destiny and spin her own free hours.
> Such when I meant to feign and wished to see,
> My Muse bade "Bedford" write, and that was she.

15. rock, spindle, shears—a reference to the Three Fates: Clotho, who spun the thread of life; Lachesis, who determined its length; Atropos, who cut the thread with her shears. *Rock* means distaff (H&S).

LXXXIX
To Edward Allen*

> If Rome so great, and in her wisest age,
> Feared not to boast the glories of her stage,
> As skillful Roscius and grave Aesope, men
> Yet crowned with honors, as with riches, then;
> Who had no less a trumpet of their name,   5
> Than Cicero, whose every breath was fame;
> How can so great example die in me,
> That, Allen, I should pause to publish thee?
> Who both their graces in thyself hast more
> Outstripped than they did all that went before;   10
> And present worth in all dost so contract,
> As others speak, but only thou dost act.
> Wear this renown. 'Tis just, that who did give
> So many poets life, by one should live.

Edward Allen—leading actor, famous for creating such roles as Faustus and Tamburlaine.   3. Roscius, Aesope—Roman actors; the former famed for comedy, the latter for tragedy.

XCIV
To Lucy, Countess of Bedford,
with Mr. Donne's Satires*

> Lucy, you brightness of our sphere, who are
> Life of the Muses' day, their morning-star!
> If works—not th'authors—their own grace should look,

Donne's Satires—published 1633, but written much earlier and circulated in manuscript.   1. Lucy—from Latin *lux*, "light, brightness."   3. look— look for, seek.

Whose poems would not wish to be your book?
But these, desired by you, the maker's ends   5
Crown with their own. Rare poems ask rare friends.
Yet satires, since the most of mankind be
Their unavoided subject, fewest see;
For none ere took that pleasure in sin's sense,
But, when they heard it taxed, took more offence.   10
They, then, that living where the matter is bred,
Dare for these poems, yet, both ask, and read,
And like them too, must needfully, though few,
Be of the best; and 'mongst those, best are you.
Lucy, you brightness of our sphere, who are   15
The Muses' evening, as their morning-star.

11. where . . . bred—in the midst of the society being satirized.

XCVI
To John Donne

Who shall doubt, Donne, where I a Poet be,
When I dare send my epigrams to thee?
That so alone canst judge, so'alone dost make;
And, in thy censures, evenly, dost take
As free simplicity to disavow,   5
As thou hast best authority t'allow.
Read all I send; and if I find but one
Marked by thy hand, and with the better stone,
My title's sealed. Those that for claps do write,
Let pui'nees', porters', players' praise delight;   10
And, till they burst, their backs, like asses load.
A man should seek great glory, and not broad.

1. where—whether.   8. the better stone—Romans marked joyous days on their calendars with a white stone.   10. pui'nees'—juniors', inferiors'.

CI
Inviting a Friend to Supper

Tonight, grave sir, both my poor house and I
Do equally desire your company;
Not that we think us worthy such a guest,

But that your worth will dignify our feast
With those that come, whose grace may make that
                                              [seem   5
Something, which else could hope for no esteem.
It is the fair acceptance, sir, creates
The entertainment perfect—not the cates.
Yet shall you have, to rectify your palate,
An olive, capers, or some better salad   10
Ush'ring the mutton; with a short-legg'd hen,
If we can get her, full of eggs, and then,
Lemons and wine for sauce; to these, a cony
Is not to be despaired of, for our money;
And, though fowl, now, be scarce, yet there are clerks, 15
The sky not falling, think we may have larks.
I'll tell you of more, and lie, so you will come—
Of partridge, pheasant, woodcock, of which some
May yet be there; and godwit, if we can—
Knat, rail, and ruff too. Howsoe'r, my man   20
Shall read a piece of Virgil, Tacitus,
Livy, or of some better book to us,
Of which we'll speak our minds, amidst our meat;
And I'll profess no verses to repeat;
To this, if aught appear which I not know of,   25
That will the pastry, not my paper, show of.
Disgestive cheese and fruit there sure will be;
But that which most doth take my Muse, and me,
Is a pure cup of rich Canary wine,
Which is the Mermaid's, now, but shall be mine—   30
Of which had Horace or Anacreon tasted,
Their lives, as do their lines, till now had lasted.
Tobacco, nectar, or the Thespian spring,
Are all but Luther's beer, to this I sing.
Of this we will sup free, but moderately,   35
And we will have no Pooly 'or Parrot by;
Nor shall our cups make any guilty men;
But at our parting we will be as when

8. cates—dainty foods.   13. to—besides.   cony—rabbit.   19–20. godwit . . . ruff—edible birds.   33. Tobacco—sometimes taken in a drink rather than smoked.   33. Thespian Spring—associated with the Muses.
34. Luther's—i.e., German.   36. Pooly, Parrot—notorious informers.

We innocently met. No simple word
That shall be uttered at our mirthful board　　　　　40
Shall make us sad next morning, or affright
The liberty that we'll enjoy tonight.

CII
*To William Earl of Pembroke**

I do but name thee, Pembroke, and I find
It is an epigram on all mankind;
Against the bad, but of, and to the good,
Both which are asked, to have thee understood.
Nor could the age have missed thee in this strife　　　5
Of vice and virtue; wherein all great life
Almost, is exercised; and scarce one knows
To which, yet, of the sides himself he owes.
They follow virtue, for reward, today;
Tomorrow vice, if she give better pay;　　　　　10
And are so good and bad, just at a price,
As nothing else discerns the virtue'or vice.
But thou, whose noblêsse keeps one stature still,
And one true posture, though besieged with ill
Of what ambition, faction, pride can raise;　　　　15
Whose life, ev'n they that envy it must praise;
That art so reverenced, as thy coming in,
But in the view, doth interrupt their sin;
Thou must draw more; and they that hope to see
The commonwealth still safe, must study thee.　　　20

**Pembroke*—William Herbert, Earl of Pembroke (1580–1630) to whom Jonson in the 1616 folio dedicates all of his epigrams. He gave Jonson twenty pounds annually to buy books.　　4. asked—required.　　11. And are . . . price—they are precisely as good or bad as the price dictates.

CXVIII
On Gut

Gut eats all day and lechers all the night,
So all his meat he tasteth over twice;
And, striving so to double his delight,
He makes himself a thoroughfare of vice.
Thus, in his belly, can he change a sin,   5
Lust it comes out, that gluttony went in.

CXX
Epitaph On S. P.* A Child of Q. El. Chapel

Weep with me, all you that read
    This little story;
And know, for whom a tear you shed,
    Death's self is sorry.
'Twas a child that so did thrive   5
    In grace and feature,
As Heaven and Nature seemed to strive
    Which owned the creature.
Years he numbered scarce thirteen
    When Fates turned cruel,   10
Yet three filled Zodiacs had he been
    The stage's jewel;
And did act—what now we moan—
    Old men so duly,
As, sooth, the Parcae thought him one,   15
    He played so truly.
So, by error, to his fate
    They all consented;
But viewing him since—alas, too late—
    They have repented.   20
And have sought, to give new birth,
    In baths to steep him;
But being so much too good for earth,
    Heaven vows to keep him.

*S.P.—Salomon (Solomon) Pavy acted in Jonson's early comedies written for
the Children of Queen Elizabeth's Chapel.   15. Parcae—the Fates.

II. FROM *The Forest* (1616)

II
To Penshurst*

Thou art not, Penshurst, built to envious show
Of touch, or marble, nor canst boast a row
Of polished pillars, or a roof of gold;
Thou hast no lantherne whereof tales are told,
Or stair or courts; but stand'st an ancient pile,   5
And these grudged at, art reverenced the while.
Thou joy'st in better marks, of soil, of air,
Of wood, of water; therein thou art fair.
Thou hast thy walks for health, as well as sport:
Thy Mount, to which the dryads do resort,   10
Where Pan and Bacchus their high feasts have made,
Beneath the broad beech and the chestnut shade;
That taller tree, which of a nut was set,
At his great birth, where all the Muses met.
There, in the writhèd bark, are cut the names   15
Of many a sylvan, taken with his flames.
And thence the ruddy satyrs oft provoke
The lighter fauns to reach thy Lady's Oak.
Thy copse, too, named of Gamage, thou hast there,
That never fails to serve thee seasoned deer,   20
When thou wouldst feast or exercise thy friends.
The lower land, that to the river bends,
Thy sheep, thy bullocks, kine, and calves do feed;
The middle grounds thy mares and horses breed.
Each bank doth yield thee conies; and the tops   25
Fertile of wood, Ashore, and Sidney's copse,

*Penshurst—home of the Sidney family in Kent. Sir Robert Sidney (1563–
1626), lord of the manor at this time, was a brother of Sir Philip, the poet.
2. touch—expensive black basalt or marble.   4. lantherne—glassed room at
top of the house.   6. these . . . the while—the more sumptuous palaces are
envied, while you are reverenced.   10. Mount—high ground overlooking the
main house.   14. his—Sir Philip's.   16. sylvan—denizen of the woods.
taken with his flames—inflamed by Sir Philip's love poetry.   17. provoke—
summon, invite.   18. thy Lady's Oak—a tree under which the mistress of
the manor went into labor with one of her children.   19. Gamage—Sir
Robert's wife, Barbara Gamage.   23. bullocks, kine—cattle.
26. Ashore . . . copse—two groves.

To crown thy open table doth provide
The purpled pheasant with the speckled side.
The painted partridge lies in every field,
And, for thy mess, is willing to be killed.   30
And if the high-swoll'n Medway fail thy dish,
Thou hast thy ponds, that pay thee tribute fish,
Fat, agèd carps, that run into thy net.
And pikes, now weary their own kind to eat,
As loath the second draught or cast to stay,   35
Officiously, at first, themselves betray.
Bright eels, that emulate them, and leap on land,
Before the fisher, or into his hand.
Then hath thy orchard fruit, thy garden flowers,
Fresh as the air and new as are the hours.   40
The early cherry, with the later plum,
Fig, grape, and quince, each in his time doth come;
The blushing apricot and woolly peach
Hang on thy walls, that every child may reach.
And though thy walls be of the country stone,   45
They're reared with no man's ruin, no man's groan;
There's none that dwell about them wish them down;
But all come in, the farmer, and the clown;
And no one empty-handed, to salute
Thy lord and lady, though they have no suit.   50
Some bring a capon, some a rural cake,
Some nuts, some apples; some that think they make
The better cheeses bring 'em; or else send
By their ripe daughters, whom they would commend
This way to husbands; and whose baskets bear   55
An emblem of themselves in plum or pear.
But what can this, more than express their love,
Add to thy free provisions, far above
The need of such, whose liberal board doth flow,
With all that hospitality doth know?   60
Where comes no guest but is allowed to eat,
Without his fear, and of thy lord's own meat;
Where the same beer and bread and self-same wine,

31. Medway—river bordering the grounds.   35. draught—sweep with a
net.   stay—await.   36. Officiously—dutifully.   44. walls—fruit trees
trained on walls.   48. clown—peasant.   50. suit—request.

That is his Lordship's, shall be also mine.
And I not fain to sit—as some, this day,   65
At great men's tables—and yet dine away.
Here no man tells my cups; nor, standing by,
A waiter doth my gluttony envy;
But gives me what I call and lets me eat;
He knows, below, he shall find plenty of meat.   70
Thy tables hoard not up for the next day.
Nor, when I take my lodging, need I pray
For fire, or lights, or livery; all is there
As if thou, then, wert mine, or I reigned here.
There's nothing I can wish, for which I stay.   75
That found King James, when hunting late, this way,
With his brave son, the Prince, they saw thy fires
Shine bright on every hearth, as the desires
Of thy Penates had been set on flame,
To entertain them; or the country came,   80
With all their zeal, to warm their welcome here.
What great I will not say, but sudden cheer
Did'st thou, then, make 'em! and what praise was
                                                      [heaped
On thy good lady then, who therein reaped
The just reward of her high housewifery;   85
To have her linen, plate, and all things nigh,
When she was far; and not a room but drest
As if it had expected such a guest!
These, Penshurst, are thy praise, and yet not all.
Thy lady's noble, fruitful, chaste withal.   90
His children thy great lord may call his own—
A fortune, in this age, but rarely known.
They are, and have been, taught religion; thence
Their gentler spirits have sucked innocence.
Each morn and even, they are taught to pray   95
With the whole household, and may, every day,
Read in their virtuous parents' noble parts
The mysteries of manners, arms, and arts.
Now, Penshurst, they that will proportion thee

66. yet dine away—Jonson accused Lord Salisbury of treating him this way
(*Conversations with Drummond*).   67. tells—counts.   73. livery—service.   79. Penates—Roman household gods.   98. mysteries—(1) enig-
mas, (2) crafts.   99. proportion—compare.

With other edifices, when they see   100
    Those proud, ambitious heaps, and nothing else,
    May say, their lords have built, but thy lord dwells.

IV
To the World.

A farewell for a gentlewoman, * *virtuous and noble*

False world, good night, since thou hast brought
    That hour upon my morn of age,
Henceforth I quit thee from my thought,
    My part is ended on thy stage.
Do not once hope that thou canst tempt   5
    A spirit so resolved to tread
Upon thy throat and live exempt
    From all the nets that thou canst spread.
I know thy forms are studied arts,
    Thy subtle ways be narrow straits;   10
Thy courtesy but sudden starts,
    And what thou call'st thy gifts are baits.
I know too, though thou strut and paint,
    Yet art thou both shrunk up and old,
That only fools make thee a saint,   15
    And all thy good is to be sold.
I know thou whole art but a shop
    Of toys and trifles, traps and snares
To take the weak or make them stop;
    Yet art thou falser than thy wares.   20
And knowing this should I yet stay,
    Like such as blow away their lives,
And never will redeem a day,
    Enamoured of their golden gyves?
Or having 'scaped, shall I return   25
    And thrust my neck into the noose
From whence, so lately, I did burn,
    With all my powers, myself to loose?
What bird or beast is known so dull,
    That fled his cage or broke his chain,   30

a gentlewoman—i.e., the fictional speaker of the poem. We do not know
whether she had a counterpart in real life.   24. gyves—fetters.

And tasting air and freedom, wull
  Render his head in there again?
If these, who have but sense, can shun
  The engines that have them annoyed,
Little for me had reason done,   35
  If I could not thy gins avoid.
Yes, threaten, do. Alas, I fear
  As little as I hope from thee;
I know thou canst nor show nor bear
  More hatred than thou hast to me.   40
My tender, first, and simple years
  Thou did'st abuse and then betray;
Since, stirr'st up jealousies and fears,
  When all the causes were away.
Then in a soil hast planted me   45
  Where breathe the basest of thy fools,
Where envious arts professèd be,
  And pride and ignorance the schools,
Where nothing is examined, weighed,
  But as 'tis rumored, so believed;   50
Where every freedom is betrayed
  And every goodness taxed or grieved.
But what we're born for, we must bear;
  Our frail condition it is such
That what to all may happen here,   55
  If't chance to me, I must not grutch.
Else, I my state should much mistake
  To harbor a divided thought
From all my kind, that for my sake
  There should a miracle be wrought.   60
No, I do know that I was born
  To age, misfortune, sickness, grief;
But I will bear these with that scorn
  As shall not need thy false relief.
Nor for my peace will I go far,   65
  As wand'rers do, that still do roam,
But make my strengths, such as they are,
  Here in my bosom, and at home.

31. wull—will.   34. engines—devices.   36. gins—snares.
56. grutch—complain.

IX
Song
to Celia

Drink to me only with thine eyes,
    And I will pledge with mine;
Or leave a kiss but in the cup,
    And I'll not look for wine.
The thirst that from the soul doth rise,   5
    Doth ask a drink divine;
But might I of Jove's nectar sup,
    I would not change for thine.

I sent thee, late, a rosy wreath,
    Not so much honoring thee,   10
As giving it a hope that there
    It could not withered be.
But thou thereon did'st only breathe,
    And sent'st it back to me;
Since when it grows, and smells, I swear,   15
    Not of itself, but thee.

2. pledge—drink a toast.   9. late—lately, recently.

XV
To Heaven

Good and great God, can I not think of thee,
But it must, straight, my melancholy be?
Is it interpreted in me disease,
That, laden with my sins, I seek for ease?
O, be thou witness, that the reynes dost know,   5
And hearts of all, if I be sad for show,
And judge me after, if I dare pretend
To aught but grace, or aim at other end.
As thou art all, so be thou all to me,
First, midst, and last, converted one, and three;   10

2. But . . . be—Without others immediately assuming I am melancholy?
5. reynes—kidneys, thought of as the seat of feelings or affections.

My faith, my hope, my love; and in this state,
My judge, my witness, and my advocate.
Where have I been this while exiled from thee?
And whither raped, now thou but stoop'st to me?
Dwell, dwell here still. O, being everywhere,   15
How can I doubt to find thee ever, here?
I know my state, both full of shame and scorn,
Conceived in sin, and unto labor born,
Standing with fear, and must with horror fall,
And destined unto judgement, after all.   20
I feel my griefs too, and there scarce is ground
Upon my flesh t'inflict another wound.
Yet dare I not complain, or wish for death
With holy Paul, lest it be thought the breath
Of discontent, or that these prayers be   25
For weariness of life, not love of thee.

14. raped—carried away by force.   24. with holy Paul—see Rom. 7:24.

III. FROM *Underwood* (1640)

II

A Celebration of Charis* in
Ten Lyric Pieces

1. *His Excuse for Loving*

Let it not your wonder move,
Less your laughter, that I love.
Though I now write fifty years,
I have had, and have my peers.
Poets, though divine, are men;   5
Some have loved as old again.
And it is not always face,
Clothes or fortune gives the grace,
Or the feature, or the youth;

*Celebration of Charis—if there was a real Charis, she has never been identified.   1. 5. divine—alluding to the Poet-Priest of ancient times.   6. as
old again—at one hundred, i.e., twice fifty.

But the language and the truth,   10
With the ardor and the passion,
Gives the lover weight and fashion.
If you then will read the story,
First, prepare you to be sorry
That you never knew till now   15
Either whom to love or how;
But be glad, as soon with me
When you know that this is she
Of whose beauty it was sung,
She shall make the old man young,   20
Keep the middle age at stay,
And let nothing high decay,
Till she be the reason why
All the world for love may die.

2. *How He Saw Her*

I beheld her, on a day,
When her look out-flourished May;
And her dressing did out-brave
All the pride the fields then have;
Far I was from being stupid,   5
For I ran and called on Cupid:
"Love, if thou wilt ever see
Mark of glory, come with me;
Where's thy quiver? bend thy bow—
Here's a shaft, thou art too slow!"   10
And (withall) I did untie
Every cloud about his eye;
But he had not gained his sight
Sooner than he lost his might
Or his courage; for away   15
Straight he ran, and durst not stay,
Letting bow and arrow fall;
Nor for any threat or call,
Could be brought once back to look.
I, fool-hardy, there up-took   20
Both the arrow he had quit,
And the bow, with thought to hit
This my object. But she threw

Such a lightning, as I drew,
At my face, that took my sight   25
And my motion from me quite;
So that, there, I stood a stone,
Mocked of all, and called of one—
Which with grief and wrath I heard—
"Cupid's statue with a beard,   30
Or else one that played his ape,
In a Hercules-his shape."

3. *What He Suffered*

After many scorns like these,
Which the prouder beauties please,
She content was to restore
Eyes and limbs, to hurt me more;
And would, on conditions, be   5
Reconciled to Love, and me:
First, that I must kneeling yield
Both the bow and shaft I held
Unto her; which Love might take
At her hand, with oath to make   10
Me the scope of his next draught,
Aimèd with that self-same shaft.
He no sooner heard the law,
But the arrow home did draw
And—to gain her by his art—   15
Left it sticking in my heart;
Which when she beheld to bleed,
She repented of the deed,
And would fain have changed the fate,
But the pity comes too late.   20
Loser-like, now, all my wreak
Is, that I have leave to speak,
And, in either prose or song,
To revenge me with my tongue,
Which how dexterously I do,   25
Hear and make example too.

---

3. 6. Love—Cupid.   11. scope—target.   draught—drawing of the bow
string.   21. wreak—revenge.

4. *Her Triumph*

See the chariot at hand here of Love,
  Wherein my lady rideth!
Each that draws is a swan or a dove,
  And well the car Love guideth.
As she goes, all hearts do duty   5
               Unto her beauty;
And enamoured, do wish so they might
               But enjoy such a sight,
That they still were to run by her side,
Through swords, through seas, whither she would ride.   10

Do but look on her eyes, they do light
  All that Love's world compriseth!
Do but look on her hair, it is bright
  As Love's star when it riseth!
Do but mark, her forehead's smoother   15
               Than words that soothe
                 [her!
And from her archèd brows, such a grace
               Sheds itself through the
                 [face,
As alone there triumphs to the life
All the gain, all the good of the elements' strife.   20

Have you seen but a bright lily grow,
  Before rude hands have touched it?
Have you marked but the fall o' the snow,
  Before the soil hath smutched it?
Have you felt the wool o' the beaver,   25
               Or swan's down ever?
Or have smelt o' the bud o' the brier,
               Or the nard i' the fire?
Or have tasted the bag o' the bee?
O so white! O so soft! O so sweet is she!   30

4. 9. still—always.   10. Through—pronounced *thorough*, in two syllables.   14. Love's star—Venus.   20. the elements' strife—"the four elements, earth, water, air, and fire, were thought to be constantly at war" (Hunter), and from this clash came all of the harmony and order of the universe—
discordia concors.   28. nard—a sweet-smelling herb.

5. *Her Discourse with Cupid*

Noblest Charis, you that are
Both my fortune and my star,
And do govern more my blood
Than the various Moon the flood!
Hear what late discourse of you,   5
Love and I have had, and true.
'Mongst my Muses finding me,
Where he chanced your name to see
Set, and to this softer strain,
"Sure," said he, "if I have brain,   10
This, here sung, can be no other
By description, but my Mother!
So hath Homer praised her hair;
So Anacreon drawn the air
Of her face, and made to rise,   15
Just above her sparkling eyes,
Both her brows, bent like my bow.
By her looks I do her know,
Which you call my shafts. And see!
Such my Mother's blushes be,   20
As the bath your verse discloses
In her cheeks, of milk and roses,
Such as oft I wanton in!
And, above her even chin,
Have you placed the bank of kisses,   25
Where, you say, men gather blisses,
Ripened with a breath more sweet
Than when flowers and West-winds meet.
Nay, her white and polished neck,
With the lace that doth it deck,   30
Is my Mother's! Hearts of slain
Lovers made into a chain!
And between each rising breast,
Lies the valley called my nest,
Where I sit and proyn my wings   35
After flight, and put new stings

5. 4. various—changing.   12. Mother—Venus.   14. air—expression.
35. proyn—preen.

To my shafts! Her very name
With my Mother's is the same."
"I confess all," I replied,
"And the glass hangs by her side,   40
And the girdle 'bout her waist,
All is Venus, save unchaste.
But alas, thou seest the least
Of her good, who is the best
Of her sex; but could'st thou, Love,   45
Call to mind the forms that strove
For the apple, and those three
Make in one, the same were she.
For this beauty yet doth hide
Something more than thou hast spied;   50
Outward grace weak love beguiles.
She is Venus when she smiles,
But she's Juno when she walks,
And Minerva when she talks."

38. the same—in the *Odyssey* (VIII.364) Vulcan's wife is Venus; in the *Iliad*
(XVIII.382) she is Charis. Some writers therefore thought that the two god-
desses were the same.   42. save unchaste—except that, unlike Venus, she is
chaste.   47. For the apple—Venus, Juno, and Minerva asked Paris to
judge which of them was most beautiful; the winner was to receive a golden
apple.

6. *Claiming a Second Kiss by Desert*

Charis, guess, and do not miss,
Since I drew a morning kiss
From your lips, and sucked an air
Thence, as sweet as you are fair,
    What my muse and I have done: 5
Whether we have lost or won,
If by us the odds were laid
That the bride, allowed a maid,
Looked not half so fresh and fair,
With th'advantage of her hair   10
And her jewels, to the view
Of th'assembly, as did you!
    Or that, did you sit or walk,
You were more the eye and talk

Of the court today, than all   15
Else that glistered in Whitehall;
So as those that had your sight
Wished the bride were changed tonight,
And did think such rites were due
To no other Grace but you!   20
    Or, if you did move tonight
In the dances, with what spite
Of your peers you were beheld,
That at every motion swelled,
So to see a Lady tread   25
As might all the Graces lead,
And was worthy, being so seen,
To be envied of the Queen.
Or if you would yet have stayed,
Whether any would upbraid   30
To himself his loss of time,
Or have charged his sight of crime,
To have left all sight for you.
    Guess of these, which is the true;
And, if such a verse as this   35
May not claim another kiss.

6. 16. Whitehall—palace of James I.   17. had your sight—saw you.
20. Grace—Some writers gave Charis as the name of one of the three Graces,
constant attendants of Venus.

7. *Begging Another, on Color of Mending the Former*

For Love's sake, kiss me once again;
    I long, and should not beg in vain.
    Here's none to spy or see;
        Why do you doubt or stay?
    I'll taste as lightly as the bee   5
That doth but touch his flower and flies away.

    Once more, and, faith, I will be gone;
    Can he that loves ask less than one?
        Nay, you may err in this,
            And all your bounty wrong;   10

7. (title). *Color*—pretense.

This could be called but half a kiss.
What w'are but once to do, we should do long.

I will but mend the last, and tell
Where, how it would have relished well;
   Join lip to lip and try;   15
     Each suck other's breath.
And whilst our tongues perplexèd lie,
Let who will think us dead or wish our death.

17. perplexèd—entangled.

8. *Urging Her of a Promise*

Charis one day in discourse
Had of Love and of his force,
Lightly promised, she would tell
What a man she could love well;
And that promise set on fire   5
All that heard her, with desire.
With the rest, I long expected
When the work would be effected;
But we find that cold delay,
And excuse spun every day,   10
As, until she tell her one,
We all fear she loveth none.
Therefore, Charis, you must do't,
For I will so urge you to't,
You shall neither eat nor sleep;   15
No, nor forth your window peep,
With your emissary eye,
To fetch in the forms go by,
And pronounce which band or lace
Better fits him than his face.   20
Nay, I will not let you sit
'Fore your idol glass a whit,
To say over every purl
There, or to reform a curl;
Or with secretary Sis   25

8. 7. expected—awaited eagerly.   18. the forms go by—the shapes of men
going by.   23. purl—loop of lace.   25. secretary—confidential maid.

To consult if fucus this
Be as good as was the last.
All your sweet of life is past;
Make accompt, unless you can—
And that quickly—speak your man.   30

26. fucus—a cosmetic.   30. speak—describe.

9. *Her Man Described by Her Own Dictamen*

Of your trouble, Ben, to ease me,
I will tell what man would please me.
I would have him, if I could,
Noble, or of greater blood.
Titles, I confess, do take me;   5
And a woman God did make me.
French to boot, at least in fashion,
And his manners of that nation.
   Young I'd have him, too, and fair,
Yet a man; with crispèd hair   10
Cast in thousand snares and rings
For Love's fingers, and his wings—
Chestnut color, or more slack
Gold, upon a ground of black.
Venus and Minerva's eyes,   15
For he must look wanton-wise.
   Eyebrows bent like Cupid's bow,
Front, an ample field of snow;
Even nose, and cheek withall
Smooth as is the billiard ball;   20
Chin as woolly as the peach,
And his lip should kissing teach,
Till he cherished too much beard,
And make Love or me afeard.
   He would have a hand as soft   25
As the down, and show it oft;
Skin as smooth as any rush,
And so thin, to see a blush
Rising through it e're it came;

9. (title). *Dictamen*—statement.   10. crispèd—curled.   13. slack—dull.
18. Front—forehead.

All his blood should be a flame   30
Quickly fired, as in beginners
In love's school, and yet no sinners.
  'Twere too long to speak of all;
What we harmony do call
In a body, should be there.   35
Well he should his clothes too wear;
Yet no tailor help to make him;
Drest, you still for man should take him,
And not think h'had eat a stake,
Or were set up in a brake.   40
  Valiant he should be as fire,
Showing danger more than ire;
Bounteous as the clouds to earth,
And as honest as his birth.
All his actions to be such   45
As to do no thing too much.
Nor o'er-praise nor yet condemn,
Nor out-value nor contemn,
Nor do wrongs nor wrongs receive,
Nor tie knots nor knots unweave,   50
And from baseness to be free,
As he durst love truth and me.
  Such a man, with every part,
I could give my very heart;
But of one, if short he came,   55
I can rest me where I am.

40. brake—stiff framework.   42. danger—bravery.

10. *Another Lady's Exception Present at the Hearing*

For his mind I do not care;
  That's a toy that I could spare.
Let his title be but great,
His clothes rich and band sit neat;
Himself young and face be good;   5
All I wish is understood.
What you please you parts may call;
'Tis one good part I'd lie withall.

10. 4. band—collar.

III.
The Musical Strife, in a Pastoral Dialogue*

She

Come, with our voices, let us war,
   And challenge all the spheres,
Till each of us be made a star,
   And all the world turn ears.

He

At such a call, what beast or fowl,   5
   Of reason empty is?
What tree or stone doth want a soul?
   What man but must lose his?

She

Mix then your notes, that we may prove
   To stay the running floods,   10
To make the mountain quarries move,
   And call the walking woods.

He

What need of me? do you but sing,
   Sleep, and the grave will wake.
No tunes are sweet, nor words have sting,   15
   But what those lips do make.

She

They say the angels mark each deed
   And exercise below,
And out of inward pleasure feed
   On what they viewing know.   20

*Probably the poem that Drummond said was "the most common place of his
[Jonson's] repetition." Others include *Forest* IX and *Underwood* II.7.
2. the spheres—i.e., the music of the spheres; cosmological harmony.
9. prove—try.   12. call . . . woods—make the woods walk to them; the
music of the legendary Orpheus did all these feats.   18. exercise—
action.

He

O sing not you then, lest the best
  Of angels should be driven
To fall again, at such a feast,
  Mistaking earth for heaven.

She

Nay, rather both our souls be strained   25
  To meet their high desire;
So they in state of grace retained,
  May wish us of their choir.

VIII
The Hour-Glass

Do but consider this small dust,
  Here running in the glass,
    By atoms moved;
Could you believe that this,
  The body ever was   5
    Of one that loved?
And in his mistress's flame, playing like a fly,
  Turned to cinders by her eye?
Yes; and in death, as life, unblest,
  To have't expressed   10
Even ashes of lovers find no rest.

IX
My Picture Left in Scotland

I now think Love is rather deaf than blind,
  For else it could not be
        That she
Whom I adore so much, should so slight me,
  And cast my love behind;   5
I'm sure my language to her was as sweet,
        And every close did meet

7. close—end-stopped line of verse.

In sentence of as subtle feet,
  As hath the youngest He
  That sits in shadow of Apollo's tree.   10

Oh, but my conscious fears,
    That fly my thoughts between,
    Tell me that she hath seen
    My hundreds of gray hairs,
    Told seven and forty years,   15
  Read so much waste, as she cannot embrace
  My mountain belly and my rocky face,
And all these, through her eyes, have stopped her ears.

8. sentence—pithy saying.   feet—referring to poetic meter.   16. waste—
with pun on waist.

XXIII
An Ode. To Himself.

Where dost thou careless lie,
  Buried in ease and sloth?
Knowledge that sleeps doth die;
And this security,
  It is the common moth   5
That eats on wits and arts and oft destroys them both.

Are all th'Aonian springs
  Dried up? lies Thespia waste?
Doth Clarius' harp want strings,
That not a nymph now sings?   10
  Or droop they as disgraced,
To see their seats and bowers by chatt'ring pies
                                        [defaced?

If hence thy silence be,
  As 'tis too just a cause,
Let this thought quicken thee,   15

7–8. Aonian . . . Thespia—both associated with the Muses.   9. Clarius—
Apollo.   12. pies—magpies.

Minds that are great and free
  Should not on fortune pause,
'Tis crown enough to virtue still: her own applause.

What though the greedy fry
  Be taken with false baits   20
Of worded balladry,
And think it poesy?
  They die with their conceits,
And only piteous scorn upon their folly waits.

Then take in hand thy lyre,   25
  Strike in thy proper strain;
With Japhet's line aspire
Sol's chariot for new fire,
  To give the world again;
Who aided him, will thee: the issue of Jove's brain.   30

And since our dainty age
  Cannot endure reproof,
Make not thyself a page
To that strumpet the stage,
  But sing high and aloof,   35
Safe from the wolf's black jaw and the dull ass's hoof.

19. fry—small fish.   27. Japhet's . . . aspire—with Prometheus' descen-
dants, seek.   30. issue . . . brain—Minerva, who was born from the head of
Jove.

XXIX
A Fit of Rhyme against Rhyme

Rhyme, the rack of finest wits,
That expresseth but by fits
              True conceit;
Spoiling senses of their treasure,
Cozening judgment with a measure,   5
              But false weight.
Wresting words from their true calling,

2. fits—(1) parts of a poem or song; cantos, (2) paroxysms.   5. Cozening—
cheating.   measure—meter.

Propping verse, for fear of falling
             To the ground.
Jointing syllabes, drowning letters,   10
Fastening vowels, as with fetters
             They were bound!
Soon as lazy thou wert known,
All good poetry hence was flown,
             And Art banished.   15
For a thousand years together,
All Parnassus Green did wither,
             And wit vanished.
Pegasus did fly away,
At the Wells no Muse did stay,   20
             But bewailèd
So to see the fountain dry,
And Apollo's music die,
             All light failèd!
Starveling rhymes did fill the stage,   25
Not a poet in an age,
             Worth crowning.
Not a work deserving bays,
Nor a line deserving praise,
             Pallas frowning.   30
Greek was free from rhyme's infection,
Happy Greek, by this protection,
             Was not spoilèd.
Whilst the Latin, queen of tongues,
Is not yet free from rhyme's wrongs,   35
             But rests foilèd.
Scarce the Hill again doth flourish,
Scarce the world a wit doth nourish,
             To restore
Phoebus to his crown again   40

10. Jointing—disjointing.   syllabes—syllables.   16. a thousand years—
Greek and Latin poetry did not rhyme; medieval poetry did.   17. Parnassus—mountain sacred to Apollo and the Muses.   19. Pegasus—the Muses'
winged horse.   20. Wells—Hippocrene, spring on Mount Helicon, also associated with the Muses.   27. Worth—to regularize the meter, editors
print "worthy" or "worth a."   28. bays—a wreath of bay leaves was the
ancient reward given finer poets.   34–35. Whilst . . . wrongs—some neo-
Latin poetry rhymed.   36. foilèd—defeated.   37. the Hill—Parnassus.